Treasure State
TYCOON

Treasure State
TYCOON

Nelson Story and the Making of Montana

JOHN C. RUSSELL

MONTANA HISTORICAL SOCIETY PRESS

HELENA

Front cover photograph of Nelson Story: Schlecten Bros., photographer. Museum of the Rockies, Bozeman, MT

Cover and book design by Diane Gleba Hall.

Typeset in Legacy Square.

Printed in Canada.

Copyright © 2019 by the Montana Historical Society Press, 225 North Roberts Street, P.O. Box 201201, Helena, MT 59620-1201. All rights reserved.

Distributed by Farcountry Press, 2750 Broadwater Avenue, Helena, MT 59602 (800) 821-3874

19   20   21   22   23   24   10   9   8   7   6   5   4   3   2   1

ISBN 978-1-94052-794-9 (paperback : alkaline paper)
ISBN 978-1-94052-795-6 (hardcover : alkaline paper)

Library of Congress Cataloging-in-Publication Data

Names: Russell, John C., 1956– author.

Title: Treasure state tycoon : Nelson Story and the making of Montana / by John C. Russell.

Description: Helena : Montana Historical Society Press, [2018] | Includes bibliographical references and index.

Identifiers: LCCN 2018033376| ISBN 9781940527949 (softcover) | ISBN 9781940527956 (hardcover)

Subjects: LCSH: Story, Nelson, 1838–1926. | Ranchers—Montana—Biography. | Capitalists and financiers—Biography. | Frontier and pioneer life—Montana. | Bozeman (Mont.)—Biography. | Bozeman (Mont.)—History.

Classification: LCC F731 .R87 2018 | DDC 978.6/66202092 [B] —dc23

To Peggy—loving wife, best friend.

THE MONTANA HISTORICAL SOCIETY gratefully acknowledges the financial support provided for this publication by

Anne and Alex Bernhardt Foundation
Chris and Nora Hohenlohe
Elise R. Donohue Charitable Trust
Friends of the Montana Historical Society
Liatis Foundation
Thomas Teakle Trust

After all, the longest life is short, and does not amount to much, but it is a good thing not to find that out until late in life or we would not attempt to do anything.

—NELSON STORY to A. J. Noyes, c. 1900

Contents

Preface

Until now, a full-length biography of Nelson G. Story has never been written—save for a grandiose draft by Nelson's grandson Byron, son of Thomas Byron "Bine" Story. But a chance encounter with Byron's brother Malcolm in 1976 sparked my curiosity about their grandfather. The result is this book.

While pursuing my undergraduate degree in history at Montana State University, I worked part-time as a property inspector for a title insurance company. On the job one day, while checking a parcel on Bozeman's South Willson Avenue, I was approached by a gray-haired, mustachioed man in his mid-seventies, dressed in a plaid jacket and wearing a Stetson hat. After some idle chitchat, he pointed at the nearby Sigma Alpha Epsilon fraternity house. "I was raised there, you know." Being relatively new to town, I had no idea the imposing structure had once been a private residence. "Back before the war to end all wars," he added.

"You know that theater downtown?" he asked.

"Yeah, the Ellen?"

"Right. That's named for my grandmother. I can remember us kids taking sleigh rides with her in the winter." The topic quickly changed to Ellen's husband. "Now Nelson, he's the one who brought the first herd of longhorn cattle into Montana. This was after he mined gold over in Alder. Brought them up on the Bozeman Trail when Red Cloud was raisin' a fuss. He rode with the vigilantes in Alder, helped hang a few deadbeats, and had more run-ins with the Sioux while operating his ranch over on the Yellowstone. Later he had some properties down in Los Angeles. My uncle eventually took them over, and I worked for him down there for a while in the twenties. But I missed Montana too much, so I came home to run the ranch."

Malcolm Story, the grandson of Nelson Story Sr. Courtesy Loneman Photography, Bozeman

I never spoke one-on-one with Malcolm Story again. He died in 1994, the same year I began gathering the pieces of Nelson's biography. I'll always feel indebted to him though, and not just for the pleasant and intriguing conversation on South Willson. Malcolm was always willing to grant interviews with researchers and historians. The most significant interview was done in 1967 and is housed in the Merrill G. Burlingame Special Collections of the Montana State University Library. A few years later, he gave family papers, letters, and the entire testimony of a lawsuit brought by Rose Story Hogan against her brothers—Bud, Bine, and Walter—to the Gallatin Historical Society in Bozeman. All these materials are informative, especially when combined with legal documents in local repositories. Rounding out my research sources are newspapers, diaries, dissertations, correspondence, and taped interviews I conducted with family descendants, but without the materials proffered by Malcolm this book would not have been possible.

A project such as this is very involved, but it was worth the effort. I learned not only about Nelson Story, but also about the people he associated with and the events that occurred in Montana during his lifetime. Every historical event has subchapters, and many came to light during my research. Hopefully, this volume will lead the reader to a greater understanding and appreciation of the early years of the Treasure State.

Acknowledgments

IN ADDITION to Malcolm Story, I wish to thank Keith Ashley of Pomeroy, Ohio, who supplied background information on the Story family, and Debra Wiley of Inglewood, California, who sent maps and articles relating to Nelson Story's real estate investments in Los Angeles. I am also grateful to the entire staff of the LDS Family History Library in Salt Lake City, Utah, and Susan K. Forbes of the Research Division at the Kansas Historical Society in Topeka. There are also many people to thank at the Montana Historical Society in Helena, particularly library manager Brian Shovers and staff members Roberta Gebhardt, Jeff Malcomson, Barbara Pepper-Rotness, and Zoe Ann Stoltz. Sincere thanks also to former editors Molly Holz and Randall Williams, publications director Diana Di Stefano, associate editor Laura Ferguson, former photo editor Glenda Bradshaw, and editor Jo Ann Reece of Norman, Oklahoma.

In Bozeman, Jennifer Bordy of the Gallatin County Clerk of District Court Office was very helpful, as was Eric Semerad of the Gallatin County Clerk and Recorder's Office. Thanks also to research coordinator Rachel Phillips of the Gallatin Historical Society; head librarian Kim Allen Scott and his assistants, Gary Barnhart and Heather Hultman, of the Merrill G. Burlingame Special Collections at Montana State University; and Courtney Kramer, former historic preservation planner for the city of Bozeman. Special thanks also to Judy Evans of Chicago; Bud and Mary Burkhart, Martha Drysdale, and Meta Strickler, all of Bozeman; and Rob Story of Emigrant. I also wish to acknowledge Byron and Kay McAllister, Jinny Stratton, and

Kim Scott for making suggestions to improve the manuscript. Lastly, I thank my wonderful wife, Peggy, who encouraged me through the years, read countless drafts of the manuscript, and helped make the final product a better read.

If any inaccuracies are found in these pages, I alone am responsible.

Introduction

The White Mantle of Charity

W ILLIAM FRIEND DAY, pastor of St. James Episcopal Church in Bozeman, Montana, had spent nearly a week contemplating the eulogy he would deliver the afternoon of March 17, 1926. In his short time at St. James, Day had already presided over five funerals, each time offering comfort to the deceased's family, and, by extension, to the community itself. He always emphasized the person's achievements and Christian attributes, avoiding any mention of failings or character flaws that might have been unbeknownst to those outside the immediate family. But this service would be for a man whose successes and shortcomings were both solidly in the public domain. Nelson Story had been the most dominating figure in the town's sixty-two-year history, and Day knew any effort to omit his failings would render the tribute disingenuous.

Reverend Day had migrated to Lewistown, Montana, from his native England in 1912. His uncle Frank was one of the many thousands drawn to the gold fields of Alder Gulch in the early 1860s. A blacksmith by trade, Frank eventually purchased a three-thousand-acre ranch near Lewistown, and in 1883 opened a hostelry, the Day House. The institution came to be frequented over the years by a number of notable Montanans, among them cattleman and civic leader Granville Stuart, legendary cowboy Teddy Blue Abbott, Congressman Martin Maginnis, Governor Joseph Toole, and U.S. senators Wilbur Fisk Sanders, Thomas C. Power, and Thomas H. Carter.[1]

It was through his uncle Frank that William became familiar with Montana's history and the lives of its most famous residents, Nelson Story included.

Seven years after arriving in the Treasure State, Day took a position as a chemist with the Montana Milling Company and moved to Bozeman, where he also moonlighted as an instructor at Montana State College while studying for the ministry. Here he befriended two of Story's sons, Nelson "Bud" Jr. and Thomas Byron "Bine" Story. Bud was elected a vestryman at St. James the same year Day became junior warden. Bine served on Montana Milling's board of directors and sang with Day in the Bozeman Symphony Orchestra.[2] Between the tales he had heard from Frank and his conversations with the Story boys, Day was able to piece together Nelson's life, finding much to admire about the man, but an equal amount to give him pause.

Nelson Story left his native Ohio in 1858 to settle in the most violent region in antebellum America: "Bleeding Kansas." Here he cleared brush, broke sod, set fence posts, and freighted. Later he went to Pikes Peak, and then to Idaho Territory's Alder Gulch, where he and his wife, Ellen Trent Story, initially lived in a canvas tent near his mining claim. While many successful prospectors returned east with their gold dust, Story stayed in the West and used his earnings to branch into other economic interests. Like Leland Stanford, whose commercial fortune produced during the California gold rush later generated railroad investments and a political career, or fellow Alder Gulch miner John Creighton, who rose from telegraph superintendent and merchant to banker and railroad investor in Nebraska, Story understood the importance of diversification in building his wealth. He used his gold earnings to expand into cattle ranching, freighting, banking, milling, real estate, and, perhaps most importantly, government contracts to supply the Crow Tribe as they, and other Native peoples, were forced onto reservations and rendered almost entirely dependent on supplies from the whites.

Many other western tycoons followed the same model. John Iliff, by coincidence a fellow Ohioan drawn to Pikes Peak, began as a storeowner in Denver, but came to develop an extensive cattle ranching enterprise. His herds in Colorado and Wyoming supplied mining operations, railroads, and Indian reservations, earning him the moniker "the first cattle king of the plains."[3] In Montana, Charles A. Broadwater came to the Deer Lodge Valley in 1862, first making money as a horse trader, then freighting supplies to the gold fields, and later developing connections with politicians and eastern

Nelson Story, c. 1890 Gallatin Historical Society Museum, Bozeman

entrepreneurs to secure government contracts for Army forts. Next were his mining and real estate investments, followed by banking and the presidency of James J. Hill's Montana Central Railroad.[4] Broadwater's friend-turned-rival, Samuel Hauser, was also drawn west by gold, in his case the strike near Bannack in 1862. Within a few years he joined a banking partnership in Virginia City and established the First National Bank in Helena in 1866. Hauser, who became governor, also had investments in cattle, real estate, railroads, and silver mines.[5] A. B. Hammond, who came to Montana in 1867, rose from woodcutter and store clerk to the eventual control of the Missoula Mercantile Company. From there he branched into lumber, railroads, banking, real estate, and a host of other interests that made him one of the West's premier capitalists.[6] Isaac Baker and his brother George, together with Thomas C. Power and his brother John, established successful mercantile operations for gold miners in the Missouri River town of Fort Benton, leading to investments in the fur trade, freighting, milling, and steamboats, as well as contracts with the governments of both Canada and the United States. Power went on to become a United States senator. Others, like the Conrad brothers, William, Charles, and John, who bought out George Baker's interest in his brother's firm, can also be added to the list of self-made men and early Montana industrialists.[7]

These men, like Nelson Story, possessed the timing, ingenuity, and instinct to profit during Montana's territorial development and transition into statehood. While some relied on eastern capital, others, like Story, bullied or strong-armed their way to influence. Story built his fortune on freighting, cattle, and numerous other enterprises. The individual successes of men like these resulted in noticeable advantages for their respective communities, such as civic improvements, regional influence, and employment. For these reasons, their foibles were often overlooked as secondary to the advantages they brought.

Story fit the mold of the stereotypical Western tough. As a young man in Ohio in the 1850s, he severely wounded a rival suitor. In the gold fields of Alder Gulch he had a direct role in hanging a suspected murderer in the 1860s, thus launching the infamous reign of the vigilantes, and he later used a shotgun to maim a claim jumper. While driving his longhorn herd from Texas to the rangelands abutting the Yellowstone River in 1866, he defied Kansas Jayhawkers, clashed with bands of Lakota Sioux, Cheyenne, and Arapaho warriors, and outsmarted the U.S. Army. As a cattleman, he never shied from blizzards, violence, or rustlers.

By the mid-1880s, Story's family lived in a palatial mansion in Bozeman, and they later occupied a winter home in the trendy Adams District of Los Angeles, where savvy investments padded his already significant fortunes. Story's wealth helped Bozeman evolve from a struggling, even perilous, frontier town into one of the major agricultural centers of the Treasure State. Because his businesses improved as Bozeman grew, he was a tireless promoter of the community and white settlement in the region. Story even financed an expedition to drive the Sioux from the Yellowstone Valley to facilitate the building of the Northern Pacific Railroad. Though that effort failed, it laid part of the foundation for the Sioux War of 1876, Custer's debacle at the Little Bighorn, and the subsequent surrender of non-treaty Indians. He also backed an effort to bring steamships up the Yellowstone in hopes of reducing the costs of transportation and shipping to eastern markets. When he and other promoters failed to make Bozeman the state capital, Story assured a sound financial start for the town's consolation prize, the Montana State College of Mechanic and Agriculture Arts—today's Montana State University. A Free-Silver Republican, he delivered well-received speeches on monetary policy and politics and was once promoted for the U.S. Senate.

Americans tend to respect self-made men, and Nelson Story was one of them. William Day's eulogy would have no trouble trumpeting the deceased's accomplishments. But reckoning with another side of his legacy would also be necessary and far more difficult. Nelson Story's business acumen and public charity was overshadowed by deceitfulness in his professional life and harshness in his personal affairs. In short, he was mean and underhanded. His life code, as expressed to his son Bine, was a self-centered distortion of the Golden Rule: "Do unto others as they would do unto you, but do it first."[8] Story, like so many others, reaped unwarranted profits in his Indian agency contracts by inflating prices and travel expenses, supplying substandard goods, and even stealing government annuities and reselling them to the same tribe or to nearby merchants, all the while eluding prosecution through bribery and intimidation.

Bozeman newspapers extolled his business triumphs, deflecting accusations of tyranny and sycophancy. Many of his critics wrote anonymous letters deriding Story, rightly noting that, since his "ill-gotten gains" trickled down to the community, his shortcomings were glossed over. "The secret of it all is, he has money, and no matter how obtained, money will buy toadyism and fawning," wrote one detractor.[9] He drove one rival into near bankruptcy and another, who had called Story a "miserable man" who treated others like chaff, to the brink of insanity.[10] He used a cane, the butt of a pistol, or a shotgun to assault anyone he suspected of even posing a threat. His own family, including his wife, was not immune from his verbal and physical abuse.

Indeed, Story was a man of controversy and contradictions. Although infamous for his temper, he often demonstrated a streak of benevolence. In the 1894 *An Illustrated History of the State of Montana*, essayist and fabulist Joaquin Miller wrote that Nelson Story's face was a problem, "a combination of poetry and prose, an expression of earnest determination and a tinge of bitterness mingled with kindness." When aroused, Story's eyes flashed "almost with fierceness, but when speaking of human suffering or listening to the cares of others, [his expression] is luminous and tender almost to weakness."[11] Reverend Day was aware of these attributes: Story showed compassion and generosity to destitute friends or strangers and donated freely to churches, schools, and other civic improvements, especially when it served his own purposes. Rarely a churchgoer, he enjoyed lectures by Christian scholars, read widely, and possessed a keen grasp of history and economics, as well as an appreciation of poetry. Story lavished Ellen with the finest clothing, jewelry, and possessions money could buy. His three sons received superior educations and, when needed, immeasurable financial support. He spoiled his daughter Rose, underwriting many of her day-to-day expenses even after she married a man Story grew to despise.

Story's life illuminates a number of realities underlying the history of the nineteenth-century American West. Nearly every settler community throughout the region has some kind of museum, plaque, or statue to honor its pioneer heritage. Such depictions usually emphasize the hopeful side of the past, highlighting legacies and offering lessons that reaffirm comforting notions about shared values and American ideals. Like other Western barons of the Gilded Age, however, Nelson Story presents a stark reminder that duplicity and cunning were often as central to the region's development as were determination and courage. To be sure, he demonstrated hard work, thrift, and the value of far-thinking, diversified enterprise. Nonetheless, his successes would have been unthinkable were it not for the role of federal money in making fortunes and building communities, the forcible removal of Indians to reservations, and a patriarchal culture that fostered vigilantism, political corruption, and prostitution.

Bozeman businesses, in a sign of respect, closed for the afternoon on March 17, 1926. The funeral would not be held in the church, which, all things considered, made sense. Instead, Reverend Day welcomed mourners to the Story Mansion, which had been lavishly decorated with flowers from as far away as California. After a women's choir sang the hymns "Nearer, My God, to Thee" and "Rock of Ages," Day made his best effort to reconcile the contradictory life and legacy of Nelson Story. His eulogy included the words "sturdy," "virile," "strong," and "energetic," but closed with a request that Story's failings be hidden "beneath the white mantle of charity for the errors of mankind."[12]

Chapter One

A Friendless Youth, 1838–1863

"I LOCATED in Denver in '59, just after the celebrated Gregory Gold Mine, about 40 miles from the present site of Denver, was discovered, and I built the third sluice box for cleaning gold that was put up in the state of Colorado," Nelson Story recounted to a *Washington Post* reporter in the late 1880s. "Denver then consisted of less than a dozen shanties, so I presume I may be called one of the pioneers."[1] A pioneer of Denver, yes. Builder of the third sluice box in what was still Kansas Territory? Maybe.

Like thousands of others, Story was drawn to the east slope of the Rockies by the Pikes Peak gold rush. He and a few partners paid three hundred dollars for three placer mining claims near the mouth of Nevada Gulch, but their inexperience doomed the effort. While hundreds of men accumulated riches, Story earned nothing. He learned a few lessons from the failure, however, and would fare much better further north, where he hit pay dirt a few years later.[2]

Story first went to Kansas Territory at the age of twenty, leaving his native Ohio for Fort Leavenworth in 1858. Like most western migrants, he was seeking a new life, one in which he could be his own man and live according to his own terms. In so doing, he would ride the cusp of major events in the American West, much as his ancestors had during America's infancy.

In 1637, ancestor William Story left his home in Norwich, England, sailed across the Atlantic, and settled in Ipswich, Massachusetts, where he became a successful carpenter, surveyor, and extensive landowner, with a reputation blemished only by the accusation he once stole a large amount of a neighbor's green oak for his sawmill.[3] He played a minor role in one of colonial America's more infamous chapters when, in 1692, he signed a petition denouncing charges of witchcraft against John and Elizabeth Procter of nearby Salem.[4]

William's son Seth served under Major Sam Appleton in King Philip's War (1675–78) and later became a church deacon. In 1775, Seth's grandson John marched with other Ipswich Minutemen toward Lexington and Concord to face the British.[5] John's son and Nelson's grandfather, John Story Jr., who was once described as "a very erect, squarely built man," was a cod and mackerel fisherman. He helped build and sail a merchant vessel that was impounded by the British while en route to the West Indies, and after an imprisonment of fifteen months, he escaped and made his way back to Massachusetts.[6] A few years later, and for reasons unknown, the local religious community in Ipswich asked John to leave. He did, taking his wife, Priscilla, and five children to Enfield, New Hampshire, sometime between 1793 and 1796. Three of John's sons migrated to Ohio shortly after the War of 1812. A fourth, Ira, followed in 1836, traveling by oxcart with his wife, Hannah (Gile) Story, and their young boys Addison, Elias, and foster son Harvey. They settled on 160 acres in Bedford Township, Meigs County. Another son, Byron, arrived in 1837. And on April 4 of the following year, Hannah gave birth to Nelson Gile Story.[7]

Meigs County's diversified economy offered opportunities to both farmer and laborer. Its fields produced various grains, hay, apples, peaches, and plums, while at the same time supporting local livestock operations. There were coal mines, gristmills, sawmills, cooper shops, and tanneries. Manufacturers in the community of Burlingham produced wagons, hoop barrels, staves, and railroad ties. Distilleries and saloons, considered "promiscuous places" by a minority of residents, fared well in the community.[8] A group of enraged women once raided a tavern and broke bottles, mirrors, and furniture, but despite their best efforts Burlingham retained the dubious nickname of "Bungtown," so-called for the orifice in a whiskey cask.[9]

The primary crop on the Story farm was corn. The rugged, sunrise-to-sunset workday gave Nelson an aptitude for agriculture and honed his physique. He grew to five feet, eleven inches tall, weighed close to two hundred pounds, and had blond hair and gray-blue eyes. With the exception of a bout with typhoid fever and a lifelong problem with hemorrhoids, the strong, broad-shouldered man enjoyed good health. The same, however, did not hold for the rest of his family.

Older brother Addison died just shy of his fourth birthday, before Nelson was even born. Two younger brothers, Daniel and Walter, also succumbed to childhood diseases. Then came the death of Story's mother on April 1, 1855, less than three months after she gave birth to a girl, Sarah, who herself died the following year.

In the spring of 1856, Ira wed the recently widowed Ruhamy Jesseman Russell, who was already a mother to seven children by her deceased husband. The union soon produced two girls: Hannah, born in 1856, and Lucinda, born in 1857. Nelson did not get along with his stepmother, and the very year of his father's marriage, he jumped at the chance to enroll for the fall term at Ohio University in Athens, where he studied English grammar and arithmetic and paid his tuition by performing odd jobs and teaching at a nearby elementary school.[10] When his father became ill shortly thereafter, Nelson returned to help on the farm. But Ira died on May 24, 1857, as did little Hannah a few months later.

The unrelieved tragedy of these formative years impressed upon Nelson a profound sense of life's fragility and perhaps explains his ambivalence to organized religion. His short-lived time at Ohio University revealed the ambition for which he would become well-known, but even if he had completed his college education, the Panic of 1857 dampened prospects in the lower Ohio Valley. To make his way in the world, Story felt he needed a new environment and a fresh start. His mind was set on moving, a decision hastened one late summer evening in 1857 by a violent confrontation—the first of many that would shape his life.

Since returning from Athens, Story had been courting a local girl whose two overly protective brothers distrusted Nelson. Unable to persuade their sister to end the relationship, they visited the Story home to make their disapproval known. After calling Nelson outside, the older brother took a swing at him. Nelson pulled a Barlow pocketknife and cut the boy's arm from wrist to elbow.[11] The assailant fled the scene hollering in pain, and the incident cemented neighbors' opinions that Nelson was a short-tempered and vicious young man. To them, his initials stood for "No Good" Story.

To avoid an ultimatum like the one that had driven his grand-father out of Ipswich, Story decided to head west. He set his sights on Fort Leavenworth in Kansas Territory, where, in the words of one writer, "prices were fast rising, money plentiful, and everybody speculating."[12] As the U.S. Army's main western depot, Leavenworth served as a jumping-off point for westbound settlers, particularly those using the Santa Fe Trail, and opportunities in freighting and mercantilism abounded. Story's choice of destination was also influenced by the New England Emigrant Aid Company, an organization recruiting antislavery settlers to ensure the territory's admission to the Union as a free state under the Kansas-Nebraska Act.[13] The society promised cheap land, and thousands of settlers—many of them Whigs or disaffected Democrats who had joined the Republican Party—answered the call. With the society's assistance, they founded antislavery towns like Lawrence, Topeka, and Manhattan.[14] But the issue remained far from settled.

In an 1855 territorial election, thousands of pro-slavery voters from neighboring Missouri crossed the border and illegally cast ballots, resulting in a pro-slavery legislature. In response, "Free Soilers" organized a shadow government in Lawrence. When Missouri guerillas attacked the town in May 1856, destroying a hotel and a free-state printing press, abolitionist John Brown, his sons, and a small group of followers executed five pro-slavery settlers at Pottawatomie Creek. Missouri ruffians responded by invading Osawatomie and killing one of Brown's sons. A pro-slavery mob then ran free-soil settlers out of the town of Leavenworth, forcing many to seek sanctuary at the fort. The violence continued throughout the summer, with dozens killed and millions of dollars in property destroyed.

Free-soil delegates captured a legislative majority in the territorial election of October 1857, but before they were seated, convention delegates in Lecompton framed a pro-slavery constitution and submitted it to voters for ratification. Because slavery opponents boycotted the vote in which Missourians once again illegally participated, the constitution easily passed. Though the new legislature rejected the results in January, President James Buchanan asked Congress to admit Kansas as a slave state. But Congress, led by Illinois senator Stephen A. Douglas, adopted a compromise measure, the so-called English Bill, mandating a new vote on the Lecompton Constitution in August.[15]

This chaotic situation did not deter Nelson Story. In early 1858, he raised money for his travels by selling two bull calves for thirty-six dollars. While initially planning to take a riverboat down the Ohio and up the Mississippi and Missouri Rivers to Leavenworth, he changed his mind due to rumors that pro-slavery mobs were blocking river traffic. Instead, he joined a wagon train as a bullwhacker, walking much of the way across Ohio, Indiana, and Illinois. He most likely picked up the Mormon Trail at Nauvoo, Illinois, crossing Iowa to reach the Missouri River at Nebraska City, where he briefly found employment in a mercantile store. From there he followed the river south to Leavenworth. Days after his arrival, a group of pro-slavery men physically attacked him after he denounced the Lecompton Constitution in a street conversation. This quick lesson in frontier politics quieted Story's opinion on slavery for the balance of his stay.[16]

Story would not be in Kansas when voters rejected the Lecompton Constitution in August. The previous year, President Buchanan had appointed Alfred Cumming of Georgia to succeed Brigham Young, president of the Church of Jesus Christ of Latter-day Saints, as governor of Utah Territory. Appalled by the church's practice of polygamy, Buchanan sought to end Mormon control over the territory. To curb any resistance to the transition of power, twenty-five hundred federal troops escorted Cumming from Leavenworth to Salt Lake City. Departing July 18, Cumming and the first contingent of some fifteen hundred soldiers took up winter quarters near Fort Bridger, Wyoming. In anticipation of armed hostilities, Young activated the territorial militia and ordered the construction of fortifications in Salt Lake. He eventually yielded to Buchanan's decision in early 1858, however, averting any major conflict. The military detachment, now under the command of General Sidney Albert Johnston, proceeded on to Salt Lake City in late June, establishing Camp Floyd in the nearby Cedar Valley.[17]

In July 1858, the government's transportation master at Fort Leavenworth, Percival G. Lowe, assembled wagons, wagon masters, teamsters, and other workers to freight supplies, particularly winter clothing, to Camp Floyd.[18] Nelson Story, whom Lowe later remembered as "a friendless youth of twenty," was one of the ninety-three teamsters he hired at the rate of thirty dollars per month.[19]

Lowe's train of some eighty mule-drawn wagons, divided into three groups, began its westward journey on July 31. Teamsters took turns driving, assisting, and resting as the caravan followed the Platte River. Before long, they encountered setbacks. Pulling heavy loads through the route's sandy soil exhausted the draft animals, but worse yet were the illnesses that struck the caravan. Malaria incapacitated dozens of men, including Story. Upon reaching Fort Laramie, Story and another teamster, Mike Flood, were so sick they had to remain in the infirmary. After battling shakes and fever for three weeks, Story returned to Leavenworth, where for the next several months he made wages breaking sod, hauling timber, and selling fence rails and posts.[20]

While Story was in Lowe's employ, a small prospecting party, led by William Greeneberry "Green" Russell, found a promising amount of placer gold on the far western edge of Kansas Territory. The discovery was on Dry Creek, not far from the Platte River tributary of Cherry Creek. By fall, the migration of prospectors to the "New Eldorado" began, many of whom pitched their tents in or near a newly established community named for Kansas territorial governor James Denver. Russell's strike was a life-changing event for an untold number of people, among them Nelson Story.

In early 1859, freighters William Hepburn Russell and John Jones built a line of twenty-seven stagecoach stations between Leavenworth and Denver on a route that followed the Kansas and Solomon Rivers west before eventually reaching Cherry Creek. When the firm announced plans to transport flour, coffee, sugar, bacon, and other supplies over the same route to the growing mining camps at the foot of the Rockies, Nelson Story signed on as a driver for one of the caravan's twenty-five mule-drawn wagons. The outfit reached Denver on June 5, nearly a month after the first stage had arrived.[21] Story encountered a great number of miners frustrated by their lack

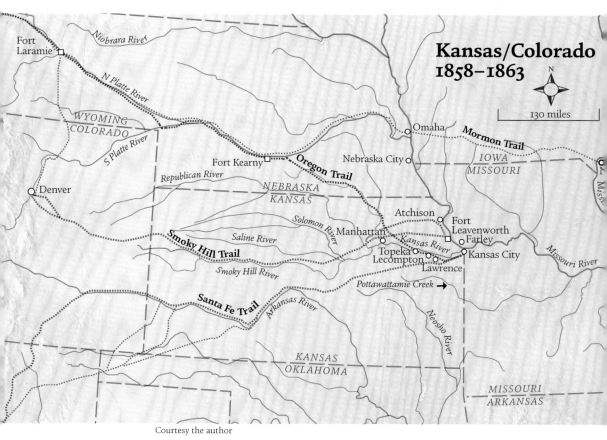

Courtesy the author

of success in Dry Creek and Cherry Creek, dismissing the find as "Pikes Peak Humbug."[22] Many decided to return home.

Had they held on a little longer, news of promising strikes nearby might have changed their minds. Earlier that summer, a party led by John Gregory began earning as much as eight dollars with each dip of the pan into the North Fork of Clear Creek. Soon came another big find, this time by Green Russell in early June. These developments prompted Nelson Story to quit his employ with Russell and Jones and head for Nevada Gulch in Kansas Territory with Asher Martin and two other men. Thousands more made the same move. Mining sites known as Jackson, Negro Gulch, French Gulch, Deadwood Gulch, and Breckenridge popped up throughout the territory, as well as the communities of Nevadaville, Montana, Black Hawk, Pikes Peak City, and Colona. Roads and stage lines were constructed, followed by schools and churches. Gambling houses, saloons, and bordellos flourished, but just as quickly these establishments were banned in some districts.[23] Surveying the camps, *New York Tribune* editor Horace Greeley claimed the entire population "sleeps in tents or under booths of pine boughs, cooking and eating in the open air . . . around a cloth spread on the ground, while each one sits or reclines on mother earth."[24]

While this rough life did not bother Story, the lack of profits did. Realizing their claims were of little value, he and Martin returned to Leavenworth. That summer's experiences convinced Story that a fortune could be made supplying miners with clothing, food, and tools. Determined to purchase his own freighting outfit, Story earned eight hundred dollars breaking sod and clearing and hauling timber from Little Stranger Creek. Among his employers was Matthew Trent.[25]

A native of Kentucky, Trent, his wife Frances, and their newborn son, John, migrated to Missouri in the early 1840s to settle on an eighty-acre farm near Farley in Platte County. Here, four more children were born, including Ellen on July 22, 1844. In 1854, the family moved to Leavenworth. While not slave-owners themselves, given their roots in the Bluegrass State and Virginia before that, the Trents may well have been part of the pro-slavery migration to Kansas. While working for Trent in 1859, Story was quickly captivated by fifteen-year-old Ellen's dark eyes and raven-black hair.[26]

By the spring of 1860, Story had saved enough of his earnings to buy wagons and an oxen team. With a few hired men, he loaded them with supplies, returned to Denver, and sold the goods in various camps. During the return trip to Leavenworth that fall, Story and his crew were attacked near the Republican River by Otoe

Indians, who ran off most of the stock. Story recalled that he and his men completed the final leg "with one sore-footed steer and a horse hitched by rope around the horn of a saddle."[27]

Story remained in Leavenworth for the next twelve months, again breaking sod and hauling bridge timber from the Missouri River to Little Stranger Creek. The Confederate bombardment of Fort Sumter and President Abraham Lincoln's subsequent call for volunteers did not draw Story into military service, even as fighting erupted in neighboring Missouri. He had other objectives in mind. In the spring of 1862, he purchased two condemned ox-drawn wagons from the army and freighted foodstuffs, coffee, candles, sugar, sundries, and hardware to Denver, clearing twelve to fifteen cents a pound. While he prepared to return to Leavenworth, two of his oxen mysteriously disappeared. Suspecting the animals had been stolen for meat, Story visited a nearby butcher shop, where indeed, he recognized the missing animals' hides. He sued the owner for damages, but lost the suit and was ordered to pay the court costs. Infuriated, Story skipped town, pursued by a sheriff's deputy. The lawman took a wrong turn in eastern Colorado, and Story made it back to Leavenworth via the Smoky Hill Trail. Story then purchased groceries and supplies in Kansas and promptly returned to Denver, where he rented a building and established his own mercantile store.[28]

Story had tired of long days on the trail, but the primary reason he quit freighting was to win the hand of Ellen Trent. Ellen saw Nelson as an ambitious man who would surely someday find success; that he never gambled and rarely drank only added to his appeal as a potential husband, so she accepted his proposal.[29] The details of their marriage remain a mystery. According to the family Bible, the pair wed in Leavenworth on September 28, 1862, but Mary Long Alderson, an acquaintance who later wrote a brief biography of Ellen, dated the marriage to August 1. No legal record exists, either in Leavenworth County or the newly created Neosho County to the south, where the Trents would soon relocate. Years later, Malcolm Story dismissed the matter by claiming that his grandparents had a civil ceremony because "preachers were hard to come by in those days" and noted that the two "stuck together a damn sight better than lots of them that have fancy weddings today."[30] The Trent family had no objection to the union. Frances had just given birth to another child, a girl named Jeanette, and eighteen-year-old Ellen leaving the nest meant one less mouth to feed. After the nuptials— if there were any—the couple struck out for Denver. There, Nelson operated the store while Ellen kept house on the second floor.[31]

If Ellen thought Denver would be their permanent home, she was mistaken. Miners disappointed by the prospects in Colorado Territory had been fanning out into the Rocky Mountains, testing quartz veins with their picks and exploring creeks with gold pans and cradles. Silver, and some gold, was discovered in Utah Territory, near Virginia City and Carson City, the same year as the first strikes in Colorado. To the northwest, in Washington Territory, gold had been found years earlier near present-day Drummond, Montana, in a stream that became known as Gold Creek. In 1858, James and Granville Stuart, two brothers returning east from the California gold fields, worked Gold Creek with moderate success. Then in July 1862, a party of Colorado miners led by John White found gold along Grasshopper Creek, a tributary of the Beaverhead River in Dakota Territory, roughly 115 miles southwest of Gold Creek. The camp was named Bannack after the neighboring tribe of Indians who supplied the men with venison. Word spread, and by mid-winter 1863, nearly five hundred settlers populated the site. Another five hundred arrived that spring. Hopeful miners hastily constructed sluice boxes and cradles, while teams of oxen and pack trains soon crowded Bannack's streets.[32]

Knowing that additional veins had been found in Colorado after the Pikes Peak rush and the subsequent discoveries in Nevada Territory, Story formulated a plan as soon as he learned of the strikes in Bannack. He believed that more finds were certain to follow in the nearby area, promising further population growth and numerous business opportunities. If he could stake the right claim in this new, far-flung territory, he just might accumulate the seed money needed to finance a lucrative freight and merchant operation. This was an opportunity to get in on the ground floor, and the allure was too tempting. Although Ellen may have hesitated to move again after having left home only a few months earlier, she acquiesced to her husband's wishes.[33]

Others who shared Story's vision wasted no time. Settlers from all walks of life established stores, hotels, farms, and ranches near the mining camps. On December 30, 1862, a group of recent arrivals established the Gallatin Town Company at the headwaters of the Missouri River, some one hundred trail miles northeast of Bannack. The Crows called the headwaters Aashalaxxua, or "where the rivers mix," a reference to the confluence of the Missouri's primary tributaries: the Jefferson, the Madison, and the Gallatin, all named by Lewis and Clark in 1805 during their famed expedition to the Pacific Coast.[34] The Three Forks, as it is known, marks the northwestern edge of the Gallatin Valley, an oval-shaped, 325-square-mile area that, thanks to a rich alluvial soil covering a third of the valley, would prove to be one of the most fertile in North America.[35]

Some settlers predicted that the new Gallatin City would become a major territorial metropolis, servicing migrants who, after traveling by steamship to Fort Benton, could portage around the Great Falls of the Missouri River and complete the upriver journey on light-draught boats.[36] Among those hoping to hitch their fortunes to the upstart community was John Merin Bozeman, whose actions over the next two years would have a profound effect on Nelson and Ellen Story. In 1860, Bozeman set out from Georgia for the gold fields of Pikes Peak, leaving behind his wife and three daughters. Having no luck in Colorado, he made his way to Gold Creek and then Bannack, but quickly grew tired of prospecting. By moving to Gallatin City, Bozeman suspected he might find some alternative means of profiting, and his exploration of the surrounding country reinforced that belief.

Indeed, the burgeoning settlement was favorably situated on the tip of a rich and productive landscape. The southern end of the Gallatin Valley, some thirty-plus miles southeast of the Three Forks, is bounded by the Gallatin Mountain Range. To the east stand the Bridger Mountains, named for mountain man Jim Bridger, a frequent traveler through the region years before the first gold strike. To the southwest lies the Madison Range, and further west, the Tobacco Roots. Varieties of pine blanket the mountainsides, alders and aspens dot the lower elevations, and cottonwood trees grow along the rivers and streams. The valley itself ranges from four to five thousand feet in elevation and has an arid or "continental" climate, with rainfall averaging just under fifteen inches per year. Summertime highs can reach one hundred degrees, but winter lows often dip far below zero.[37]

The Gallatin River has east and west branches that merge roughly ten miles below the Three Forks. The West Fork originates far to the south in high mountainous country that is now Yellowstone National Park, where snowfall averages nearly 150 inches annually. Called Cut-tuh-o'-gwa, or "swift water," by the Shoshone, it winds its way for sixty-plus miles through the picturesque Gallatin Canyon before entering the valley and meandering another thirty miles to merge with the East Gallatin, whose own headwaters reside in the Gallatin Range. Both are fed along the way by numerous creeks and streams.[38]

The Blackfeet called the valley Ahkoto-waktai-Sakum, or "Many Come Together Country."[39] Various tribes who occupied the region over the last several thousand years hunted deer, elk, and antelope, fished trout from its streams, and picked wild berries in the lower elevations. They also pursued bison in the Yellowstone River valley that lay to the immediate east.[40] Like the Gallatin River, the Yellowstone originates in present-day Yellowstone National Park and courses through spectacular canyons before making its way through a sixty-mile-long scenic valley flanked by two mountain ranges, the Gallatin on the west and the Absaroka on the east. This stretch, now known as Paradise Valley, ends at the river's "great bend" to the east. Numerous streams from the Absaroka Mountains, including the Stillwater and Clarks Fork Rivers, feed the Yellowstone for the next one hundred miles. Then the river winds to the northeast for more than three hundred miles, joined along the way by tributaries including the Bighorn, Tongue, and Powder Rivers, before merging with the Missouri.

John Bozeman (n.d.), was one of the founders of the community that later bore his namesake. Nelson Story was suspected having a hand in Bozeman's untimely death. MHS Photograph Archives, Helena 941-362

John Bozeman concluded that farms and ranches in the Gallatin Valley could feed the nearby mining camps and that bringing settlers to the area might prove lucrative. Other than following the Missouri River, the only means of accessing the territory via established routes was to travel west along the Oregon Trail and turn north at Fort Hall on the Snake River. But during Bozeman's time in Bannack, he learned from mountain man John Jacobs about an old trail, used by various tribes and trappers, that ran from the Platte River in Wyoming to the Yellowstone River and cut diagonally across the Bighorn Basin. Since the Oregon Trail followed the Platte, Bannack-bound travelers could branch off for the Yellowstone and pass through the Gallatin Valley on their way to the gold mines. This route was a few hundred miles shorter, better watered, and well wooded. With this knowledge, Bozeman saw an opportunity.

The country through which he hoped to lead western migrants, however, was occupied and utilized by a number of indigenous tribes that lived along the Yellowstone or hunted in the Bighorn Basin. The Apsáalooke or Crows, a Siouan nation numbering three thousand in population, were divided into two bands: Mountain Crows, who lived along the Yellowstone, and River Crows, who lived further north near the Missouri River.[41] Under terms of the Fort Laramie Treaty of 1851, "Crow Country" was bordered on the south by the Wind River Range and on the north by the Musselshell River. The eastern boundary was the Powder River, the western a line from the Wind River Range to the headwaters of the Yellowstone, then north to the mouth of Twenty-Five Yard Creek, then on to the source of the Musselshell.[42] To the immediate east were the Cheyenne, on lands between the Powder and Missouri Rivers. Further east lived some sixteen thousand Lakota Sioux, whose migration into the Powder River country in the early 1800s pushed the Crows west of the Big-horn River.

That these groups might object to a flow of settlers through their homelands caused John Bozeman little concern.[43] Standing a few inches above six feet and weighing two hundred and twenty-five pounds, he was, according to an acquaintance, restless, fearless, and "brave to a fault."[44] Bozeman talked Jacobs into an informal partnership to develop the trail, convincing the frontiersman that guiding miners and settlers for a fee would be less demanding and ultimately more profitable than panning for gold.[45]

On March 20, 1863, Bozeman, Jacobs, and Jacobs's eleven-year-old daughter Emma set out on horseback, traveling eastward through a gap in the mountains near the Gallatin Valley's southeast corner. Cutting between the Gallatin Range to the south and the Bridgers to the north, the pass ascends nearly one thousand feet through heavily pine-forested foothills and reaches an apex of fifty-eight hundred feet before descending one thousand feet over the next twelve miles to the great bend of the Yellowstone. Once there, the party followed the river for more than a hundred miles before turning southeast. Their destination was Fort Laramie on the Oregon Trail, where they hoped to recruit enough migrants to blaze the shortcut.[46]

Three days before Bozeman and the Jacobses began their journey, Nelson and Ellen Story, along with two hired men, three yoke of cattle, fourteen Mexican jack pack mules, and two wagons loaded with goods, departed Denver.[47] Traveling north through Fort St. Vrain, they picked up the Oregon Trail at Fort Laramie, crossed South Pass, and arrived at Fort Bridger, where they heard news of problems ahead. Knowing that a larger group could deter attacks by Natives defending their territory, the Storys decided to wait for more Bannack-bound travelers. They were soon joined by several others, including Jack Gallagher, James and Anne Sheehan with their baby daughter Katherine, James's ten-year-old daughter Mary from a previous marriage, and a cousin named Ellen. Mary, nicknamed Mollie, was captivated by Ellen Story and remembered her later as "beautiful" and "sixteen years of age," though Ellen was actually eighteen.[48]

Leaving Fort Bridger, the train proceeded to Fort Hall, crossed the Snake River and headed north. Mollie recalled that the Storys were alone in using slow-moving oxen to pull their wagons—everyone else relied on horses or mules—so each night they were last to pull into camp. Nelson often let Mollie ride one of his Mexican jacks around camp at the end of the day, but the groups' experience was far from carefree. "Men on horseback rode beside the wagon train, reconnoitered, guarded the rear . . . [and were] especially vigilant in Indian country," Mollie wrote of the trip. "Word was brought to camp one day that the train ahead of ours had come upon some murdered bodies. We passed by a mound of fresh earth with a board marker on which a penciled message stated that an unidentified body had been found and buried."[49] The train never saw the Indians they believed responsible for the violence, but some horses were stolen from camp one night. Upon reaching Bannack Pass on the Continental Divide,

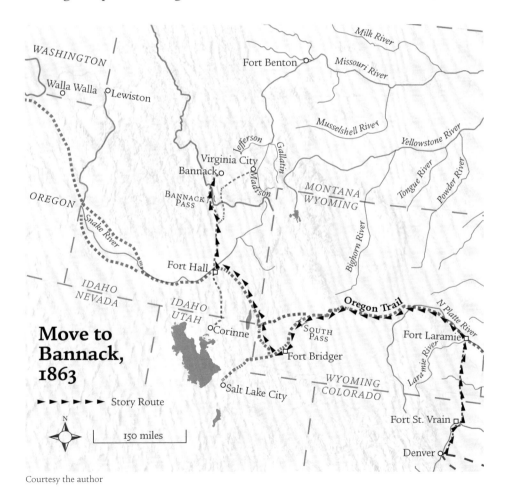

Courtesy the author

they descended northwest through the Beaverhead Mountains for some sixty-odd miles to Bannack. They arrived on June 4, bringing an end to weeks of what Mollie described as "the monotonous miles of jolting . . . perilous ascents and descents" and "dread of lurking Indians."[50]

The Storys expected a bustling community in Bannack, but instead found the town nearly deserted. There were but few men, women, and children.[51] After absorbing the bleak setting, Ellen turned to her husband and vented her frustration: "Is it to reach this kind of place that we have toiled and suffered during these last three months?"[52] Although she often spoke her mind, this was one instance when she did so without a cruel reprisal from her husband. While Ellen set about cooking a dinner of beefsteak, Nelson went out to see where everyone had gone.

Story's hunch that additional strikes would follow Bannack had been correct. He soon learned that in late May a party of six miners led by Bill Fairweather had discovered major gold deposits in a stream near the divide of the Madison and Jefferson Rivers on the northern edge of the Gravelly Mountain Range, some seventy miles to the east. They had come upon the site while en route to Bannack after a Crow war party forced them to abandon a prospecting trip in the Yellowstone Valley. The first day's panning washed out $12.80 of the precious yellow metal; the second day yielded another $18. One of the men, Henry Edgar, named the site Alder Creek for the numerous alder bushes along the stream, and the group agreed to tell no one about the find when they returned to town for needed provisions.

But the secret would be short-lived. The men drew attention to themselves when they used gold dust to buy supplies, and one of them, Thomas Cover, supposedly leaked the word to a friend. When the gang departed for Alder Gulch, hundreds of anxious miners followed behind. Recognizing their predicament, the Fairweather party convened a meeting with their pursuers at Beaverhead Rock, forty miles from Bannack. Here, all agreed to honor the claims of the original six before staking any of their own. They then proceeded another fifteen miles to the Stinking Water (Ruby) River and then southeast another twenty miles to Alder Gulch. One of the greatest placer gold rushes in U.S. history had begun.[53]

Leaving Ellen in Bannack, Story and his two hired men set out the next day along the same route that had seen the earlier exodus. He staked a claim of one hundred feet on each side of lower Alder Gulch, and, after a week of panning, returned to Bannack for Ellen.

Prospector Henry Edgar (photographed above in 1870), one of the original miners to stake a claim at Alder Gulch in 1863. Museum of the Rockies, Bozeman x85.3.462

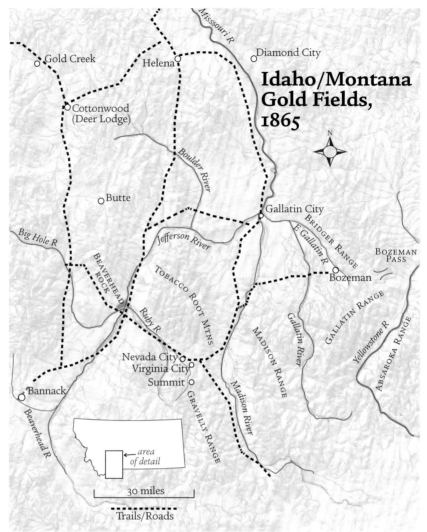

Idaho/Montana Gold Fields, 1865

Courtesy the author

A small tent beside Alder Creek served as the Storys' first home in what was then Idaho Territory, and Ellen was one of the first women to take up residence in the gulch.[54] Hundreds of other tents and brush wickiups were soon erected, followed by crudely constructed cabins. Two primary hubs of settlement emerged: Nevada City and, a few miles to the south, Varina, named in honor of Jefferson Davis's wife, until a pro-Union mining court judge insisted the name be changed to Virginia City.

As an observer noted, six thousand "money-mad human beings of every nationality and country on earth" soon resided in Alder Gulch, including miners, merchants, businessmen, Civil War deserters, drifters, gamblers, felons, and prostitutes.[55] Virginia City's first constructed building was a bakery, but the second was a saloon, where a drink of whiskey sold for fifty cents and a bottle of champagne for twelve dollars.[56] More drinking establishments followed, as did casinos and bordellos. One visitor surmised that few places in the world "held so much riches and sin as Virginia."[57] Miners, believing their claims inexhaustible, spent their earnings freely. Shootings became commonplace. "Went to a miner's meeting Monday evening," wrote John Grannis. "Lemuel Reid got killed. I helped carry him home."[58] Mollie Sheehan, whose family came to Alder a few days after the Storys, remembered that "loafers lolled at the doors or slouched in and out of saloons and hurdy-gurdy houses too numerous to estimate. Frequently the sounds of brawling, insults, oaths echoed through the gulch. . . . When my stepmother sent me down the street on errands she often said, 'now run, Mollie, but don't be afraid.'"[59]

Charged with maintaining order in this rough-and-tumble environment was Sheriff Henry Plummer, a native of Maine who had been a town marshal in Nevada City, California.[60] While he had arrested his share of arsonists and robbers and cracked down on opium dens, he had also been imprisoned in San Quentin following a conviction for second-degree murder. After receiving a pardon from the governor, Plummer made his way to Washington Territory and then came to Bannack in December 1862. Over the next few months he was involved in two shootings, killing a man in the first and suffering wounds in the second.[61] Despite this checkered past, Plummer was elected sheriff in late May.

On June 29, 1863, the chaotic violence in Alder Gulch reached a turning point when an argument erupted between Plummer's deputies. Three of them, Buck Stinson, Asa Hayes Lyons, and Charley Forbes, accused a fourth, D. H. Dillingham, of spreading a rumor that they planned to rob two local miners. The loud quarrel escalated into a gunfight, and Dillingham was mortally wounded.[62] The other three were put on trial before a mining court—an ad hoc affair where all district members in attendance, no matter the number, often served as the audience and jury.[63] A blacksmith headed the prosecution; three physicians sat as judges. After the evidence was presented, the three accused men were confined for the night. The next morning a voice-vote of the assembled miners acquitted Forbes and convicted Stinson and Lyons. Coffins were built and graves dug, while other miners constructed a gallows. The two condemned men asked that letters written the night before to their mothers be read into the record. Their request was granted. Women in the audience began to weep while listening to the words, and the entire crowd agreed to reconsider the sentence. While a new vote was conducted, Stinson and Lyons managed to secure their guns and a pair of fast horses. They fled the area, causing one of the civilian guards to refer to the hastily built gallows as a "monument of disappointed justice."[64]

That eventful summer, Nelson's brother Elias came to Alder Gulch. A few months earlier, his eighteen-year-old wife Catherine Beatty Story had died in childbirth. Deeply grieved, Elias left the baby, Elias Jr., with Catherine's parents and set out for the West to recover.[65] His arrival in July coincided with the discovery of gold near the head of Alder Creek, seven miles south of Virginia City.

At an elevation of 6,742 feet, the new district was aptly dubbed Summit due to its shallow bedrock, which frequently yielded sizable nuggets worth anywhere from one to one hundred dollars and a few larger ones ranging from six hundred to seventeen hundred dollars in value. The Storys were among hundreds who relocated to the new site, where Elias helped Nelson build a sod-roofed cabin that would serve as a home and mercantile store. Ellen supplemented the family income by selling her homemade dried apple and peach pies while Nelson ran a pack train through Alder Gulch and occasionally delivered mail between Summit and Virginia City.[66] As the number of log homes, saloons, and hurdy-gurdy houses grew, Summit soon became a "lively, noisy place."[67] Alder Gulch now had a new nickname, Fourteen-Mile City, referring to the rough distance from Nevada City to Summit.[68]

Chapter Two

A Land of Fair Promise, 1863–1866

JOHN BOZEMAN's initial attempt at becoming a wagon master had not gone as planned, and, in fact, was a near disaster. Yet he was not dissuaded from his plan. While Bozeman and the Jacobses were camped on the Powder River, Indians—probably Crows—took most of their supplies and clothing, forcing the three to complete the trek mostly on foot. The shoeless and footsore party reached an Oregon Trail trading post called Deer Creek Station, some one hundred miles shy of Fort Laramie, in late May or early June. After recuperating from their ordeal, they recruited eighty-nine westward travelers to follow them to the gold fields via the Gallatin Valley. Forty-six wagons left Deer Creek on the morning of July 6.[1]

Two weeks later, as the party took a noon rest on Rock Creek near present-day Buffalo, Wyoming, a party of 150 Sioux and Cheyenne Indians approached on horseback and told the emigrants that they would be killed if they proceeded any further. With little hesitation, the train turned around and headed back toward Deer Creek. The majority of the group decided to return to the Oregon Trail with Jacobs and the French trader John Boyer as their guides, but Bozeman and nine others decided to ride through the Bighorn Mountains. Traveling only at night and fighting hunger after their packhorse fell off a cliff, the group reached the Clarks Fork of the Yellowstone, then headed northeast to a gap in the divide between the Yellowstone and Gallatin Valleys that Bozeman and the Jacobses had crossed in March. One of the ten, George Irvin, named it the

Bozeman Pass in honor of their leader, saluting his indefatigability, "stalwart presence," and "love of adventure."[2] Once he learned of the developments in Alder Gulch, Bozeman knew the territory would become even more attractive to western settlers. He continued on to Virginia City that fall, hoping to garner financial backing from local businessmen to support another guiding effort during the 1864 travel season.

One of Idaho Territory's newly appointed supreme court justices, Sidney Edgerton, also arrived in Alder in the autumn of 1863, accompanied by his twenty-nine-year-old nephew, attorney Wilbur Fisk Sanders. A native of New York, Sanders had just resigned his officer's commission in the Sixty-fourth Ohio Volunteer Infantry because of poor health. Hoping to revive his law practice, he had agreed to head west with his uncle, serving as his secretary. It would not be long before the two men would assert their authority over the chaotic gold fields of Alder Gulch.

Henry Plummer's dismal arrest record was raising suspicion. His position as sheriff allowed him to keep track of those miners who had struck it big and when they planned to leave the territory. Many suspected that Plummer passed this information along to road agents like Whiskey Bill Graves, Boone Helm, "Clubfoot" George Lane, and "Dutch" John Wagner.[3] Twice that fall, masked gunmen robbed the stagecoach running between Virginia City and Bannack. Neither the passengers nor the driver could identify the assailants.[4]

Sidney Edgerton, 1860. As territorial justice for Idaho Territory, Edgerton sought to establish law and order in the mining communities around Alder Gulch. He later served as first territorial governor for Montana Territory. Library of Congress

In December, a hunter found the body of young Nicholas Tiebalt, known as "the Dutchman," in the nearby Stinking Water Valley.[5] The boy had been shot and killed ten days earlier while leading a team of mules to Summit. The robber had taken two hundred dollars in gold from his pockets and made off with the mules. When Tiebalt's body arrived in Nevada City, a posse that included Elias Story was formed to hunt down the killer and headed first to a horse and mule rental service run by George Ives. Several other men were at the camp, including "Long John" Franck and George Hilderman. Under questioning, Franck pointed at Ives and said he was the killer. The posse returned to Nevada City with all three men in custody on the evening of December 18, and the next morning Ives faced trial before a mining court. Wilbur Fisk Sanders was appointed lead prosecutor, and five attorneys were chosen to represent Ives. After more than two days of testimony, much of it from Franck, a twenty-four-man jury convicted Ives.[6]

As the trial concluded early in the evening of December 21, Nelson Story pulled into Nevada City with a wagonload of potatoes. After dinner, he joined the crowd of fifteen hundred onlookers as Ives's sentence was handed down. Colonel Sanders moved that Ives be hanged immediately to prevent other road agents, including some who had already emerged from the crowd to bid farewell to the condemned, from attempting to free him. Nevada Mining District sheriff Robert Hareford formed a guard to escort Ives to a nearby makeshift gallows.[7]

"The air was filled with apprehension," Story wrote years later, "and upon hearing Sander's speech, and warning of rescue, the writer, being fully equipped with pistol and carbine, stepped forth into the guard without being invited, for all the guard were made up of volunteers."[8] They transported Ives to a small, vacant space between two one-story log buildings, where they affixed a noose to two logs that extended from one building to the other and ordered Ives to stand on a large dry goods box.

The guards arranged themselves on all sides of the opening, facing the crowd. On Story's left stood Summit boarding-house keeper Benjamin Ezekial. As Sheriff Hareford adjusted the noose around Ives's neck, the condemned man continued to proclaim his innocence, asserting that Alex Carter was the true killer and prompting four of Ives's friends, armed with revolvers, to threaten the volunteer guard. For a brief moment both sides held their ground, until, according to Story, "I took Ezekial by the right shoulder and gave him the order to take hold of the box on which Ives stood. We took the box from under Ives, and down he came with a crash into the rope. Ezekial and I stepped back into our places, our guns in hands, cocked, ready for action."[9]

Wilbur Fisk Sanders, Sidney Edgerton's nephew, c. 1865. Along with Edgerton, Sanders helped organize the vigilantes to bring an end to lawlessness and crime in Virginia City, Bannack, and Nevada City.
R. A. Lewis, photographer. MHS Photograph Archives, Helena 944-847

Many in the crowd dove to the ground, expecting a shootout. But the guns remained quiet, and an uneasy silence descended over the scene as Ives dangled in the background. After a doctor pronounced him dead, his distraught friends immediately insisted that the hanging had in fact been a murder. The most vociferous of the bunch, a drunken attorney, was locked up in the same cabin as Hilderman and Franck. When Bill Hunter, whose nearby saloon allegedly served as meeting place for the gang, began denouncing the hanging, Story and fellow guard Charlie Brown chased him to his establishment:

> There was a door in the southwest corner leading to
> an adjoining apartment. The door opened outward
> and Hunter made for it with Brown reaching for him.
> As Hunter and Brown passed the west end of the bar
> counter, out jumped a man, the barkeeper, his hat and
> coat off, with a big revolver in his hand pressed close
> to Brown's back. I gave him a vigorous thrust with my
> carbine, which brought him right about face, looking into
> the muzzle of my gun. I ordered him to give up the pistol.
> Brown pursued Hunter to the back door, and Hunter,
> after passing through, slammed the door back against
> Brown. Brown, with one thrust of the double-barreled
> gun, knocked the door from its hinges into the next
> room, where there was no light. Brown did not pursue
> further but turned to see the barkeeper give up his pistol.
> No less than a hundred were in the saloon at the time,
> many of whom were road agents. Brown and I kept our
> guns presented at the crowd as we backed to the door
> which had been closed behind us. Brown opened the
> door, as both my hands were full (a gun in one and a
> pistol in the other) then we stepped out. We were obliged
> to return to the camp fires without our prisoner, but very
> thankful to return with whole bodies.[10]

Following the execution of Ives, George Hilderman, though also convicted in Tiebalt's murder, was allowed to leave the territory. Interrogators coerced information from "Long John" Franck by putting a rope around his neck and hoisting the horse trader up and down from a tree limb. Under the tortuous treatment, Franck talked, detailing the activities of a band of criminals who called themselves the "Innocents." Franck's cooperation, which revealed the identities of some of the road agents, spared him the same fate as Ives.[11]

Thus began the reign of the vigilantes, engineered primarily by Sanders and Edgerton and modeled after a similar movement of extralegal justice during the California gold rush. Men from Virginia City, Nevada City, and Bannack held secret meetings to establish bylaws and regulations for the vigilance committee. Twenty-four men, several of them Freemasons, signed a pact "uniting ourselves in a party for the laudable purpose of arresting thieves & murderers & recovering stolen property" and pledging "that we will reveal no secrets, violate no laws of right & never desert each other."[12] Members elected Virginia City mayor Paris Pfouts committee president. James Williams served as executive officer, Wilbur Fisk Sanders official prosecutor, and John Lott treasurer. Though Story did not sign the bylaws and regulations, he was one of hundreds of recruits, often divided into companies of fifty, mustered to eliminate the thirty-eight suspected Innocents.[13]

Barely had the ink dried on the vigilance committee's founding documents when Williams led a posse out of Nevada City in search of Alex Carter. The group rode a good one hundred miles northwest to the Deer Lodge Valley, but Carter gave them the slip near the mining camp of Cottonwood (present-day Deer Lodge). While returning to Virginia City, the vigilantes captured two men, George Brown and Red Yeager, who they believed had warned Carter. Both were hanged on January 4. A week later, the vigilantes executed Sheriff Plummer and two of his deputies, Edward Ray and Buck Stinson.[14] On January 14, five road agents were rounded up and hanged in Virginia City. Among them were Boone Helm and "Clubfoot" George Lane, as well as Jack Gallagher, who had traveled to Bannack with the Storys.

The next day Nelson, and most likely Elias, joined a group of twenty men riding out of Nevada City. At the Big Hole River, some went to a nearby ranch and hanged a suspected road agent before rejoining the main party. The group rode on to Cottonwood, enduring frigid temperatures and deep snow. On January 19, they hanged William Bunton, who maintained his innocence as he was led to a butcher's block that served as a hanging scaffold.[15] Jose Pizanthia, known as "The Greaser," put up a fight when the vigilantes came to his cabin, killing one man and wounding a second. In retaliation, Edgerton furnished a howitzer and the vigilantes blasted three holes in the cabin. Pizanthia was shot several times, dragged out by a clothesline, and hanged from a pole. After onlookers used his body for target practice, the corpse was tossed onto a bonfire. Allegedly, hurdy-gurdy girls later futilely combed Pizanthia's ashes for gold dust.[16]

The twenty-first victim of the vigilantes was saloonkeeper Bill Hunter. After eluding Story and Brown, Hunter had snuck out of Virginia City on January 13 and taken refuge in a small cabin near the mouth of the Gallatin River. A small posse of vigilantes caught up with him on February 3 and hanged him from a nearby cottonwood tree. Though they had promised Hunter a decent burial, the executioners left his body suspended by the noose until passersby cut down and interred Hunter several days later.[17]

Many of the Innocents, who survived the purges of January and February 1864, wisely fled the territory. Thomas Dimsdale, editor of the newly formed Virginia City newspaper, the *Montana Post*, defended the vigilantes by exaggerating the Innocents' crimes and the number of their victims. As for Story, he believed the ends justified the means. One observer noted that "when civil authority loses its virtue, vigilance or safety committees have a salutary effect."[18] Story agreed. Alder Gulch needed law and order, and, as he saw it, vigilantism was the answer for "undesirables."[19] As was the case throughout his life, Story never gave his actions or convictions a second thought.

The episode marked a turning point in the history of the territory. Justice Sidney Edgerton insisted that vigilantism had been an unavoidable consequence of the sprawling geography of Idaho Territory, as the territorial capital, Lewiston, was at least five hundred trail miles to the northwest of the booming gold towns and often inaccessible due to heavy snow. Assisted by Ohio congressman James Ashley, Edgerton lobbied to divide the territory along the crest of the Bitterroot Mountains and, further south, along the Continental Divide. Congress, hoping that the imposition of greater order in the region would maintain the flow of gold into the treasury, concurred. On May 26, 1864, President Abraham Lincoln signed the bill creating Montana Territory.[20]

At the same time as these events were unfolding, John Bozeman, who briefly rode with the vigilantes and helped repulse a robbery of a wagon train en route to Salt Lake City, focused on organizing and guiding another emigrant train across the Bighorn Basin and into the Gallatin Valley. His efforts to secure investors panned out when several Virginia City businessmen agreed to back him. Together, they founded the Missouri and Rocky Mountain Wagon Road and Telegraph Company to create a trail to the mining camps and establish ferries and tollgates along the route.[21]

In early 1864, Bozeman recruited two partners, Daniel Rouse and William Beall, to lay out a townsite in the southeastern corner of the Gallatin Valley. On July 7, Rouse and Beall staked claims twelve miles from Bozeman Pass on a fork of the East Gallatin River that would become known as Bozeman Creek. They also established several roads in the new townsite: Main Street, running east-west, and Rouse Avenue and Bozeman Avenue, both running north-south. Beall staked a 160-acre claim west of Bozeman Avenue, and Rouse did the same on the east side. They also laid out a claim for John Bozeman on the south side of Main Street.[22]

In the meantime, Bozeman assembled a train of roughly eighty wagons at Richard's Bridge on the North Platte River, one hundred miles west of Fort Laramie. It departed a few days later and was soon joined by another train of twenty-five wagons.[23] Accompanying Bozeman was Mitch Boyer, the twenty-five-year-old son of John Boyer and his Santee Sioux wife. One of the best scouts and hunters in the West, Boyer was fluent in French, English, Sioux, and Crow.[24] The caravan of 360 people made a safe and mostly uneventful six-week journey to the Gallatin Valley. Bozeman had convincingly demonstrated that the Jacobs-Bozeman Cut-Off, or Montana Road, was weeks faster than the Oregon Trail. The new route quickly became known as the Bozeman Trail.

Following a quick review of the progress made by Rouse and Beall, Bozeman and his wagon train, less those who opted to stay in the Gallatin Valley, proceeded west on what would become the Virginia City Road. At the eight-mile mark, it crossed the West Gallatin River, and eighteen miles later it reached the Madison River. Like the Gallatin, the Madison originates in today's Yellowstone National Park, but it is wider and shallower with a slower current. Bearing to the south-southwest, the train followed the river upstream for eleven miles before turning southward through the Madison Valley for another sixteen miles, then west to a pass on the northern edge of the Gravelly Range leading into Virginia City. In all, it was the shortest route between the Gallatin Valley and Virginia City, a trip of roughly seventy miles.

Other wagon trains arrived in the Gallatin Valley that summer. In an effort to avoid tribal hunting grounds, Jim Bridger, with the sponsorship of the Missouri and Rocky Mountain Wagon Road and Telegraph Company, guided a caravan that cut through the west side of the Bighorn Mountains, following the Yellowstone River north to the great bend, then proceeding north along Twenty-Five Yard Creek (Shields River) and south through Bridger Canyon to the Gallatin Valley.[25] John Jacobs led a train on roughly the same route. A. A. Townsend's group of 150 wagons and more than four hundred people had a tougher time. A party of Cheyenne and Sioux warriors attacked the train in July on the north bank of the Powder River. Two men were killed, and two others went missing during a six-hour fight. But the train reached the valley nonetheless on August 1; among its passengers was Rosa Van Vlierden, the first white woman to settle in the Gallatin.[26]

Arriving in the valley with a small wagon train that followed the Bridger Trail, Methodist minister William Alderson and his brother John were astonished to see "not a log or pole in sight," but rather a lone wedge tent made of wagon canvas and occupied by William Beall, whose only other possessions were a pair of blankets, a camp kettle, and a week's worth of food.[27] According to William Alderson's diary entry of July 15, the valley was "so pleasant and inviting that we concluded to lay over and look around."[28] After meeting Beall and Rouse, the Aldersons abandoned plans for Virginia City and staked a claim.

William White Alderson, n.d. A Methodist minister, Alderson traveled the Bozeman Trail and was one of the first settlers to stake a claim in the Gallatin Valley. Hamilton Studio, Bozeman, photographer. MHS Photograph Archives, Helena 940-009

Once John Bozeman led his wagon train into Virginia City, he immediately returned to the Gallatin Valley. On August 9, a meeting of the newly formed Upper East Gallatin Claim Association defined the town's boundary and established rules for filing claims. On motion of the meeting's secretary, William Alderson, the association named the emerging community Bozeman. Weeks later, association member and Republican James Burtsch, resentful of Bozeman's southern heritage, tried to change the name to Montana City, but after a "vigorous . . . spirited" discussion, the motion was defeated.[29]

Those who arrived in the Gallatin in the summer of 1864 had an array of choices for prospecting or staking a homestead. Miners found modest amounts of gold some ninety miles northwest of Bozeman, leading to the founding of Butte.[30] Gold was also discovered in Last Chance Gulch, roughly the same distance north-northwest of Bozeman, in an area near the Prickly Pear Valley. That autumn, streets were laid out in the upstart "Crab Town," which later became Helena.[31] Another discovery, thirty miles east of Helena at Confederate Gulch, led to the creation of Diamond City.

Bozeman was ideally located and quickly became more inviting than the floundering Gallatin City at the Three Forks. Travelers coming over the Bozeman Pass could continue on to Virginia City, swing north to gold fields around Helena, or make the Gallatin Valley their home. No matter their final destination, westward migrants required rest and provisions when they arrived, and efforts immediately began to accommodate those needs. John Stafford and W. S. Rice erected a one-and-a-half-story hotel substantial enough to host the 1864 Christmas Eve Ball, and other wooden structures popped up on Main Street.[32] Simple homes were constructed, containing, in William Alderson's words, "such homemade articles of furniture as ordinary ingenuity could devise or urgent necessity demand."[33] When one homesteader's wife came from the East to join her husband, she sat patiently for several minutes in a small, dirt-floor shed before asking to see the main house. Only then did she learn that the presumed shed was actually the main house.[34]

Farmers dug irrigation ditches from the East Gallatin River, and L. B. Lyman sowed what was probably the first crop of wheat in Montana. The Alderson brothers planted one thousand pounds of seed potatoes, obtained from Daniel Rouse for a horse worth $250. Tom Cover and Perry McAdow erected a flour mill just east of town, and eventually appropriated eight hundred miner's inches of water from Bozeman Creek that flowed via Mill Creek.[35]

To the southwest, Nelson Story had accumulated enough dust from the gold fields of Alder Gulch to invest $13,000 in additional claims by the spring of 1865, and to hire several men to mine his interests in lodes named Monson, Julia Ferina, and Farragut. That fall, he purchased a one-half interest in three of Benjamin Frank Christenot's claims in the Pine Grove District for $2,500. The two also mined four different claims at Summit that were part of the Oro Cache Lode, with Christenot owning a two-thirds interest, Story one-third. It was here they found their greatest success.[36]

Taking its name from the Spanish word for gold and the French word for hidden, the Oro Cache consisted of a large series of quartz veins embedded with gold.[37] Between December 1864 and March 1865, Christenot supervised the excavation of more than eighty-one-and-a-half tons of rock, yielding more than eight thousand dollars in gold. But once he learned that simple mining methods were barely able to capitalize on the full potential of the site's unique deposits, Christenot constructed a Spanish arrastra, a type of crude stone mill consisting of four stone drags and one stamp for breaking rock. The mule-powered arrastra allowed him to extract thousands of dollars more in gold from the pulverized quartz. While Christenot arranged for more expensive equipment to be shipped from the East, specimens from the Oro Cache, now dubbed "the richest gold lode ever discovered in any country," went on display at the William & Nolan Company Bank in Virginia City.[38] The lode's success attracted attention as well as would-be claim jumpers. When Bill Carter and an accomplice tried to move in on the site, Nelson confronted the two men with a shotgun. Using his companion as a shield, Carter reached for his revolver, but Story fired first and shot Carter's right hand off. Carter, stunned, tried futilely to pick up his gun, not realizing his hand was missing.[39]

Hard times followed the incredible discovery at Oro Cache. That winter and spring, heavy snow and subzero temperatures stalled freight trains from Salt Lake City and Walla Walla, leading to inflated prices in Alder Gulch. By May of 1865, a one-hundred-pound sack of flour that sold for $28 six months earlier cost a staggering $85. Armed gangs seized all the sacks they could find and sold them in twelve-pound allotments to residents, those with families receiving priority.[40] Merchants sold butter at $1.50 per pound, syrup for $9 a gallon, onions at forty-five cents a pound, and potatoes for twenty-five cents apiece.[41] Story charged a carpenter $9 in gold dust for one hammer. A few days later, he purchased two eggs from the same man and was billed $3. "I remember having sold you a hammer at one time," said Story as he squared up. "Here is your money. Glad I didn't buy any more eggs."[42] Children supplemented family incomes by cleaning sluice boxes, selling flowers on street corners, and collecting gold dust swept from store floors. A paper shortage led others to sell sharpened sticks to butchers, who gave them to customers for carrying home their meat. The pressures of inflation lingered over the summer, though flour costs returned to normal, aided in part by shipments from Bozeman after Gallatin Valley farmers harvested twenty thousand bushels of wheat.[43]

Fourteen-Mile City was losing its luster. Story's mining claims were all but exhausted, and he soon concluded that Bozeman offered a more promising future for his mercantile operation. Virginia City's population was dwindling as many headed to the new camps, and by the end of 1865, only two thousand residents would remain. Though the gulch was safer than it had been when he first arrived, lawlessness continued to plague the mining camps throughout the territory and there were sporadic vigilante hangings, particularly near Helena.[44] Story, more interested in pursuing his financial goals, refrained from further involvement in the movement. "He didn't stay with any cops and robbers deal," said Malcolm. "He wanted to pursue mercantilism and merchandising . . . get into something solid."[45]

As the region's population grew and its economy diversified, larger developments began to shape the future of Montana Territory. In the summer of 1864, President Lincoln appointed Sidney Edgerton the first territorial governor, and very shortly Edgerton lost any hope he might have held for Republican dominance. Democrat Sam McLean defeated Wilbur Fisk Sanders in an election for territorial delegate to Congress, and Edgerton's radical partisanship alienated many Democrats. The territorial legislature could barely agree on laws regarding mining, roads, and public education.[46]

Nevertheless, a bipartisan agreement on February 2, 1865, led to the creation of nine counties. Gallatin County included the Gallatin Valley and the Yellowstone Valley to the Clarks Fork of the Yellowstone, with Gallatin City the county seat. The legislature also moved the territorial capital from Bannack to Virginia City in Madison County. Anticipating increased emigrant traffic, legislators gave the Missouri and Rocky Mountain Wagon Road and Telegraph Company—at times referred to as the Broad Gauge Company—a twenty-year charter that included ferry, toll, and townsite privileges. In March, the company hired William Davies to build three ferryboats where the Bridger and Bozeman Trails crossed the Bighorn, Clarks Fork, and Yellowstone Rivers. Bridges soon spanned smaller streams, and branch trails extended to the Milk River, Fort Benton, and other gold fields in western Montana.[47]

Davies established a boatyard in mid-April on the Yellowstone, and within a month his crew constructed two ferryboats for crossings on the Clarks Fork and the Bighorn Rivers. Unfortunately for Davies, there were no customers in need of crossing. Fearing for emigrant safety, the government had barred civilian traffic through the Powder River Basin and deployed three army columns under General Patrick Connor to conduct punitive raids against the Sioux, Cheyenne, and Arapaho Tribes.[48] The action only made matters worse. The presence of the army infuriated the Sioux and their allies, especially when Fort Reno was constructed in August on the Powder River, three miles below the mouth of Dry Fork. Warfare intensified all along the trail and raised worries in the Gallatin Valley.

"It was a land of fair promise, of course, with its extensive acreage of nutritious pasturage," wrote William Alderson, "but even that was only available at the risk of encountering at any day or hour, a band of hostile Indians to dispute the white man's right of possession."[49]

In late August, a band of Sioux killed two men on the eastern side of the Bozeman Pass, triggering a panic that prompted several families to flee to Bozeman for sanctuary.[50] Among them were A. H. and Rosa Van Vlierden and their two young daughters. "We had an Indian pony which my husband brought up while I dressed myself and [the] children," Rosa wrote years later. "Then I mounted the pony, took one little girl in front of me and the other behind me, my husband walking beside as we started for town. Never will I forget the horror and the loneliness of that night. The wolves and coyotes were howling around us, and it seemed as though everything we saw was an Indian."[51] The Van Vlierdens arrived safely and joined others holed up in the Stafford and Rice Hotel. A letter signed by more than a dozen people and published in the *Montana Post* requested men from Virginia City to come "promptly to the scene of inhuman murder and butchery." Despite the gross exaggeration, or maybe because of it, the plea went unanswered.[52]

After the scare abated, Alderson brought in the first harvester to Montana, a Woods model shipped via Fort Benton. He and his brother imported seed potatoes from Utah at twenty cents a pound, yielding a 4,100-pound potato crop that they sold in Diamond City for a half-bit, or twelve and a half cents, per pound. Other local producers also raised potatoes and a few vegetables, marketing them in Diamond City, Virginia City, and Helena.[53] Caleb "Squire" Fitz and his son opened a store in 1865, the back portion of which was used as a children's classroom by teacher Samuel Anderson. Tom Cover and Perry McAdow's new threshing machine raised the flour mill's capacity to one thousand sacks per week.[54]

Observers noted the valley's ongoing transformation. John Grannis wrote that the farms and plowed fields so closely resembled those back east they made him homesick.[55] In October, James Sawyers, while laying out a wagon road from the mouth of the Niobrara River to Virginia City, wrote in his diary that the Gallatin Valley presented a fine appearance, "and when irrigated produces abundant crops, the yield of grain on the numerous farms in the valley being very large this season."[56] Such impressions earned the valley its first nickname, "the Genesee of Montana," for the fertile region in New York state.[57] Thomas Dimsdale believed anyone who undertook farming in the new territory would enjoy a "sure market" and a "splendid price for every pound of produce that can be raised."[58]

The Gallatin Valley's recent growth and the promise of future development convinced Story that the time was right to capitalize a mercantile operation with his earnings from the gold fields.

By the 1870s, the Gallatin Valley was beginning to flourish as an agricultural center. Its alluvial soils made the valley ideal for growing grain and vegetable crops. Museum of the Rockies, Bozeman x80.6.862

Hoping to stock his shelves with the finest implements and supplies, he believed the best products and prices would be found back in Leavenworth, and a favorable exchange rate made the opportunity even more enticing. The federal government had issued so-called greenbacks to finance the Civil War, but they were unsecured by any specie. With the war now over, one greenback was worth about seventy cents. Having amassed a sum of thirty thousand dollars in gold from his various claims, Story realized he could see those earnings increase immediately given the weak dollar.

He also saw further opportunity to profit from a journey across the plains. In Texas, longhorn cattle populations, unattended during the war, had exploded, and an estimated five to six million animals now roamed the ranges.[59] At the end of the conflict, these animals found eager consumers and fetched high prices in newly reopened northern markets. A longhorn worth as little as five dollars in the Lone Star State could be worth anywhere from eighteen to thirty dollars at western army posts and Indian reservations. In Chicago, one could get forty dollars a head, and elsewhere the rate reached fifty dollars.[60] Story rightly believed that the value of a herd in Montana could be nearly twice that of a herd in Chicago. While trailing cattle such a great distance was no doubt a risky proposition, the ability to supply beef to mining camps, towns, and nearby Indian tribes held the promise of a massive windfall.[61]

Story was willing to take the chance. Even the impending birth of his first child did not change his mind. A mercantile, freighting, and cattle operation in Montana Territory would allow Story to provide his family with the very best and open doors to countless other opportunities. It was something to build a future on, something solid.

SIDNEY EDGERTON headed east in September 1865, ostensibly to look after personal affairs in Ohio and Montana's interests in Washington. This left territorial secretary Thomas Francis Meagher as acting governor. But since Edgerton had failed to obtain a leave of absence, he was removed from office a few months later.[62]

Other prominent Montanans journeyed east that fall and winter for a variety of reasons. Territorial chief justice Hezekiah Hosmer made a trip to Washington, D.C., to fend off "mettlesome legislation" in Congress that would allow the government to raise revenue by auctioning off mining lands.[63] Hosmer, like most westerners, opposed the plan, as it would force miners to bid for claims they had already established.[64] Paris Pfouts was bound for New York, Boston, and Philadelphia in an effort to raise capital to expand mineral exploration in the territory. Territorial marshal George Pinney, and businessmen Benjamin Christenot and Tom Cover also went east for personal reasons, as of course did Nelson Story. Prior to their respective departures, all agreed to rendezvous in New York and travel together to the nation's capital, where they would promote statehood for Montana.[65] In the interest of supplying the treasury with gold and silver during the waning days of the Civil War, Congress had expedited the process for Nevada in 1864, making it the thirty-sixth state. The loose-knit Montana delegation hoped history would repeat itself.[66]

Some left the territory via Fort Benton and the Missouri River, and others on Mackinaw boats down the Yellowstone.[67] Most departed by November, but it seems Story waited until December. He left Ellen, then eight months pregnant, and the Summit store under the care of Elias, and purchased a ticket to Atchison, Kansas, on the Benjamin Holladay Stage for $350. The ticket price included twenty-five pounds of luggage, but the stage would not accept liability for the loss or theft of bullion, gold dust, and bank or treasury notes.[68] Story, therefore, kept a 140-pound tin box containing his gold by his side at all times.

He spent a few days in Salt Lake City, taking in performances by Shakespearian actress Julia Dean Haynes at the Brigham Young Theater, before departing for the Midwest. After a five-day journey via Forts Bridger and Laramie, Story reached Denver, where he took his gold to the Kountze Brothers Bank for shipment to Wall Street.[69] After another monotonous, jolting ride of one week, living primarily on the stage-stop standard fare of beans, sourdough bread, and coffee, Story reached Atchison and boarded the Hannibal and St. Joseph Railroad. Following a brief family visit in his hometown of Burlingham, he arrived in New York and received forty thousand dollars in greenbacks for the gold dust, ten thousand dollars of which was paid in cash and the balance under a letter of credit. Fearful of being robbed or otherwise losing his fortune, Story sewed the cash into his coat, and he kept a lariat nearby to lower himself from his second-floor hotel room in the event of a fire.[70]

As planned, he joined the Montana delegation shortly thereafter, and the two dozen members traveled to Washington for an audience with President Andrew Johnson on February 7, just days after Thomas Meagher proposed statehood in a letter to the president.[71] Delegate spokesman George Pinney told Johnson that Montana's gold and silver, "which the Almighty had long kept hidden and garnered in our hills and ravines, have been revealed or discovered at a time when the nation needs new channels of flowing wealth to supply her treasury."[72] He then went on to extol the territory's agricultural resources.

Johnson assured the delegation he would be a "willing and cordial helper" in transitioning territories like Montana toward statehood, but the effort was unsuccessful.[73] Having commanded New York's

Irish Brigade at Antietam and Fredericksburg, Governor Meagher's loyalty to the Union was evident, but his resistance to vigilantism and his Catholic heritage rubbed some, especially Freemasons, the wrong way. And he was a Democrat. Republicans, Wilbur Sanders chief among them, worried statehood might give the Irish patriot ambitions of becoming a U.S. senator, tipping the balance of power in Montana to the Democrats. In reality, Meagher harbored no such political aspirations. While he did convene a constitutional convention in Virginia City that April as a necessary step toward statehood, his opponents made sure the resultant document never reached Congress, claiming it was lost or destroyed in a fire.[74]

Chapter Three

Holding the Herd, 1866

A

FTER shaking hands with the president, Story headed back west. He visited the Civil War battlefield at Stones River, Tennessee, where, during the winter of 1862–1863, many of his childhood friends and acquaintances fell while serving in the Eighteenth Regiment, Ohio Volunteer Infantry. Then, in Leavenworth, Kansas, he arranged the purchase of canned goods, seed, farming supplies, tack, and even fruits, items either essential to or coveted by farmers in the Gallatin Valley. Story promised the merchants he would return for his order in a few months, and then he hired two acquaintances, Bill Petty and Tom Allen, purchased a pair of wagons, and headed for Texas. After a five- to six-week journey, the three men reached Fort Worth in late March, where they acquired a herd of six hundred longhorns for just under ten dollars a head, as well as supplies, horses, and four mules.[1]

A typical cattle drive in the 1860s required one cowboy for every one hundred head of cattle, plus a cook, a horse wrangler, and a trail boss. The going wage at the time was forty dollars per month, and the trail boss, in this case Story, would supply each drover with six horses.[2] Having already secured the services of Petty and Allen, he hired six additional men, who, in his judgment, would be the most honest and loyal. One of these hires was Jose Pablo Tsoyio, part Mexican and part Native American, who would be known throughout his short life as Mexican Joe.[3] Tsoyio had spent years as a guide on the Santa Fe Trail and had also worked as a buffalo hunter and skinner. He knew how to read a trail and could sign-talk. Although Story was the trail boss, Tsoyio would be the group's guide, at least during the first part of the journey.[4]

The drive began in mid-April. Having branded the cattle with an ox-yoke T on the left ribs and a circle on the left hip to denote trail cattle, Story, wearing knee length boots and sporting two holstered Colt Navy Revolvers, led his herd and men northeast out of Fort Worth to pick up the Texas Road, or Shawnee Trail, used since 1842 to trail longhorns to Kansas City.[5] The first leg was a rugged, wooded stretch that ran through Sherman, Texas, before crossing the Red River at Colbert's Ferry and entering Indian Territory.[6] Two men rode point, keeping the herd in the right direction. The rest of the drovers, divided into pairs, served as either "swing drivers" to keep the cattle in line or as "drag drivers" on the flank to prevent sick, tired, and laggard cattle from falling too far behind. A cattle drive averaged fifteen miles a day, but Story's men pushed the herd hard during the first several days in order to tire the animals and prevent them from trying to return to their accustomed ranges. After the first week, the pace slowed to no more than ten miles a day, giving the cattle more time to graze and water.[7]

Texas longhorns, thin and long-legged, can travel long distances and endure tough conditions, but like all cattle are easily spooked. When the herd approached a stream, the riders would move the animals through the water quickly, as they could be skittish about crossing, particularly if sunlight reflected in their eyes or if the wind caused the surface to ripple. Given cattle's ability to smell water from miles away, a shift in the wind could make the herd turn around to a previous watering hole or charge ahead to a new one. If drovers sensed an impending storm, they would try to keep the animals calm by riding around the herd and singing songs. Should thunder and lightning trigger a stampede, riders would fire their six-shooters and attempt to swing the lead cattle into a circle, or "mill." It was not an easy task, and it carried the serious risk of being trampled underfoot. Not until the stampede halted could cowboys resume the calming effect of their singing and boast that they had "held the herd."[8]

Story and Tsoyio rode out ahead of the drovers each afternoon to find the next creek or stream, as the availability of water often determined the evening's campsite. Once a location was selected, the supply wagon was brought in first, and only when the cattle and horses had been bedded down were the men fed.[9] Staples were corn meal, sorghum molasses, beans, bacon, salt, sugar, and coffee,

Longhorn cattle are driven across a river in Kansas Territory, c. 1866.
Kansas State Historical Society, Topeka 00264503

occasionally supplemented by wild game killed during the day. After dinner, all the men took turns watching the herd, with shifts ranging from two to four hours. As was the case during storms, the cowboys sang to keep the cattle calm. Lack of sleep was perhaps the greatest hardship at night. Some rubbed tobacco in their eyes just to keep them open. Breakfast on a trail drive was usually served at or just before daylight.[10]

When Story and his train reached the Chickasaw Indian settlement of Boggy Depot in Oklahoma Territory, rainstorms caused stream levels to rise throughout the area. There was little relief from the weather as they crossed the Canadian and Arkansas Rivers, and Story later joked that the herd swam more than it walked.[11] The ground became so soggy that the men often slept in their saddles. Upon reaching Fort Gibson, also in the Cherokee Nation, they were stopped by tribal representatives. Previous herds had damaged their lands, so the Indians sought concessions: ten cents a head to proceed, the return of any stray Cherokee cattle that might join Story's herd along the way, and a promise to stay on the main trail. Story agreed to the first two demands, but told Cherokee officials he could not abide by the third. Hundreds of thousands of Texas cattle were driven north in 1866, most destined for the railhead at Sedalia,

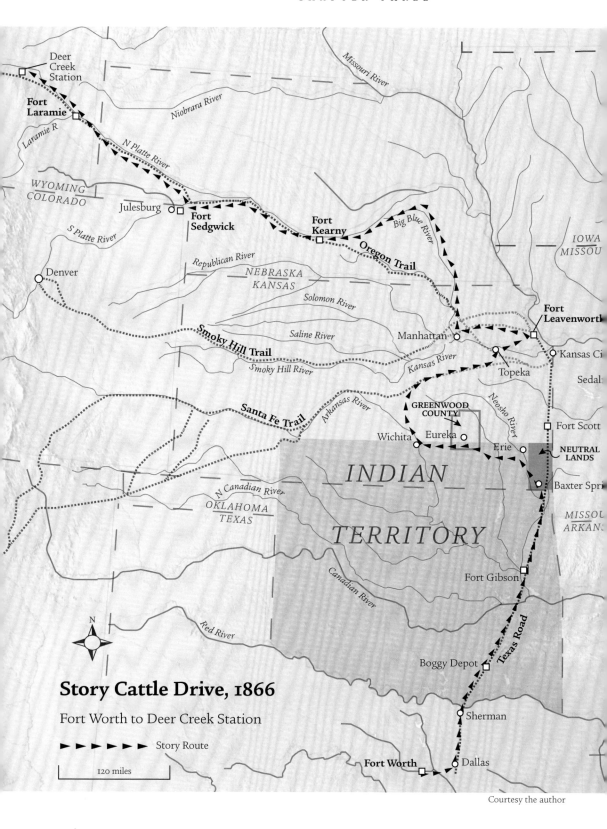

Story Cattle Drive, 1866

Fort Worth to Deer Creek Station

▶▶▶▶▶ Story Route

⊢——⊢ 120 miles

Missouri. As a result, good grass was scarce, and Story insisted he be allowed to take his herd off the main trail to graze. The Cherokees were peaceful farmers, and the well-armed cowboys probably dissuaded them from pressing the point. Story could run his cattle wherever he saw fit.[12]

When the herd reached the Neosho River in late May, Story and his men had logged just over four hundred miles. A few cattle had been lost to predators, but none to rustlers. Once the men turned the herd north-northwest along the Neosho, the enterprise would meet its first major challenge. But Story's resolve, as it would many times over the course of the drive, averted disaster and kept the cattle and his men together.

Missourians and Kansans claimed to have suffered serious losses to their native herds from Texas tick fever, an often-fatal disease that destroyed an animal's red blood cells. As a result, strict quarantine laws banned northern-bound longhorns from April 1 to November 1, when the disease was thought to be most infectious. Missourians especially took advantage of the tick fever scare and established roadblocks. The most notable was in the Cherokee Neutral Lands, a fifty-mile-long and twenty-five-mile-wide stretch in the southeast corner of Kansas, which was originally created as a barrier between Osage Indians and settlers, but by the 1860s had come to be a no-man's-land separating Kansas and Missouri. Located near Baxter Springs (formerly Baxter's Place), the Neutral Lands blocked drovers from herding more than one hundred thousand head of cattle to northern markets in the summer of 1866. Herds were often stampeded at night and held for ransom. If the owner refused to pay, the thieves kept the cattle, cashing them in at Sedalia. Rather than challenge the barricade, many cattlemen cut their losses and sold their herds to locals, only to learn later they had been paid with bogus drafts and checks.[13] Those who challenged the barricade often exacted a heavier toll. Many were flogged by Kansas Jayhawkers, and a few were killed.[14] Some managed to reach Sedalia by driving their herds east along the Arkansas line and swinging back to the north-northwest, while others opted to drive west along the southern Kansas border, then swing to the north-northeast to St. Joseph, Missouri.[15]

Story knew of the quarantine when he left Fort Worth, but believed he would be able to continue north via Fort Scott by paying a toll. Not until he and his men actually approached Baxter Springs did he learn how high that price would be and the perils of defying the barricade. Armed men posing as members of the Granger's

Association demanded two dollars per head for the longhorns to continue. Story was outraged, but would neither turn back nor pay the Jayhawkers their "ransom." Nor would he just sit and do nothing while his animals starved. Story added a few hundred cows and calves to his herd, some purchased and some pilfered from frustrated cattlemen, hired four more drovers, and then headed west, hoping to avoid as many established counties as possible before swinging back to the northeast for Leavenworth.[16]

THE JUNE 23, 1866, edition of Burlington's *Kansas Patriot* included the following announcement:

> *A man was arrested in Greenwood County, lately, for attempt-*
> *ing to drive through it a drove of Texan Cattle. He was taken*
> *to Eureka, sentenced to pay a fine of seventy-five dollars*
> *(which was paid), and made to drive his cattle back.*[17]

Whether the man in question was Nelson Story cannot be known, as civil appearance court docket records for Eureka, Kansas, only date back to 1867. Still, a compelling case can be made that it was, as it would corroborate information contained in family letters and recollections.

By 1866, Story's in-laws, the Trents, had settled in Neosho County's Centreville Township, not far from present-day Erie, Kansas. Ellen's sister Jeanette, then five years old, later claimed that Nelson visited the family during the drive, and that she tearfully ran after him as he left, hoping he would stay or take her to Montana. Centreville bordered the Neosho River, a stream Story most likely would have followed north-northwest after leaving the neutral strip. In letters Bine Story wrote to his son Byron, he insisted that his father told him he reached Leavenworth by way of the Arkansas and Smoky Hill Rivers. Such a route would make sense, given the location of Kansas settlements barring Texas cattle. In moving west, Story would have to keep the herd in Indian Territory that then included a ten-mile-wide strip on the southern border of Greenwood County.[18] The northern edge of the strip was roughly four miles south of Eureka, so he could have accidentally crossed the border into Greenwood County sometime in June. If Story was, in fact, the subject of the *Patriot's* notice, one thing is certain: he would not "be made to drive his cattle back."

Story eventually reached the Arkansas River near present-day Wichita, then angled north to the Santa Fe Trail. This was familiar country, land he had traversed when freighting out of Fort Leavenworth, but it did not ease the fatigue and concern caused by the events at Baxter Springs. Somewhere along this stretch Story awoke one morning to find missing a hundred-dollar bill that he was sure he had placed in his bedroll. He searched every one of his men, but the money was never found. Chances are he simply lost the note.[19] It was the only time Story demonstrated distrust for his cowboys, but not enough to garner their resentment. Staying on the Santa Fe Trail, the drive turned northeast to Topeka, where the herd crossed the Kansas River on a pontoon bridge, and then ambled on to within twenty miles of Fort Leavenworth. This circuitous route from the neutral strip totaled 450 miles, and would have taken nearly a month to complete.[20]

While his men made camp, Story and a few others rode into Leavenworth for his supplies. Here he learned that the army had issued General Order No. 27. Intended to protect westward emigrants crossing Native lands, the mandate designated several forts as assembly points, where travelers wishing to proceed were required to be in

Freight teams pass through Manhattan, Kansas Territory, c. 1867. Story acquired fifteen freight wagons, 150 oxen, and several more drovers before leaving Kansas Territory. Kansas State Historical Society, Topeka d408

a train of at least twenty wagons or thirty armed men.[21] For those headed to the Bozeman Trail, the assembly point was Fort Kearny in Nebraska. In Leavenworth, Story purchased fifteen wagons to haul groceries and supplies and added 150 head of work-oxen. He also hired eleven more men, including twenty-year-old Tommy Thompson, a freighter from New York State. Tom Allen decided to stay in Leavenworth, meaning Story had twenty-two men in his employ. He figured he could find seven more along the Oregon Trail and in the meantime still manage to move the herd.[22] Story also bought thirty civilian model Remington "Split-Breech" carbines. Operated by a rotating block system, these single shot rifles could be reloaded quickly and easily. They were superior to the muzzle-loading Hawken rifle and army Springfields in range and accuracy. The rifles sold for thirty-five dollars apiece in the East, but commanded one hundred dollars on the frontier. Given the dangers that awaited, Story agreed to the price, and also purchased enough .56-50 Spencer rimfire cartridges to fill one of the supply wagons.[23]

Supplied and armed for the journey ahead, Story's men broke camp on July 10 and led the herd southwest along the Smoky Hill Trail to the Big Blue River, and then turned north.[24] One hundred forty trail miles later they reached the Platte, headed west, and arrived at Fort Kearny in early August. The terrain beyond Fort Kearny was much like that in Kansas: well-watered, flat, and favorable to the steady movement of the herd. In ten days, the drive reached the junction of the North and South Platte Rivers, where it followed the latter stream until reaching Fort Sedgwick near Julesburg, Colorado. After a brief rest, the drive set out to the northwest and passed Courthouse Rock, Chimney Rock, and Castle Rock, "the dreary bottomlands of the North Platte Valley" before crossing the Laramie River to reach Fort Laramie.[25]

Between Forts Leavenworth and Laramie, Story managed to hire an additional seven hands, bringing his total armed strength to thirty. Exactly where they joined up is unknown, but it would be fair to assume they came on board at or near Fort Kearny. Story hired two more men at Fort Laramie, bullwhackers John Catlin and Steve Grover, both Union veterans who had been waiting to join a larger train to Montana where they hoped to start a freighting operation.[26]

Officers at Fort Laramie told Story that Oglala chief Red Cloud and his Lakota bands had abruptly left a major treaty council at the fort earlier in the summer. Nine days later the Eighteenth Infantry, commanded by Colonel Henry Carrington, left the fort to build more outposts along the Bozeman Trail. They reached Fort Reno

Oglala Lakota chief Red Cloud (right, c. 1870) objected to the trespass of American settlers and prospectors into tribal lands not ceded under the 1851 Fort Laramie Treaty. Just months after Story's cattle drive, Red Cloud and his allies burned the forts along the Bozeman Trail. Indian Neg 10576, Wyoming State Archives, Cheyenne

in time to witness a raid on June 30 in which Native warriors captured a horse and mule herd. Undaunted, Carrington led the Eighteenth seventy miles northwest to Piney Creek, where he established Fort Phil Kearny on July 14. A few days later, Red Cloud's warriors launched a weeklong series of raids along the trail that left twenty-four soldiers and civilians dead, including five traders ambushed six miles from the new fort.[27] Indians also harassed Fort Reno, as well as a third post, Fort C. F. Smith, which was constructed in August on the Bighorn River north of Phil Kearny.[28] Given these events, the officers suggested Story remain on the Oregon Trail and take the same route into Montana he and Ellen had traveled in 1863. He rejected the idea, however, after calculating the additional mileage and the possibility of snow trapping the herd in high country. Besides, his train exceeded the size mandated by Order No. 27. Story would keep to his original plan.

Out of Laramie, the Story cattle drive followed the Oregon Trail along the North Platte River for some eighty-plus miles to Sage Creek, where it picked up the Bozeman Trail in mid-September. As the train moved along, Story and his men noticed small war parties observing the herd from a distance.[29] Occasionally they spotted newly dug graves, burned wagons, and dead livestock, all resulting from the violence that had erupted just weeks earlier. Story stopped sending the supply wagon ahead to pick out the evening's camping spot. Everyone stayed together, and Story had three of his best marksmen escort the horse herd to protect it from attack.

Upon reaching the Dry Fork of the Cheyenne River, Story rested his men and animals. He ordered all containers capable of holding water to be filled, as this was the last major watering hole until Fort Reno and the Powder River, sixty miles further up the trail. Story was determined to reach the Powder River in three to four days, meaning the pace would have to be hastened. Instead of traveling ten miles a day, Story hoped to average closer to twenty.

The first day ended near midnight when the herd bedded down at Antelope Creek, just over twenty miles away. On the second day, some of the younger cattle began to bawl from thirst, and most of the animals refused to graze. Weaker ones began to fall behind. Story rode drag, trying his best to keep them moving with the main body. Some collapsed; those who were unable to continue were shot. Late

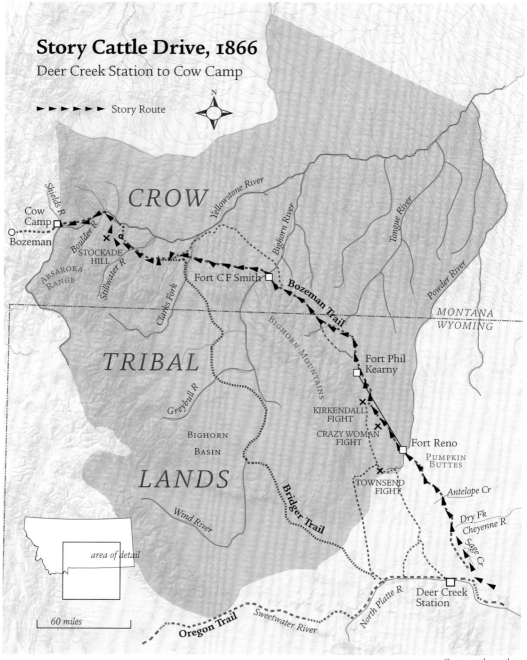

Story Cattle Drive, 1866
Deer Creek Station to Cow Camp

►►►►►► Story Route

N

CROW

TRIBAL

LANDS

Shields R

Cow Camp
Bozeman

Boulder R

STOCKADE HILL

Stillwater R

ABSAROKA RANGE

Clarks Fork

Yellowstone River

Fort C F Smith

Bozeman Trail

Bighorn River

BIGHORN MOUNTAINS

Tongue River

Powder River

MONTANA
WYOMING

Greybull R

Fort Phil Kearny

KIRKENDALL FIGHT

CRAZY WOMAN FIGHT

Fort Reno

PUMPKIN BUTTES

TOWNSEND FIGHT

Antelope Cr

BIGHORN BASIN

Bridger Trail

Wind River

area of detail

Dry Fk
Cheyenne R

Sage Cr

North Platte R

Deer Creek Station

60 miles

Oregon Trail

Sweetwater River

Courtesy the author

in the evening, the train, having covered twenty-four miles, reached the Dry Fork of the Powder River, just west of Pumpkin Buttes.[30]

At dawn of the third day, Story's men moved the herd along the Dry Fork, where scattered pools of water allowed the animals to drink and recover some strength. Late in the day, they came upon the Powder River, and the smell of water caused the longhorns to stampede for the river's edge, where the men let them wade and range up and down the bank. As evening fell, a party of seventy-five Sioux warriors approached. Through signs interpreted by Tsoyio, the leader of the band communicated peaceful intentions. Story was leery, but allowed them to approach under the careful eye of his men and their loaded Remingtons. The Indians told Story he was tres-passing on their hunting grounds, but that they would allow him to proceed if he gave them several head of cattle. Emboldened by the fact Fort Reno was a short ride away, Story refused. He declared that his party did not want to stay in the area and that he would pass through quickly and would not return. Noting the strength of his force, the warriors surrendered the point, and the encounter ended after only twenty or thirty minutes.[31]

It was now late in the day, and Story decided to move the herd further along the Powder, closer to Fort Reno. John Catlin recalled that as the men moved the herd, they came upon a French trapper and his young son who were making camp: "We invited them to turn back and camp with us for greater safety. The Frenchman said he wasn't half-afraid of Indians as he was some white men. That set us going and, telling him to be careful, we moved along."[32]

On the morning of September 21, Story allowed his men some extra rest before proceeding after lunch. The cattle, still enjoying the waters of the Powder and the nearby grasses, also needed a break. Some of the cowboys took advantage and returned to their bedrolls. A few others, led by Bill Petty, went hunting. Story, Thompson, and George Dow rode to the rear of the train to double-check the condi-tion of the wagons.

Although Story's men did not know it, the same group of Sioux warriors who had visited the train the day before had continued their watch. Realizing the cowboys had let their guard down and spread out, they attacked. A group of twenty swooped down and opened fire on the hunting party, wounding Petty and George Over-holt. They then went after the cattle. At the sound of the gunfire, Story, Thompson, and Dow swung their horses around and galloped back toward the front of the train. By the time Story had emptied both of his pistols at the retreating Sioux, he had two wounded

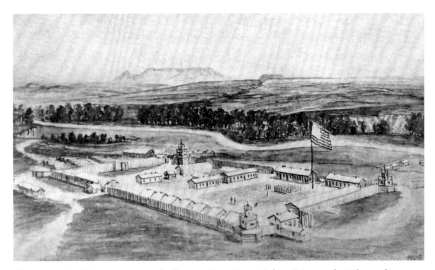

Story's cattle drive was attacked near Fort Reno (above) in early July and one drover was killed, yet the soldiers from the fort did little to intervene in the conflict.
Sub neg 5378, Wyoming State Archives, Cheyenne

men and half a dozen dead cattle. Angry over his carelessness, Story ordered his drovers to round up the cattle and move the entire train half a mile closer to Fort Reno. Petty's gunshot wound was dressed, and pincers were used to extract two arrows from Overholt's back. Tommy Thompson rode on to Fort Reno to procure an ambulance. The men were on high alert for the entire evening, and the fear of another attack proved too much for one of the high-strung Texans. Story claimed he died from "sheer fright."[33] Though officers and soldiers in Fort Reno now knew about Story's predicament, they did not lend assistance. The inaction was fully in keeping with one traveler's assessment of the station, written only a month earlier:

> They have 150 men here. All they do is steal from emigrants, eat Uncle Sams' [*sic*] rations & play cards. If a dozen Indians come around they shut themselves up in the Fort and watch them. There is no fight to them.[34]

As the sun rose the next morning, the Sioux attacked again. Thirty warriors stampeded the herd and killed one of the cowboys. Before Story's men had time to react, the Indians had disappeared, as had forty head of cattle. Having two men wounded and six cattle killed the day before were one thing. The death of a cowboy and the theft of forty cattle was another. Story wanted his animals back. He strapped on his revolvers, saddled his mount, and ordered five other men to join him.[35] Among them was war veteran John Catlin, who was both impressed and worried by Story's grit: "Accustomed as the Civil War had made me to following almost any daredevil leader, there were a good many times when Nelson Story had me guessing."[36]

Story and his small force followed the trail left by the stolen cattle, and as the tracks became fresher the Sioux attacked again. Their force was shaped like a crescent, with the warriors on the flanks hoping to cut off any potential escape routes. As Story later put it, he and his men "wheeled and with dignity and haste, retreated."[37] Some of the party, including one man who had chosen to ride a mule, were nearly overrun until Story took refuge behind a boulder and fired his revolvers at their pursuers. The men in camp laid down covering fire, and everyone returned safely.

When darkness fell, Story resumed the chase, this time taking all but just a few of his men. After locating the warriors' camp, they quietly dismounted and approached. Just as the warriors were roasting one of the captured steers, Story and his men attacked. The rapid-firing Remingtons gave Story's cowboys the upper hand. An unknown number of Sioux men were killed. All the cattle, save a few that had already been butchered, were recovered.

Story and his force returned to camp at dawn and immediately pushed on to Fort Reno. Before leaving, Story sent Catlin and another man back to check on the Frenchman and his son that they had met two days earlier. "We found the bodies of the man and boy, scalped and mutilated," wrote Catlin. "Their wagon was burned; their horses were gone; their provisions were scattered over the ground. We buried the bodies and went back to the train."[38]

John Catlin, n.d. At Fort Laramie, Story hired Union veteran John Catlin, above, to be one of his bullwhackers. During the drive, Catlin discovered the mutilated body of a murdered Frenchman and his son along their route. MHS Photograph Archives, Helena 941-473

At Fort Reno, once described as a "toy-like log stockade," the commanding officer, Captain Joshua Proctor, told Story the attacks were an omen, and that he would be wise to turn back to the Oregon Trail. But Story was in too big of a hurry, and despite the risk of more casualties ahead, decided to stay the course. Leaving Petty and Overholt at the fort to recover from their wounds, Story and the remaining twenty-seven men pointed the herd toward Fort Phil Kearny.[39]

On they rode north through Reno Draw and across Ninemile Creek. A day and a half out of Fort Reno, they came upon the site of the Crazy Woman Fight, where on July 20 the Sioux had attacked a military train. The graves of two dead soldiers caught the eye of Story's men. At the end of the third day, they came upon the scene of the Kirkendall Fight, in which a party of six freighters had been attacked just north of Buffalo Wallows Springs, with one of them killed. No doubt Catlin and Steve Grover were glad they had waited at Fort Laramie for a train the size of Nelson Story's.

Groups of Sioux and their allies continued to observe the drive from a distance. At the end of the fourth day out of Fort Reno, a contingent of soldiers stopped Story with orders from Colonel Carrington that the drive could not continue because the road north was unsafe. Story rode on to Phil Kearny with the soldiers to meet face-to-face with Carrington, who described the bloodletting on the trail that summer. Story retorted that he was aware of the potential risks, and that his men had already been in skirmishes and managed to successfully defend themselves with their arsenal of Remingtons.

He claimed that the entire herd would be lost to marauders and blizzards if he was forced to sit and wait. Unsympathetic, Carrington told him to stay put. To make matters worse, Carrington upped the requirements outlined in General Order No. 27, requiring that Story have forty armed men in his party before proceeding.[40]

Neither Story nor his men felt particularly compelled to defy some three hundred–plus U.S. Army troops, so they chose to make camp. When Story sent a message to Carrington asking

Colonel Henry B. Carrington (left) ordered Story's outfit to remain at Fort Phil Kearny until he had at least forty men, but Story and his men defied the orders in a bold nighttime escape with the herd.
Courtesy PBA Galleries, San Francisco

to move his herd closer to the fort, he was again rebuffed. Carrington said he needed that pasturage for the army's animals.[41] Story now suspected that the fort commander wanted to confiscate the herd in order to feed his troops.[42] Catlin shared that belief: "There were three miles of fine meadow grass between us and the post. The troops had a few mule teams that were being used to transport logs and hay and General Carrington had one saddle horse left that the Indians had not captured. That three miles of grass was for the saddle horse, I suppose."[43]

Settling in for the unanticipated delay, the men built two corrals, one for the beef cattle and one for the work oxen. Several days later, though, Story ran out of patience when one of his night herders was killed, scalped, and according to Catlin, "shot so full of arrows that he looked like a big pincushion."[44] Convinced the camp was unsafe and that the men might as well take their chances on the trail, Story and Catlin rode to the fort for another audience with Carrington.

Story bluntly told Carrington that his herd had now been halted for better than two weeks with no sign of any other emigrant trains coming up the trail. It was nearly November, and the Bighorn Mountains already had several layers of new snow on the highest peaks. It would soon be the same along Piney Creek. Story sought permission to proceed but was again turned down. Carrington ordered him to wait for another train, while also requesting some of the cattle at low government prices. Story quickly rejected the proposed transaction.

Upon returning to camp, Story assembled the men and explained the situation: it was too dangerous to remain at Fort Phil Kearny, and the winter was coming. Story wanted to get his cattle to the Yellowstone Valley and see his wife and young daughter, Alice Montana Story, who had been born in early February, so he offered a choice to his drovers. If they could make Fort C. F. Smith, ninety-plus miles further up the trail, they would be out of the heart of Sioux territory. If they disobeyed Carrington and the army confiscated the herd, however, Story would be unable to compensate the crew. He then called for a vote.

Story and twenty-five of the men agreed to proceed onward by slipping out under cover of darkness. The only dissenter among the group was George Dow, whom Story immediately had bound, gagged, and placed in the back of a wagon. That evening, the men drove the cattle in a wide circle around the post and picked up the trail north out of Fort Phil Kearny without being detected. They pushed the herd hard to put as much distance between themselves and Carrington as possible. When dawn arrived, the men rested and made camp. Dow was freed and told he could return to the fort if he wished, but the prospect of traveling more than fifteen miles back through Sioux country convinced him to remain with the group.[45]

Before long, Carrington learned of Story's furtive exodus. Furious that his men had not detected the cattleman's move, he issued two new orders. The first required all subsequent civilian trains to be quartered within the stockade. The second tasked a fifteen-man detail with catching up to Story and escorting him safely through Sioux country. As the soldiers prepared to leave, however, Carrington, not wanting the fort to be undermanned, rescinded the order. Nelson Story was on his own, just as he wanted.[46]

In order to reduce their vulnerability to the Sioux, the cowboys moved the cattle by night and rested during the day. They maintained their vigilance, and were actually aided by an early snowstorm that discouraged any raids.[47] "We were attacked only two or three times and each time was when we were resting during the day," said Catlin. "We easily stood off the reds and had no trouble at all. Close to the fort there were more than three thousand Indians. As we moved toward the Bighorn country they became fewer."[48] One week out of Fort Phil Kearny, the herd reached Fort C. F. Smith, the final bastion along the Bozeman Trail. Commanded by Captain Nathaniel Kinney, the fort was but a few months old and garrisoned by only two companies of infantry. Kinney saw no reason to interfere with Story, and soldiers at the fort even helped ferry his supply wagons across the Bighorn River. A band of warriors, most likely Sioux, tried to stampede the cattle late one evening, but failed.[49]

Turning almost due west, the cattle train now headed toward Bozeman, just under two hundred trail miles away. The weather was unusually mild in the Yellowstone Valley, but knowing conditions could quickly change, Story continued to push his men and the herd toward the Gallatin Valley, right through Crow territory. They crossed the Clarks Fork of the Yellowstone, where Story observed a partially burned boat and assumed it had been transporting people east when it was attacked by Indians.[50] About a week out of Fort C. F. Smith, one of Story's men rode ahead of the outfit to hunt. It was late afternoon, and Story and Tsoyio were looking for a campsite when they heard a distant rifle shot. Racing toward the sound, they arrived in time to see a band of fifteen or twenty Sioux ride toward the wounded hunter. Two warriors, one on either side, lifted him up between them and, joined by the others, galloped to the top of a distant hill. There they killed the drover by shooting an arrow through his chest, and scalped him before Story and Tsoyio could

Nelson, Alice, and Ellen Story, 1866. After most of a year on the trail, Story was eager to reunite with his family, including his daughter who had been born just after he left. Gallatin Historical Society Museum, Bozeman

drive them off. The unfortunate cowboy was buried on top of the hill where he died.[51]

As Story and his men crossed a high plateau a few miles south of the Yellowstone, another war party, possibly Blackfeet, came into view. The men dismounted and positioned their supply wagons side by side. They started to dig defensive trenches, but the rocky ground stalled their efforts and they instead constructed three-foot-high stone breastworks. After a brief exchange of gunfire, the warriors retreated.[52]

A day later, the Story train forded the Yellowstone near present-day Springdale, passed Sheep Mountain, and then reached the Shields River. Just north of the great bend of the Yellowstone, near present-day Livingston, sat an abandoned cabin right on the boundary of Crow Country. Story ordered Tommy Thompson and a few others to construct cabins and corrals at the site while he, Catlin, and the remaining drovers took the herd and supply wagons into Bozeman, where they arrived on December 3. While most of the cattle, some seven hundred–plus, were left to graze east of town, the men drove the remaining three hundred to Virginia City, where butchers paid up to one hundred dollars per head. Here Story reunited with Ellen, Alice, and Elias, and immediately had them pack up the family belongings and accompany him back to Bozeman.[53]

The Story cattle drive covered more than 2,100 miles in just under eight months. Though cattle continued to trickle into the territory, it would be nearly ten years before large herds would again traverse the Bozeman Trail, affording Story an unparalleled dominance over the Montana beef market.[54]

Chapter Four

Blue Coats and Shoulder Straps, 1866–1869

I N THE EIGHT YEARS since he left Ohio, Nelson Story had been constantly on the move: Ohio to Kansas, the trail miles he racked up to Colorado and Bannack, his trip to the East Coast and down to Fort Worth, then north with the cattle. He had logged more miles than many people of his day traveled in a lifetime, but he was just getting started.

Story still had plenty of grubstake money, and he used it to initiate a spree of land acquisitions in and around Bozeman.[1] The most significant purchase was the 148-acre Van Vlierden ranch north of town, near where Bozeman Creek merges with the East Gallatin River. This property would serve as his ranching headquarters, where he, Ellen, and Alice moved into a double log house in mid-December while a hired crew built the Storys a cabin on Main Street. Joining the Storys in the log house were schoolteacher Sarah Sanford and Methodist minister Matthew Bird, as well as his wife, Jane, and their one-and-a-half-year-old son, Fletcher. The Birds had arrived with a wagon train in early September, and while en route and camped near Fort Reno, the reverend's evening prayer service had calmed nervous travelers' fears of an Indian attack.[2]

Once the cabin on Main Street was completed, Story set up a small mercantile store in an adjacent building, where he sold groceries, hardware, whiskey, and tobacco obtained in Leavenworth. The wagons he had driven up from Kansas formed the core of an upstart freighting operation, and he occasionally shipped supplies to Virginia City and sold nails at a dollar a pound, candles at seventy-five cents a pound, bacon at fifty cents a pound, "and other goods in proportion."[3]

John Bozeman's prediction that the Gallatin Valley's plentiful streams and location at the gates of the mountains would make it the "Garden of Montana" was coming true. While Story brought his cattle north, farmers growing wheat, potatoes, and vegetables expanded the valley's network of irrigation canals. Some producers

Freight wagons on Main Street, Bozeman, 1872
Museum of the Rockies, Bozeman
x80.6.368

were averaging thirty bushels of wheat an acre. In the fall of 1866, Tom Cover and an armed escort hauled three wagonloads of Gallatin Valley potatoes, some 6,450 pounds, to Fort C. F. Smith, selling them to the army for $1,548. A few months later, Cover and Perry McAdow shipped several wagonloads of flour to Virginia City and Helena.[4]

The valley soon proved capable of supporting a number of economic enterprises. The Penwell brothers, having procured the water rights to five hundred miner's inches from the "never-freezing" Ross Creek, began construction of the Union Flouring Mills on the

eastern edge of Springhill in the foothills of the Bridger Mountains.[5] Loren Tuller and Charles Rich's merchant operation, which began in a walled tent, moved its headquarters into the bottom floor of the Masonic Lodge cabin. Their bookkeeper was Davis Willson, a cousin of Rich's who also taught school. Missourian Achilles Lamme, a great-grandson of Daniel Boone, partnered with Lewis Howell to open a store, and Lamme's future brother-in-law, John Mendenhall, established a saloon. William Beall, after building a planing mill and furniture shop south of Bozeman, began construction of the Methodist Episcopal Church.[6] Progress was slow, given the inflated cost of materials. Common cut nails ran fifty cents a pound, and lumber as much as $100 for one thousand feet. But thanks to a community fundraiser that included a $25-dollar donation from Nelson Story, the quaint 864-square-foot log structure, with slab seats and a sawdust floor, began hosting services in early 1867. Located next to Story's Main Street property, the church doubled as Gallatin County's district court for a two-week period in 1867, and the resultant rental income of $240 served as the foundation for continued improvements over the next two years.[7]

As settlers scratched and clawed to build a community, the town's namesake applied himself only when necessary. In 1866, John Bozeman helped George and Elmyra Frazier build the town's first frame structure, the City Hotel, but eventually assigned his interest to the Fraziers in exchange for free meals. His meager income came from a ferry operation just west of the mouth of the Boulder River, occasional mail deliveries to Virginia City, and a small store stocked with the three frontier staples: whiskey, tobacco, and bacon.[8] Bozeman sold most of his real estate, save for a home and small farm on Main Street. In a letter written to his family in December 1866, he confessed that he had "made a great amount of money in this country but have had some bad luck and spent a good deal."[9] The roots of his misfortune stemmed from the card table, and gambling debts led him to partner with William Davies in a Mackinaw and flatboat fleet on the Yellowstone for travelers returning to the states.[10] Davies believed that Bozeman's faults resulted from the socioeconomic culture of the Old South, "where labor was a disgrace to a white man," and observed that he "had no use for money except to bet with, and the most congenial place on earth to him was the saloon, with a few boon companions at a table, playing a game of draw."[11] Bozeman's raw strength and bravado appealed to women, but incurred the jealousy of married men. He was disliked by pro-Union northerners, and newly arrived Confederate veterans also had little fondness for Bozeman, resenting his absence during the so-called War of Northern Aggression.[12]

Though Story acknowledged John Bozeman's courage and daring, he considered the trailblazer an odious fop. One friend Bozeman did have was fellow Georgian William McKenzie, who first met him along the Oregon Trail during the latter's arduous trek of 1863.[13] On January 1, 1867, Bozeman and McKenzie, still tipsy from the prior night's New Year's Eve revelry, strolled arm-in-arm into Story's store, closely followed by a dog. Fred Fridley, a friend of Story's and staunch Republican, seated on a store keg, noted that the animal was a very fine dog. "Yes, he is," replied Bozeman. "And he can lick any other dog in town, and I can lick any Black Republican in town." "Damn you Bozeman," replied Fridley, jumping out of his chair, "I suppose you mean me!"[14]

With fists flying, the two men wrestled each other to the floor. As Fridley bit into Bozeman's thumb and rolled on top of him, McKenzie picked up a scale weight and lifted it over Fridley's head. Story jumped into the fracas wielding an ax handle, forcing McKenzie to withdraw. At that moment, George Dow walked into the store, saw the fight, and immediately went to fetch Mrs. Fridley, who was just down the street. She burst into the room and stopped the brawl by grabbing her husband's ear and marching him home.[15] This sort of fracas did little to endear Bozeman to Story.

IN EARLY FEBRUARY, Story returned his unsold cattle to his recently established cow camp just north of the great bend. Though a few head were lost to heavy snow and extremely cold temperatures over the Bozeman Pass, Story's herd in the upper Yellowstone Valley still amounted to nearly seven hundred animals. Tommy Thompson served as foreman, and although most drovers collected their pay and moved on, Frank Mounts, George Dow, and Jose Tsoyio remained.

Story's herd was not the first to reach Montana, but it was among the earliest to take advantage of the free ranges of the upper Yellowstone Valley. Jesuit missionaries kept cattle to help feed the Flathead Indians, and other herds were driven into western Montana from California, Utah, and Oregon as early as the 1850s. Most notable among these early cattle operations was that of Richard Grant and his sons John and James, while others included those of Neil McArthur, James and Granville Stuart, and Reece Anderson. Herds in the Beaverhead and Bitterroot Valleys transformed the futures of men like Conrad Kohrs, who started out as a twenty-five-dollar-a-month butcher in Bannack, and ended up a wealthy rancher.[16]

But the Yellowstone region would prove especially advantageous for livestock operations. It received less snowfall than the Gallatin Valley, and the rich, deep soil of the rolling terrain yielded plentiful bunch and gamma grasses. This land had fed buffalo for centuries, and it would soon prove to be one of the finest cattle-raising regions in North America. Over the next several years other ranchers ventured in with their herds, allowing Story to supplement his longhorns with shorthorn cattle.[17]

A few weeks after Story's cow camp had been established, a deadly ambush near Fort Phil Kearny incited considerable alarm throughout the region. Returning to Bozeman after delivering vegetables and butter to Fort C. F. Smith, part-Sioux trader and interpreter John Richard Jr. reported that Captain William Fetterman and his command of eighty soldiers had been attacked by a band of Sioux, led in part by the young warrior Crazy Horse, on December 21. Every last soldier had been killed.[18] The disturbing news, coupled with accounts of stolen horses in outlying parts of the Gallatin Valley, initiated what became known as the Indian Panic of 1867. Tom Cover rode to Virginia City to request guns and ammunition from Governor Meagher.[19] In a letter to the governor, John Bozeman claimed that the Gallatin Valley was "in imminent danger of hostile Indians, and if there is not something done to protect this valley soon, there will be but few men and no families left."[20]

Thomas Cover witnessed John Bozeman's death and may have had a hand in it. MHS Photograph Archives, Helena 940-040

When Cover returned to Bozeman, he learned from Richard that Fort C. F. Smith was low on flour. Despite his recent pleas to the governor for additional resources to secure the region, he must not have been too worried about Indians, as he opted for another trip to Fort Smith, and perhaps also to Forts Phil Kearny and Reno to market Gallatin Valley wheat, beef, and produce.[21] The three-member county commission had recently granted Cover and John Bozeman permission to build another ferry across the Yellowstone River, so Cover asked Bozeman to accompany him on the journey in order to scout locations. Though hesitant, Bozeman agreed to go. But before leaving town, he asked Elmyra Frazier to send some of his personal effects to his mother in Georgia, in the event that he did not return.

On the first night of their trip, April 17, Bozeman and Cover met

William McKenzie, Al Lund, Richard's younger brother Louis, and John Baptiste "Big Bat" Pourier, who were on their way to Bozeman with a load of buffalo robes received in trade with the Crows. While the seven men prepared to bed down in a double cabin adjacent to Story's cow camp, a band of Blackfeet led by Mountain Chief drove off their herd of twenty horses. Lund, Richard, and Pourier mounted the three remaining horses tethered near the cabin and chased the raiders to a point just above the mouth of the Shields River. Following a short fight, the trio returned to the cabin with all but one of the stolen mounts.

As the men finally settled in for the night, a nervous John Bozeman told McKenzie that he had a premonition that he would die if he continued on with Cover. Bozeman offered McKenzie his horse, saddle, and outfit if he would take his place. But McKenzie demurred, saying he wanted to get to the town of Bozeman, where he could bathe and finally wear a fresh change of clothes. "I laughed at his idea that he couldn't go thro' the Indian country," McKenzie recalled, "and told him the only thing for him to do was to keep the Indians away from him."[22] He found Bozeman's anxiety out of character, for ordinarily the Georgian "was afraid of nothing on earth."[23]

John Bozeman's friend William McKenzie, above, noticed an uncharacteristic nervousness in Bozeman the night before his ill-fated trip into the Yellowstone Valley. M. A. Leeson, *A History of Montana, 1739–1885*

After traveling twelve miles the next morning, Cover and Bozeman stopped for lunch. They had just completed their meal of venison when, according to Cover, the five Blackfeet who had attempted to steal their horses the night before approached. In a letter written to Governor Meagher a few days later, Cover claims Bozeman initially thought they were Crows and let them into camp. But upon closer look, he whispered to Cover, "I am fooled. These are Blackfoot. We may, however, get off without trouble." Cover left his rifle with Bozeman and went to secure the horses, when one of the Blackfeet took aim and shot Bozeman, who attempted to return fire before being killed by a second bullet.[24]

Cover himself was hit in the left shoulder, but recovered his rifle near his companion's body, only to find the gun was jammed. After retreating some "fifty paces," however, Cover was able to open fire, "bringing one of the gentlemen to the sod." He then charged the two nearest warriors, forcing their retreat toward the other pair saddling Bozeman's horse and packhorse. Seizing the opportunity to evade his attackers, Cover made his way to a stand of willows four hundred yards away, "giving the Indians a shot or two as I fell back. I remained in the willows about an hour, when I saw the enemy cross the river, carrying their dead comrade with them." Cover then returned to Bozeman's body, confirming the Georgian "was out of all earthly trouble."[25]

Cover returned to Story's cow camp on April 19. After an explanation of what had happened, Thompson rode to Bozeman to tell his boss, while McKenzie tended to Cover. While dressing the gunshot wound, he noticed powder burns directly under the skin, suggesting that the shooter had been at close range, not at the distance Cover had described in his account. McKenzie also wondered how someone with a repeating Henry rifle had not been able to kill all five Blackfeet.[26]

When Story arrived several hours later, he too noticed the olive- and green-colored powder burns. Cover claimed the bullet entered from the back of the shoulder, but it appeared to Story that it had entered from the front. Without revealing his mounting suspicions, Story ordered Jose Tsoyio to examine the scene of the fight and report back as quickly as possible. If there were marauding Blackfeet on the Yellowstone, Story needed to take precautions with the herd. In the meantime, Pourier escorted Cover to Bozeman.[27]

The next day, Tsoyio returned to the cow camp and relayed his findings to Story. His report remained unknown to the public for nearly eighty years, until 1946, when Bine Story shared it with the then-editor of the *Bozeman Chronicle*, Jefferson Jones. According to Bine, Tsoyio found no Indian pony tracks at or near the campsite, and though there was blood around Bozeman's body, there was none where Cover claimed to have shot one of the warriors:

> Joe picked up the trail of the Bozeman-Cover horses and followed the three trails east along the river. He told father that he noticed that small rocks the size of the palm of your hand had been removed from the sod some fifteen or twenty feet from the campsite. Joe said that he continued his advance eastward and found the stones lying on the surface. The heel marks of Cover's boots abounded. It was Joe's impression, he told my father, that Cover had been throwing stones at the horses to get them to go on down the river. Figuring the horses might still be in the area, Joe told father he went out on a sandbar and gave several shrill whistles thinking the horses would neigh. Spanish Joe came back to his tethered horse and

mounted it and this time he rode up onto the bluffs where he examined the tableland beyond the rim for more than a mile. There were no tracks of any kind— either horse or Indian.[28]

Tsoyio's report and Story's subsequent interviews with friends of Bozeman and Cover led him to conclude that Cover had murdered Bozeman and used the five Blackfeet who had raided Story's cow camp as convenient scapegoats. Bozeman had been a frequent visitor to Cover's cabin in recent weeks, raising Tom's suspicion that he was after the affections of his wife Mary. As for the shoulder wound, Story was certain it was self-inflicted to lend credence to Cover's version of events.[29] But he nonetheless kept silent on the matter for decades, only sharing his private views twice, once to Bine and once to the son of an employee.[30] In all of his public correspondence, Story held to Cover's account.[31] So, too, did he guard his true opinions of Bozeman, in one letter praising the then-mythic Georgian's "commanding appearance . . . good reputation," and "jovial . . . demeanor."[32]

A day after Tsoyio returned from the scene of Bozeman's death, Story, McKenzie, John Alderson, Daniel Rouse, and "Big Bat" Pourier went to secure the body. They did not bring the corpse back to town, claiming the road was too muddy, and instead buried Bozeman where he fell.[33] His estate was settled in probate court, where Story purchased the deceased's interest in a ranch for $380. Cover, who claimed Bozeman never paid him for threshing fifty-seven bushels of barley and eighty-four bushels of oats, received $39.75. A year later, Cover sold his interest in the McAdow Mill to Perry's brother William, and relocated to California with his wife.[34]

Bozeman's death triggered yet another panic among the residents of the Gallatin Valley. Rumors circulated that various tribes, angered about persistent encroachment onto tribal hunting lands, were allying among themselves in advance of a major attack on settlers in the region. Governor Meagher forwarded a citizen's petition to equip one thousand volunteers to Ulysses S. Grant, commanding general of the U.S. Army, who sent it along to Secretary of War Edward Stanton. In a note appended to the telegram, Grant suggested that if Montana volunteers were called into action, they could petition Congress for compensation.[35] If the threat turned out to be exaggerated, however, the War Department should pay nothing. Meagher also requested troops from Camp Cooke, downriver from Fort Benton, but was turned down. In a letter to the *Montana Post*, Davis Willson called on the government to assist settlers facing this "perilous situation," as "a few, who are able, are sending their families away; but there are many who have expended all their means and energies in the past two or three years in simply developing what little they have."[36] Nelson Story could have sent Ellen and Alice to Virginia City or Helena, but instead arranged for them to board with Sheriff John Guy and his wife.

General William Tecumseh Sherman, commander of the Military Division of the Missouri, the administrative district that included Montana Territory, told Meagher that troops would be sent to the territory, but if the situation were as dire as reported, the governor could muster volunteers for "self-protection."[37] Still, Sherman remained skeptical of the danger, and feared that government resources would be exploited by opportunistic settlers. Major W. H. Lewis was dispatched from Utah to investigate, and days after arriving in Virginia City, received a message from Sherman authorizing him to muster a battalion of eight hundred men who would furnish their own horses and arms at forty cents a day. Lewis replied that he could not recruit men on those terms, as Meagher had already enrolled some 150 volunteers in the territorial militia with promises of higher wages.[38] Meagher appointed attorney Thomas Thoroughman to command the Montanans, and gave him the rank of major general. Thoroughman established three camps: one near the Bozeman Pass, another near Story's cow camp in the Yellowstone Valley, and the third near present-day White Sulphur Springs.

Most of the Montana militiamen were tough, seasoned frontiersman. Volunteer Thomas Leforge, known as a "hard knot," once used a jack knife to amputate two of his frostbitten toes one winter morning after a hunting trip. But even he was appalled by the militia's conduct. Mostly they raced horses, gambled, and fought among themselves. After trying to instill discipline among the ranks, one commanding officer was drowned in the Shields River and another shot by his own troops. U.S. Army officers thought little of the Montana militia. In mid-June, forty-two militia men, joined by Mitch Boyer and John Richard, escorted a ten-wagon supply train from Bozeman to Fort C. F. Smith.[39] But the post commander would not allow them to cross the Bighorn River and enter the fort. "They are a hard set," wrote First Lieutenant George Templeton "and although they have a colonel, a capt. and two lts., they don't mind any of them, but do just about as they please."[40]

In the midst of these developments, Governor Thomas Francis Meagher, like John Bozeman before him, met a mysterious end. On

July 1, while in Fort Benton awaiting a shipment of arms for the militia, he suddenly disappeared, apparently drowned in the Missouri River. It remains unknown, however, whether he fell by accident, was pushed, or committed suicide. Given his many political enemies, Meagher was most likely murdered, perhaps at the behest of Wilbur Sanders. Compounding the mystery further, Meagher's body was never found.[41]

Despite the fears of residents, the much-anticipated attacks on the Gallatin Valley never materialized. The Sioux and their allies instead concentrated their efforts further east, where on August 1, two soldiers, one civilian, and at least twenty Lakota and their allies died in the Hayfield Fight near Fort C. F. Smith. The following day saw seven whites and an undetermined number of warriors killed in the Wagon Box Fight near Fort Phil Kearny. When General Alfred H. Terry, commander of the Department of Dakota, arrived in Helena that August, however, he determined that the perceived threats had been overblown. After interviews with new territorial governor Green Clay Smith and Helena merchants, Terry reported that "nothing which has happened within the Territory during this spring and summer, in my judgment, justified the alarm which was felt."[42] Per his orders, all 513 volunteers were mustered out by early October.[43]

General Sherman's suspicions were validated by Terry's findings. An emerging consensus held that the crisis had been manufactured by merchants in Bozeman, Helena, and Virginia City to plunder the federal coffers. John Bozeman's death offered a timely opportunity to do so, as an ebb in placer mining, together with fewer emigrants on the Bozeman Trail, had cut into the bottom lines of many businessmen. Davis Willson, in a letter to relatives back east, admitted in early May that many understood the situation to be a convenient fiction "got up for the purpose of making money."[44] And a profitable summer it was for Montana merchants outfitting volunteer troops. Horses normally valued at $80 a head sold for $200; hay worth $35 a ton was priced at nearly twice that amount. Beef, bacon, sugar, coffee, hardware, and medical supplies were all inflated at the same rates.[45] Nelson Story obtained a government voucher for $7,260 in "provisions" that were never delivered.[46] "It was a marvelous opportunity to raid the treasury," historian Robert Athearn would later write, "and in a country where government funds were looked upon as fair game, the financial dredging proceeded with utmost avidity."[47]

Despite the rampant profit-seeking by local merchants, General Sherman understood that the army's presence was necessary on the western portion of the Bozeman Trail, provided "forage can be had at some price below its weight in gold." The territory was, he wrote, "growing daily in importance, and its interests and routes leading thereto . . . require the supervision of some one officer."[48] General Terry agreed, insisting to Secretary Stanton that the Gallatin Valley "should be guarded by a military post; such a post is demanded and justified by the importance of the productions of the valley, and by the fact that its inhabitants being agriculturists, living dispersed on farms, and having their families with them, are far less capable of protecting themselves than are the inhabitants of the mining regions."[49]

The number of claims against the government, coupled with plans to build a new fort, brought about a quiet reexamination of John Bozeman's death. A handful of locals concluded that neither the Blackfeet nor Tom Cover were responsible. Instead, they believed, the culprit was likely a powerful merchant who stood to gain from heightened government spending in the valley, and that merchant was Nelson Story. According to their line of thinking, Story saw Bozeman as a rival who threatened his business interests. Killing him would eliminate a competitor while also adding a more renowned name to the list of those killed by Indians, forcing the government to send in supplies or, better yet, troops. What's more, descendants of Tom Kent, a purported wrangler of Story's, claim that Story paid him to murder Bozeman.[50]

However intriguing the theory may have been, it holds little water. John Bozeman was not a threat to Nelson Story's interests. He was in debt, and barely paid attention to the tolls and ferries along his namesake trail, much less his and Davies's Mackinaw operation. Bozeman was content playing cards and eating free meals at the City Hotel while virtually ignoring his farm and mercantile store. Tom Cover, Perry McAdow, and even William Tracy and William Alderson possessed more get-up-and-go, yet Story felt no need to eliminate them to protect his interests. In fact, they became his business allies. Had Bozeman's friend William McKenzie bought into the conspiracy, his future partnerships with Story would have never materialized. It is more likely that Story suspected a conspiracy was afoot against Bozeman, but allowed events to play out, and then joined the campaign for troops and supplies by insisting on the Blackfeet's culpability.

In any event, military officials agreed to erect a fort on the Yellowstone River near the mouth of the Shields River, not far from Story's cow camp.[51] Tasked with building the post were two companies of

Fort Ellis near Bozeman, 1871 W. H. Jackson, photographer. MHS Photograph Archives, Helena 947-240

the Thirteenth Infantry commanded by Captain Robert S. LaMotte, and when they arrived in the Gallatin Valley on August 27, LaMotte—likely at the urging of the local populace—decided to site the fort just a few miles east of Bozeman for "the protection of the agricultural settlers of Gallatin Valley rather than that of the prospectors and gold seekers of Yellowstone."[52] With the help of citizen employees, soldiers began construction of an officer's quarters, regular barracks, and a ten-foot-high log stockade behind which residents could take shelter in the event of an attack. LaMotte named the post Fort Ellis in honor of Colonel Augustus Van Horne Ellis, a Union officer killed at the battle of Gettysburg.[53]

The construction of Fort Ellis brought tranquility to the Gallatin Valley, which continued to witness further development. Union veteran James Chesnut mined coal along the Bozeman Pass, Jacob Spieth and Charles Krug opened Bozeman's first brewery, and John Tomlinson established a lathe and shingle mill along the West Gallatin River.[54] William Beall, with five hundred dollars raised by a five-mill tax, began erecting a permanent schoolhouse. Within months, the town of 150 had forty wooden dwellings.[55] *Helena Herald* correspondent Harry O'Neill counted four stores, two blacksmith shops, one hotel, a brewery, and "the sign of advanced civilization—a poor whisky shop."[56] Bozeman was now the major supply center for Montana's gold camps, and Davis Willson beamingly wrote that "blue coats and shoulder straps, government freighters, contractors, jobbers, woodcutters, hay makers, teamsters, butchers and barbers throng the metropolis like grasshoppers in August." Though Gallatin City had been relocated just south of the Three Forks on a stage route, Bozeman became the county seat in an election held that December.[57]

Meanwhile, Loren Tuller sold his interest in the store partnership with Charles Rich to Davis Willson's brother Lester, a Civil War veteran who rose from entry-level recruit to brigade adjutant general in the Sixtieth New York Volunteer Infantry. Now known as Willson & Rich, the business moved into a new, two-story frame building spacious enough to also accommodate a public hall and dining room. On Christmas Eve, it hosted a grand Masonic Ball, the first in town to require tickets and offer a printed program. Guests danced the minuet, quadrille, Spanish waltz, Money Musk, Highland Schottische, and Virginia reel.[58] Since many of the women in attendance were unmarried, landing a dance partner was easy, and afterward a celebratory meal was served at the Frazier City Hotel. "Oh," opined O'Neill in the *Helena Herald*, "who wouldn't live in [the] Gallatin?"[59]

WITHIN A YEAR of its construction, Fort Ellis was garrisoned by three companies of the Thirteenth Infantry, presenting Nelson Story, Willson & Rich, and other merchants a convenient market for supplies and foodstuffs.[60] But Story remained intrigued by Fort C. F. Smith because its remote location would allow him to charge much higher prices. When word arrived that the new commander, Lieutenant Colonel Luther P. Bradley, wanted vegetables to prevent his men from getting scurvy—already a problem at Forts Reno and Phil Kearny—Story and Perry McAdow jumped at the opportunity. They reached the fort in October, where Bradley negotiated a contract with McAdow to deliver chopped wheat and vegetables, and agreed to pay Story ten thousand dollars for 110,000 pounds of potatoes.[61] While Nelson procured extra wagons and oxen, Elias purchased the potatoes from Gallatin Valley farmers for one thousand dollars. Story returned to Fort Smith on November 19 with his cargo loaded on twenty-eight wagons. McAdow arrived the next day with twelve wagons of wheat and vegetables, amounting to some 250,000 pounds of goods. Story still had two wagons of potatoes left after he closed the deal, and these he sent on to Fort Phil Kearny.[62] Frontier officers and enlisted men often referred to merchants as "Commodore" upon their arrival, but after word spread of Story's outrageous profit margins, he became known as "that old pirate."[63]

Fighting continued along the Bozeman Trail as the Sioux and their allies continued to harass supply trains and reinforcements sent to Fort C. F. Smith from Forts Reno and Phil Kearny, whose presence they regarded as a violation to their treaties. The Crows, fearing that the government planned to cede their hunting grounds to the Sioux, attacked settlers along the upper Yellowstone in April of 1868 and stole thirty wagon sheets and five head of horses from Story's cow camp. Story moved his herd back over the Bozeman Pass to graze near Fort Ellis, only to see two hundred head run off by Crows and Blackfeet. He pursued the herd with a civilian force and twenty-five soldiers, and despite a sudden snowstorm recovered the animals, though three eventually died of arrow wounds.[64] Throughout, Story issued orders to the soldiers as though they were his personal employees, and they later complained about his "insulting and ungentlemanly manner."[65] During the chase, one of Story's herders, nineteen-year-old Lee Wyett, was killed in an ambush ten miles from Fort Ellis, a casualty that Davis Willson said "cast a horrifying gloom over the community."[66]

Red Cloud's goal to push the army out of the Powder River Basin was realized that spring when a federal peace commission sent to Fort Laramie agreed to close the Bozeman Trail forts. The government ordered all portable stores at Fort C. F. Smith transported to Omaha, although some ended up at Fort Ellis, and those items that could not be transported were to be auctioned. Story immediately recognized an opportunity to buy various goods at reduced prices from the army and then sell them to civilians in Helena and Bozeman. As one of few individuals in Montana Territory possessing the cash, wagons, and resolve necessary to extend his enterprises across the Bozeman Trail, he also hoped to buy the fort's buildings to establish a trading post.[67] On May 29, 1868, Story, McKenzie, Louis Richard, and Jim Leighton arrived at C. F. Smith to bid on the government property. But because there were too few bidders, the auction was postponed until June 15.

When that appointed day arrived, only Story, McKenzie, and a crew of teamsters showed up. By then, the officers in charge were desperate to get rid of anything they could not transport by horse and wagon. In the words of one soldier, Story purchased items at "ridiculously low figures."[68] In addition to four thousand pounds of white lead, ten thousand pounds of nails, and seven mowing machines, Story bought a steam-powered sawmill for five dollars and stoves ranging from twenty-five cents to one dollar each.[69] He also procured harnesses, blankets, paint, firewood, wagons, assorted tools, medicines, shoes, caps, clothing, and the roughly forty build-ings on the site—a total investment of ten thousand dollars.

Story had hoped for a military escort from Fort Ellis, but Captain LaMotte rejected the request, noting that it was not the army's responsibility to escort "every citizen who might wish to send a train into the Indian Country on speculation."[70] Though Story threatened to go over LaMotte's head, he dropped the matter. While Frank Mounts, Daniel Rouse's brother Elisha, Al Lund, and three others remained to look after the buildings, Story, McKenzie, and the hired teamsters loaded twenty-seven wagons with as much of the merchandise as possible and headed west.[71] Indians attacked Story's train at the Clarks Fork, killing teamster Allen Howard. After selling some items in Bozeman, the train proceeded on to Helena. Nelson, accompanied by Ellen and Alice, followed in a buggy, and he began selling his wares that August. The stoves purchased for one dollar fetched one hundred dollars, and other items produced similar profits. Story and McKenzie maintained a lucrative trade in Helena until the following spring, when a fire destroyed the balance of their inventory. Even still, they realized a gross profit of thirty-five thousand dollars.[72]

For a brief time, Nelson Story profited by selling food supplies to Fort C. F. Smith, above. The newly constructed fort burned to the ground in 1867. Sub Neg 20590, Wyoming State Archives, Cheyenne

Between late July and mid-August, the U.S. Army abandoned Forts C. F. Smith, Phil Kearny, and Reno. Indians confiscated whatever supplies had been left behind at the posts and burned Forts Phil Kearny and C. F. Smith to the ground, ruining Story's hopes of establishing a trading post. Not only did the second Fort Laramie Treaty close the forts, it also delineated reservation boundaries. As of 1868, the Sioux Reservation would encompass all the land in what would become South Dakota, west of the Missouri River. This was bordered by unceded Indian Territory: the Powder River country that lay between the Sioux Reservation and the Bighorn Mountains and on which the Sioux and Cheyennes depended for hunting. The Mountain Crow Reservation was reduced from thirty-eight million acres to eight million. The Crows ceded their lands in Wyoming and accepted the Yellowstone River as their territory's northern and western boundary. The eastern boundary was established at the 107th meridian, the southern at the Wyoming-Montana boundary line. Crow chiefs, initially reluctant to accept the treaty, acquiesced when promised an agency in the Yellowstone Valley where they would receive food, supplies, and protection from their Sioux adversaries. The agency was to be sited near Otter Creek, just east of present-day Big Timber. The River Crows were not party to the treaty of 1868, instead agreeing to share a reservation north of the Missouri with the Gros Ventres.[73]

The treaty created additional free range between the Yellowstone and Musselshell Rivers, but Story opted not to use it all year long. During the summers, his cattle herd grazed lands thirty miles south of the cow camp, along the west bank of the Yellowstone at the base of the Gallatin Mountain Range, where it was safer from raids. During the winter months, Story moved the animals back to the north, where there was less snow. The new summer range was near Emigrant Gulch, a mining hub that had produced some $180,000 in gold since 1864. Operations there were only intensifying, as miners continued to find promising deposits. The scenic area also became a favorite of recreationists, particularly fishermen. Captain LaMotte ignored any concern about Indians that summer, and led a group of officers and civilians from Fort Ellis on a two-day fishing expedition to the Yellowstone near Story's new cow camp.[74]

IN THE SPRING OF 1869, Story began construction of a single-family frame house he wanted ready by fall. The site was adjacent to the log cabin and mercantile store and, to give Ellen and Alice greater comfort and minimize their exposure to the workmen, he moved them to John Guy's newly built hotel, the Guy House. The Storys rented the only room with a carpet at a rate of eighteen dollars per week. Meanwhile, Gallatin Valley farmers planted their crops and looked forward to a prosperous, and hopefully peaceful, year.[75]

Such hopes evaporated in March when seventy-five Sioux warriors came up the Yellowstone Valley and drove off 150 head of cattle owned by Perry McAdow near the Shields River.[76] Thirty Fort Ellis soldiers and a dozen civilians, including Jose Tsoyio, skirmished with the Sioux near Bozeman Pass, reportedly killing four of them. Plans for a larger detachment to pick up the chase the next day, however, were scuttled by a spring snowstorm.[77]

A resolution adopted at a subsequent town meeting called for more armaments and reinforcements, specifically cavalry.[78] The document exaggerated the threat by warning that the valley may have to be abandoned in the absence of additional forces. Over the past year, territorial newspapers had clamored for more troops, with the *Helena Herald* claiming that the current Fort Ellis detachment could "barely keep the savages out of Bozeman."[79] The resolution bemoaned the size of the force, which consisted of a mere 150 officers and soldiers, with only twenty horses suitable for prolonged marches. Copies of the resolution were sent to Sherman, recently appointed general of the army, and General Alfred H. Terry.[80]

A few weeks after the meeting, a party of ten to twelve Blackfeet raided the upper portion of the Gallatin Valley and drove off several horses and ten head of beef cattle. Again, soldiers out of Fort Ellis gave chase, accompanied by at least a dozen ranchers. They caught up with the raiders some forty-plus miles north of Story's cow camp. The subsequent fight was a bloody one: nine Blackfeet and one soldier were killed, and two soldiers and one volunteer were severely wounded. All of the dead Blackfeet were scalped, and the *Helena Herald* praised the soldiers and volunteers, believing their actions would deter "other prowling gangs of fiendish robbers and assassins" from entering the valley.[81]

The attacks of March and April, coupled with the citizen's petition, led the government to assign four companies of the Second Cavalry to Fort Ellis. These reinforcements arrived in July and were led by Lieutenant Colonel Albert Brackett, who was also made the new post commander.[82]

Given his profitable venture with Fort C. F. Smith, Nelson Story took notice of the planned Crow Agency in the Yellowstone Valley.

Company B, Troop F, 2nd Cavalry, Fort Ellis, Montana Territory, c. 1867–1872.
MHS Photograph Archives, Helena 947-242

Here, too, he saw opportunity, and he was well-positioned to secure government contracts for agency provisions. With his cattle herd, supplying beef would be no problem, and his wagons could transport other foodstuffs and goods easily purchased in the Gallatin Valley. All he needed was a connection to get his foot in the door. As it turned out, just such an individual was then living in Bozeman, and his name was Leander M. Black.

"Colonel" Black left his native Kentucky in 1859 for the Pikes Peak gold rush. Arriving via the Smoky Hill Trail, he first worked Cherry Creek, and then a claim at the Gregory Mine. Like Story, his first efforts at panning yielded little, and his inexperience became obvious when another miner made a fortune off his abandoned claim. In Denver, Black purchased a separate mine for one hundred dollars, only to find it worthless. Dejected, he went to Nebraska and worked as a carpenter on the Pawnee Reservation. Agent James Gillis was so impressed by Black's work ethic and skill that he appointed him acting agent while Gillis tended to business in Washington, D.C.

Black returned to Denver in 1860 to cut and sell hay at eight to ten cents per pound, and thanks to a government contract, his profits over the next few years allowed him to purchase teams and wagons. In 1864, he was hired to provide supplies and transportation from Denver to Fort Leavenworth for African American troops. Upon his return to Denver, he sold foodstuffs and supplies purchased in Leavenworth at a 300 percent profit. A year later, Black was nominated for the territorial senate, or "upper house," by Governor John Evans. A reluctant politician, Black responded by asking "where in the hell is the upper house?" Though he did not actively campaign, he won the seat by a four-to-one margin.[83]

After an unsuccessful attempt at securing statehood for Colorado, Black left the senate to freight corn from Nebraska City to Fort Laramie during Brigadier General Patrick E. Connor's 1865 Powder River campaign. After transporting an initial haul in July, Black used his twenty-one wagons, two hundred oxen, and twenty-six employees to haul lumber to Fort Sedgwick. Upon reaching Sedgwick, Black paid teamster wages to the soldiers who had helped drive his wagons, but the escort commander, Captain John Shanks, seized the money. Black appealed to officers at the fort, who forced Shanks to return the wages to his men. Black then headed for Denver while the train returned east to Nebraska City. While en route, Shanks ordered the train stopped and detained for thirty-four days on the dubious grounds that Black had given aid to army deserters. The charges were eventually dropped, but winter had set in by the time the train could proceed, preventing Black from fulfilling his corn contract.[84] Still, he had established political ties in the West and the nation's capital, where Tennessee congressman Horace Maynard referred to him as "a man of high character and standing."[85]

Chapter Five

Black and Story, 1869–1871

I N 1869, General Alfred Sully was appointed superintendent of Indian Affairs in Montana, and one of his first orders in that new role was to move the planned location of Crow Agency west from Otter Creek to Mission Creek, some thirty miles from Fort Ellis. The decision came at the request of the Crow chiefs, who feared that its construction at the original site would drive buffalo away from their hunting grounds.[1] Sully named Lieutenant Erskine Camp as Crow agent that May, but his arrival via steamboat was delayed until November due to low water on the Missouri River. In turn, Sully received permission from the new administration of President Ulysses S. Grant to appoint Leander Black as interim or "special" agent, the final approval coming from commissioner of Indian Affairs and Grant's former Civil War aide-de-camp, Seneca Indian Ely S. Parker. Black received a contract to construct the agency as well as the trading license for the soon-to-be-built post.

Black's connection to the region began in 1866. At the time, he was a principal contractor for the Army of the Platte, a lucrative arrangement that afforded him a net worth of at least $250,000 and allowed him to own two homes, one in Colorado and the other in St. Joseph, Missouri. Foreseeing the imminent closure of the Bozeman Trail forts, Black saw an opportunity to profit in Montana, and that summer furnished supplies to the militiamen during Governor Meagher's "Indian War." His total bill to the government for arms, horses, and miscellaneous supplies exceeded the staggering sum of $150,000.[2]

A one-time partner of Nelson Story, Leander Black would eventually become one of Story's bitter business rivals. M. A. Leeson, *A History of Montana, 1739–1885*

After receiving the appointment, Black left his wife Mary and four children in St. Joseph and came to Bozeman. He met with a delegation of Crow chiefs at Fort Ellis in mid-August to assure them that fresh supplies, including ammunition, were on the way, and that the agency would be ready before winter.[3] Black wasted little time. On September 1, he and Sully loaded a sawmill purchased in Chicago onto a wagon train and headed to Mission Creek. Black's hired crew completed the agency before the end of November.

The crude fort was constructed of cottonwood logs and shingles, and featured a ten-foot-high stockade extending two hundred feet in length on each side. On opposite corners stood blockhouses, each armed with a howitzer. The site, located on a bluff one mile south of the Yellowstone River, afforded ample protection from the Sioux. Though Sully named the agency Fort Ely S. Parker, it was commonly referred to as either the Mission Agency or the Crow Agency. On November 20, Lieutenant Camp arrived with annuities for the Crows, who were promised additional buildings, a teacher (the first would be Isaac Newton Parker, Ely's younger brother), clothing, and a pound of meat and a pound of flour each day for every individual older than four years of age. Black constructed a warehouse at the fort, which in the subsequent three years would receive two-thirds of the flour produced in the Gallatin Valley, shipped to the Crows by one of Black's bull trains.[4]

With an eye toward profiting from the new agency, Nelson Story befriended Leander Black, and with his help procured a contract to supply beef to the Crows in 1869. Together the two enjoyed a monopoly provisioning subsistence supplies. By year's end, Black and Story formed a partnership, each proffering a one-half interest in their own commercial property. This included Story's 148-acre ranch, 350 head of stock cattle, three ponies, his Main Street store, and several hay scales. Black granted Story a one-half interest in the trade, peltries, goods, and other capital at Mission Agency, and a warehouse, barn, and store on Bozeman's Main Street. Each man also put up four thousand dollars in cash.[5] Within a year, Black and Story's retail store offered nearly everything needed on the frontier, including dry goods, clothing, groceries, millinery goods, toiletries, liquors, wines, and bar fixtures. The closure of the Bozeman Trail inflated shipping costs, but the partners passed these expenses on to their customers: sugar went for thirty cents a pound, salt for fifteen cents a pound, a pair of blankets for as much as fifteen dollars, a box of two dozen matches for two and a half dollars, and a gallon of coal oil for two dollars.[6] The store also stocked family goods, earthenware, hardware, cutlery, and jewelry: "everything the ladies admire or could desire . . . for cash or country produce."[7]

Black hired Mitch Boyer and Carl Stanley to run the simple, two-room trading post located within the Mission Agency stockade. Though he and Story had exclusive trading rights, competition arose from Yellowstone Crossing, a post established near the great bend of the Yellowstone River when William H. "Billy" Lee built a ferry there in 1869. Another rival was the sutler at Fort Ellis, but that quickly ended when Sully ordered him to refrain from any business that interfered with the agency.[8]

By October, Nelson Story had realized huge profits from his association with Black, adding nearly fifty thousand dollars to his net worth. But this alliance of enterprising egocentrics unraveled when Black accused Story of pocketing more than his share of the proceeds. Story, enraged, but equally suspicious of Black, quit the partnership. Each man returned their one-half interests, and Black told friends he was relocating to Washington, D.C., as he was "out with Story and wouldn't have anything more to do with him."[9] As it turned out, neither man was done with the other. Though they remained at arm's length, their actions over the following years would shape the community of Bozeman and put the two on another collision course.

THIS PERIOD saw a number of significant changes for the Story family. During the construction of Fort Parker and while Nelson formed his partnership with Leander Black, Elias Story returned to Ohio. Meanwhile, Nelson, Ellen (who was then five months pregnant), and Alice moved into the new home on Main Street. The Texas-style frame house was more spacious than their log cabin, and was among the first residences in Bozeman to have a brick chimney and a doorbell. Ellen, having endured life in tents and cabins since leaving Leavenworth, was especially pleased, often referring to the home as the "cottage."[10] Men outnumbered Bozeman's female residents by a three-to-one margin, so Ellen was always happy to welcome new women to the community. She quickly befriended William Tracy's seventeen-year-old wife, Sara Jane, after her arrival in 1869. Sara barely knew her way around the kitchen, but "with the

A boy plays on a wagon scale outside the first Story home in Bozeman. Montana State University–Bozeman MSU-2160

help of kind Mrs. Story . . . I soon learned to keep our table quite well supplied."[11] Another friend was Emma Weeks Willson, who joined her husband Lester in Bozeman that same year. An accomplished musician, Emma owned the first piano ever shipped to the Gallatin Valley. She became the town's "songbird," and her clear voice and melodic piano playing attracted audiences to her home on warm, dry days. Among the assembled listeners were members of the Bannock tribe whenever they passed through Bozeman to hunt bison in the Yellowstone Valley.[12]

But Ellen's happiness with her new home and growing circle of female companions was tragically interrupted on September 12, 1869, when three-year-old Alice died of cholera.[13] Childhood mortality was an all too common occurrence on the frontier. Nearly one-fifth of all infants perished before the age of one, and at least another one-fourth died between the ages of one and four.[14] The loss of Alice, in parlance of the day, ushered in a "season of sorrow" for Ellen.[15] Her pain was partly subdued a few months later with the birth of another girl they named Ellen. Nelson also hired a domestic servant, twenty-five-year-old Elizabeth McClarren, to take on some of the household work so that Ellen could spend more time with the new baby.[16]

Montana Territory's population now counted 20,595, and of the 1,586 in Gallatin County, 168 resided in Bozeman. With sixty-five wooden buildings, including livery stables, stores, cabins, and houses mostly built along Main Street, the town was taking shape. Theophilus Brunett finished a saloon and wholesale liquor store by paying the construction crew in cheap "red-eye" whiskey, with the ironic result that the contractor and his men owed Brunett money at the end of the job. Walter Cooper, a New York native who had enjoyed some success as a miner and game hunter, established a firearm and sporting goods business. The community's first jail, paid for with subscriptions raised by Sheriff John Guy, was established to the immediate north of Main Street, where a new, two-story brick hotel, the Metropolitan, was under construction.[17] On New Year's Eve of 1869, Horatio Maguire, having raised $2,200 with the help of schoolteacher T. B. Gray, published the inaugural issue of the town's first newspaper, the *Montana Pick and Plow*.[18] Thanks to the influx of federal funds through Fort Ellis and the Crow Reservation, Bozeman possessed economic stability as both an agricultural and trade center.

Nelson Story, c. 1870 Museum of the Rockies, Bozeman 2011.24.1

Whereas the Crows were considered friendly, most of Bozeman's residents viewed the Sioux and Blackfeet as perpetual enemies and deserving of removal or extermination. In January of 1870, the new commander of Fort Ellis, Major Eugene Baker, led a force north to conduct retaliatory punitive raids against the Piegan Blackfeet, specifically targeting Mountain Chief and his band. The order came from Lieutenant General Philip Sheridan, commander of the Division of the Missouri, in response to claims from Superintendent Sully that settlements like Bozeman faced the danger of being overrun. Others, however, including Colonel Philippe Régis de Trobriand, commander of the Military District of Montana, felt Sully's

Ellen Story, c. 1870 Museum of the Rockies, Bozeman 2011.24.2

worries were exaggerated at the encouragement of local businessmen hoping to profit from an increased military presence in the territory. On January 23, Baker, reportedly drunk, attacked a peaceful village on the Marias River headed by Chief Heavy Runner, who had just signed a peace treaty with the United States. Heavy Runner and 217 members of his tribe, nearly all of whom were women and children, were killed in the slaughter. With temperatures nearing thirty degrees below zero, the soldiers burned the Blackfeet lodges and destroyed their provisions. The remaining 140 Piegans, mostly women and children, were taken prisoner, but the American troops quickly abandoned them with little food or adequate clothing after determining that they were infected with smallpox.[19]

While the *Pick and Plow* praised Baker for his "severe castigation" of the "red-skinned thieves and murderers," the *New York Evening Post* called the attack inexcusable, a "slaughter of the unarmed, the helpless, and the innocent," destined to leave "so dark a stain on our history."[20] But the opinions of East Coast editors fell on deaf ears in the Gallatin, with many seconding General Sheridan's purported statement that "the only good Indian is a dead Indian."[21]

Major Eugene Baker and Fort Ellis officers, c. 1870. At General Philip Sheridan's orders, Baker (sixth from right) led an unprovoked attack on a friendly Blackfeet band in the winter of 1869 and slaughtered over two hundred noncombatants. Library of Congress.

Meanwhile, Sioux war parties continued to move through the Yellowstone Valley. One, believed to have been led by Sitting Bull, killed two settlers and captured three hundred horses during a raid of several Gallatin Valley ranches in late July. In September, remnants of an expedition from Wyoming came to Bozeman after three of its members were killed by Sioux. The 150-man Bighorn Mining Expedition had failed to find gold in the Bighorn Mountains, and as it dispersed, about half the force tried their luck in eastern Montana, again with no success. The Sioux attack hastened their exit from the Yellowstone Valley, and once in Bozeman the miners abandoned their chief weapon, a six-pound smoothbore cannon dubbed the "Bighorn Gun."

A few of the men moved into an old cabin next to the city jail, among them Henry Comstock, namesake of the famous Nevada gold and silver mine. Comstock had sold his mining interests for ten thousand dollars, and then went broke after poorly managing two general stores in Carson City and Silver City. This failure, plus the later realization he had sold his mining interest at an undervalued amount, put Comstock into a deep depression. On the morning of September 27, he walked out of the Bozeman cabin into a nearby three-foot-deep hole that had been dug to supply dirt for the jail's new roof. Here he calmly drew his pistol, placed the barrel above his temple, and fired. Nelson Story, having known Comstock only briefly, was touched enough by his plight to arrange a proper burial.[22]

NATIONAL EVENTS would have an impact on the Gallatin Valley, too. When Ulysses Grant moved into the White House, abolitionists and philanthropy groups pressed the new administration for fairer treatment of the nation's indigenous people. For much of the early nineteenth century, the Indian Department, later the Office of Indian Affairs (OIA), was part of the War Department. Congress eventually created the post of commissioner of Indian Affairs to oversee the OIA, which in 1849 became a branch of the Interior Department. By the late 1860s, Indian advocates claimed that graft and corruption hindered the distribution of annuities, and that a more humane system would evolve if agencies were placed under the care of Christian denominations, with an ultimate aim to "civilize" the Indians and grant them citizenship.[23] The president went along, and on March 24, 1869, Congress enacted what came to be known as Grant's Peace Policy. Reservations were divided among various Christian denominations, each responsible for submitting candidates for the position of agent. A Board of Indian Commissioners, assisted by the army, would oversee the purchase and distribution of annuity goods to the tribes.[24]

Under the new policy, administration of the Mission Agency was assigned to the Methodist Church.[25] On September 23, 1870, Lieutenant Camp was relieved and replaced by Fellows David Pease, a former freighter and fur trader who, while running the sutler store at Fort Pierre, Dakota Territory, in the mid-1860s, was accused of illegally selling guns and ammunition to the Indians. He was cleared of the charges, and in 1869 became temporary agent at the Blackfeet Reservation. As for Sully, he was replaced a few weeks later by Joseph Viall of Keokuk, Iowa.[26]

During the fiscal year 1870–1871, Black transported annuity goods from the Union Pacific Railroad depot at Corinne, Utah, to various Montana agencies. The Crow Reservation alone received $130,000 in supplies. Black's continued involvement was largely the result of the friendly rapport he had established with Ely Parker. This relationship hit a road bump when, in a letter dated February 13, 1871, Blackfeet agent M. M. McCauley complained to Parker that Black tried to get him to falsify vouchers totaling $45,000 in exchange for "job security." Black eluded major investigation by befriending Viall. In fact, Black agreed to act as one of two sureties on Viall's $100,000 performance bond. Shortly afterward, Viall recommended granting Black the contract to supply all Indian agencies in Montana for fiscal year 1871–1872. Parker approved the deal, but it was soon rescinded following allegations of irregularities in awarding supply contracts for various Missouri River tribes. Though eventually cleared of fraud charges by the House Committee on Appropriations, Parker was considered incompetent. He resigned on August 1, 1871, after Congress expanded the Board of Indian Commissioners' control over all expenditures made by the Indian Service. With Parker gone, Black and Story failed to win contracts to supply the Crows for fiscal year 1871–1872, though Black did oversee a few minor shipments of flour. As for Story, he only furnished $10,000 in supplies to the Mountain Shoshone, or Sheep Eaters.[27]

Pease and Viall, joined by Major Baker and other officials, met the Crows for the first time on November 25 with a delivery of annuity goods. There were now an estimated twenty-three hundred Mountain Crows and thirteen hundred River Crows, and both groups, particularly the Mountain Crows, had grown increasingly dependent on the agency for protection. Just a few months earlier, they sustained

Indian agent Fellows David Pease (left) with George Daw, E. Goughnour, Andy Billman, and B. F. "Sandy" Ten Broek. Pease and Story, who supplied the trading post and agency serving the Crow Indian Reservation, profited from unscrupulous contracts. Whithorn Collection, Yellowstone Gateway Museum, Livingston YGM_2006.044.3835

thirteen casualties when their camp of 160 lodges was attacked by the Sioux near the Little Bighorn River. The Crows blamed the defeat in part on a shortage of ammunition, a problem they hoped would be remedied by the agency. One of Pease's first actions was to hire additional workers, including a physician, engineer, farmer, miller, carpenter, and two blacksmiths. New employees included Pierre Shane and Mitch Boyer, as well as Pease's cousins S. B. Bowen and Zed Daniels, who each served for a time as agency farmer. Thomas

Fort Parker, on the Yellowstone River (above, c. 1870), was the site of the Crow Indian agency, where Story enriched himself through shady contracts. W. H. Jackson, photographer. MHS Photograph Archives, Helena 955-902

Leforge occasionally worked at the agency for the standard laborer's pay of fifty dollars a month, plus room and board.[28]

Nelson Story's curtailed involvement with the Crow Agency allowed him more time to pursue other enterprises. As he had demonstrated on the cattle drive from Texas, a promising investment could induce Story to travel a long way, and the spring of 1871 saw an abundance of mustangs in southern California. Ranchers there viewed the wild horses as a nuisance because they competed for rangeland with revenue-producing stock, particularly cattle. But mustangs, because of their small size and swift speed, made excellent cow ponies. Despite the great distance and with Ellen pregnant yet again, Story and Tommy Thompson left Bozeman in March for Corinne, Utah, and from there took a train to San Francisco. They traveled on to Los Angeles, where they spent a month inspecting mustangs and enjoying trips to the nearby Spanish missions.

In late April, Story purchased close to nine hundred mustangs. He hired enough men to drive the herd and headed north for the

Central Overland and California Trails. But after fifty miles, worsening saddle sores forced him to hand control of the herd over to Thompson. Story returned to Los Angeles, caught a stage to Santa Barbara, then a steamboat to San Francisco, a train to Cheyenne, and finally a stagecoach to Bozeman. Two weeks later, he received a telegram from Thompson stating that Mormon farmers near Austin, Nevada, refused to allow the herd to pass unless they received a fee of four hundred dollars. Story traveled to Austin by stage and train, and told the Mormons he would not pay the requested sum, but would instead forfeit three hundred head. The offer was accepted, and Story and his men escorted the remaining mustangs to Humboldt Wells. Story returned home once again by stage, while Thompson and the others completed the drive. Story had the animals branded by mid-September, and ran them on the Horseshoe Hills north of Bozeman.[29]

While Story was bouncing back and forth between Montana and Nevada, the *Pick and Plow* folded. Leander Black purchased the property from Horatio Maguire, and in September, leased it to another newspaperman, Kentuckian Joseph Wright, a Confederate veteran who had worked for the Virginia City *Democrat,* founded the *Montanian*, and assisted with the *Pick and Plow*.[30] On September 13, 1871, he published the first issue of the *Bozeman Avant Courier*, a seven-column, four-page sheet dedicated to assisting industrious and hardy pioneers "in opening this new and comparatively undeveloped territory"[31] Though Wright promised to run a politically independent newspaper, the *Avant Courier* became the champion of local entrepreneurs, particularly Leander Black and, to a lesser extent, Nelson Story.[32] The paper's name was a French translation of "forerunner," or "precursor," a reference to the much-anticipated arrival of the Northern Pacific Railroad, "now with unparalleled celerity coming over plains and mountains, through canyons and across rivers, to our territory."[33]

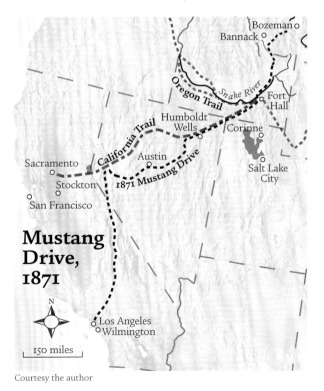

Courtesy the author

Leander Black's wife and children moved to Bozeman in the summer of 1871, but returned to St. Joseph in November so that his two oldest girls, Ella and Sarah, could complete their education. Black's son Madison remained in Bozeman, as did Black himself, postponing the promised relocation to Washington, D.C. Black's shipping business brought nearly five hundred tons of goods to Montana in 1871, netting him thousands. He platted a new residential section on the southeast side of town and purchased the Guy House, renaming it the Northern Pacific Hotel for the soon-expected railroad.[34] Black also sold his Mission Agency trading post to Story and construction contractor Charles W. Hoffman, who had built adobe houses at the agency for $32,000, before finally leaving for the nation's capital.[35]

In Black's absence, contract bids to supply Montana's Indian agencies were opened in Helena. Story was awarded the beef contract, but those for all other supplies, including flour, went to John Baldwin of Council Bluffs, Iowa. Baldwin and associate Grenville Dodge, a Civil War veteran and friend of President Grant, had partnered in banking and real estate in Council Bluffs since the 1850s before branching out into Indian supply contracts. Black, whose flour bid lost out, was furious, and he blamed Viall. He withdrew as one of Viall's sureties, and through the *Courier* railed against the "Iowa Indian Ring." Crow contracts had pumped half a million dollars into the Gallatin Valley economy in prior years, and Black claimed Viall's agreements with his fellow Iowans would rob the local coffers of some two hundred thousand dollars. The superintendent's actions also infuriated Story, who thwarted the efforts of the "sanctimonious psalm-singers" from Iowa by purchasing the contract from Baldwin. Viall also incurred the anger of territorial governor Benjamin Potts by refusing to replace an agent who was not a Republican. Recalled to Washington, D.C., in November, Viall resigned effective December 10, after a meeting with Interior Secretary Columbus Delano.[36]

Before returning to the Gallatin Valley, Black secured for Bozeman its own branch of the First National Bank, an accomplishment he hailed as "unmistakable evidence of the growing prosperity of Bozeman."[37] So, too, was it a testament to his individual prominence, now at an all-time high. He and Walter Cooper built the Cooper/Black Building on Main Street, which housed Cooper's weapons manufactory and Black's mercantile operation, and he still owned interests in a saloon, hotel, livery stable, and a freighting firm.[38] Black purchased a Concord coach that he proudly drove around town, the horses adorned in gold-plated harnesses.[39]

HAD HE WANTED, Nelson Story could have also harnessed his horses in gold. His cattle herd, freight operation, Mission Agency trading post, and government contracts put him on a close economic footing with Black, but he demonstrated little interest in flaunting his wealth.

On November 27, 1871, Ellen gave birth to a girl she and Nelson named Rose. A few months later, after the death of Frances Trent and Matthew's remarriage, eleven-year-old Jeanette Trent arrived in Bozeman by stagecoach, an unusual but not unheard-of feat for a girl her age.[40] The reasons for her leaving Kansas remain unclear, but a few descendants hold that Jeanette's dislike for her stepmother and Matthew's belief that his daughter would be happier in Montana were the driving factors. Jeanette was barely acclimated to Bozeman when, on April 14, two-year-old Ellen died from scarlet fever, a tragedy William Alderson, who conducted the funeral, labeled a "very sorrowful and affecting time."[41] Months later, Englishwoman Mary Blackmore, traveling with her wealthy husband William on an excursion to Yellowstone National Park, died in Bozeman of peritonitis. She was buried on the same south-side hill where Story's two daughters rested and where John Bozeman had been reinterred in 1870.[42] At William Blackmore's urging, Story, Lester Willson, Charles Rich, and John Mendenhall paid landowner Elisha Rouse $250 for the seven-and-a-half-acre site that became Blackmore Cemetery. Most if not all of the money came from Blackmore.[43]

A permanent, public cemetery represented another milestone in the community's development. Others included a 45 percent increase from 1871 to 1872 in the value of taxable county property. George Thomas introduced a new, superior grade of flour at his Madison Mills in Gallatin City, Perry and William McAdow, now operating under the name Gallatin Mills, had enlarged their operation by adding a large warehouse, and millwright John Tomlinson borrowed two thousand dollars from Nelson Story to import machinery and establish a feed-and-flouring mill on Cottonwood Creek in the community

In 1871, Ellen Story's eleven-year-old sister, Jeanette Trent (photographed here c. 1880), arrived in Bozeman to live with the Story family. Museum of the Rockies, Bozeman x85.3.113

of Salesville, ten miles southwest of Bozeman. New York native John Vreeland Bogert and several others founded the Young Men's Library Association, raising funds for books and periodicals while also sponsoring lectures, dramas, and minstrel shows.[44] "The valley is now dotted with cheerful, comfortable dwelling houses," observed the *Courier*, proclaiming that "Bozeman only needs the railroad to make it complete in all the elements of civilization."[45]

Engineers from the Northern Pacific Railroad continued in their work, but hardly with the "unparalleled celerity" heralded by the *Avant Courier*. A November 1871 survey of the Yellowstone Valley concluded that the land north of the river was most conducive for laying track, but a major snowstorm that left twenty-three soldiers and several civilians severely frostbitten forced the surveyors and their Fort Ellis escort to postpone their exploration. The following August a party, headed by John Haydon and escorted by infantry and cavalry under Major Baker, was attacked by Sioux and Arapahos while encamped on the Yellowstone near the mouth of Pryor Creek. Led by Crazy Horse and Sitting Bull, the warriors were unable to run off the command's horses, and eventually retreated under heavy fire. On the white side, the raid resulted in the deaths of an army sergeant and a civilian attaché. Two privates were wounded. On the Sioux-Arapaho side, two were killed and six wounded.[46] Major Baker, either drunk or severely hungover, failed to properly deploy his forces to pursue the fleeing warriors. The expedition concluded its work in late September, and Baker eventually received reassignment to Omaha, Nebraska, and was succeeded at Fort Ellis by Major Nelson Sweitzer.[47]

In the meantime, others outside the territory recognized the opportunity presented by a rail connection to Montana. Brigham Young's son John, and Connecticut capitalist Joseph Richardson, envisioned the construction of a narrow-gauge line from the Union Pacific Railroad in Utah to Helena, roughly following the Corinne-Virginia City Road. The two felt they could complete the project ahead of the Northern Pacific and open the territory's markets to the nation, albeit by a more circuitous route. Even after the Northern Pacific was finished, the Utah Northern Railroad would provide an alternate route for goods and passengers coming into or leaving Montana. But in order for the venture to be viable, subsidies in the amount of one million dollars in territorial bonds were needed. Nelson Story was somewhat leery of the idea. After all, his cattle traveled to the Chicago stockyards via Bismarck, not Corinne. Still he, Lester Willson, Achilles Lamme, and other

Bozeman businessmen offered their tentative endorsement, provided that details of the railroad's construction would be released before the legislature took any action.

While the railroad question stood in limbo, Story, Willson, and a handful of others set into motion an effort to bring order to the growing town of Bozeman. Horse thefts and petty infractions were on the rise, so much so that in November 1872, a grand jury concluded the city jail needed additional guards. Story was among those who registered a silent protest to the deteriorating state of affairs by not paying taxes.[48] The tipping point came on January 30, 1873, when John St. Clair, a pimp known as "Steamboat Bill," murdered a Chinese prostitute. Justice of the Peace Samuel Langhorne tried to placate the community by releasing St. Clair on his own recognizance, but reversed the order in the ensuing uproar. St. Clair and his alleged accomplice, Billy Roe, were tossed into jail, where Z. A. "Tripp" Triplett was also being held for the October murder of restaurant proprietor John Gempler.

On the evening of January 31, a large group of men gathered at O'Dell's saloon and billiard hall and gave voice to the same sentiments that had emerged in Alder Gulch years earlier. "Gallatin County was then enormous, and sparsely settled," recalled one witness to the ensuing events. "Court was held at infrequent intervals, and these two men, whose guilt was established beyond doubt, would have been held for months at the county's expense, and then subjected to a jury trial at great additional cost. Instead of this, and fearing that the outbreak of lawlessness might be followed by worse happenings, the individuals took the law into their own hands."[49] Backed surreptitiously by Story, Willson, and John Mendenhall, they emerged from the meeting as the "Committee Three Hundred," and like their vigilante predecessors, pledged to "reveal no secrets."[50]

The next day, an anonymous note was delivered to the offices of the *Avant Courier*, informing "the good people of Gallatin County through the columns of your noble paper, that all action of desperados . . . is now and forever played out in this community. So mote it be."[51] The letter's closing lines were a ritual phrase commonly repeated by Freemasons at the end of prayer. Given the fraternal organization's connection to the Alder Gulch vigilantes, the suggestion of impending violence was clear. That evening, Willson & Rich store clerk Peter Koch, sensing something afoot, refused to sell a customer thirty feet of rope. Despite Koch's noble intentions, the item was procured elsewhere, allowing a "rope jury" to gather later that same night. While a few men forcibly detained Sheriff Guy

The Committee Three Hundred, a vigilante group backed by Story and other prominent businessmen, was responsible for the hanging of two alleged murderers, Z. A. Triplett and John St. Clair, on January 31, 1873. Joshua Crissman, photographer. Museum of the Rockies, Bozeman x85.3.1032

and Judge Langhorne at two separate locations, the rest of the mob stormed the log jail, pulled the three prisoners from their cells, and took them to a meat-dressing rack in a nearby abandoned slaughter-house, where they hung Triplett and St. Clair.[52] They advised Roe to leave town, and, needing no further encouragement beyond the lynching he had just witnessed, he immediately complied. By the time a cavalry detachment from Fort Ellis was alerted and reached the scene, Triplett and St. Clair were dead, their bodies dangling on the meat rack in full view of worshippers attending early church services the next day.[53] When two Chinese men were arrested days later for killing a Chinese prostitute, officials determined that they should be incarcerated at Fort Ellis in order to prevent a similar scene. Thus ended what Joseph Wright of the *Avant Courier* deemed a "week of horror."[54]

Chapter Six

Close Observers, 1871–1875

IN MARCH OF 1873, Montana's new Indian superintendent, Iowan James Wright, made his first visit to Mission Agency. A devout Methodist Episcopalian minister, he wasted no time in his attempts to bring change to the Crow Reservation. He ordered those white men openly cohabitating with Crow women to either marry their mates or leave. As a result, "six noble whites of pure Caucasian blood led to the hymeneal altar an equal number of forest virgins of the Crow Indian Tribe," wrote the *Courier*, "[with] the Rev. Matthew Bird, performing the solemn and interesting ceremonies."[1] Wright demanded employees perform an honest day's work for a day's wage, and in order to monitor goings-on at the agency he appointed his son-in-law, Robert Cross, as head farmer. Other hires included George Town and Horace Countryman, who quickly found himself on Nelson Story's bad side for supplying inadequate hay to cattle Story was illegally grazing on the reservation.[2]

A fire the previous fall had severely damaged Mission Agency's employee housing complex, one of several recently finished buildings that included a schoolhouse, warehouse, agency building, and physician's quarters.[3] The incident had interrupted the operation of Story and Hoffman's trading post, but only briefly. By now business was in full swing. They stocked the store with meat, flour, vegetables, potatoes, coffee, sugar, beads, jewelry, tools, canned goods, tack, and even ammunition.[4] John Waddell headed the enterprise, and Tom Leforge received $250 in cash and trade goods to direct the

Crows to the post store rather than to those run by non-government traders. Since Story and Hoffman did not sell liquor, Leforge liked the arrangement.[5] "My sympathies naturally were with the licensed traders," he recalled. "While I knew that the traders reaped an enormous profit, I always saw to it that my Crow clients were not cheated beyond the bounds of the regular robberies established by custom."[6]

With the store in competent hands, Story set his sights on impending contracts that were to be submitted in New York. This coincided with final congressional approval of $513,343 for the 1867 Montana war claims. The investigation into the claims had taken some time. In 1871, General James Hardie traveled to Montana and negotiated the final settlement, which whittled the original claims of $980,313.11 by nearly half. Black was awarded $36,161, and Story, though his voucher of $7,260 was rejected, received $1,060 for "miscellaneous stores and subsistence."[7] Complicating the process was

Crow chiefs and head men in front of the Mission Agency building, 1871. Left to right: Etcharekash-characha (Poor Elk), Kamnebutse (Blackfoot or Sits in the Middle of the Land), Apatske (Long Ears), Isaseeh (He Shows His Face), and Mitchoash (Old Onion). Kamnebutse was a chief of the Mountain Crows. W. H. Jackson, photographer. MHS Photograph Archives, Helena 955-758

the loss of the original vouchers at General Sherman's headquarters in Chicago, where they were destroyed by the great fire of October 1871.[8] The Democratic press had then urged the government not to accept any substitute vouchers and perhaps repeal the legislation itself. The *New York Sun* accused the "patriotic Montana people" of fabricating Indian outrages so as to furnish troops "supplies at the most extravagant prices."[9] Counterattacks by the *Courier* and the *Helena Gazette* foiled any efforts at repeal, and claimants were given a year to request reimbursement either in person or through power of attorney.[10]

While preparing to head east, Story and his associates reversed their position on the Utah Northern Railroad after Samuel Hauser of Helena and attorney Sam Word of Virginia City convinced Governor Potts to convene a special legislative meeting to consider bonds only from those counties through which the railroad would pass.[11] Story opposed any subsidies, territorial bonds, or tax exemptions for the railroad.[12] Missoula businessmen who favored the Northern Pacific promised Story to "bind ourselves to collide with the first express train that passes on the North and South Railroad."[13] The legislature overrode Potts's veto and passed a bill that allowed counties along the rail route to invest in capital stock, but financial support for the Utah Northern nonetheless waned. Major investors in San Francisco and Salt Lake City balked, demanding an outright and absolute subsidy from the Montana legislature.[14]

To further reinforce the primacy of the Northern Pacific's route along the Yellowstone, Story hired carpenter Alexander Jamison to construct ten Mackinaw river boats, each twelve feet wide and thirty feet long, with a per-boat cargo capacity of fifteen tons. The so-called Yellowstone Fleet would not only move goods to market, but hopefully encourage Northern Pacific officials to accelerate their efforts by demonstrating that commerce could be conducted through the Yellowstone Valley.[15] Even Leander Black sided with Story, the *Courier* hailing the fleet's launch in May as the onset of "a free channel of commerce which grasping corporations cannot control," a veiled reference to the Utah Northern and its investors.[16]

By late April, Story was able to set out from Bozeman, and once in New York he submitted bids with the Board of Indian Commissioners to deliver beef and bacon to the Crow and Blackfeet Tribes. Around the same time, a new phrase, the "Montana Indian Ring," began circulating in newspapers as lucrative federal contracts engineered by western businessmen and politicians raised the suspicions of journalists and the public alike. A *New York Sun* correspondent

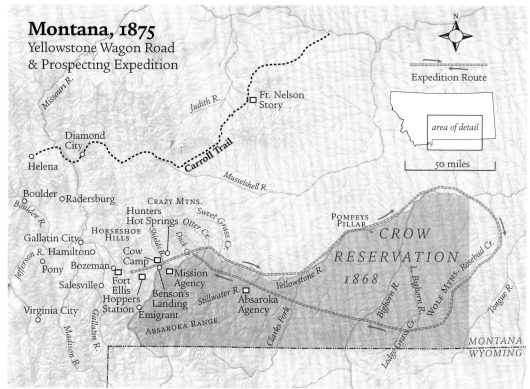

Montana, 1875
Yellowstone Wagon Road & Prospecting Expedition

N

Expedition Route

area of detail

50 miles

Missouri R.

Judith R.

Ft. Nelson Story

Diamond City

Carroll Trail

Helena

Musselshell R.

Boulder Radersburg

Boulder R.

CRAZY MTNS.

Hunters Hot Springs

Sweet Grass Cr.

Otter Cr.

POMPEYS PILLAR

HORSESHOE HILLS

Shields R.

Duck Cr.

CROW

Gallatin City

Cow Camp

RESERVATION

Jefferson R. Hamilton

Pony Bozeman

Mission Agency

1868

Yellowstone R.

Bighorn R.

L. Bighorn R.

WOLF MTNS.

Rosebud Cr.

Salesville

Fort Ellis

Benson's Landing

Stillwater R.

Absaroka Agency

Clarks Fork

Tongue R.

Virginia City

Hoppers Station

Emigrant

ABSAROKA RANGE

Gallatin R.

Madison R.

Lodge Grass Cr.

MONTANA
WYOMING

Courtesy the author

wrote a scathing piece accusing Leander Black, Joseph Viall, and former territorial representative William Clagett of lining their pockets with a $750,000 appropriation for the Teton Sioux and Milk River tribes. Story came under scrutiny when he won the contracts to deliver the Crow and Blackfeet tribes 295,000 pounds of beef at $2.33 per hundred pounds and 105,000 pounds of bacon at thirteen cents per pound.[17] Those who proffered lower bids complained to the commissioner of Indian Affairs, Edward Parmelee Smith. In a report made to the Department of the Interior, Smith alleged that Story supplied a better class of cattle and that the cost of Montana beef was actually less than it had been in previous years. Though the bid of the complaining party was in fact lower, he charged that it was "obscure and informal, and could not have been modified without doing injustice to other bidders."[18] Charges against Black and Viall were never filed, and, thanks to Smith's head-scratching explanation, Story kept his contracts.[19]

Upon his return to Montana, Story delivered thirty-seven hundred pounds of flour to the Crow Agency in July under the contract he had secured from John Baldwin. Fellows Pease paid more than the contract had specified, stating that no other supplier could offer a better deal. Later, when Story delivered 180 head of cattle that exceeded the established per animal weight by 250 pounds, he was paid for the total weight, which Pease justified by claiming that Yellowstone Valley cattle were often unusually large.[20] Whenever Pease needed exigency supplies, meaning those not called for in an advertised, competitive contract reviewed by the Board of Indian Commissioners, he bought them from Story. These included farm tools, seed, horses, foodstuffs, and even tea and hominy. In his final annual report written in September, Pease informed the Indian commissioner that delays in food supply shipments from the East compelled him "to purchase sugar, coffee, etc. from N. Story, in order to subsist these Indians in accordance with treaty stipulations."[21] In 1873, $34,791 in supplies and cattle were purchased from Story, who used some of the funds to construct a new brick warehouse on Bozeman's Main Street to store goods for the agency. Meanwhile his partner, Charles Hoffman, received contracts for most of the construction work on the agency and enjoyed a monopoly in supplying the agency firewood and other materials. Board of Indian Commissioners secretary Thomas Cree, in testimony before the Standing Committee on Indian Affairs, would rightly note that Bozeman businessmen lived off the Office of Indian Affairs and the U.S. Army.[22]

The businessmen were not alone. Ever since the agency's establishment on Mission Creek, the Crows lodged numerous complaints about encroachments by white hunters and miners. Their claims were corroborated by Pease, who admitted trespassers on Crow land were "killing and driving the game . . . destroying the best of their grazing country by bringing into the country herds of cattle and horses; roaming at will from one end to the other; [and] searching for gold and silver mines."[23] The government's solution was to relocate the Crows and redraw the reservation boundary. Or so it hoped. That summer, Indian Commission representatives Felix Brunot, General Eliphalet Whittlesey, and Thomas Cree arrived in Montana to negotiate a new treaty that would place the Mountain and River Crows on one reservation in the Judith Gap area, some 140 trail miles northeast of Mission Creek.

Due to a battle in which the Crows and their Nez Perce allies defeated the Sioux on Pryor Creek, the conference did not start until August 11. Story, Hoffman,

Fellows D. Pease, c. 1875 Sarony's Imperial Portraits, New York, photographer. MHS Photograph Archives, Helena 944-301

Fellows Pease, James Wright, some agency employees, and a contingent from Fort Ellis all participated.[24] The commissioners told the Crows that the government would purchase the current reservation and help relocate the tribe to a new location near the Judith River, but Crow leaders protested, saying the land allocated for the new reservation was not large enough to hold both the Mountain and River Crows and that it was too often frequented by other tribes. "We were born on this side of the Yellowstone and were raised here," said Chief Blackfoot. "There is plenty of good land here. Timber and grass and water are plenty, and there is much game in the mountains."[25] Blackfoot then raised the issue of continued encroachments by miners in the Emigrant Gulch area.

The Crows were also informed that Fellows Pease would be replaced by Wright, whose prior position of Montana Indian superintendent was abolished by Congress through the 1873 Appropriations Act. The change, presumably arranged by the Methodist Church, which felt Wright would be more likely to succeed in efforts to Christianize the Indians, was to occur in mid-September.[26] Pease had been popular with the Crows, and they were disappointed by his departure. "We know Pease's face," Chief Iron Bull told the commissioners. "All the people, old men, young men, women, and children, know Pease. If you put anybody else here as agent, we will not feel like living here anymore."[27]

The proposed relocation to the Judith and the planned removal of Pease left the two sides at an impasse. Story and Hoffman inadvertently became part of the solution when Iron Bull told commissioners, "We do not want Story and Hoffman, our traders, to go away. There is a tall man in the store called [Robert] Cross; he makes bad faces to us; he is a hard man; we do not know him."[28] Wright promised the Crows that Story and Hoffman would establish a new trading post in the Judith Basin, and that Pease, as special agent, would escort a Crow delegation to Washington to iron out relocation details with the Indian Office. On August 16, the tribal chiefs acquiesced and agreed to relocate.[29]

Like Iron Bull, many in Bozeman felt Pease had dealt honestly with the Crows, and they appreciated that he had made sure contracts were won by local merchants. The switch, some suspected, was made to restore the "pickings and stealings within the pale . . . of the Iowa Indian Ring."[30] And though the community welcomed the new mining and lumber opportunities in the Yellowstone Valley that the relocation would open up, there was genuine concern the move would embolden the Sioux and lead to more bloodshed. These fears were bolstered on September 3, when two ranch hands were killed by the Sioux within a half mile of the agency.[31]

Iron Bull's endorsement was a significant boon for Story, and he hoped to win a similar vote of confidence from the Methodist Church and, to an extent, the U.S. Army. He and Ellen often attended performances by the Fort Ellis Dramatic and Minstrel Association and hosted officers and their wives at dinner parties, where Ellen's jelly

Iron Bull and his wife, 1873. Iron Bull was one of the Crow chiefs who supported Pease and Story's involvement with the agency, even when the agent and the trader were accused of fraud. MHS Photograph Archives, Helena Lot 035 B11, F5.07

cakes were always pronounced a triumph.[32] Story's socializing, however, did little to ease the army's reservations that his establishment of a trading post in the Judith Basin would lead to continued abuse of agency contracts. As for winning the favor of the Methodists, Story did not have to wait long for an opportunity. That fall, local minister Thomas Corwin Iliff started an $8,000 fundraising campaign to build a new brick church in Bozeman.[33] "With that inspiration," wrote Iliff, "I called upon Mr. Nelson Story, a leading citizen and a man of considerable means, now a millionaire but not a church man, who surprised me by making a subscription of $1,000 which gave much impetus to the project."[34] Story's generosity allowed the cornerstone to be laid on September 15, and he also agreed to sit on the church's board of trustees.

DURING THE CIVIL WAR, agricultural and industrial activity in the North yielded huge profits. This led to rampant financial speculation fueled by a high protective tariff and the accelerated growth of the railroad industry. As banker and purchasing agent for the Northern Pacific, Jay Cooke sold bonds to finance the railroad's construction, but he unwisely used funds from his banking firm to finance short-term debt. A tightening money market, however, prevented Cooke and his partners from luring outside investors, and the endeavor collapsed. On September 18, the New York branch of Jay Cooke & Company closed, soon followed by the Philadelphia branch, triggering the calamitous Panic of 1873. Thousands of businesses across the United States failed, and other railroads went bankrupt. The Northern Pacific line stalled at Bismarck in Dakota Territory.[35] The Episcopal bishop for Montana, Daniel Tuttle, told a church contributor that fall, "I fear that Jay Cooke's failure is going to retard greatly the building of the N.P.R.R. So am I exceedingly sorry for Montana's sake."[36] The Panic also stalled construction of the Utah Northern at the Idaho-Utah border.

Despite the disastrous state of the economy, Story and Hoffman proceeded with their plans for a new trading post in the Judith. They recruited Peter Koch to build and manage the post for a salary of one hundred dollars per month plus expenses.[37] Having worked one and a half years as a woodcutter on the Musselshell and then as a quartermaster clerk at Fort Ellis before joining Willson & Rich, Koch possessed a unique combination of relevant experience for the job, and was widely recognized as a diligent and reliable employee.

In mid-October, Story dispatched an eight-to-ten-wagon bull train to Mission Creek to be loaded with flour, bacon, sugar, coffee, tobacco, soap, dried apples, blankets, axes, and clothing for the Judith.[38] Story's wagon boss, William Carr, noticed that the goods were annuities taken from the agency warehouse and rightfully designated for distribution to the Crows. George Town later corroborated the thievery, stating the wagons were definitely loaded with government sugar. When he mentioned it to a fellow worker, he was told to "ask no questions."[39]

Story's bull train and a lighter unit led by Wright's son-in-law Robert Cross left the agency on November 6. Guided by Mitch Boyer, it turned north from the Yellowstone, skirted the east side of the Crazy Mountains, and headed for the Judith Basin.[40] During the journey, Cross boasted to Horace Countryman that he and Story planned to make a lot of money off the post. They were going to "clean-up," he predicted, by selling the pilfered items to the tribe as well as hunters and trappers in the Judith. He also revealed that Agent Wright and his wife were in on the swindle so they could "live comfortably the rest of their days."[41] When officials at Fort Ellis learned of Town's and Countryman's statements, their suspicions that the agency's relocation to the Judith would lead to further fraud with less oversight only intensified.[42]

On November 14, Cross's train reached the west bank of Big Spring Creek, adjacent to present-day Lewistown. While waiting for Story's slower-moving bull train to catch up, the men passed the time playing cards, leading them to name two of Big Spring's small branches Big Casino and Little Casino Creeks.[43] In the meantime, Cross selected the new agency's location while Koch chose a site for the trading post, which he dubbed Story's Fort, opposite the agency on Little Casino Creek.[44] Once Story's train arrived, Koch and his party constructed a row of rough-cut log buildings one hundred feet long, including a warehouse, store, kitchen, and two "Indian houses." The structures were "built for use," according to Koch, "and not for show."[45]

On December 5, Fellows Pease returned from Washington with the Crow delegation that included Iron Bull, Blackfoot, and several others.[46] The *Avant Courier* predicted that the chiefs, having witnessed firsthand the extent of American civilization and the marvels of the nation's capital, would persuade "their astonished squaws and less-favored brothers of the breech-cloth" that resistance to continued white settlement was futile.[47] On December 16, Pease headed to the Judith with the Crow chiefs to inspect the location. After twelve days surveying and exploring, he and Lieutenant Gustavus Doane, commander of a military escort from Fort Ellis, affirmed Cross's selection of a site for the new agency. Meanwhile, James Wright sent a messenger to the River Crows on the Judith River, inviting them to receive their annuities at Mission Creek. When the River Crows replied their ponies were too thin to make the trip, Wright ordered the annuities be sent to Story's new fort for distribution.[48]

NELSON STORY's Mackinaw boat operation did little to resolve the barriers to the further development of the Yellowstone Valley as a corridor for commerce. The continued activity of Sioux war parties in the area meant that goods and people traveling to and from Montana were predominantly routed through Fort Benton or Corinne. Story by now had incorporated and become president of the Yellowstone Transportation Company, and though he continued to build boats at Yellowstone Crossing, which by then was known as Benson's Landing after Billy Lee sold it to Amos Benson, he raised fifteen thousand dollars to finance more ambitious plans.[49] In January 1874, Story, Lester Willson, John Bogert, Walter Cooper, and Charles Rich issued a call for volunteers to join the Yellowstone Wagon Road and Prospecting Expedition, which aimed to establish a wagon road from Bozeman to the mouth of the Tongue River, where steamships could transport goods to and from Bismarck.[50]

By early February, 125 men had volunteered.[51] The organizers spent five thousand dollars to equip them with four hundred rounds of ammunition per man, more than two hundred horses, mules, and oxen, and supplies enough to last four months. Story donated wagons, beef cattle, a mule, and a five-yoke oxen team. Governor Potts loaned a brass howitzer, and Walter Cooper provided at least one hundred oyster cans stuffed with scrap metal that could be fired out of the Bighorn Gun.[52]

The federal government opposed the expedition. Even Lieutenant Colonel George Armstrong Custer, commander of the Seventh Cavalry at Fort Abraham Lincoln near Bismarck, feared that it could "precipitate difficulties with the Indians."[53] Such a result, however, would not have been unwelcome by the expedition's sponsors. Conflict with the Sioux and Cheyennes would compel the government to establish forts in the Yellowstone Valley, encouraging the Northern Pacific to resume construction. This was confirmed by the *Courier*, noting that in the settlement of the West, "the people lead, and the

Executive committee members of the Yellowstone Wagon Road and Prospecting Expedition: Back, left to right: Samuel Langhorne, unknown. Front, left to right: Walter Cooper, Nelson Story, Horatio Nelson Maguire. Gallatin Historical Society Museum, Bozeman 5019

government and its soldiers follow."[54] The force assembled sixteen miles from Bozeman on February 10, and began its march two days later, careful to remain on the north side of the Yellowstone, thereby avoiding Crow treaty lands. When the expedition reached Duck Creek, it was joined by a smaller force led by schoolteacher J. L. Vernon, who claimed to have discovered gold in the Wolf Mountains the prior year.[55]

As the Wagon Road and Prospecting Expedition slogged its way east, rumors circulated in Bozeman that Sitting Bull and his band were buffalo hunting near the Bears Paw Mountains, northeast of Fort Benton. Some feared that the Crows, unhappy with the government's attempt to push them from the Yellowstone, might join their traditional enemy and raid white settlements. And with so many of the area's fighting men on the expedition, Gallatin Valley settlers, despite the presence of Fort Ellis, worried the community would be defenseless against such an attack. In early March, dozens of citizens, including Story, sent a petition to Governor Potts requesting that he activate a militia and hire the Crows as scouts so as to dissuade them from joining the Sioux. Potts never acted on the petition, and for good reason. The reports were baseless.[56]

Meanwhile, the Mountain Crows balked at relocating to the Judith. It was too small, and they suspected that the River Crows had become Sioux allies. Their refusal coincided with the emergence of designs among Helena freighters to establish a wagon road through the Judith Basin to a point on the Missouri River twenty-five miles west of the mouth of the Musselshell, where passengers and freight could be unloaded and transported to Helena. The road was laid out that spring by the Diamond-R Freighting Company, with the trail and the river port named for one of the firm's owners, Matt Carroll.

Nelson Story suspected that the Carroll Trail, together with the Mountain Crows' intransigence, would likely doom plans for a new reservation. His brother Elias had just returned to Montana with his new wife, Lucy Caper Story, and their two-year-old daughter, Nora, while Elias Jr. remained in Ohio to attend school. Elias took ownership of the Crow Agency trading post with Nelson and Hoffman retaining the supply contracts.[57] Story, in effect, planned to keep his operations at Mission Creek. When the U.S. Senate refused to ratify the relocation treaty, Story and Hoffman sold their interest in the Judith post to Theodore Dawes, who took over in March and renamed the site Fort Dawes.[58]

Potential trouble for Story began to brew elsewhere. On March 10, the U.S. House of Representatives passed the first of two resolutions calling for an inquiry into charges of fraud and unfairness in the awarding of supply contracts at Indian agencies in the West. This meant another examination of Story's 1873 beef and bacon contracts for the Blackfeet and Crows. Story headed for Washington to defend his bids, joined by John Bogert and Fellows Pease, who hoped to raise financial support for the Wagon Road and Prospecting Expedition.[59]

When the hearings before the U.S. House Committee on Indian Affairs began, congressmen heard a litany of complaints regarding contracts that had not been awarded to the lowest bidder. One of the complainants was James Booge of Sioux City, Iowa, upset because his bid of ten and a half cents a pound for bacon to the Crow and Blackfeet agencies had been rejected in favor of Story's. On June 2, Commissioner of Indian Affairs Edward P. Smith testified that Story's bid of thirteen cents a pound was preferable because Booge would have had to ship from Sioux City, and his bid did not account for freight costs. Smith also claimed Booge's signature on the bid appeared to be fraudulent, suggesting it was a so-called straw bid, in which signatures of the original bidders were erased. Another complainant was Helena businessman Richard Lockey, whose offer of $2 per hundred pounds of beef to the Blackfeet lost out to Story's at $2.33 per hundred pounds. Smith claimed he awarded the contract to Story based on the recommendation of the Board of Indian Commissioners.[60] After the hearings concluded, Assistant Secretary of the Interior Benjamin Cowen concluded there was no criminality in the awarding of the contracts, much less "fraud, irregularity, or unfairness."[61]

The Indian Commission awarded the Crow Agency beef contract for fiscal year 1875–1876 to Willson & Rich at $1.94 per one hundred pounds. This came at the urging of Leander Black, who otherwise did not fare so well in Washington. After Congress appropriated $10,000 for a wagon road to the newly created Yellowstone National Park, Black sought an exclusive government contract to build station houses through the Paradise Valley to Mammoth Hot Springs. Along with John Bogert, Lester Willson and a few others, he formed the Bozeman City & Yellowstone National Park Wagon Road and Hotel Company to also construct additional roads and "a commodious hotel" near Mammoth.[62] The bill to incorporate the organization with a capitalization of $500,000, introduced on April 27, never made it out of committee, in large part due to the opposition of territorial representative Martin Maginnis, who claimed it would be an unfair monopoly. Without the government charter, the partners gave up their effort, and the road went into the possession of James George, known as "Yankee Jim."[63]

Story arrived back in Bozeman in late May, once again ending a business trip by seeing his new child for the first time, a boy, Nelson "Bud" Jr., born May 12, 1874. Unshaken by congressional scrutiny, Story immediately finalized plans to deliver 22,640 pounds of dried buffalo meat and 34,750 pounds of pemmican to the Assiniboines and Sioux at the Milk River Agency. The request came from Story's friend William Alderson, then the new agent at Milk River, and Story collected $7,582 upon delivery.[64]

The Yellowstone Wagon Road and Prospecting Expedition had returned to Bozeman a few weeks before Story. The addition of Vernon's men and a few recruits from the Mission Agency had bolstered the expedition's size to nearly 150 men, and though it had several engagements with the Sioux, it failed to establish a wagon road, much less induce railroad construction or steamship navigation into

Montana. Like the militiamen, many of the expedition's members were a "hard set." J. L. Vernon, tagged by the *Courier* as a "bilk of the first water with the cheek of the devil," deserted near Pompeys Pillar. He and James Rockfellow took off with two horses and Story's mule, and forwarded a message to Story from Mission Agency requesting more supplies for the expedition, which they presumably intended to keep for themselves. With Story in the East, the plea went unanswered. The two eventually stole a skiff in Fort Benton and headed east on the Missouri River.[65] Later they quarreled, and Vernon cut Rockfellow up with a knife. Neither was heard from again.[66] The balance of the expedition spent most of March futilely prospecting for gold before proceeding to Rosebud Creek. Their largest fight occurred in the Little Bighorn Valley, when hundreds of warriors attacked the train on Lodge Grass Creek. The Bighorn Gun, with its deadly, shrapnel-filled canisters, proved a formidable weapon, and the Sioux withdrew. Their leader, Sitting Bull, impressed by his opponents' bravery, later remarked "that he had never seen such men."[67]

Before returning to Bozeman, the expedition's members presented the Crows with eight Sioux scalps as trophies. They also mutilated their victims by cutting off fingers and ears, but kept these gory souvenirs for themselves.[68] They left food containers laced with strychnine in their abandoned camps and poisoned Indian food caches, but the Sioux later claimed they avoided the suspicious-looking items. The men also booby-trapped a fake grave with a howitzer shell. When the Sioux investigated, the twelve-pound shell exploded, but no one was killed.[69]

Volunteer Zack Yates was killed during one of the fights, and a few others were wounded. John Bogert tried to put a positive spin on the effort by claiming that sixty Sioux had been killed and one hundred wounded, prompting Governor Potts to boldly state that "three hundred white men and the Crow Nation could settle the Sioux question in one season."[70] Talk of another expedition was quickly quashed when the army threatened to disarm and arrest any participants.[71]

All told, Story and the other expedition sponsors were disappointed with the results. The government had not dispatched troops to the area and no forts had been established, much less a shipping hub near the Tongue River. Many in Bozeman resigned themselves to the fact that the Northern Pacific would not reach their community until the economy rebounded. Story most likely held the same view, but events only a year later would give him enough hope to invest yet again in a plan to open the Yellowstone Valley.

AT MISSION AGENCY, Matthew Bird took over regular Sunday services from Reverend Iliff, as well as control of the reservation school. Though Sunday congregations rarely numbered more than a dozen, Wright considered the influence of the Methodist Episcopal Church beneficial.[72] He was also pleased that the government had abandoned its plans to relocate the Crows to the Judith Basin, which was already home to trading houses and whiskey shops. Wright now hoped the government would take immediate steps "to move the agency farther from the reservation line," noting, "There are good locations forty to sixty miles east of here."[73]

Wright's biggest concern with the agency's original location was the whiskey trade centered at nearby Benson's Landing, where Amos Benson and Dan Naileigh operated a saloon, as did Horace Countryman and his partner Hugh Hoppe. Liquor produced crime and sickness on the reservation, and led to such a dramatic rise in prostitution that the agency, in Iliff's words, became little more than a "squaw whorehouse" to service white men.[74] Wright further argued that the current agency site lacked adequate farming and hunting land, was too far removed from always-needed timber, and was difficult to defend against the Sioux. Lastly, the area's constant winds made the location "uncomfortable."[75]

As they did with Nelson Story, Fort Ellis officers harbored suspicions of Wright, believing his requests for relocation merely amounted to a ploy to hide his thievery. Already Wright had diverted Crow subsistence supplies to agency employees and pocketed their ten-dollar room-and-board fee. Whenever Wright needed exigency supplies, he, like Pease, turned to Story. In the summer of 1874, he paid Story just over thirty thousand dollars for flour, coffee, sugar, rice, potatoes, and hominy, leading the commissioner of Indian Affairs to issue an order abolishing such exigency purchases, effective in October. Wright saw to it the government paid Story for horses he was supposed to deliver to the Crows, but instead Story, with Wright's help, sold them to other ranchers while the two split the profits.[76] On another occasion, Story received thirty-five dollars a head for two hundred horses, when in fact he only delivered one hundred. Story had his foreman run the animals around a hill twice for inspectors, who either naively believed they were getting two hundred head, or found the farce so comical they went ahead and paid Story the full amount. One year later, Story purchased the same horses back from the government at ten dollars per head.[77]

Billy Frazier, son of George and Elmyra and a part-time Story employee, admitted later that Story was dishonest in his agency dealings, but insisted that any smart man would have done the same:

> I remember one time I took a load of oats down to the agency for him. It rained while I was on the way . . . I took the wagon sheet off my load and let it rain . . . we sold the oats by the weight when we delivered them at the agency; wet grain weighed heavier than dry. When I left Bozeman my load weighed 8,000 pounds; when I weighed in at the agency it weighed 11,000 pounds. Oats sold at three cents a pound and that meant $90 difference to me. I showed Story my bill of lading when I got back to Bozeman. He asked me why the oats weighed more in the agency than when they did when I left Bozeman. I told him and offered to split the $90 with him. He just laughed and told me to keep it.[78]

William Carr helped Story deliver 164 cattle to the reservation, but objected when ordered to combine them with agency cattle. He knew that doing so would allow Story to sell the Crows livestock that had already been purchased by the government, and when he pointed this out to Story, he received a terse reply: "I expect you to do as I request as you are in my employ."[79] Carr complied. Story also had Carr take a separate yoke of large steers to the agency scales, so as to increase the calculated average weight for the herd, which would result, of course, in more money for Story. Carr later reported the deception to James Wright, who said the weather was too severe to weigh the cattle again. After Carr's concerns about the Judith Basin supplies and the agency cattle tampering reached Bozeman, William Alderson advised Story to find a new wagon boss, as Carr "was too close an observer."[80] Story replaced Carr with Nelson Sill.

Carr stayed on as a reservation herder, and noticed the Crows received only half of the promised annuities that summer. He was certain that Story and Wright stole the balance to sell in Story's store, and also believed that Wright pocketed the difference between the $5.50 in government funds he paid per sack of flour and the $3.50 each was worth.[81] When Carr placed a bid to deliver wood to the agency at $4.50 per cord, Wright rejected the offer as too expensive. Yet a few weeks later, Elias Story received a contract at $10 per cord. Indeed, Story and Wright were bilking the government, and, like the soldiers at Fort Ellis, Carr had no doubt that Wright's true reason for relocating the agency to the east was to diminish any oversight from Bozeman. Story's public support for the plan only reinforced that assumption.

While Story reinvigorated his operation at Mission Creek, Theodore Dawes, with the help of his brother William, continued to operate the store in the Judith. But Dawes's investment became untenable in early June when the Indian Office ordered all traders not adjacent to an actual agency to forfeit their permits for the sale of arms and ammunition. According to Horace Countryman, thievery and deceit had allowed the store to survive as long as it did. He claimed Dawes and Cross stole supplies from the Mission Agency to sell in the Judith, and that Wright and Elias Story had cached six thousand government-owned needle-gun cartridges in a gulch near the agency, which they would later sell in Nelson Story's sutler store.[82] The allegations were never proven, but Wright had seen enough. He submitted a letter of resignation to Commissioner Smith in June, citing the danger of Sioux war parties and the "vile loafers, blacklegs, and cutthroats" who were plotting to murder him and his family.[83] In truth, he merely needed to escape from the mounting scrutiny. Wright's resignation was accepted, but he would stay on until his successor arrived before taking a transfer to Fort Hall.

Sioux war parties would not leave the agency alone that summer. Since many of the Crows were in the Judith collecting annuities or hunting, one hundred Sioux met minimal resistance as they advanced on the agency in July, forcing Wright to hire additional guards.[84] Others stole six horses from herder George Town near Benson's Landing, and a few weeks later crossed the Bozeman Pass and stole at least fifty horses from Fort Ellis and a few nearby ranches.[85] Story and thirteen civilian volunteers gave pursuit with a company of the Second Cavalry led by Captain Edward Ball, but after two days the soldiers returned home, believing the Indians had scattered in the mountains. Story and the civilian force, however, caught up with some of the raiders at the Boulder River, where a brief exchange of volleys ended with no casualties. Later, the body of herder Hardy O'Dare was found nine miles from the Mission Agency, horribly mutilated and full of arrows.[86] A few days afterward, Tommy Thompson rode into Bozeman and reported that nine Indians, presumably Sioux, were eyeing Story's herd. Several volunteers returned to the Yellowstone with Thompson, but the Indians made no attempt to steal any animals.[87] Critics of Agent Wright blamed him for the Sioux attacks, saying a proper distribution of annuities would have kept the Crows on the reservation and discouraged Sioux activity in the region.[88]

IN THE FALL OF 1874, Leander Black became president of the Eastern Montana Agricultural, Mineral, and Mechanical Association. With Nelson Story as vice president and John Bogert as secretary, the association raised eight thousand dollars in capital stock to construct a fairgrounds and race track north of town. Story, a lover of horse racing, purchased a "superb" trotting horse from Utah that he hoped would dominate early competition.[89] Once again, Story and Black put aside their enmity, as they had when dealing with the Iowa Indian contractors, to enhance the community. But more trouble between the two was brewing elsewhere.

In early October of 1874, Black abruptly shut down the *Avant Courier*. He insisted that it was purely a business matter, and that Joseph Wright and coeditor John Bruce owed him two thousand dollars. Wright, however, saw the decision as retaliation for his editorial support of the territorial referendum, approved in August, moving the capital from Virginia City to Helena, which Black opposed.[90] Black rejected an offer of fifteen hundred dollars from Wright and Bruce to buy the paper. Story, who liked Wright for his pro-business stance, offered to form a stock company to buy the paper, but backed off when Black raised his asking price to three thousand dollars. Black then turned the property over to his son Madison and John Bogert. The two renamed the paper the *Bozeman Times* and hired Ezekiel Wilkinson of Helena as editor, and his two sons, Raleigh and Henry, as publishers.[91] The paper promised to be "independent in politics, open to all, seeking to make itself not only useful, but indispensable, trustworthy, and original."[92]

John Bogert had a tangled relationship with Nelson Story, Leander Black, Lester Willson, and Charles Rich. As Fort Ellis's official contractor in 1871, he devised a scheme whereby fort suppliers received scrip redeemable only at the Willson & Rich store, where they received the equivalent in store goods.[93] Bogert reimbursed the store in cash, helping Willson & Rich realize a total of seventy thousand dollars in

Among the Bozeman founders to profit through shady schemes were Lester Willson, left, and his partner Charles Rich. For a time, suppliers of Fort Ellis could only redeem their scrip by exchanging it for merchandise at the Willson & Rich store.
Montana State University–Bozeman MSH-1407-B01-F-13-img01

transactions for 1871.[94] Achilles Lamme, whose operation was patronized by Missourians and other Confederate sympathizers, cried foul at the arrangement. With the assistance of fellow southerner Leander Black, Lamme pressured Bogert to cease the practice.[95] Bogert, in partnership with his father, then began selling merchandise to the Crow Agency, but after only limited success sought out an alliance with Leander Black in hopes of growing his business.

Story was rightfully concerned by the development, as Bogert was undoubtedly aware of the rampant duplicity and fraud at the agency. The suspicions of William Carr and Horace Countryman were being whispered around town, but Wright had until then managed to keep the accusations out of the newspaper. But the Blacks and John Bogert might not be so kind. Story saw Wright as an ally and wanted to keep him in business. Together with Lester Willson and John Mendenhall, he purchased equipment and a new office for the *Avant Courier*, allowing it to resume printing on November 7, nearly a week before the inaugural issue of the *Bozeman Times*.

John V. Bogert, portrait, c. 1883. Aware of the fraudulent goings-on at the Indian agency, Bogert sought to turn a profit by helping Willson and Rich monopolize contracts with Fort Ellis. Museum of the Rockies, Bozeman x85.3.127

Locals wondered if the young community was large enough to support two newspapers. Wright, in the November 13 edition, called the *Times* an experimental paper, a test to see if its rival publication couldn't be "crushed out." He added that the *Avant Courier,* contrary to rumors, was not the organ of any ring, "nor is it engaged in any private schemes."[96] Events over the next few years, though, would bring that assertion into question. Wright had always written favorably of men like Story, Black, and Bogert, but now owed his allegiance entirely to Story. Grateful his livelihood had been saved, Wright would repay Story in print, and add further homage to his benefactor by naming his newborn son Nelson Story Wright.[97]

The federal government approved the relocation of the Crow Agency, and on November 30, Agent Wright's replacement, Dexter Clapp, arrived in Bozeman. Clapp was a Methodist minister who had enlisted as a captain in the 148th Regiment of New York Volunteers during the Civil War, later rising to the rank of brigadier general. From 1871 to 1873, he served as U.S. consul to Argentina and earned a reputation as a very capable administrator.[98]

Clapp immediately traveled down the Yellowstone to scout locations for the new agency. He picked a site at the junction of the Stillwater River and Rosebud Creek, seventy-three trail miles from the Mission Agency. "It is twenty miles from the reservation boundary and thus protected from whiskey traders," wrote Clapp. "It has good farming land; it is away from the terrible winds of the Yellowstone Canyon."[99] He later suggested that the Crows be allowed to raise their own cattle, since they "are as good herders as they are poor farmers."[100] He also made clear to agency employees that criticism of his administration would not be tolerated, and violators would be dismissed. Story became an immediate confidante of Clapp, and quickly filled another agency supply contract by purchasing five hundred sacks of flour from Achilles Lamme at five dollars each.

In May of 1875, the move was underway as Clapp hired a crew of thirty mechanics and laborers to build a road and haul equipment from Mission Creek to Rosebud Creek. Major Sweitzer protested, telling his superiors that the only beneficiaries would be the traders and the cattlemen who wanted the range on the western edge of the reservation. "The plea is to get away from whiskey traders," he wrote, and "no moving of agency will do that. Whiskey traders ply their trade principally when the Indians are in the Buffalo Country and the Crow Indians do not stay at their Agency and will not as long as the buffalo last."[101] The Crows, too, had misgivings about the plan. First, they feared it would drive game animals east into Sioux hunting grounds and, second, that it would render the Crows more vulnerable to Sioux raids. Nonetheless, the transfer of agency materials began on May 22. In addition to the several wagons traveling overland, a flatboat loaded with provisions was sent down the Yellowstone. Deputy U.S. Marshal Frank Murray accompanied the wagon train, and described the monotony with his droll diary entries:

> Monday, 24th—All at work grading road. Archie
> McDonald run over by a Texas bull. No one hurt but
> the bull.
> Tuesday, 25th—Rainy and cold. All take an invigorating
> walk through half a mile of mud to breakfast. March to
> the Yellowstone; all wet, moody and thirsty, but plenty
> of whisky—in Bozeman.
> Wednesday, 26th—Hunting for signs of the boat, when
> news comes of its loss, and nothing saved but McMillen
> and a bed-quilt.[102]

No lives were lost when the flatboat capsized, but all the provisions, save the bed-quilt, were.

At the time, Story was in Washington, D.C., where he received the fiscal year 1876 pork contract for the Crow Agency at fourteen cents per pound and collected payment for thirteen thousand sacks of exigency flour furnished to Fellows Pease, despite claims by a few army officers that only three thousand sacks had been delivered.[103] Virginia City businessman William Kiskadden received the beef contract at $1.70 on the hoof, and the flour contract at $3.25 per hundred pounds. In all, the contracts amounted to one and a half million pounds of beef and five hundred thousand pounds of flour. A provision permitted Kiskadden to double-sack the flour, allowing for two layers of burlap to guard against breakage on the rough road to the agency. Leander Black, who first met Kiskadden in Denver in the 1860s, was one of two sureties on a $25,000 bond that guaranteed Kiskadden's obligations to the Crows as well as flour deliveries to the Blackfeet, Lemhi, and Fort Hall Agencies. The Kiskadden contract, signed May 26, was in effect Black's contract.[104]

Story returned to Bozeman on May 30, and a few days later, ground was broken for the new Absarokee Agency on Rosebud Creek. Both Story and Black made attempts to court Clapp and ensure the continuation of their favorable commercial relationships with the agency. Story and his brother Elias came out the winners. Clapp paid Elias Story $425 for four horses worth half that amount, as well as an $800 voucher for 13,334 needle cartridges Clapp said he needed because he could not secure assistance from Fort Ellis for the post's defense, though it appears he never requested any. Clapp also gave Elias a $97 voucher for tobacco, though an adequate supply had already been furnished by the

Elias Story, n.d. With little over-sight from the Indian Bureau, Agents Pease, Wright, and Clapp collaborated with Nelson and Elias Story—and others—over the years to ensure handsome profits from the Story brothers' contracts to supply the Crow Reservation agencies. Gallatin Historical Society Museum, Bozeman 18003

government's annuity. Furthermore, Clapp paid Nelson $300 for work oxen and plows, but they were never used during the year.[105]

Black was not as tactful in his approach to the new Crow agent. According to Clapp, Black told him that together they could split as much as fifty thousand dollars on the Kiskadden contract. "He further said that if I would not thus work with him, that his friends or partners would have me removed."[106] Black noted that his friend, Captain Edward Ball at Fort Ellis, also had aims of enriching himself, and added that he counted Nelson Story as an enemy, "and would certainly make him a great deal of trouble on his pork contract."[107] In short, Black made plain that he had cheated the government in the past and possessed great confidence he could continue in his efforts unabated. In doing so, he failed to win over Clapp, but he did set the stage for a showdown with Nelson Story.

Chapter Seven

Thieves and Scoundrels, 1875

ACTIVITIES in the Yellowstone Valley in 1875 triggered trouble in the region and opened new opportunities. In June of that year, the *Josephine*, a U.S. Army–chartered steamship tasked with scouting potential sites for military posts to guard the Northern Pacific Railroad, successfully navigated up the Yellowstone River to near present-day Billings. Previous efforts had been thwarted by the river's shallow water, particularly at Wolf Rapids, twelve miles below the mouth of the Tongue River. Piloting the *Josephine* was Grant Marsh, and among the army officers onboard was the president's son, Lieutenant Colonel Frederick Dent Grant. Its successful navigation resurrected Story's hope that tourists, settlers, and supplies could be delivered as near to Bozeman as Fort Benton was to Helena, trimming hundreds of miles off the Missouri River route and making Bozeman the foremost freight depot in the territory.[1] An effort to establish a port on the Yellowstone came the following month, when an expedition of forty-five men led by Fellows Pease left Bozeman and headed to the mouth of the Bighorn to build a stockade for trappers and prospectors. The expedition was divided in two groups: one a mounted overland party, and the other aboard a fleet of four of Story's Mackinaw boats loaded with supplies and armaments, including the Bighorn Gun.[2]

On the second day out of Benson's Landing, one of the boats, the *Bozeman*, wrecked just above Hunters Hot Springs. Valuable supplies disappeared into the current, but some of the rifles and the

Bighorn Gun were retrieved from the bottom of the river.[3] A day later another boat, the *Prairie Belle*, struck a snag at the mouth of the Stillwater and sank. No lives were lost in either mishap, but the group was now desperately low on salt and sugar. "We have now the cargo of one boat left," read a letter from Paul McCormick to John Bogert at the *Bozeman Times*, and "we may get to the mouth of the Bighorn with our lives, but we shall be nearly destitute. We can only pray to be successful in saving the *Maggie Hoppe*, the only boat that has not been under water."[4]

Pease and his men reached the mouth of the Bighorn on June 24, where they found the surrounding hills occupied by Sioux, who had just fought a three-day battle with the Crows and Nez Perces. Although the Crows could claim victory in the encounter, they had moved off to the north. Within a few days, however, the Sioux disappeared, allowing the men time to construct Fort Pease, which consisted of a blockhouse and a few small log houses within a 235-square-foot parcel. Pease himself remained only long enough to select the site, thereafter taking two others downriver to Fort Buford and Bismarck for supplies, and then ostensibly on to Chicago and New York to raise capital for the venture.[5]

These developments were heartening news to proponents of the east-west railroad route. The success of the *Josephine* and construction of Fort Pease suggested that communities could be established in the eastern reaches of the territory. Despite the Panic of 1873, nearly $5 million in goods were exported from Montana in 1874, including more than $4 million in gold, silver, and copper. Imports had an estimated worth of $1.27 million.[6] Forecasts predicted that nearly one hundred thousand pounds of buffalo robes and elk skins would be shipped out of Bozeman within the year. Relocation of the Crow Agency gave Story and other stockmen larger ranges, and his herd now used the Tom Miner Basin near Emigrant for summer pasture. A railroad line could transport these fat cattle to eastern markets.[7] But its construction would only resume when the nation's economic health improved, and the "Sioux question" was finally answered.

THE TRANSFER to the Absarokee Agency entered its final stages in the summer of 1875. Story often had thirteen freight wagons transporting goods and supplies at any given time, services for which he would earn just under two thousand dollars.[8] The Sioux, unhappy that the new Crow Agency would be closer to their territory, watched the relocation from a distance until July 2, when thirty warriors attacked a camp of choppers and teamsters near the mouth of the Stillwater and escaped with a mule and several oxen. Later that same day, the Sioux ambushed and killed Jose Tsoyio while he was herding stray agency cattle. Agent Clapp's report to Captain D. W. Benham at Fort Ellis noted that Tsoyio "must have made a good fight, as the bushes where he took refuge showed many bullet marks."[9] With the exception of a piece of his scalp, Jose's body was never recovered.[10]

Two days later the Sioux ran off eight agency mules and fourteen that belonged to "other parties."[11] They then raided Benson's Landing and killed herder Jim Hughes, whose companion escaped with only a flesh wound and reported the attack at Fort Ellis.[12] In response, a posse formed in Bozeman and set out to warn other ranchers, including William Martin and Alfred Myers, who had a ranch on Brackett Creek, a tributary of the Shields. Meanwhile, Lieutenant Lovell Jerome led a detachment of cavalry from Fort Ellis to Benson's Landing.[13] Despite pleas from cattleman Joe Lindley to pursue the Indians who had killed Hughes, Jerome did not move his force for two days, when he joined a civilian party from Bozeman.[14] On July 9, twenty miles from the Absarokee Agency, the Sioux attacked three messengers returning to the Gallatin Valley from Fort Pease. Sam Shively was killed and Patrick Hyde wounded, while Nelson Weaver escaped injury. Several cabins in the upper Yellowstone were ransacked, including Lindley's.[15]

Although Fort Ellis was home to more than two hundred soldiers, only ninety-two were available for duty when those on assignment, detached service, hospitalized, imprisoned, or facing discharge were deducted from the total.[16] Governor Potts asked the War Department to send in additional troops, and appealed to Interior Secretary Columbus Delano "to afford the Crow Agent and the people of Gallatin & Yellowstone Valleys protection, from the raids of the worst Band of Indians on the American Continent."[17] Delano forwarded the letters on to President Grant, but no action was taken.

On July 13, as Nelson Story was preparing to ship supplies from Mission Creek to Rosebud Creek, a ferry carrying a small contingent of soldiers and civilians from Fort Ellis sank near Benson's Landing. Four soldiers and two civilians, Stonewall Jackson Hunter and Benjamin "Berry" Smith, an African American teamster employed by Story, drowned. One civilian was rescued by the ferryman, and two soldiers swam to a nearby island where they were eventually rescued by Story, Agent Clapp's brother Charles, and Andrew Dusold, an Indian Affairs inspector accompanying Story's supply train.[18]

On July 21, the Sioux stole forty-three head of oxen from the agency's corral, including eight belonging to Story. The next day, when Story's train was roughly six miles from the agency, Sioux warriors hiding in ambush opened fire. No one was hit, and Story, Dusold, and several others attacked the Sioux position, forcing them to flee. Twenty-one men dispatched from the agency escorted the train in safely, and as soon as it was within the agency's confines, Story, Mitch Boyer, Dusold, Clapp, and sixteen others rode out in an attempt to retrieve the stolen oxen. Eight of the animals were found dead on the trail, and of the nine recovered, all but one was wounded.[19]

To the east, Fort Pease was under constant surveillance by the Sioux. One man, James Edwards, was killed in an ambush a mile from the fort on July 12. With little hope for the deployment of additional men into the Yellowstone that summer, a boat with eight reinforcements and supplies left Benson's Landing on July 24 to give some measure of relief to the beleaguered post.[20]

Three days later, while Story and Clapp were in Bozeman to welcome Secretary of War William Belknap during his tour of western posts and agencies, thirty Sioux ambushed James Hildebrand and Charlie Gale while they were herding Story's cattle sixteen miles south of the agency.[21] Hildebrand was fatally wounded and quickly bled to death. Gale, positioned behind a boulder, prevented the raiders from stealing the cattle until three other Story employees, including wagon master Nelson Sill, arrived to help.[22] The thirty-seven-year-old Hildebrand was a native of Ireland, and according to Leforge "had been regarded as a good man, very capable, an important factor in Nelson Story's business organization."[23]

The conflicts continued into August. One near Benson's Landing killed a Bannock scout and left another man with a gunshot wound to the hip.[24] Clapp urged the government to take action to "effectually quiet the hostile Indians of the Yellowstone country, and give to the Whites peace, and to the Crows opportunity for the progress of civilization."[25] His requests went unfulfilled, as the army claimed that a shortage of troops prevented the deployment of any additional forces. Clapp fumed over the lack of assistance from Fort Ellis, convinced that the military's inaction stemmed from its disapproval of the agency's relocation.[26]

The Crows finally drove the Sioux from the region, allowing work on the new agency to continue. By early September, a warehouse, carpenter and blacksmith shops, and employee houses, mostly made of adobe brick, were completed. A sawmill and lime-kiln were fully operational, the main agency building was nearly finished, and an irrigation ditch supplied water to hundreds of acres. The Mission Agency officially closed on September 6, as all employees, their families, and supplies had been transferred to the new agency. Clapp gave Story a $1,260 voucher for freighting materials, some of which had already been delivered.[27] Story began building a trading post at the Absarokee Agency, and under Elias's management it took in $70,000 in buffalo robes and peltries by the end of the year. Horace Countryman and Hugh Hoppe relocated their operation as well, building a new trading post at the mouth of the Stillwater. Countryman referred to the site as his ranch, but in reality it was a meager frontier outpost trafficking in illegal whiskey.[28]

TERRITORIAL FARMERS had long believed themselves short-changed when supplying post contractors like Story with goods for Fort Ellis or the Crow Agency. They formed a grange in 1873 to command higher prices, and then decided in 1875 to skip the middlemen and negotiate directly with post commanders. The grange received several contracts by undercutting the competition's hundred-pound bids of grain—in the case of hay and oats, by $5 and $3.50 respectively. But 1875 was a bad grasshopper year, lowering crop yields and driving up prices. As a result, the grange could not fulfill the agreed-upon terms, and the War Department soon decided to stick with the contractors.[29]

The degree to which men like Story controlled the contracting process on reservations across the West led to mounting accusations of government fraud. One-quarter million Native Americans were now the responsibility of some seventy-plus agencies under Grant's Peace Policy, and it was widely believed that many of the agents in charge accepted lower quantities and grades of foodstuffs for the tribes, and on some occasions lined their own pockets with the proceeds of inflated payments.[30] "They will take a barrel of sugar to an Indian tribe and get a receipt for ten barrels," decried Representative Maginnis. "For a sack of flour, the Indians sign a receipt for fifty sacks. The agent will march three hundred head of cattle four times through a corral, get a receipt for twelve hundred head, give part of them to the Indians, sell part to a white man, and steal as many back as possible."[31] Story and Clapp were suspected of stealing annuity and subsistence supplies, including clothing they allegedly sold to merchants in Bozeman and elsewhere. Story was also accused of diverting sugar destined for the Dakota Agency to the Crow Agency, where Clapp not only issued a voucher for it, but then allowed Story to sell it to Montana merchants.[32]

Story and his ilk did not see themselves as depriving the Indians of anything, instead choosing to believe that they were merely taking advantage of a foolhardy government program. Thomas Leforge claimed that the Crows did not care for agency beef and seldom ate it anyway. Like most plains people, they preferred buffalo and often fed the federally supplied alternative to their dogs. Bacon was fried only for the lard that could season wild game or tan skins. Indians ate little flour and often sold their allotted sacks to whites or emptied the contents and used the bag for other purposes. "A flour sack, with its decorative colored printing," explained Leforge, "was to an Indian woman a beautiful piece of material for working up into clothing or hanging upon the interior wall of the lodge."[33] Leforge's simplistic justification for the abusive practices of traders failed to consider, however, the increasing dependence of the Crows on government annuities as game populations in the Yellowstone dwindled and the encroachment of white settlers disrupted traditional subsistence practices.[34] In his indifference to the welfare of any tribe, Billy Frazier expressed a hard-eyed view that, although cruel, was likely representative of popular opinion: "The more Indians who starved to death, the fewer we had to fight."[35]

The Indian Commission issued a statement that summer defending government policies as "eminently humane and Christian." Since nearly all currently serving agents had been appointed by their respective denominations, they were considered trustworthy enough to root out any alleged fraud. The commission believed the system was under assault by "bad men," and denied the existence of any "rings or combinations."[36] *Avant Courier* editor Joseph Wright scoffed at the commission's claim that the Sioux were beginning to show "great promise in the line of peace, order, and quiet," and invited commissioners to come "take a trip but a few miles from our town, and if you return in the flesh, you will find that your 'Humane Policy' was dropped at the first crack of a Sioux rifle."[37]

General Philip Sheridan, unconvinced by the commission's faith in the system, ordered army officers to inspect all agency supplies and to "be on their guard lest the quantity and quality of the supplies be changed before the delivery at the agencies, and in this way their inspection of the original stores be taken advantage of to cover up fraudulent acts."[38] Captain Edward Ball, perhaps as a result of Black's influence, received an appointment as inspector for the Crow

Agency, allowing him to scrutinize and examine all shipments from area contractors, Nelson Story included. At Commissioner Smith's behest, Ball, Indian Affairs inspector Colonel Erwin C. Watkins, and two U.S. marshals came to the new agency in September and, upon finishing their investigation, submitted fraud charges against Nelson Story and Dexter Clapp to a grand jury.[39]

A panel of seventeen jurors from Madison and Gallatin Counties was assembled in Bozeman, and by the weekend of October 16, spectators and newspaper reporters filled the Metropolitan and Northern Pacific Hotels. Among them were Black's attorney Sam Word, still miffed at Story's role in delaying the Utah Northern, and Martin Maginnis. One visitor noted that the town had a neat and tidy appearance, and even the *Avant Courier* seemed pleased with the community's behavior: "There has been but one or two fights, and few drunks. In the first stage of the proceedings, the pet bear chained in the rear of Gov's saloon, which has borne a good moral character, got gloriously drunk, which no doubt disgusted some."[40] That Monday, the jury took up the case.[41]

Samuel Word, n.d Dana of New York, photographer. MHS Photograph Archives, Helena 945-695

Henry Blake, a Boston attorney and Civil War veteran who had immigrated to Montana in 1866, served as presiding judge. A former editor of the *Montana Post* and later part-owner of the *Montanian* newspaper, Blake was elected Virginia City's representative to the territorial legislature in 1874, and the following year President Grant appointed him an associate justice for the territorial supreme court.[42] Merritt Cicero Page led the prosecution. A native of New York, Page graduated from Yale University in 1862, where classmates remembered him as "a shrinking, almost listless fellow," who had few friends.[43] He studied law in New York City, and in 1865 moved to Chattanooga, Tennessee. There his career floundered, and in 1868 Page set out for Laramie City, Wyoming, where, in addition to practicing law, he also served as temporary mayor. After losing money in a mining venture, Page came to Radersburg, Montana, in 1869. His law practice there did well, and, with the influence of Wilbur Fisk Sanders, Page won appointment as U.S. district attorney for Montana in 1872. Together with William Clagett, he had investigated alleged frauds at other Montana Indian agencies, but had yet to seek an indictment.

As the community awaited the courtroom drama, Nelson Story laid plans to stifle the investigation and upend the trial through bribery and a campaign of shaping public opinion. He revealed to associates that he was willing to spend as much as ten thousand dollars to beat the charges. To that end, on October 14, Peter Koch offered two hundred dollars to George Town on the condition that he not volunteer any information about the supply goods taken to the Judith Basin, instead only answering questions posed directly by Page. Town refused, telling Koch neither he nor Story had enough money to buy his silence. Months earlier, however, Town had defaulted on a ninety-seven-dollar loan from Story, which Koch promised would be forgiven altogether with no ill will from Story in exchange for his cooperation. Town gave in, and later accepted the two-hundred-dollar bribe.[44]

Peter Koch,
c. 1900 Museum of
the Rockies, Bozeman
x85.3.556

Meanwhile, through Koch, Lester Willson, and Charles Rich, Story spread word that the grand jury was trying to blackmail him. These actions were followed closely by an anonymous letter to the Virginia City *Madisonian* newspaper. "Witness," as the writer called himself, claimed that Bozeman was infested by "thieves and scoundrels," specifically Nelson Story and his strikers. "Do innocent men fear any blackmailing?" posed Witness, continuing:

> Why did Nelson Story say, publicly, he would not be indicted for $10,000? . . . Why is it that about this time a few around Bozeman, who had heretofore been loud-mouthed in their denunciation of Indian Frauds, were suddenly hushed? . . . Why is it that all at once Mr. Story has occasion to draw on the little bank here for "greens" to such an extent that it telegraphed to Helena for currency to enable it to honor his drafts?[45]

On Friday, October 22, the jurors appeared ready to issue indictments. But whenever they questioned Page on their duties and the limits of law, he acted preoccupied and offered only vague answers. Foreman Loren Olds then asked Judge Blake to appoint separate legal counsel to advise the jurors. Page objected, and stunned the court by claiming the jury was "packed" by Story's enemies. He demanded they be discharged. Judge Blake asked the U.S. marshal for Montana, William Wheeler, to query jurors if any lawman had questioned them ahead of time about the so-called Indian Ring. Wheeler did so, and although each juror answered with an emphatic "no," Page's request was granted.[46]

With the jury dismissed, Story continued his influence campaign through the *Avant Courier*, which maintained that most of the jurors were friends of Sam Word, chosen only because they promised to find Story guilty. The paper further accused the jurors of plotting to remove Page when they asked for additional legal counsel, forcing the prosecutor to end the "attempted outrage" of unscrupulous men "to levy blackmail upon the citizens of Bozeman."[47]

Judge Henry N. Blake, c. 1887. Judge Blake presided over the legal investigation into Story's and Clapp's business dealings and urged the jury to let no guilty man go unpunished. MHS Photograph Archives, Helena 941-161

The *Madisonian* had a different take. It accused Page of being a tool of the Indian Ring and accepting a bribe from Story. The paper also questioned his abilities as a lawyer and claimed that in previous cases he had appeared in court "drunk as a boiled owl."[48] The paper demanded Page "in behalf of justice, and the people you have outraged, that you step down and out of a position they believe you have so shamefully abused and disgraced."[49] Marshal Wheeler denied the jury had been "packed," noting that he and his deputies selected jurors in proportion to the population of Gallatin and Madison Counties and adding that those chosen were legally qualified, honorable, and respectable men.[50] As for the jurors, each signed a petition forwarded to U.S. Attorney General Edwards Pierrepont demanding Page's dismissal. The jurors called Page a "stumbling block" to justice, "the hired attorney of parties who have notoriously trampled the laws of Congress under foot."[51]

The war of words continued in the press. The *Avant Courier* answered with the assertion that "innocent men are frequently dragged before courts through the machination of enemies. While fearing no legitimate investigation of his affairs as contractor (which is provided for by the government), Mr. Story, like any other honest man who has a reputation he values, does not care about having it bandied in a jury box or court room even upon false and groundless charges."[52] However, Story's behavior throughout the affair offered little reason to believe in his innocence. His bribery scheme gives veracity to the statements of Horace Countryman, William Carr, George Town, and "Witness," as well as the suspicions of Fort Ellis army officers and other government officials. As the letter from Witness mentioned, why would Story fear blackmailing and dole out hush money if he was innocent?[53]

In the aftermath of the trial, controversy surrounding the Crow Agency erupted yet again when Bozeman residents learned that the government, per the recommendation of Dexter Clapp and with the approval of President Grant, had annexed a large strip of land north of and adjacent to the agency as Indian Territory. Clapp claimed that the land, stretching from the Great Bend to just east of the mouth of the Bighorn River, was necessary as a buffer for whiskey traders, as alcohol was making its way into the new agency. But observers were skeptical. Thomas Leforge doubted Clapp's rationale, claiming that most of the Crows did not drink.[54] Many, including Martin Maginnis, who expressed his thoughts in a letter to Secretary Delano on September 27, suspected the annexation was simply a ploy to reduce competition for Story's agency store and to better conceal the activities of the Indian Ring.[55] Fears mounted that it would also impede navigation of the Yellowstone, wagon road construction, and the approach of the Northern Pacific. Such suspicions soon made their way into print, as Witness, now calling himself "Truth-Teller," wrote to the *Madisonian* that "men can steal with impunity when behind formidable barriers."[56]

Story and Clapp convened a town meeting in Bozeman on November 9. Despite their assurances that the annexation would not hinder development of the Yellowstone Valley, the assembly passed a sternly worded resolution denouncing the annexation as the "last encroachment upon our rights and business interests." It went on to enumerate a variety of government "failures," including closure of the Bozeman Trail and relocation of the Crow Agency, promised to use "all lawful and feasible means" to work against the reservation's extension, and declared that "of this determination all private interests, cliques and combinations may take due notice, and govern themselves accordingly."[57] Before the meeting adjourned, a subcommittee was appointed to draw up a petition urging President Grant to reverse the annexation.

The *Courier*, at the urging of Story, characterized the resolution as too severe and based on incorrect assumptions. "We regard indignation meetings and resolutions as having little effect toward accomplishing the desired end," opined the paper.[58] This campaign led petitioners to strike the words "private interests, cliques and combinations" from the document at a subsequent meeting on November 13. The reworded resolution simply claimed that the Crows already had enough land and that the government should not countenance any action to thwart settlement or interrupt travel through the Yellowstone Valley. The petition was unanimously approved, and copies sent throughout the county.[59] In all, more than sixty had signed by the time it reached President Grant.[60]

To offer further public reassurance that the annexation would not hinder commerce, Story announced that the Yellowstone Transportation Company would buy a steamship to transport goods as far perhaps as Pompeys Pillar, where they could then continue on to Bozeman via wagon road. He pointed to the success of the *Josephine* and, believing that the government would soon build military posts in eastern Montana, Story envisioned warehouses, a permanent settlement, and an eventual stagecoach line, as well as company offices in St. Louis and Chicago. Achilles Lamme signed on as a partner in the venture, and with his son traveled east to find a steamship. Word arrived in December that he had hired a crew to build a "first class" light-draught steamship on the Ohio River at Jeffersonville, Indiana. Powered by two steam engines, the 153-by-30-foot side-wheeler's depth of four and a half feet would allow it to haul 167 tons and offer deluxe accommodations for twenty passengers. Lamme wanted to christen the vessel the *Bozeman*, but Story, not wanting to further immortalize the late Georgian, named it the *Yellowstone* after the first steamboat to reach the mouth of its namesake river in 1832.[61]

Story predicted that the boat would have nearly the same impact on Bozeman as would the arrival of the railroad and that it would double the territory's population within a year. In a promotional letter sent to the *New York Tribune*, Peter Koch claimed that the steamship and wagon road would reduce the journey to Montana by close to three hundred miles compared to the alternative route through Corinne, offering tourists an easier journey to Yellowstone National Park. "Affording increased facilities to tourists is, however, a secondary object," wrote Koch. "The principal objects to be attained are the opening of Eastern Montana to settlement and the lowering of freights."[62] But Story and Lamme either ignored or overlooked an important aspect of the *Josephine's* voyage: the boat carried a very light cargo load in a year of unusually high water. Under more typical conditions, any attempt to navigate beyond the mouth of the Bighorn River was ill-advised.[63]

While Story and Lamme made plans to open the territory to further development, probes into Montana's Indian agencies continued. After Horace Countryman bypassed Dexter Clapp and obtained a Crow Agency trading license from Judge Blake, Clapp asked Commissioner Smith to overturn the decision. Clapp denounced Countryman as a whiskey trader unfit to be in Indian country, "a man of bad character and of infamous reputation."[64] Smith came down in support of Clapp, asserting that only the agent in charge could issue a license. Meanwhile, William Alderson stood accused of switching brands on sugar barrels at the Assiniboine Agency, and had fallen out of favor with Commissioner Smith for giving the Assiniboines food, clothing, and other provisions meant for the Sioux. Without admitting any guilt, Alderson resigned on January 1, 1876, and returned to Bozeman several months later.[65]

Combined with the controversial annexation, these developments launched a new series of attacks on the Indian Ring. On February 3, the *Bozeman Times* inveighed against these "corrupt scoundrels . . . birds of prey, which have so long robbed the whole country; caused all the Indian massacres and robberies in Montana and the whole western country."[66] John Bogert sent a letter to the *New North-West* of Deer Lodge in February, accusing Clapp of ordering the Crows to attack and rob whites who got too close to the reservation. The agent, according to Bogert and the *Times*, cleverly avoided detection by conveying his orders through interpreters, and that "99 out of 100" area residents believed it to be true.[67]

Clapp denounced the accusations as malicious and atrocious, then turned around and issued Nelson Story two more vouchers: one for $968 for supplies ostensibly delivered three years earlier and another for $850 for oxen used in the construction of agency buildings in January and February, despite the fact that it would have been too cold at the time for such work. Elias Story received vouchers amounting to under $2,000 for some three hundred cords of wood.[68] It was another handsome and yet suspicious windfall for the Story brothers.

Chapter Eight

A Diligent Inquiry, 1875–1877

THOUGH CLAIMING a net worth of one hundred thousand dollars in 1875, Leander Black still felt the effects of the 1873 panic. Several Bozeman merchants had filed liens on his property to collect payments. Among them was Nelson Story, who had already successfully sued Black for a six-hundred-dollar promissory note.[1] Black resigned as president of the First National Bank, and in the ensuing vacuum, Story joined the bank's board of directors. Black also had another concern—his role as a surety on the Kiskadden contract.[2]

William Kiskadden's first flour shipment of 35,770 pounds on August 20 of the previous summer went to the Mission Agency. The second, on September 21, went to the new agency on Rosebud Creek.[3] By terms of the contract, Kiskadden was to receive ninety-one and one-quarter cents per hundred pounds in transportation costs for flour delivered to the new agency.[4] On October 12, 1875, Kiskadden wrote to Indian Commissioner Smith, complaining that the rate was inadequate, and requested it be raised to two dollars and nineteen cents per hundred pounds.[5] To bolster his case, he cited a letter from Captain Edward Ball to Leander Black describing the road to the new agency as rough, hilly, and "impracticable for freight wagons," especially those with a full load.[6] Kiskadden made three more shipments before the end of the year while his request to Smith went unanswered. In all, he delivered 186,886 pounds to the Absarokee Agency.[7]

Without any assurance that the transportation fee would be raised to reflect his actual costs, Kiskadden was hesitant to complete any further shipments. To aid in resolving the issue, Leander Black hired a team of men to improve the road between the old and new agency, and was reimbursed for $599 in costs by Clapp. Still worried that he may have to forfeit all or part of his surety bond, however, Black then persuaded Kiskadden to transfer the contract to Nelson Story.[8]

Despite their differences, Black knew that Story was the only man with the resources to fulfill the contract. The two discussed the matter for several days in December, and then held a formal meeting in Dexter Clapp's private room at Bozeman's Metropolitan Hotel on January 4, 1876. Black agreed to pay Story the contract rates: $1.70 for every one hundred pounds of beef and $4.16 for every one hundred pounds of flour. He also promised Story one-half of any increase in transportation costs to the new agency. Though time would prove him wrong, Story thought the deal represented something of a reconciliation with Black, and as a gesture of goodwill loaned him $2,500 to help settle some outstanding debts.[9]

In the following months, however, Story's contracting work came under increasing scrutiny due to the efforts of Captain Ball. In a February 18 report to the new commissioner of Indian Affairs, John Q. Smith, Ball claimed that upon arriving at the agency with a delivery of fifty-seven barrels of mess pork, Story observed that seventy-five thousand dollars in Crow appropriations remained unexpended, and he wanted as much of it as possible by the end of the fiscal year. He promised Ball one thousand dollars if he would pass the pork at 450 pounds per barrel and certify 300,000 pounds of flour under the Kiskadden contract, for which Story would be paid eighteen thousand dollars. According to Ball:

> He intimated to me that with my assistance the money could be expended so as to make it profitable to us, meaning, as I suppose, the agents, himself, and myself. I then asked Mr. Story what the poor Indian would have to subsist on, should such transactions as he proposed take place. He replied that there were plenty of buffalo and they could live on buffalo meat, as it was good enough for them.

The captain then told Story he had never taken, nor would he ever entertain, such a bribe. His only promise was to inspect the pork and, later, the flour. If they met the specifications of the contracts, they would pass. If not, they would be rejected. [10]

Ball found that only seven of the barrels were of the standard size that would contain 450 pounds of pork, while the remaining fifty were whiskey barrels only capable of holding an average of 231 pounds. Of these, Ball opened three and found most of the contents inedible, as they included nearly the entire hog, including the head, shoulders, backbone, and tail, tossed in with the mess pork. "The contractor," he noted, "did not care to have me examine any more barrels than those I had examined, he knowing full well that they were all alike, and that I knew it." Ball rejected all fifty-seven barrels. [11]

As of February 11, Story had delivered 1,217 ninety-eight-pound sacks of flour, each double-sacked. [12] Ball mistakenly put the count at 1,197, and claimed Story asked him to inflate the shipment to 2,000 by counting sacks in the agent's storehouse that had been delivered by Kiskadden in December. "This difference of eight hundred and three sacks I feel satisfied that Mr. Story, with the assistance of the agents, to make up by taking from the already inspected flour . . . and secondly, by re-sacking some of the already inspected flour." The flour in the storehouse was also double-sacked as allowed under the Kiskadden contract, but Ball wanted to present the fact as evidence of intended deception:

> You can readily see how it could be done. The inspector examines the flour by running a small probe into the sacks, and if the flour is good he places his brand on the sack. This does not penetrate the inside sack; but leaves it clean. The inspector goes away, and on his return the flour will have the outside sack stripped off and an unbranded sack presented for inspection. Fortunately for me Mr. McAdam [McAdow] who put up the flour, informed me of this unusual way of sacking it, which put me on my guard. [13]

Story completed the beef portion of the contract by delivering 598,889 pounds by the end of March. [14] Regarding this transaction, too, Ball levied accusations of fraud:

> Mr. William Carr, a reliable citizen of Bozeman, told me on the 14th instant that he knew positively that large numbers of beef-cattle belonging to the Crow Agency are now in Mr. Story's herd near the old Crow Agency,

seventy-five miles west of the present agency, and that more are in herds on Shields River, a distance of eighty-five and ninety miles from the agency, and that he, Carr, knows most of the Indian Department cattle, and that he can go at any time and pick them out. Mr. Carr says that he knows positively of Mr. Story having put his brand on Indian Department cattle. The matter of beef-cattle does not come under my jurisdiction as inspector, but these reports have been made to me so often that I deem it my duty as an officer of the government to lay them before the Department for its consideration, and would recommend an investigation of these reports.[15]

Major James Sanks Brisbin, the new commander of Fort Ellis, shared his uncomplimentary opinions of Story, Clapp, and the Indian Department in his endorsement of Ball's report, which he forwarded to the secretary of war:

The within report is a damning record of the utter rascality now practiced by the thieves of the Indian ring. The coolness with which these scoundrels offer to bribe an honorable and honest officer of the government is astounding. . . . If Nelson Story and Dexter Clapp were arrested and shot to death by musketry, it would be no more than such men deserve. This paper is sent forward by Captain Ball through the military channels, lost if forwarded direct to the Indian Department it might be pigeon-holed, and no notice taken of the irregularities reported within.[16]

Brisbin's remarks didn't sit well with commissioner of Indian Affairs John Smith. He demanded Brisbin and Ball be interviewed to determine on what grounds "they saw fit to reflect so sharply upon my official conduct." Acting Secretary of the Interior Charles Gorham seconded Smith's request, calling Brisbin's remarks a "gross imputation."[17] General Sheridan, however, derailed any inquest by noting that officers typically included personal comments in reports to the War Department, which were not intended to be forwarded to any other department. While acknowledging that Brisbin's remarks were uncalled for and worthy of condemnation, he did not see the need for any further investigation or the associated expense.[18]

As the contents of Ball's report became public, demands for an investigation into the irregularities at Crow Agency resurfaced. In late February, a new grand jury was empaneled, with most of its members hailing from Madison County. This time, the jury would be seated in Virginia City, with Henry Blake again serving as the presiding judge and Merritt Page once more the reluctant prosecutor.[19]

When court convened, the jury asked Page to subpoena witnesses, but Page balked, claiming that a circular from Attorney General Pierrepont advised him that none should be issued unless he was confident of a conviction. On March 24, Judge Blake rebuked Page, declaring his argument invalid and stating emphatically that the evidence suggested laws had been broken and therefore testimony should be aired before the jury. Page grudgingly issued the subpoenas.[20]

General James S. Brisbin, n.d. Like Judge Blake, Brisbin believed Nelson Story and Dexter Clapp to be guilty of defrauding the government, but when Story and Clapp came to trial, no conviction could be rendered despite ample evidence of bribery, fraud, and collusion.
MHS Photograph Archives, Helena 941-243

Blake's charge to the members of the jury suggests his awareness of the rivalry between Black and Story. Though advising them to "let no guilty man escape," he also asked that they examine the motives of those seeking the indictments: "The interests of men conflict often, and attempts to gratify malice are sometimes made in the room of the grand jury." Blake wanted a fair and balanced assessment of not only the events at the Crow Agency, but also the aftermath of the previous inquest. "I wish you to make diligent inquiry," he implored the jury, "and ascertain if any efforts were made to impede the investigations of the grand jury at the last term of the Court, held in Bozeman, by influencing or intimidating any witness by corruption, force or threats. Such acts obstruct the due administration of justice, and subject the offenders to fine and imprisonment, or both."[21]

Furthermore, Blake tasked the jury with determining whether the "inalienable right" of any citizen to explore for minerals, hunt, or even fish in the Yellowstone Valley was impeded, and if so, by whom:

> The list of those who have been murdered and wounded
> in claiming these rights is long, and increases annually.
> It has been always assumed that these crimes have been
> committed by the members of tribes of hostile Indians,

and no judicial inquiry has been made respecting them. Many intelligent persons have asserted that some of the guilty criminals belong to the tribes that are fed by, and supposed to be at peace with the United States, and that American citizens have been principals or accessories. If any citizens caused Indians to drive away the hunters and trappers, and cut and destroyed their furs, you should indict them for disturbing the peace and tranquility of the United States by their speeches or messages to the perpetrators of these crimes.

He concluded by criticizing the Indian Commission and its unsatisfactory attempts at an investigation, a "negligence" and "stumbling-block in the path of Justice."[22]

One by one, the subpoenaed witnesses from Bozeman, Judith Basin, and the Crow Agency took the stand. Though testimony before the grand jury was confidential, some of it leaked. William McAdow recalled that Story once ordered him to double-sack close to five hundred sacks of flour and stamp both bags so he could sell them separately. Despite the promise of extra compensation, McAdow refused. Captain Ball reiterated the charges levied in his report to the commissioner of Indian Affairs. He also alleged that Story was so angered by his rejection of the pork delivery that he promised to get it passed "with you in Washington," suggesting Story possessed the influence to have the captain transferred out of the territory.[23] Lastly, Ball claimed that before he left Bozeman for his court appearance in Virginia City, Hugh Hoppe, representing Nelson Story, made an offer to "make it all-right" if he promised to "keep still."[24] After such explosive testimony, Story later confronted Ball on a Virginia City street. The heated argument nearly became a gunfight before the two could be separated.[25]

Those closely following the hearing harbored no doubts that Story and Clapp would be indicted.[26] An anonymous Gallatin Valley farmer, who identified himself only as "Z," wrote to the *Rocky Mountain Husbandman* newspaper of Diamond City on March 31, contending that Story was not only cheating the Crows, but also area farmers. "If the Indians had what they are justly entitled to," the letter read, "it would make double the amount of produce to supply them, and the government would not be required to pay one cent more." Story, Z maintained, was a villain, able to buy "toadyism and fawning," and explained the respect and esteem he still enjoyed in Bozeman with an old English rhyme:

A little stealing is a dangerous part.
But stealing largely is a noble art.
Tis mean to rob a hen roost of a hen,
But stealing millions makes us gentlemen.[27]

On Tuesday, April 11, following twenty-two days of testimony, foreman Walter Cooper informed Judge Blake the jury would not issue any indictments, as the evidence was "weak and watery," and some of the allegations dated back more than two years and were therefore nullified by a statute of limitations. Eleven members voted for indictment and seven against, leaving those in favor one short of the required two-thirds majority.[28]

Blake scolded the jury, insisting that several parties should have been indicted. If any member found the testimony presented unconvincing, then that individual "would not believe any evidence if one [were to] rise from the dead."[29] The judge warned those jurors who had voted against indictments that the next grand jury may well investigate whether they had been bribed or threatened, an accusation most likely directed at Cooper, a known associate of Story's. It was no surprise that the *Courier* lauded the jury's decision, calling the situation "a tempest in a tea-pot" that ended a "fruitless investigation."[30] But the *Times* held that the Indian Ring remained guilty in the court of public opinion: "The whole country reeks with corruption, from the highest department to the lowest, and it has become an issue before the people whether corruption is still to rule the country or honesty reinstated."[31]

Walter Cooper, c. 1875. Cooper, a businessman who had past dealings with Story, served as foreman of the jury that, by one vote, failed to indict Story and Clapp. Ernsberger & Ray of Auburn, N.Y., photographers. MHS Photograph Archives, Helena PAc 99-69.3

Thanks to the Grant administration, corruption was indeed on the minds of many Americans. Though the president's secretary, Orville Babcock, had been acquitted of complicity in a tax evasion plot by whiskey distillers, Democrats continued to probe accusations of improper dealings surrounding the White House. Columbus Delano and Edward P. Smith had already left office under suspicion of wrongdoing, and charges of jobbery were leveled against Secretary of War William Belknap for his dealings with agency contractors on the frontier. The most indefensible scheme was engineered by Belknap's wife, who helped trader John S. Evans keep his franchise at Fort Sill, Indian Territory, in exchange for an annual kickback of fifteen hundred dollars. After Mrs. Belknap died, the money went straight to her husband, who by then had pocketed twenty thousand dollars.[32] Hearings began before the House Committee on Expenditures in the War Department, with Democratic congressman Hiester Clymer of Pennsylvania presiding. Belknap resigned on March 2, but Clymer continued to pursue further allegations regarding the Grant administration's handling of Indian post traderships.[33]

On March 29, Lieutenant Colonel George Armstrong Custer testified before Clymer's committee. Custer asserted that the corruption was far more common and wide-ranging than most could imagine. Belknap, he suspected, demanded kickbacks from traders all along the Missouri River, one of whom, Robert Seip, admitted to Custer an annual profit of fifteen thousand dollars from his post, for which he paid five thousand dollars annually to two influential army generals. Custer believed Orvil Grant, the president's brother, was also receiving payments from post traders whom he had recommended for appointment, and that Belknap further profited by helping traders run whiskey across the Canadian border and selling it illegally on the reservations. He also alleged that the government was billed twice for some corn shipments to upper Missouri agencies.

The sum of Custer's testimony was overwhelming. His most damaging revelation involved the Standing Rock Agency, where one winter, the Sioux were forced to eat their ponies because promised annuities, which Custer believed were stolen and sold elsewhere, never arrived. As a result, many on the reservation left to join the non-treaty bands in the Bighorn and Powder River country.[34] When asked why he had not filed any formal complaints, Custer cited a War Department order that required complaints to be first forwarded to the general of the army and the secretary of war, which stifled dissent among officers all along the frontier (with the notable exception of Major Brisbin).[35] Based largely on this testimony, the House indicted Belknap on five articles of impeachment.

While the hearings in Virginia City and Washington continued, President Grant revoked the decision to annex land north of the Yellowstone. Interior Secretary Zachariah Chandler informed Martin Maginnis of the decision in a letter that said Clapp's concern of the "pernicious traffic of liquors" near the reservation notwithstanding, the land would be returned to public domain and the territorial legislature should enact the necessary laws to keep whiskey traders away from the agency.[36]

The *Madisonian* and the *New North-West* refused to let the Crow Agency controversy die. Believing swindling, robbery, and bribery had been covered up by men "shielded with too many greenbacks to be reached," the papers called for a new grand jury and demanded that Merritt Page be replaced as prosecutor.[37] But the pleas fell on deaf ears. On May 1, 1876, Governor Potts endorsed Page's re-appointment as U.S. attorney for Montana Territory in a letter to President Grant. "Mr. Page," he wrote, "has been the most active and successful Attorney that has ever represented the government in Montana. He has been blamed by some persons for not instituting certain proceedings in Indian Cases, but as to such cases he has fully obeyed the wise instructions of the Honorable Attorney General."[38] On May 19, Grant approved the nomination.

CLEARED OF THE threat of indictment by the grand jury, Nelson Story wanted to collect the balance of the contract payments from Kiskadden, who was then in Washington, D.C., as was Leander Black. He announced that he and Ellen, who was again pregnant,

Ellen Story, c. 1875
Museum of the Rockies,
Bozeman x85.3.709

along with Jeanette, Rose, and Nelson Jr., would also make a trip east, traveling to Philadelphia for the U.S. Centennial Exhibition. In actuality, Story had business on his mind. The evening before their departure in early May, the Storys were treated to a community send-off featuring a serenade by the Bozeman Cornet Band. Also leaving town was Dexter Clapp, who had decided to resign from his post as Crow agent.[39]

Story's time in Washington got off to a promising start. Federal officials agreed to increase the stipulated transportation costs to two dollars per hundred pounds, retroactively effective to cover the whole of the Kiskadden contract.[40] And in a meeting with Black and Kiskadden at a Washington hotel, Story received two vouchers from the latter: one for $3,812.44 for 1,197 sacks of flour at $0.0325 per pound, and the other for $10,181.28 for 598,899 pounds of beef at $1.70 per hundred pounds. All seemed to be going well, so much so that Story felt generous enough to offer Black and cosigner Fellows Pease a loan through a promissory note for $1,300.[41]

Story's good fortune, however, was soon threatened by developments in the halls of Congress. In the aftermath of the Clymer hearings, the House of Representatives debated a bill transferring control of the Indian agencies back to the War Department, believing that such a measure would eliminate the need for agents, corrupt or otherwise, and require traders to certify their "character and fitness" before receiving any contracts. On June 6, Democratic representative Henry Blackstone Banning of Ohio, chairman of the House Committee on Military Affairs, placed Captain Ball's February 18 statement into the Congressional Record to bolster support for the measure. Others spoke out strongly in support of reform. "The history of American trade with the Indians is not a record we can be peculiarly proud of," said Martin Maginnis on the House floor. He continued:

> Under its cloak the corrupt rings have been formed,
> and the chief abuses of the Indian service have occurred
> behind its convenient cover. It has enabled the corrupt
> agent to keep every one off the reservation except his
> confidants and accomplices; and thus, under an almost
> impenetrable cover, and beyond the reach of detection,
> much of that unholy work has been done which has
> brought such odium on the Indian service.[42]

In such a climate, Story feared his vouchers could be rejected. To repair his reputation and preserve the validity of the payments, he answered Ball's charges in a letter to Indian Commissioner Smith. Story rejected the accusation that he had offered a $1,000 bribe to accept the pork as absurd and untrue. "Fifty-seven (57) barrels of pork," he maintained, "would not be worth under my contract more than $2,000. It is not reasonable to suppose that I would offer to pay one-half of the value of the pork to have it passed, because I had already furnished the full amount of my contract, and could not increase the quantity more than I had on hand." Story added that he had not inspected the pork packed in Bozeman and that he had promised to remove the noncompliant portions and repack the entire shipment when Ball opened the barrels and refused to accept their contents. He then pointed out the captain's "ill-will toward me . . . [which] he took frequent occasions to express." He continued, "I was warned by different parties, at different times that Ball intended to give me trouble." All told, Story concluded, "It would have been the height of folly for me to have made him a specific offer of money for nefarious purposes, even if I had been so disposed."[43]

Story went on to deny any mention of the seventy-five thousand dollars of Crow money to be had or any attempt at deception using the two thousand sacks of flour already in the warehouse:

> As for the heart-felt appeal of this man Ball for the poor Indian's subsistence, I would simply say that his statement in that respect is a myth of his own malicious concoction. As regards the charge that fraud was attempted by the means of double sacking flour, I would say that the contract for flour calls for double sacks; that all the flour made by me, I ordered the mills to double sack as provided by contract.

Continuing in his impassioned defense, Story insisted that only three hundred fifty sacks were double-sacked because he could not obtain enough sacks for the whole shipment, and that each had been branded before reaching the agency. He also rejected claims that Carr had made any allegations to Ball regarding cattle "because they know such statements to be untrue . . . nor have there been any Agency cattle with my herd to my knowledge."[44]

> As regards my character, I refer you to all the respectable people, (among whom Capt. Ball is not classed, where he is well known) of Montana, where I have resided for the last twelve years.

In conclusion, I respectively ask your attention to two facts which I have already mentioned, viz: the pork and bacon already put in and on hand for inspection exceeded the total amount of the contract, and the amount of flour at the Agency and en route, and in my warehouse at Bozeman, under contract for shipping, exceeded the amount to be delivered on the Kiskadden contract, which I was filling.

Under these circumstances; I can see no chance for fraud, nor what use Captain Ball could have been to me that should have induced me to offer a bribe.

I fully believe that Captain Ball—excited into anger because he could not plunder the Indians through the present channel—made the glaring report he made for the express purpose of furnishing fuel to be used in an effort to be made during the present session of Congress to transfer the Indian Bureau to the War Department, in which event he would probably have an opportunity to make the Indians live on Buffalo meat to the benefit of his own pocket.[45]

Story was able to keep the $3,812.44 flour voucher, but the government withheld the beef and pork vouchers pending further investigation. While awaiting the decision, the Storys made their trip to the Centennial Exhibition, where displayed items included the Remington Typographic Machine, Alexander Graham Bell's telephone, a portable bathtub, Heinz Ketchup, and even the right arm and torch of the Statue of Liberty. The festive atmosphere, however, was dampened by news of Custer's defeat in late June at the Battle of the Little Bighorn.

The 1876 campaign had not gone well for the U.S. Army. The Sioux bested General George Crook's Wyoming Column at the Battle of the Rosebud a week before annihilating Custer's Seventh Cavalry. Close to 270 officers, soldiers, and civilians died in the engagement, including lead scout Mitch Boyer. Among the first to view the carnage was Captain Ball, who arrived on the scene on June 27 with the Second Cavalry. In the ensuing hysteria, panicked Gallatin Valley residents claimed to see Indian scouts in the mountains south of town. Absurd rumors spread that Sitting Bull and his warriors would attack Bozeman.[46]

Once calm was restored, Captain Ball's supporters sent a statement to answer Story's letter to the Indian commissioner:

We, the undersigned citizens of Gallatin County, Montana Territory, believing that attempts have been and are being made here and in the city of Washington, to impeach the testimony and ruin the character of Capt. Ed Ball, Second U.S. Cavalry, now absent in the Sioux Country with his company, do hereby certify that said Captain Ball is well known to us, and we do believe him to be a gentleman of truth and honesty, and an officer who has ever discharged his duties without fear, favor, or affection.

Nearly one hundred individuals signed the petition, including Perry and William McAdow, as well as John Bogert. Those names failed to bother Story, but he was surprised and angered that Achilles Lamme had signed the document by proxy.[47]

WHILE THESE other events unfolded, construction on the *Yellowstone* was taking longer than expected; it finally arrived in St. Louis on May 3, captained by Lamme's nephew John Calhoun Bryan. After placing advertisements in the *Courier* and the *St. Louis Republican* seeking passengers and cargo, Lamme secured a contract to ship fifty tons of freight to Bozeman on the vessel's maiden voyage. The *Yellowstone* left St. Louis on May 11, but poor health forced Bryan to surrender the helm to John Massie at Washington, Missouri. In Omaha, Lamme agreed to take a large consignment of oats up the Missouri River to Fort Benton before plying the Yellowstone. Two weeks later, in Yankton, passengers and additional freight for both Fort Benton and Bozeman came on board. It was here that Lamme, growing increasingly worried about the threat of a Sioux attack, decided not to run the Yellowstone that summer and instead deliver all passengers and freight to Fort Benton, where those bound for Bozeman could complete the journey via wagon road. When the *Yellowstone* reached Fort Pierre, Lamme sold several hundred bags of flour destined for his Bozeman store to miners headed for the Black Hills. He received five dollars per bag, rightfully concluding the cash transaction was more profitable than paying freight costs from Fort Benton to the Gallatin Valley. On June 24, the *Yellowstone* docked at Fort Benton.[48]

Story exaggerated the *Yellowstone's* success, claiming it had done "bully—better than all the damn Indian contracts I ever knew."[49] But that assessment, and Story's involvement in the enterprise, would soon change. After the army confiscated the *Yellowstone* to ferry troops and supplies into eastern Montana, Story was forced to ship twenty-nine hundred pounds of material from the Midwest to Fort Benton on the steamship *Benton*, and then by wagon road to Bozeman. Shortly after Lamme returned to Bozeman in October, he learned that Story, miffed over his endorsement of Captain Ball, was withdrawing from the partnership. Lamme purchased Story's interest that, to date, had financed roughly one-third of the venture.[50]

Story now calculated his response to the petition supporting Captain Ball. He had hundreds of pamphlets published throughout Montana containing a letter titled, "Officers of the Army That Know Capt. Ed Ball." The officers, under anonymity, claimed that

Ball's real name was David Rey, and that he had abandoned his wife and children while stationed in Oregon. The letter questioned his caliber of service as a drill instructor during the Civil War before leveling charges of defrauding the government at Fort Ellis, and alleged that he became inspector of supplies at Crow Agency at the behest of Orvil Grant and Leander Black, who hoped to drive away Story and other contractors in pursuit of their own profits. He was, the letter-writers continued, a "willful, malicious liar and perjurer . . . a man of lowering dejected countenance, with a very malicious disposition . . . a professional gambler and bummer" who often laid drunk on the streets of Bozeman.[51]

Story and Achilles Lamme (above) attempted to establish a freighting route on the Yellowstone River in the mid-1870s. Gallatin Historical Society Museum, Bozeman 9698

Major Brisbin called the accusations "unjust and shameless . . . upon a brave soldier and worthy gentleman."[52] There is no proof that Ball ever abandoned his family or was prone to bouts of public intoxication. His military record indicates he did enlist as David Rey in 1844. In an 1858 campaign against the Spokane and Coeur d'Alenes, Ball got drunk while following orders to destroy all medicinal whiskey when his force abandoned camp. When he awoke, his command was gone, and Ball, after days of walking and hiding, was picked up by a rescue party.[53] Still, he was cited for distinguished service during the campaign.

IN LATE AUGUST, Peter Koch took over the Crow Agency trading post from Elias Story, and in early October, Major Lewis Carpenter replaced Dexter Clapp as agent. Meanwhile, in Washington, Commissioner Smith dispatched inspector Colonel Edward C. Kemble to the Crow Agency to examine provisions and look into Captain Ball's allegations, a development Governor Potts believed had been orchestrated by Leander Black. Assisted by Captain Benham from Fort Ellis and two federal investigators, Kemble spent ten days interviewing agency employees, many of whom were fired by Agent Carpenter for refusing to cooperate.[54]

Kemble concluded that Ball had been telling the truth and affirmed his accusations against Story and Clapp. He held that Story had, in fact, attempted to bribe Captain Ball upon delivering the inedible shipments of pork, wrongly included yearling cattle as part of his beef deliveries, double-sacked flour as a means of deceiving inspectors, and presented false vouchers, ultimately characterizing him as a "conniver of Indian frauds."[55] As for Clapp, Kemble accused him of deliberately accepting the inedible pork, determining the weight of Story's cattle by a "pernicious" method of calculation, neglecting to weigh flour deliveries, maintaining incomplete records, confining most of his purchases to Willson & Rich, and issuing questionable vouchers, including the $599 reimbursement to Leander Black for road improvements. Kemble believed Clapp and Story cheated the Crows out of their supplies, and had engineered the relocation to the Rosebud so they could operate "as remote as possible from public observation."[56] Kemble noted that both individuals, particularly Story, had earned "a most unenviable reputation among honorable and upright men."[57]

Kemble summarized his findings in a letter to Merritt Page on October 12, but the attorney still doubted that sufficient evidence existed to convict.[58] Instead, he referred the entire matter to the new U.S. attorney general, Alphonso Taft. His refusal to prosecute caused the *Bozeman Times* to declare angrily, "Under the administration of Page, justice is a farce!"[59] It also cost him his job. In a terse memo to Taft on October 25, President Grant wrote, "Remove Dist. Atty. Page of Montana."[60] Page protested his dismissal to the president on November 13:

> I have reason to believe that this is due to the efforts of Indian Inspector E. C. Kemble who recently visited this territory and on his departure threatened to have me removed from office because I refused to institute criminal prosecutions against D. E. Clapp late Agent of the Crows. My course in this matter would be, as my previous course with reference to the Crow Agency has been,

endorsed by Governor Potts and every other respectable lawyer in this territory. If Mr. Kemble has discovered any matter which is properly the subject of a criminal prosecution he has not made it known to me.[61]

Grant, now a lame-duck president, issued no response. Page's termination held.

On the same day Page expressed his protests to Grant, Nelson and Ellen Story's fifth child was born at the Pierce House in Washington, D.C. The boy was named Thomas Byron, after Tommy Thompson, but would come to be known by the nickname "Bine." Shortly afterward, Story received a letter from his new son's namesake, asking if he should move the cattle herd off Crow land. Story said no, directing Thompson to leave the animals where they were for the winter, and to move them in the spring only if Carpenter requested.[62] Evidently Story, despite Kemble's investigation and his continued inability to secure payments for his vouchers in Washington, believed he could foster as favorable a relationship with Carpenter as he had enjoyed with Clapp.

In a letter to Commissioner Smith dated December 30, 1876, Dexter Clapp refuted Kemble's charges. He claimed that he had accepted only mess pork and merchantable beef, and that he had no

Story Family, 1876. Left to right: Ellen, baby Bine, Bud, Nelson, Rose. Gallatin Historical Society Museum, Bozeman

choice but to average the weight of Story's herd because the scales he requested had not yet arrived. Clapp maintained that he kept "exact and minute" records, and that when he first came to Bozeman he tried to do business with the Bogerts as well as "different Jew merchants," but the Bogerts overcharged him and the "Jew merchants" operated the whiskey shops near the agency. For those reasons, he confined the agency's trade to Willson & Rich, whom he found reliable and fair, and believed that this decision explained the "vile and false" slanders Bogert had levied in the *New North-West*.[63] As for Black's road improvement voucher, Clapp insisted that the work had been necessary, and he scoffed at Kemble's accusations regarding any underlying motivations for relocating the agency, rightly noting it had not been his decision.[64]

On January 3, 1877, Story also replied to Commissioner Smith in writing, again calling Ball's claim "maliciously false."[65] He noted that the grand jury failed to issue indictments, and the entire proceeding "had its origin in the malice and jealousy of my rivals in business." As for the pork deliveries, Story reiterated that the barrels were packed contrary to his instructions, and that he was just as surprised as any by the inedible contents. He denied any personal knowledge of the yearling cattle, noting that the herd had been delivered by Martin & Myers. Still, the yearlings were "large and fat; there were no young calves, and the herd . . . was an unusually good one," and Clapp accepted them in the best interests of the agency. And for the double-sacking of flour, Story again noted that this was called for in the Kiskadden contract, and he ordered William McAdow to double sack only as a means to avoid loss and waste, never with the intention of being paid twice for one sack. Story further denied ever submitting false vouchers, and that the relocation of the agency was neither his nor Clapp's decision, but rather that of the Indian Office. Clapp, according to Story, "has at all times, and in the most positive manner, denied all complicity with me in wrongful act or intention, and of knowledge of any intended fraud."[66] Story blamed Judge Blake, Leander Black, and Sam Word for instigating the second court hearing, and enclosed a letter from Governor Potts citing the bitter enmity between Story and Black. Potts called Story a decent citizen and businessman, and Story furnished additional statements from other Montana businessmen attesting to his honesty, integrity, and fair dealing.

A hearing before Commissioner Smith and Interior Secretary Chandler over Kemble's report lasted through February of 1877, with much of the submitted evidence the same that had been proffered during the two hearings in Montana. Among those to testify in Washington were Leander Black, Dexter Clapp, and Nelson Story. In early March, only days before Rutherford B. Hayes was sworn in as president, Chandler ruled that the charges of Kemble and Ball could not be substantiated by the evidence. He decided that Story was entitled to payment for his pork deliveries, as well as the flour and beef under the Kiskadden contract, with the exception of 45,000 pounds of yearling cattle deemed not merchantable.[67]

The entire dispute had kept Story in the East for a year. But despite all of the controversy and legal wrangling of the previous months, Story wished to remain a Crow Agency contractor. Though the fiscal year 1878 contract for beef went to Martin & Myers, and the flour contract went to Perry McAdow, Story wrote to a few Bozeman friends about plans to open his own flour mill.[68] Skeptics believed that a Story-owned mill would make it easier for him to continue in his fraudulent ways by eliminating third-party witnesses like William McAdow.[69] Major Brisbin, incensed by Chandler's ruling, began gathering statements from Carr, Countryman, Town, and others in hopes of restoring credibility to Captain Ball. It would take Brisbin nearly two years to compile the affidavits and pen his own report, and by the time it was delivered to General Sheridan, the government had lost interest. The matter had consumed enough time and attention in Washington, and the case was considered closed.

Newspapers in Montana curtailed their coverage of the controversy. *Avant Courier* editor Joseph Wright died on December 29, 1876, and in January the two remaining editors, George Wright and Joseph Allen, sold the paper to William Alderson, who immediately hired John Bogert as associate editor.[70] As Bogert had been an outspoken critic of the Indian Ring while working for the *Bozeman Times* and *New North-West*, his appointment signaled Alderson's determination to broaden the *Courier's* appeal without dropping its pro-business, pro-Republican philosophy. Evidence suggests, however, that Bogert did not enjoy the freedom in his new post to continue his accusations against Story, Clapp, and the rest of the Ring. If he did, he certainly would have raised questions about the untimely death that spring of Merritt Page.

On May 13, 1877, days after the Storys returned to Bozeman, Page and Wilbur Fisk Sanders, on their way to the community of Pony, were fording the Madison when their buggy overturned. Sanders managed to scramble onto a bar downstream, but Page, having regained his footing in a shallow area, was swept off his feet by the swift water and drowned. Sanders's account of the incident was not questioned. There were no inquiries. After Page's body was recovered, Story helped with the funeral arrangements, and the lawyer was buried in Bozeman's Blackmore Cemetery.[71]

Upon Leander Black's return to Bozeman a few weeks later, Story demanded the flour and beef vouchers under the Kiskadden contract. Black refused, so Story took the matter to court, where he claimed to have delivered 1,578 sacks, 1,217 in January 1876, and an additional 361 in March, for a total shipment of 154,644 pounds. Per the terms of the contract, this gave Story a legitimate claim of $7,275, but his complaint inflated the amount to $9,608. After deducting the voucher he received in Washington, Story demanded $5,795.56.[72] Black, of course, saw the matter differently and argued that the vouchers Story sought were payment for flour delivered prior to the contract's reassignment to Story. Black further claimed that Story, as part of the deal by which Story assumed responsibility for the Kiskadden contract, had promised to transfer ownership of the agency storehouse and trading post over to him. Since Story denied having done so and had not followed through with the agreement, Black felt no obligation to turn over any more vouchers.[73]

The two were also at an impasse over the beef portion of the contract. Despite the government's refusal to pay for 45,000 pounds of what had been delivered, Story insisted Black relinquish the $10,181.28 voucher that had been suspended pending the investigation in Washington. Black maintained the same position as he did regarding the flour vouchers: payment for any amount delivered after January 4, 1876, was between Story and the government, and any vouchers in Black's possession were for beef delivered prior thereto.[74]

The litigation would last nearly two years, as depositions from Dexter Clapp, then living in Kansas, as well as Interior Department officials in Washington had to be recorded. The case required two separate trials, but in the end Story received most of what he demanded. The first jury gave him credit for the 1,217 sacks delivered in January, but for only a portion of the additional sacks Story claimed to have delivered in March. The award totaled $2,170.16. The second jury was more generous, awarding Story a little more than $14,000 for the beef. [75]

HISTORIAN Mark Brown could have had the Crow Agency, Nelson Story, Dexter Clapp, Leander Black, Edward Ball, Merritt Page, and other bit players in mind when he wrote that the fraud and corruption stemming from the lucrative business of supplying the agencies amounted to the most "malodorous chapter in the history of the frontier. Even honest men were harassed and subjected to libelous statements and in the end the Indian was the loser."[76] Indeed, Native peoples suffered greatly as a result, but the honest men of whom Brown makes mention are hard to come by.

Clearly, cronyism at the agency and in Washington allowed Nelson Story and Leander Black to profit illegitimately from the system, but a full reckoning of their misconduct boils down to the word of one against the other. Each had their detractors and defenders, and both could thwart accusations from an enemy either through the press or by statements of friends and colleagues. Merritt Page most likely lined his pockets by deflecting court proceedings, but the depth and nature of Captain Ball's alliance with Black will never be known. Fellows Pease may have benefited financially from his time as agent, but not to the extent that Dexter Clapp and James Wright apparently did. Accusations tying Clapp to attacks along the Yellowstone, however, are far-fetched and more likely John Bogert's retribution for being squeezed out of the spoils.

Agency fraud in the American West ruined some but enriched others. Nelson Story was counted among the latter, and since two grand juries and the Indian Commission investigation failed to establish any wrongdoing, he felt vindicated. The lingering resentment of officers at Fort Ellis, close observers like William Carr, or embittered citizens like "Z" did not bother him. The opinions he did value were those of fellow businessmen and merchants in the Gallatin Valley, and here he had no worries: the agency had poured millions of dollars into Bozeman. As long as the region remained peaceful and the federal money continued to enrich the local economy, they all looked the other way and would continue to hold men like Nelson Story in high esteem.[77]

Chapter Nine

An Empire Grand, 1877–1883

I N THE AFTERMATH of Custer's defeat at the Little Bighorn, the United States government intensified its efforts to subjugate the Sioux and Cheyenne. Battles at Slim Buttes, Wolf Mountain, Clear Creek, and Spring Creek forced tribal members to either surrender or flee to Canada. The army constructed a new outpost, Fort Custer, at the confluence of the Bighorn and Little Bighorn Rivers, and the establishment of Fort Keogh at the mouth of the Tongue River led to the creation of nearby Miles City, whose namesake, Colonel Nelson Miles, commanded the winter campaign that rounded up many of the non-treaty Indians.

One last major clash between the American military and Indians brewed to the west, where a band of non-treaty Nez Perces refused federal orders in June of 1877 to leave their home in Oregon's Wallowa Valley and settle on a reservation in Idaho. Following a violent encounter that resulted in the deaths of a few white settlers, roughly seven hundred and fifty Nez Perces led by Chief Joseph fled east, seeking refuge with their Crow allies.[1]

Army officials tasked Colonel John Gibbon, commanding officer at Fort Shaw, to intercept the Nez Perces. Company L from Fort Ellis, some one hundred and twenty-five soldiers, set out for Missoula, two hundred miles west of Bozeman, to assist.[2] While Gibbon gathered his forces, the Nez Perces rode around a crude log barricade built in the Bitterroot Valley by soldiers and volunteers from Missoula and headed south. On August 9, Gibbon's force of just under two hundred soldiers and volunteers attacked the Nez Perce camp on the Big Hole River. Initially routed, the Nez Perce regrouped and counterattacked. By battle's end the next day, twenty-nine soldiers and civilians under Gibbon had been killed and another forty wounded. Anywhere from seventy to ninety Nez Perce were dead, mostly women and children, and an untold number injured.[3] Chief Joseph's band continued eastward, killing at least a dozen white settlers on their way to Yellowstone National Park. Anxiety mounted in Bozeman, prompting one hundred men to join the Gallatin County Militia.[4]

General William Tecumseh Sherman, visiting Fort Ellis during a tour of western military posts, shrugged off any danger and proceeded on a planned tour of Yellowstone. Like Sherman, Story demonstrated little concern about the threat posed by the Nez Perces. His brothers Byron and Elias were in town, and the three decided to join Charles Rich for a tour of the park and the nearby Clarks Fork Mines. Leading the group was John Work, a former freighter and gold miner who supplemented his ranch income by guiding tourists. In late August, the Nez Perces reached Yellowstone, and as they moved to the northeast, they killed two more whites and terrorized several others, mostly tourists. General Sherman had apparently already left, and Story and his party abandoned their camp near the park's east entrance, fled across the Yellowstone River, and returned safely to Bozeman on August 27.[5] Chief Joseph and his followers continued along the Clarks Fork into southeastern Montana, only to learn that the Crows would not join them in their fight. A subsequent attempt to flee north and join Sitting Bull in Canada was unsuccessful, and Colonel Miles forced the surrender of the Nez Perces after catching up to them in the Bears Paw Mountains.

The end of the Indian Wars produced a surge of growth and interest in Montana's economy. Chief among the industries to benefit was ranching, particularly in the Yellowstone Valley. Confident that the Northern Pacific would soon resume construction, farmers and merchants anticipated easier access to eastern markets, promoters envisioned a wave of tourism, and land speculators counted on a swelling population and accelerated development. With Bozeman's isolation as a frontier outpost waning, community leaders set out to enhance their town's appearance and livability.

In December, Story was appointed city road master, and quickly initiated repairs to the Main Street Bridge over Bozeman Creek.[6] As construction concluded on the community's first brick schoolhouse, the West Side School, Story stabilized the structure by adding timbers around the building's base and iron rods under the first floor, all at his own expense.[7] The four-year effort to complete a race track and fairgrounds north of town concluded in May 1878, when Story secured sixty acres of land from William Tracy.[8] That same month, the Storys joined nearly a hundred people in the offices of the *Avant Courier* for a demonstration of William Alderson's Bell hand telephone. The crowd listened in amazement as hired musicians on an extension in the Alderson home three-quarters of a mile away played songs like "Coming By-and-By" and "Somebody's Darling."[9]

Never for want of a project, Story re-shingled the family home and added a front portico, making it a more attractive location for the parties and gatherings planned by Ellen. Jeanette, having left St. Vincent's Catholic Academy in Helena after a few years of study, now attended the Presbyterian-operated Gallatin Valley Female Seminary in the center of the valley near Hamilton.[10] This allowed her to cohost many of Ellen's well-attended social functions, known for their tables laden with food, ice cream, and coffee. Ellen's popularity and her husband's deep pockets secured her election as treasurer of the Ladies Society of the First Presbyterian Church in 1878, and Jeanette became treasurer of the Methodist Episcopal Sunday School.[11]

On September 16, Jeannette married Tom Lewis, an Ohio native, eighteen years her senior. As a wedding gift, Story assigned Lewis the $2,500 promissory note from Leander Black, allowing Lewis to buy a one-half interest in Lester Willson's store, as Charles Rich had recently quit

Frank and Jeanette Trent Benepe and children, c. 1895. After leaving her abusive first husband, Tom Lewis, Jeanette Trent married Frank Benepe, a business associate of Nelson Story. Schumacher, photographer. Museum of the Rockies, Bozeman x85.3.109

the partnership.[12] Only weeks later, however, Jeanette returned to the Story household and then left for Kansas, not to return until early April.[13] The reason for her departure was most likely domestic abuse. In a letter written to Story that December, George

Woodson denied rumors he mistreated his own wife, adding as a postscript, "I am not Tom Lewis."[14] Reconciliation proved impossible for Tom and Jeanette, and they divorced in 1879. Lewis, who eventually remarried, dissolved his partnership with Willson and together with Paul McCormick opened a store at the mouth of the Stillwater. Three years later, Jeanette married Frank Benepe, another Ohio native who came to Bozeman in 1877 and operated a grain and feed store on Main Street with partner John Davidson.[15]

Throughout the late 1870s, Story continued to diversify his portfolio. His 1877 trip to Yellowstone led him to purchase stock in and become a trustee of the Eastern Montana Mining and Smelting Company, which hoped to mine gold on the Clarks Fork.[16] Then, in August of 1878, he took on a more substantial interest in the banking industry when the First National Bank of Bozeman abruptly closed its doors. Over a period of several months, it had loaned sixty thousand dollars to its indebted associate institution, the People's Bank of Helena.[17] When the Helena bank collapsed, so too did Bozeman's First National. Helena banker Erastus Edgerton would later note that the banks, backed by notes rather than cash, "had many marks of rascality."[18]

Lester Willson was appointed receiver, and together with Story assumed operation of the First National Bank, which became known as the "Banking House of Story & Willson."[19] Liabilities to depositors totaled an estimated $67,000, but the bank held only $50,000 in assets. Willson and Story hired Peter Koch as cashier, and then filed a series of liens against Black's property to collect a $1,170.34 promissory note. Black had already sold his home, furniture, and carpeting to Koch for $2,000 in an attempt to retire his debts, and told a friend he would have to liquidate all his property.[20] The sheriff saved him the trouble by attaching all property owned by the *Bozeman Times* and much of his real estate.[21] At subsequent sheriff sales, Story picked up many of Black's downtown properties, while Metropolitan Hotel operator George Wakefield purchased the Northern Pacific Hotel for $2,300.[22] By the end of 1878, the bank had rebounded, its capital stock reaching $150,000.

Black, meanwhile, relocated to Jefferson County to start anew. He freighted supplies to gold miners along Basin and Cataract Creeks, and oversaw construction of the Boulder Road between Helena and Butte. His fortunes seemed to turn in the following years. The sale of his interest in a mine at Boulder City brought him $25,000, and he received a $6,800 settlement from the government for the detention of his wagon train in Colorado back in 1865. Then, on a trip to Helena in the summer of 1881, Black took a room at the International Hotel after complaining of stomach pain. He died on July 18 of peritonitis. Caring for Black in his final moments was John T. Grayson, Black's partner in the Anton M. Holter Silver Mine in Elkhorn Gulch. Grayson was arrested a few days after Black's death, accused of stealing papers guaranteeing Black's heirs a two-fifth interest in future mine earnings, but he was never convicted of any charges.[23]

Others during this time renewed their efforts to spur further growth in the region. Achilles Lamme still harbored dreams of establishing steamship service up and down the Yellowstone, but a series of disappointments would soon make clear that a "free channel of commerce" through the valley would remain dependent on the arrival of the railroad. On April 13, 1877, the *Yellowstone* left Yankton with supplies and lumber Lamme hoped to use to build a warehouse at Miles City. However, low water on the Yellowstone forced the boat to travel up the Missouri to Fort Benton, and the cargo was shipped overland to Bozeman, then relayed east.[24] John Alderson and Perry and William McAdow still had enough confidence in Lamme's vision to establish a sawmill and ferry on the eastern tip of the Clarks Fork Bottom, to which Grant Marsh had managed to pilot the *Josephine* in 1875. The settlement was named Coulson, and the McAdows and Alderson hoped it would become the supply point for Fort Custer and serve as a forwarding station where boat cargoes could be unloaded for shipment to Bozeman.[25]

The following summer, the *Yellowstone* managed to reach Junction City at the mouth of the Bighorn, where it unloaded its two hundred tons of freight and then continued upstream.[26] However, a broken rudder, malfunctioning boilers, and a damaged wheel stopped the craft within sight of Pompeys Pillar at a spot dubbed Camp Bertie.[27] From there, the thirty passengers and cargo, at two cents per pound, were transported to Bozeman by Nelson Story's freight train. Though disheartened, Lamme could at least claim that his vessel had carried freight further up the Yellowstone than any other boat.[28]

Misfortune struck yet again in June 1879, when the *Yellowstone* collided with rocks and sank in the Buffalo Rapids, twelve miles below Fort Keogh. Most of the 180 tons of merchandise aboard was lost. It was a huge financial blow to Lamme, and insurance covered only one-fourth of the ship's twelve-thousand-dollar value. A few steamboats continued to ply the Yellowstone to Fort Keogh or Junction

City over the following years, but, with resumed construction of the Northern Pacific in 1879, the days of steamship navigation on the river were numbered.[29]

❖

THE *Bozeman*, *Prairie Belle*, and *Yellowstone* were just a few of the boats that in recent years had wrecked on the snags, sandbars, and reefs of the Yellowstone. The river's rapid, chilly waters had taken a number of lives, and the summer of 1879 saw at least two more added to that list, one of which would haunt Nelson Story for the rest of his days.

In late July, Story and his men were herding cattle from the Crow Reservation to the north side of the river near the mouth of Sweet Grass Creek. Tommy Thompson and Stephen Gage were following six head when Story, concerned about the river's depth, mounted his horse and rode toward the pair to order them out of the stream. Before he could get their attention, however, Gage, believed to have been drunk, lost control of his horse. Thompson, nearly to the far bank, turned around to help, but when he reached for Gage's horse, both men were thrown from their mounts and disappeared under the water. Distraught, Story immediately offered a five-hundred-dollar reward for Thompson's body, and he and others, including a rancher's wife who nearly drowned when her horse tried to throw her into the water, searched in vain until sunset. Five days later, searchers found Thompson's body. It would take twelve days to find Gage's.

Reverend C. L. Richards and Bishop Tuttle conducted a funeral service for Thompson on July 24 at the Story home. Aimee Malin, Ben and Ed Fridley, and Billy Frazier served as pallbearers. A procession of carriages and mourners on foot accompanied the coffin to Blackmore Cemetery, where Thompson was laid to rest in the Story family plot.[30]

Nelson Story had lost men on the cattle drive from Texas and in skirmishes with Indians in the Yellowstone Valley, but none affected him like the death of Thompson. He was Story's most trusted and best-paid employee, earning seventy-five dol-

Tommy Thompson, Nelson Story's faithful employee since the 1866 cattle drive, was regarded as practically a member of the family. Story's second son, Thomas Byron, was named for him. Gallatin Historical Society Museum, Bozeman

lars a month plus free board. Thirty-three and single, he was like a member of the family. "We were great pals," Bine wrote later, recalling that "he used to shower me with many presents, the first among them being a hobby horse called Dexter. Although only two years and eight months old at the time of his drowning, I remember the instance very vividly."[31] Thompson's meager estate, which amounted to four horses valued at two hundred dollars and personal effects worth fifty dollars, stood as testament to his life as a devoted cowboy.[32]

Thompson's death left Story depressed and moody for months. He snapped during an evening meal in December when five-year-old Bud playfully threw a table fork at him. As Story jumped from his chair and reached for the child, Ellen tried to intervene. Story backhanded his wife across the face, leaving a bruise and a small scar above her eyebrow. After his arrest for the incident, Story avoided jail time with a guilty plea and a fine of fifteen dollars plus court costs.[33] It would not be the last time Ellen endured such treatment. While Jeanette had opted for divorce to escape abuse at the hands of her husband, Ellen chose not to, likely for the sake of her children and, for better or worse, the security of home and family.[34] She always felt a deep connection to her siblings, so as a minor atonement Story sent money to his brother-in-law Winfield Trent, allowing him and his wife to leave drought-ridden Kansas and resettle in Bozeman. Ellen again became pregnant in April, and when the child, a girl, arrived on January 28, 1881, she was named Alice in memory of the couple's late daughter.[35]

On March 20, 1880, Bozeman's first telegraph office opened. The inaugural transmission, penned by Nelson Story and other city leaders, was sent to Bismarck that same day. Eight hundred sixty-seven of the county's 3,643 residents now lived in Bozeman, and Story held the distinction of being the county's biggest taxpayer, his 1880 assessment valued at $2,437.[36] The town's school population had grown by 107 pupils over the previous year.[37] Story supervised and helped pay for further improvements to the West Side School, and the next twelve months saw the construction of dozens of new homes and buildings, including a thirty-thousand-dollar courthouse and jail, a malt house, a warehouse, numerous frame and Gothic homes, and a new Presbyterian church. By the end of the year, Bozeman had three hotels, two boardinghouses, one restaurant, seven stores, four wagon and blacksmith shops, two drugstores, a medical dispensary, and the First National Bank. Other buildings located on or near Main Street included livery stables, billiard halls, a brewery, and a meat market.[38] There were also brothels, the two largest of which stood on the northeast side of town, one catering to white clientele and the other to Chinese. Louisa Couselle was proprietor of the former, located at the intersection of Main and Rouse, which took the nickname "Couselle Corner." Since relocating to Bozeman from Helena in the early 1870s, she had amassed a small fortune and owned several town lots and two farms on the city's outskirts. Her wealth allowed her to extend mortgages to several citizens, including Kitty "Roberta Warn" Warren, a former employee who used the money to open an operation of her own.[39]

BY THE EARLY 1880s, the buffalo herds of the Great Plains had been dramatically reduced, from an estimated sixty million animals at the time of Lewis and Clark, to barely one thousand. Coupled with the confinement of Indian tribes to the reservations, this dramatic collapse rendered the grazing lands of central Montana ripe for exploitation, and cattlemen wasted little time moving in. Some 17,000 head were driven past Bozeman and into the Yellowstone Valley in 1880, representing only a fraction of those that would boost the territory's cattle population to 274,316 head by year's end.[40]

Along the Shields River, Martin & Myers and Joe Lindley still grazed cattle, as did Walter Graniss and, further to the south, J. J. Hopper. These and other operations made Benson's Landing, where James Bailey served as postmaster and Perry McAdow now operated the ferry, an important location along the Yellowstone. Further to the east, Alfred Myers, having procured a beef contract to supply the army at Fort Custer in 1877, ran a herd along Rotten Grass Creek. Helena investors Alfred Guthrie and John Ming owned a herd on Pumpkin Creek south of Fort Keogh, while English brothers Moreton and Richard Frewen founded the 76 Outfit on the upper Powder River east of the Bighorn Mountains.[41] Conrad Kohrs, John Bielenberg, the Moore brothers, and William Gordon ran cattle along the Smith and Musselshell Rivers. The Judith Basin proved especially attractive, and Thomas C. Power established the Judith Cattle Company there in the late 1870s, followed by A. J. Davis, Samuel Hauser, and Granville Stuart, founders of the DHS Ranch on the southeast side of the Judith Mountains in 1880.[42] James Fergus and Joseph Rosenbaum of Chicago established additional ranches. Other herds from Nebraska, Nevada, Oregon, and Texas flooded into Montana, bringing the total number to an estimated 613,882 head in 1885.[43]

Nelson Story, too, had a hand in the open-range ranching boom. Having purchased additional cattle from Al Lund and fifteen head of high-grade Durham bulls from Charles Anceney, whose cows and bulls had their pedigree listed in the *American Herd Book*, Story now possessed close to six thousand head of cattle and two thousand head of horses. He also had a new foreman for his operation, twenty-three-year-old T. P. McDonald, who had helped run his father's stock business in Missouri.[44] During the winter of 1880, McDonald and Story drove the cattle into a fifty-mile-wide area in east-central Montana bordered by Raspberry Butte on the west and Lake Basin on the east. Watered by creeks like Big Timber, Little Timber, and Sweet Grass, the area saw lighter snowfall and enjoyed a milder climate than the upper Yellowstone. Major Brisbin, who came to be known as "Grasshopper Jim" due to his keen interest in agriculture, noted the "grazing cannot be excelled in any country in the world. . . . In the springtime the stock is fat, and it is fair to say that no better beef can be found."[45]

It cost only $3.50 to produce a four-year-old steer in Montana that would sell for $20 to $28 at market. With an annual calf crop of one thousand to fifteen hundred head, Story's capital gains each year averaged 25 percent. And it was now easier than ever to get livestock to market. By the end of 1881, close to twenty thousand head of cattle would be driven from the Yellowstone to the advancing Northern Pacific railhead.[46] Alternatively, operators could lead their animals along the Yellowstone River to Fort Custer, then south via the Bozeman Trail to Pine Bluffs, the site of a Union Pacific station fifty miles east of Cheyenne. From either point, the cattle could be shipped to the Chicago Union Stock Yards.[47]

Story's mustangs, no longer able to paw for grass in the Horseshoe Hills outside Bozeman, had been moved to the Yellowstone Valley. With the assistance of Billy Lee, they were bred with Percheron stallions imported from the Midwest. The offspring, once broken, were healthier and sturdier.[48] "Every year Mr. Storey [sic] sells off a large number of young horses at from $50 to $75 per head," wrote Brisbin, "and will allow buyers to pick at $100, yet his herd increases and is now worth a large fortune."[49]

The growth of the livestock industry and the corresponding increase in strays and rustlers led to the 1879 establishment of the Montana Stockgrowers Association in Helena. On February 19, 1881, Story, Charles Anceney, Joe Lindley, William Martin, Alfred Myers, and others drafted a charter to form the Stockgrowers Association No. 1 of Gallatin County. Story was elected president as well as a member of the five-member Committee of Arbitration to resolve disputes between ranchers over strays.[50] The organization's constitution and bylaws included a provision for the hiring of detectives to investigate rustling or missing animals. Later in the year, all members published their brands in the *Avant Courier*, with a promise of a five-hundred-dollar reward for the apprehension of and sufficient evidence to convict anyone stealing cattle from an association member. Among those printed in the Bozeman paper was that of Story & Lee: the letters S D marked on the side of cattle, and N S on the shoulder of each horse.

As the cattle industry spilled out onto the plains of central Montana, the Utah Northern Railroad, now the Utah & Northern, was approaching Butte. The company never managed to secure subsidies from the territorial government, vindicating Nelson Story's prediction that Montana's natural resources would be enough of a draw.[51] Meanwhile, the Northern Pacific Railroad, now under the control of transportation financier Henry Villard, continued its westward extension. A contingent of railroad officials, including vice president General Thomas Oakes, came to Bozeman on August 4, 1881. During a banquet at the Northern Pacific Hotel, Oakes quashed any rumor that the railroad might bypass the growing town, an announcement met with "enthusiastic demonstrations of approval," and in one of several champagne toasts that evening Story promised the Northern Pacific land on the town's north side.[52] He, Walter Cooper, and William Alderson had already raised two hundred thousand dollars in cash and obtained a 55 percent interest in the McAdow brothers' property, allowing the railroad to start construction of a six-stall masonry roundhouse, wood-frame depot, and maintenance yard the following January.[53]

As the railway extended across the plains, more towns sprouted up along its route. One was a new community near Coulson, where the town's namesake, former Northern Pacific president Frederick Billings, together with several investors, formed the Minnesota and Montana Land and Improvement Company to develop the "Second Denver" of the West. Another was in Bozeman's backyard, a site near Benson's Landing named for Northern Pacific stockholder and executive Crawford Livingston.[54] Walter Cooper, Peter Koch, and George Wakefield, working as the Bozeman and National Park Railway Company, hoped the railroad would make Bozeman a pivotal junction by constructing a branch line from Bozeman to Yellowstone National Park via Gallatin Canyon. Their plans were upended, however, when six businessmen from the Twin Cities negotiated a contract to build a standard gauge railroad to the park from Livingston.[55] Story, Koch, and his fellow investors blamed park superintendent Colonel Philetus Norris for the disappointing development, and were pleased with his replacement in April 1882 by Patrick Henry Conger, former superintendent of the Sioux Reservation in Yankton, Dakota Territory.[56] Journalist Eugene Smalley of the *New York Tribune,* visiting in May, astutely contended that Bozeman should count itself fortunate simply for having the railroad pass through. "Population attracts population and capital attracts capital," said Smalley. "The road will develop it [Bozeman] as a central distributing and trading point, and a desirable residence for people who have made money on cattle ranches and farms, or in mining operations."[57]

Smalley's vision proved prescient, and Nelson Story shrewdly positioned himself to benefit handsomely from the development. Throughout the 1870s, Story acquired numerous tracts of land in and around Bozeman, including several adjacent to his north-side ranch. He also loaned John Tomlinson $4,838.26 for his flour mill in Salesville, and then bought Tomlinson out altogether in 1879 for $9,000.[58] Story sold the property to Tomlinson's head miller John Krise and his partner James Shed, but foreclosed in August of 1881, when the two defaulted on their $18,000 loan.[59] This made Story, in his words, an "unwilling miller."[60]

Despite the professed reluctance, Story had long been considering the acquisition of a flour mill to fulfill his Crow Agency contracts, and he also knew that the Northern Pacific would soon open numerous markets to Gallatin Valley agricultural products. Furthermore, recent changes in the industry made it a more lucrative venture. For years, "low" or "flat" milling, in which two revolving stones ground grain into flour, had been standard practice, but 1871 saw the invention of "high" milling and the gradual reduction process. By this method, a series of grindings, rather than just one, removed more impurities from the wheat and retained all of the gluten, the protein that gives bread its necessary rising strength. The resultant flour was whiter, purer, and had a longer storage life. This new processing technology facilitated Minnesota's emergence as the most important flour-milling center in the world, and would allow western states like Montana to offer a tastier, healthier product. Once again, Nelson Story had entered an industry at a historically opportune moment.[61]

In the spring of 1882, he confiscated the sills, timbers, burrstones, and other gristmill machinery from the Tomlinson operation and took the material to his ranch. After spending fifteen thousand

Threshing, Gallatin Valley, c. 1880s H. M. Rice, photographer. Museum of the Rockies, Bozeman 2017.4.67

dollars on new equipment from the Jonathan Mills Manufacturing Company of Cleveland, Story hired millwright Justin Riehl of Chicago to oversee construction of a new facility. He also began digging ditches and flumes to carry water to the site from Bridger and Lyman Creeks, eventually adding more from Bozeman Creek via Mill Creek.[62]

By the early 1880s, Nelson Story cast a large shadow over the town of Bozeman. He owned roughly one-fourth of its real estate, some

twelve hundred acres, and his rental income was $1,000 per month. His 1882 tax bill of $3,187.98 was, according to the *Courier*, "more taxes than the average Montanian [*sic*] is worth."[63] When a downtown fire destroyed some of his properties in August, Story sold the newly vacant lots for $3,000, producing a tidy $500 profit. The First National Bank, capitalized at $100,000, became the Gallatin Valley National Bank in 1882, and by purchasing Lester Willson's shares Story became majority stockholder and board president.[64] His net profits from the bank in 1882 totaled $26,000.[65] Nephews Charles and Walter Delisle Story, sons of Byron, came from Ohio to work in the bank, as did Indiana native and Wabash College graduate Charles Hartman, a soon-to-be attorney and future political ally of Story.[66]

Over time, Story, Willson, and other civic leaders identified a number of improvements they thought necessary for Bozeman to continue in its growth. In May, Story spoke at a series of public meetings to warn residents of the threat posed by smallpox if the manure piles, filthy hog sties, and outhouses polluting both Bozeman Creek and the town's groundwater were not addressed.[67] Unsanitary conditions such as these most likely contributed to the deaths of his two daughters, so Story took the matter seriously.[68] He joined the fifteen-member Board of Health to force businesses and residents to clean any nuisance or filth "injurious to health, or indecent, or offensive to the senses." The "Smelling Committee," as it came to be known, also encouraged county commissioners to erect a hospital and a "pest-house," and recruit nurses to the area.[69]

Within a month, observers noted the "praiseworthy and thorough" enhancement of the town's appearance.[70] Outhouses had been relocated, with many owners adding a "draw" and sanitizing with ashes or dirt. Other efforts to beautify the community proved effective. Families fenced their yards, made additions to their homes, and spruced up their properties with minor paint jobs and the planting of shade trees. Patrick Worsham remodeled the Northern Pacific Saloon, while John Smith began work on a two-story resort that would include an elaborate bar and billiards room. Frank Otto Maerdian, then staying in Bozeman before leaving for the Mussel-shell, called the town a "very nice place" in a letter to his sister: "There are two churches, court house, fine large brick school and the nicest lot of small dwelling houses all painted white with green lawns and level as a floor."[71]

An influx of outside money and interest contributed to the excitement in Bozeman. The approaching railroad contributed to the town's cultural development by attracting touring entertainers. The Boston Comic Opera performed scenes from *The Pirates of Penzance*, *H.M.S. Pinafore*, and *The Chimes of Normandy* in August. F. Jay Haynes began taking promotional photographs in the "Wonderland" of Yellowstone National Park. Tourism to the region increased, and more well-to-do Midwesterners and Easterners hired Bozeman out-fitters to take them to the park through Gallatin Canyon. Wisconsin native Thomas Quaw settled several miles northwest of town on a planned railroad sidetrack that he named Belgrade to honor Serbian investors in the Northern Pacific Railroad.[72] Confident of Bozeman's future, A. K. Yerkes published the first issue of the Democratic-leaning *Bozeman Weekly Chronicle*, with editor Samuel Langhorne promising fairness and balance, as "the news did live until it was owned by the *Courier*."[73]

William Davies captured the optimism of the period with his "Song of the North Pacific," published in the *Courier*:

> I come with a rush and a roar
> I'll run from shore to shore
> I will build in the land an empire grand,
> Such as was never seen before.[74]

Anticipation for the railroad's arrival mounted in the spring of 1883, but the season proved a trying time for Nelson and Ellen Story. Of minor consequence was nephew Walter's hopelessness as a bank bookkeeper; Bine noted that "he could never get the same answer twice."[75] As a result, "W. D." found himself reassigned to the Yellowstone to take charge of the horse herds at the Lee & Story Ranch. Charles's employment with the bank also proved short-lived, but for more unfortunate reasons. In February 1883, he abruptly left town, at which point Nelson received notice that funds were missing from the bank and responded with dispatches sent far and wide seeking his arrest. Charles was taken into custody in Miles City, where $9,540 was found in his pockets.[76] "Charlie" told the Miles City sheriff that he had used his uncle's signature to withdraw $10,000 from the First National Bank in Helena, intending to spend it on gambling, liquor, and a Bozeman prostitute. He showed little remorse, and penned a confession to his uncle that concluded, "I have staked all and lost; do what you please with me."[77] Nelson did nothing. When the authorities returned him to Bozeman, Charlie sat in jail until Byron arrived from Ohio, paid his son's debts, and took him back to Meigs County.[78]

Like many mothers in the nineteenth century, Ellen Story—pictured here in about 1885—lost several children from infectious diseases. Of her four daughters, only one survived beyond a few years of age.
Hamilton Studios, photographer. Museum of the Rockies, Bozeman x65.3.28

But the most tragic event that spring was the loss of another child. Young Alice died of membranous croup on March 3, marking the onset of another season of sorrow for the Storys. Given Nelson's recent efforts to improve the town's sanitation in hopes of reducing disease among its residents, Alice's passing must have been especially painful.[79]

On March 21, 1883, the first Northern Pacific train descended into Bozeman. Flags, banners, and evergreens decorated Main Street businesses to mark the occasion. Soldiers from Fort Ellis, the Bozeman Cornet Band, members of the 1874 Wagon Road Expedition, as well as citizens on horseback and in carriages paraded through town. An audience of three thousand gathered in front of the courthouse to hear the secretary of the newly formed Board of Trade, John Bogert, read congratulatory telegrams from territorial governor John Schuyler Crosby, General Sherman, Bishop Daniel Tuttle, Wilbur Fisk Sanders, and various Northern Pacific officials. The keynote speaker, former *Pick and Plow* publisher Horatio Maguire, predicted further growth and prosperity for Montana, the "Empire State of the West."[80] The ceremony ended with fired salutes, another procession down Main Street, and a banquet.

The city of Bozeman was incorporated on March 26. Nelson Story won election as one of eight aldermen, and John Bogert became the town's first mayor.[81] Story, Walter Cooper, and John Dickerson continued development of a new residential area on the town's west side that featured a four-and-a-half-acre park, the city's first. Spieth and Krug began replacing their wood-framed brewery with one made

Among the town's many improvements made in 1883 was Story's roller skating rink. It was later converted into classrooms for the Bozeman Presbyterian Academy as well as Montana State College. MHS Photograph Archives, Helena 940-544

of brick, reserving the second floor for use as a meeting and dance hall.[82] Construction of the new East Side School on North Church Avenue was nearing completion, and Story opened a skating rink on Main Street where patrons, according to the *Courier*, would make better headway if "they would fasten the rollers to their hip pockets and hire a cheap boy to haul them around. They evidence a decided preference for the floor with that portion of the anatomy brought into prominence by wearing a Seymour coat."[83] Even the city cemetery received a minor upgrade when Story arranged for a marble headstone on John Bozeman's grave, a gesture mocked by the *Dillon Tribune* with the reminder that "Injun Ring money, when devoted to buying up newspapers or Federal grand juries, or building monuments, is judiciously expended."[84]

But not all changes to Bozeman during this period were welcome. As the city grew, observers noted a rise in public drunkenness, brawling, and profanity. Vagrants entered homes to demand food from housewives when their husbands were absent. The level of discord was evidenced by one of the city's first ordinances, a ban on vulgar or indecent language, cock and dog fights, public intoxication, nudity, and crossdressing. The *Courier* had already warned "quarrelsome newcomers" that nearby cottonwood trees "would bear fruit to perfection if once put to the test," and in June, an anonymous group revived memories of the Committee Three Hundred by chalking or painting the cabalistic numbers "7-444," a hybrid of the "3-7-77" used by Helena vigilantes, on Bozeman sidewalks.[85] The exact meaning of the numbers remains a mystery, but as historian Mark Dillon noted, the most viable explanation stems from the San Francisco vigilante movement of the 1850s, in which members were each given a number, and those with a 3, 7, or 77 were authorized to impose death sentences. A *Courier* editorial cut to the quick of the matter: the "old and square town" of Bozeman was "tired of feeding a jail-full of loafers."[86]

In May, Northern Pacific president Henry Villard announced that a special train of statesmen, journalists, and "leading spirits of the most progressive European countries and of America" would pass through Bozeman that fall to witness the ceremonial driving of the last railroad spike near Helena, joining the two sets of tracks then making their way east from the Pacific and west from Bismarck.[87] The passenger list for the event included former president Ulysses S. Grant, Interior Secretary Henry Teller, politician Carl Schurz, and *New York Evening Post* editor E. L. Godkin.[88] The prospect of a visit from such esteemed company motivated Bozeman's leaders to expand their efforts to enhance the town's appearance. New and upgraded sidewalks were installed, leading Story to muse that, given the vast extent of his holdings, he would have to build at least a mile of walk. Meanwhile, the Bozeman Board of Health ordered residents to clean their yards or face a daily fine of five dollars.[89]

Something of a rehearsal for Grant's much-awaited appearance in Bozeman occurred in July, when General William Tecumseh Sherman, accompanied by U.S. Supreme Court Chief Justice "Mott" Waite and General Alfred Terry, commander of the ill-fated 1876 Sioux campaign, stopped at Fort Ellis during Sherman's final inspection of military posts throughout the northern West.[90] Sherman enjoyed the visit, particularly the serenade provided by the Bozeman Silver Cornet Band, but Terry was less complimentary. Writing to his sister, he observed that, despite the recent improvements, the town was "a queer place, very bustling & very ragged. Of its honest industries the principal one seems to be the selling of rum."[91]

On September 7, four "Gold Spike" trains carrying some three hundred dignitaries arrived in the Gallatin Valley. When Grant stepped down from his car, he requested a brief tour of the city. The honor of escorting the former chief executive went to Nelson Story, his carriage drawn by a "spanking team" of horses.[92] The irony could hardly be lost: a president whose administration was marred by the scandal of fraudulent contracting touring a town built largely by Crow Agency profits and chauffeured by the head profiteer. After showing Grant the Main Street business district and a quick swing along residential streets and avenues named Olive, Tracy, Church, First, and Second, Story's carriage returned to the depot. Here, Grant acknowledged the cheering crowd, especially Union veterans, by acquiescing to their call for a speech. He provoked laughter and applause by uttering one sentence: "Now, boys, you should remember that this is not a campaign year."[93] Before departing for the next day's ceremony near Helena, each guest received a gift of mementos from Bozeman, including vegetables, fruits, and bottled beer.[94]

The completion of the Northern Pacific that fall marked a turning point in the history of Montana and the Gallatin Valley. Nelson Story did not attend the ceremonial spike event. As the pivotal year of 1883 came to an end, he and Ellen welcomed another addition to their family, a boy named Walter, born on December 18.[95]

Chapter Ten

Sober and Industrious, 1884–1889

As the territory's cattle herds swelled, an influx of sheep and homesteaders arrived in Montana, and the open range began to shrink. The estimated number of sheep in the territory exploded between 1880 and 1885, from two hundred and fifty thousand to nearly eight hundred thousand, forcing many small operators to stable their cattle and spend more money for feed.[1] Cattlemen feared that only wealthy capitalists would be able to ranch in Montana unless more range became available, and Story briefly considered moving his herd to the Greybull River in northern Wyoming. He even purchased nine full-blooded pedigreed bulls in Helena for three hundred dollars each, as they were ideally suited to higher mountain ranges. But, he opted instead to stay in Montana. As was the case a decade earlier, the Crow Agency presented Story with numerous opportunities, and he would again use the reservation to his benefit.[2]

In 1880, the U.S. government attempted to acquire all reservation land west of the Clarks Fork for grazing, mining and a Northern Pacific right-of-way. But the Crows sold only a portion, some 1.6 million acres west and south of the Boulder River.[3] Long-lasting cold spells and heavy snowfall during the winter of 1881–1882 caused some cattle operations to report losses of 25 to 35 percent.[4] Seeking more favorable conditions for his animals, Story had his men take the cattle onto higher ground east of the Boulder River, on the Crow Reservation. Agent Henry Armstrong fined Story three hundred dollars for the transgression, but it was a small price to pay to prevent the herd from starving.[5] A few months later, Congress gave the Crows the right to allow grazing on the reservation, with rates set by the Interior secretary. Lessees could not erect any improvements such as fences and outbuildings, possess liquor, or carry firearms.[6] In 1884, the Briggs and Ellis Sheep and Cattle Company received a lease for twelve hundred cattle at thirty-three-and-a-third cents per head. A. J. Wilkerson of Billings paid fifty cents a head to run two hundred cattle, as did George Ash for seventy-five head.

The system was quickly abused. Briggs and Ellis, Wilkerson, and Ash purposely exceeded their allotted number of cattle, leading Story and a few others to forgo negotiating a lease and simply encroach on Crow land. By the end of 1885, there were an estimated ten thousand head grazing on the reservation. At least four thousand of them belonged to Nelson Story, whose entire herd had grown to twelve thousand. These cattle would cross the Boulder River during the summer or be lured south across the Yellowstone in the winter by hay strewn on top of the frozen river. James Dilworth, who in 1880 drove a herd from Oregon to Spanish Creek along the Gallatin River,

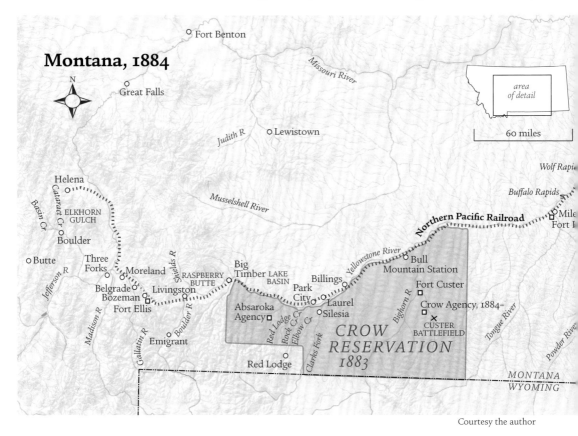

Courtesy the author

ran roughly the same number of cattle as Story. A Pennsylvanian, Dilworth had been a miller in Kansas and freighter in Colorado before establishing a ranch along the Clarks Fork of the Yellowstone, thirteen miles east of Red Lodge. This made him a neighbor of Story, who befriended Dilworth and financed much of his operation. With Dilworth's help, Story illegally built two cabins for his herders and a branding corral on the reservation. A third cabin and a corral, between Rock Creek and the Clarks Fork of the Yellowstone near present-day Silesia, became Story's winter headquarters.[7]

In addition to his membership in the Montana Stockgrowers Association, Story by now had joined the Eastern Montana Livestock Association and the Yellowstone Roundup Association.[8] All three groups sought to address many of the same concerns shared by cattlemen, and topping the list were rustlers, train-killed livestock, and of course, access to the Crow Reservation. A threat to the latter came in 1885, when John Blake of Colorado and J. C. Wilson of Kansas secured grazing rights to two million acres of the Crows' land for ten years at thirty thousand dollars per annum. Story, Dilworth, Paul McCormick, and other cattlemen cried foul, fearing they would lose the unfettered use that proved so advantageous, and Dilworth even threatened to kill Blake if he put his cattle on the reservation.[9] Civic leaders in Billings, including banker H. H. Mund, also opposed the lease, preferring instead to open the land to settlement. The outcry compelled Interior Secretary Teller to reject the deal, even after Blake and Wilson increased their offer to forty thousand dollars for the first year and fifty thousand for each subsequent year. Teller's decision held, as the government maintained that the Crows could not make such outright leases without congressional authorization.[10]

The Yellowstone Roundup Association established annual roundup districts, where various cattle owners pooled their herds twice a year. The spring roundup, usually held in late May and June, allowed cattlemen to brand the season's new calves. During the fall roundup, typically in September, hands culled those cattle destined for shipment. Late-arriving calves or any other cattle that had been missed in the spring were also branded. Each roundup could last as long as two months.

Roundups usually required about fifty cowboys per district, with the owners supplying chuck and supply wagons. Each man was given two or three pairs of blankets and a tarpaulin, and typically owned two or three clean handkerchiefs, an extra pair of socks, and a change of underclothes. Most, though not all, carried a "slicker," or oilskin coat, tied behind their saddle in case of rain. All worked in unison under an appointed foreman, sometimes referred to as "boss," "captain," or "ramrod."

Story and Dilworth pooled their hired hands from May through November, paying monthly wages of one hundred dollars for the wagon boss, sixty-five dollars for the cook, sixty dollars for night wranglers and bronc riders, forty-five dollars for top hand ropers, and forty dollars for all other hands. Cowboys were furnished with at least three horses each, ensuring every man always had a fresh mount. They began the roundup by flushing cattle from creek beds and coulees, and driving them to a series of corrals. The work demanded long days in the saddle, as cowboys had to cover the entire district. It was also hazardous, as cow ponies not completely broken would buck or roll over their riders, resulting in broken bones or, occasionally, a fatality.[11]

Nelson Jr. [Bud] and Thomas [Bine] Story, c. 1885. The elder Story sons began helping their father with his annual cattle roundup in 1886.
Museum of the Rockies, Bozeman x85.3.707

Bud and Bine Story began participating in the roundups in the 1880s, traveling by train with their father to Laurel and then walking a mile south from the station to the ranch of Lucius Nutting, where Story kept a team of geldings, a wagon, and supplies. By ferry they crossed the Yellowstone River onto the Crow Reservation, continuing another eight miles south along the Clarks Fork to Silesia, where the foreman and about a half-dozen cowboys awaited the start of the roundup.[12] Bine wrote a detailed description of the work years later:

> The cattle would be brought together . . . & held by some of the punchers while the expert ropers who practically never missed a throw, would ride into the bunch, holding a large loop & snare a calf by both hind legs, pull up his rope, at the same time starting his horse in the opposite direction the calf was taking, take his turns or "dallies" around the saddle horn & strike for the branding fire dragging the calf on its side. Its mother would imme-

diately take out after it, bawling and follow it right up to the fire where her brand would be noted, ear mark etc.—and the same be placed on the calf. . . . One man tended the branding fires & 3–4 men would be branding & tending their irons & in some cases where a man was a large owner, he had 3–4 duplicate sets of iron heating. You burn till the brand shows white.[13]

On their rare days off, the cowboys held horse races, footraces, and wrestling matches. There were occasional fights, but since most men were armed, or "heeled," few incidents escalated beyond rough horseplay. "The moral tone of a cow camp is rather high than otherwise," wrote North Dakota rancher Theodore Roosevelt. "Meanness, cowardice, and dishonesty are not tolerated. There is a high regard for truthfulness and keeping one's word, intense contempt for any kind of hypocrisy, and a hearty dislike for a man who shirks his work."[14]

Breakfast, usually consisting of biscuits, beans, grease-fried pork, and coffee or tea, was served at three o'clock in the morning. The average work day started an hour later, and lasted until eight in the evening. Lunch usually consisted of beef jerky, most often eaten while in the saddle. Dinner fare included trout, beef, calf fries, and bull calf testicles (known as Rocky Mountain oysters), as well as a gravy made from cornstarch and water, colorfully named for its resemblance to bull semen and used to thicken stews. A sauce made from flour, sugar, and water was known as "heifer's delight," while "son-of-a-bitch pudding," made from suet, raisins, and bread scraps, was a popular dessert.[15]

Nelson Story branded two thousand calves in 1884, and was one of the few cattlemen who employed Crows on his roundups. Others were leery of hiring Indians at all. Whiskey traders often bartered liquor for horses, and after the Crows traded their own mounts, some rode the ranges stealing additional animals.[16] This problem and others led stockmen like Granville Stuart to dismiss the reservation system as "sentimental bosh." He wanted each warrior disarmed, dismounted, and tilling a section of land while his children went to school to learn English and "civilized ideas." "Do this," he wrote, "and you have . . . delivered the citizens of this neighborhood from the painful but very necessary duty of killing every Indian they find off his reservation and engaged in killing and stealing stock."[17]

Stuart's demands aside, the military eventually adopted more forceful policing practices, and stricter reservation policies curbed horse stealing. But cattle thefts by both whites and Indians continued.

One roundup season in western Montana saw three thousand cattle stolen.[18] Stuart urged anyone who knew of any "thieves and dead beats" who "rob and swindle" to send their names to the Montana Stockgrowers office in Miles City. To prove he practiced what he preached, Stuart listed the names of two reported horse thieves in various Montana newspapers. One was Richard Toyne, the other John Cummings, described as a "quarrelsome and ugly" gambler and drinker. Impatient for justice, Stuart embraced Montana's vigilante tradition and formed "Stuart's Stranglers," recruiting fifteen men who, during the summer of 1884, either shot or hanged anywhere from eighteen to two dozen suspected rustlers, mostly horse thieves. The victims never faced any sort of a trial, and some may have been innocent. The "Stock Stranglers," as they were also known, received financial backing from the Montana Stockgrowers Association and a few prominent ranchers. Story was likely not one of them, as he and Dilworth opted to prosecute cattle thieves in court.[19]

In 1885, the territorial legislature authorized Governor Samuel Hauser to establish a board of livestock commissioners that would hire inspectors and detectives to curb stealing. Stuart, already the president of the Montana Stockgrowers Association, was named board president. That same year, the Eastern Montana Livestock Association and the Montana Stockgrowers Association merged. The combined organization dedicated itself to advancing stockmen's interests, protecting them from "frauds and swindles, and to prevent stealing, taking, and driving away cattle, horses, mules, and asses from the rightful owners thereof."[20] Five members from each organization formed a committee to work out the details, and Story served as an alternate for the western delegation. The association met twice a year, Miles City in the spring and Helena in August. But neither the stranglers nor the stockmen, much less the livestock commission, could put an end to the rustling.[21] It would be a while before law and order fully took hold in the rangelands; cowboys and cattlemen usually settled their own disputes, as evidenced by Stuart's admissions.

By the fall of 1885, one of Story's other enterprises, the four-story mill that opened in 1883, was now producing "a quality of flour unsurpassed."[22] New diversions of water from Bozeman and Bridger Creeks gave the mill a daily grinding capacity of three hundred sacks.[23] One flour shipment to Helena filled five railway cars, and the sheer volume of his operation prompted Story to construct a fireproof wheat storage warehouse. He had one of the largest elevators in the territory and close to forty employees, including his

twenty-one-year-old nephew Elias, who had recently relocated from
Meigs County. Story's Mill, the Union Mill (now owned by Gilbert
Stewart), and George Thomas's Empire Mill made Gallatin County
the "Minneapolis of Montana." Each operated continuously, using
a patented process whereby middlings recaptured on a sieve helped
produce a higher grade of flour.[24]

In December that year, Story took his family to Los Angeles
for a month-long vacation. Earlier in the year, he won reelection
as alderman and needed a break from the combined demands of
running his various business ventures and the goings-on at city hall.
Upon his return in January, he purchased a large number of jute
sacks for shipping flour to Europe, and ordered from Saskatchewan
several carloads of Wellman wheat, a vigorous strain that matured
early and rarely suffered from rust and blight.[25] The mill shipped five
thousand sacks of "White Rose" Montana Belle flour to Chicago at
a cost of sixty-two cents per hundred pounds. Story's net profit was
$2.25 per sack, and overall the mill earned him an annual gross profit
of $500,000.[26]

The Gallatin Valley National Bank reported assets of $354,870.01
in 1885, twice that of the rival Bozeman National Bank, and Story was
again among the biggest taxpayers in Gallatin County with $3,025.55
in county and territorial assessments. Refurbished with exterior
brick and stone and interior hardwood, the Gallatin Valley National
Bank drew praise as the finest commercial building in town.[27]

The year 1886 witnessed several other significant construction
projects in the growing town of three thousand. Story broke ground
on a new elevator at his mill-site, allowing farmers to drive their
wagons inside and unload wheat more quickly and conveniently.
A Northern Pacific Railroad side track from the depot to the mill,
the Story Mill Spur line, soon followed. The Sebree, Ferris & White
Company, which operated a freight line between Corinne and Butte,
began constructing warehouses just south of Main Street to sell
hardware and agricultural implements. Story's brother-in-law Frank
Benepe, having bought out John Davidson, resumed work on his
new brick hardware store. Lester Willson, John Mendenhall, and
attorney Charles Hartman built stylish homes on Central Avenue.
A new Catholic Church was erected on the west side, and an addition added to the Baptist Church. An assortment of other typical
improvements, among them new fences, shade trees, and fresh coats
of paint for many homes, added to Bozeman's enhanced visage.[28]

These improvements coincided with the army's August
abandonment of Fort Ellis in 1886. The end of the Indian Wars

diminished the garrison's importance, and the number of soldiers on duty had been shrinking since 1881. With the railroad having opened additional markets to Gallatin Valley products, local merchants were only selling surplus to the fort.[29] Surveyors parceled the site for potential sale to the "old settlers" who built the valley "fighting the Indians with one hand while cultivating the soil with the other," but instead the land became an agricultural experiment station.[30]

Keeping pace with these changes, Story set out to build the finest private residence in the entire territory. While Saint Paul, Minnesota, architect Cass Gilbert drew up the plans for what would become the Story Mansion, Story ordered foundation stone and 350,000 exterior bricks (a portion to be used on other projects).[31] Excavation on one of his west-side lots was completed in early May, and an adjacent brick barn was finished in September. In April of 1886, Story received Gilbert's plans, and after careful study concluded that the architect had overcharged him by several thousand dollars and that his recommendation of Indiana limestone for the exterior had inflated the mansion's cost by thirty to forty thousand dollars. He fired Gilbert and hired local architect Byron Vreeland and master mechanic William Babcock to redraw the plans. After Babcock suggested using red sandstone mined in Kasota, Minnesota, the three men boarded an eastbound train on May 3, 1886, to have a look at the material. Story liked the samples he saw, and agreed to use it for the bases, pedestals, and caps of the main entryway columns. He purchased the waterworks, heating apparatus, sash, doors, and hardware in Saint Paul, where he also hired the firm of Corleis, Chapman, and Drake to manufacture the parlor grates, mantles, wooden frames, stairs, and shutters.[32] As the *Courier* mused, Story "never does anything by halves."[33]

Two days after Story's return in late May, thirty-seven thousand pounds of iron pipe for the mansion's waterworks arrived from Saint Paul. The city council granted Story permission to connect the pipes and mains to a spring-fed pond a mile and a half to the south. Since the pond site sat at a higher elevation, gravity would propel the water to a storage tank atop the mansion. The Story family would enjoy the convenience of a waterworks before the city of Bozeman did. Working with Gilbert's original plans, Vreeland completed his drawings and hired renowned woodworker John Scahill of Boston to design the hardwood interior.[34] Though Story had the foundation torn out and reconstructed three times, the first-floor walls, including those made of brick and cut-stone trimmings, were completed by September. Winter's approach suspended work in November, but enough had been erected for a visitor to predict that the home would be "to Bozeman what Governor Hauser's Mansion is to Helena."[35]

While construction of his mansion was on hold that winter, a new set of concerns commanded Story's attention. In *The Beef Bonanza, or How to Get Rich on the Plains*, published just six years earlier, James Brisbin wrote that the laborious business of cattle ranching was lucrative, providing that the rancher "be sober and industrious, and when the storms come he must be brave, and keep his cattle together and herd them even at the risk of his life."[36] The winter of 1886–1887 provided just such a trial for Story and other cattlemen on the northern plains. The overwhelming snow and cold that season brought ruin to many, prodding some to quit the business, while others, such as Story, managed to persevere for just a few more years.

Prairie fires coupled with a lingering drought had made the already overcrowded range north of the Yellowstone extremely dry in the fall of 1886.[37] The conditions prompted Story to negotiate a lease directly with the Crows for grazing land on the reservation's west side for fifty cents per head. He and Dilworth also built a ranch near Bull Mountain Station, south of the Yellowstone and some thirty-five miles northeast of Silesia. But since the arrangement with the Crows had not been approved by the Interior secretary, Story received a one-thousand-dollar fine and Dilworth a five hundred-dollar fine from the new agent, Henry Williamson, who told one cattleman, "I do nothing without the approval of the department at Washington."[38]

The fall roundup on the lower Yellowstone involved nearly thirty thousand head from several ranches, including those of Story, Dilworth, Jeffries & Maynard, Daniel Flowerree, the Triple V and 79 Ranches, and the Cook Ranch. The ranchers secured the services of Charles Wickham as boss at a salary of $155 for six weeks. When the roundup ended, Story shipped some cattle to Chicago at an average price of $7.85 per head. He then hired Wickham to prepare his herd for winter, directing him to place fourteen thousand head inside the reservation on either Rock or Red Lodge Creek and, when that stretch was exhausted, to move the animals east of the Clarks Fork, closer to his corrals and hay at Silesia and Bull Mountain Station. Wickham, hesitant to trespass on the Crows' land, waited a month before moving only three thousand head across the Clarks Fork.[39]

After Agent Williamson ordered cattlemen to move their herds off the reservation, hired hands drove the cattle back to the north side of the Yellowstone. But Nelson Story continued to resist, even after U.S. Deputy Marshal Addison Quivey, a veteran of the Yellowstone Wagon Road and Prospecting Expedition, burned the Bull Mountain camps and corrals.[40] The *Billings Gazette* lamented the waste of "luxuriant herbage" on the reservation and the fate of "the hungry cattle that are sniffing at it from all sides."[41] Some ranchers feared a major cold snap would kill thousands of cattle and, following a public meeting in Billings in December, passed a resolution demanding the government reduce the size of the Crows' reservation "on such terms as may be deemed equitable."[42]

Granville Stuart noticed an odd phenomenon that year. Geese, ducks, and songbirds headed south earlier than usual, and those species that usually remained through the winter disappeared. For the first time in decades, snowy arctic owls were seen in the Judith Basin. A Gros Ventre Indian told Stuart these signs could only mean one thing: a very, very cold winter.[43] Indeed, a major snowstorm hit the northern plains in mid-November, leaving up to six inches of snow. Another four inches fell in early December. In January 1887, portions of the Yellowstone Valley received sixteen inches of snow in a single day, and the thermometer reached forty-six degrees below zero. Stagecoach travel was suspended for three days. Story visited the range that month, noting that "unless a Chinook puts in an appearance, many cattle will perish."[44] When he found most of his cattle still west of the Clarks Fork, Story caught up with Wickham in Park City and reminded the foreman that all the remaining cattle were to be moved. Wickham and two men drove a few more head off Rock Creek, but abandoned the effort when a spell of warm winds arrived in mid-January. Again, Wickham stalled, assuring Story that his herd would fare equally well on either side of the Clarks Fork. But later that month, another storm ravaged the area for seventy-two hours. Cattle froze stiff in their tracks.[45]

Exasperated, Story returned to Park City on January 25. With the assistance of Wickham, William Moody, "Sib" Toll, and Ralph Bailey, he set out to drive his cattle from Rock and Elbow Creeks east of the Clarks Fork. On February 9, Story received word that Dilworth had counted sixty-three dead cattle between the third and fourth crossings of the river. Story showed the note to Wickham, who disputed the claim. The next day the men drove two hundred head across the Clarks Fork. The work was hard and tedious, thanks largely to the deep and encrusted snow, and the group did not make camp until late at night. "Although I am nearly fifty," wrote Story, "I rode and walked as far as any man in the party."[46]

On February 11, the thermometer reached fifty-one degrees below zero. Chief Plenty Coups told an agency interpreter that his people heard "loud reports like cannon fire" produced by trees bursting from the frigid cold. Starved and half-crazed cattle wandered into towns searching for food.[47] That same day, Story and his group made another trek up the Clarks Fork, where in one area he counted fifty-six dead cattle and thirteen others so emaciated they had only a short time to live.

> This was the condition in which I found the country for the next ten miles. At least ninety percent of the cattle were dead, and here lay the larger portion of my cattle right in sight of as fine feed and bare ground as exists in Montana, two miles to the east of Clarks Fork; where I had early and often ordered the cattle put. My cattle had wintered here two winters, and the range was as bare of grass as the streets of Bozeman and would not sustain an animal in mid-summer, much less in winter.[48]

Story fired Wickham, and spent all of February and the first week of March along the Clarks Fork, making sporadic train trips to Bozeman where, Bine claimed, on one occasion, he "sat down and cried because he had worked so hard and seemed to be doing no good in saving the cattle."[49]

Not until a Chinook known as "Gentle Annie" arrived later in the spring could cattlemen assess the damage. Story estimated his losses at roughly 50 percent, the herd reduced from seventeen thousand head to some eight thousand, which he insisted would have been minimal had the animals been moved as directed. Wickham publicly disputed Story's claim, contending that the true figure only amounted to 10 percent, barely more than the annual average of 5 percent.[50] Although Wickham would reconsider his estimate a few days later, acknowledging that his former employer may have lost 25 percent of his cattle, the *Billings Gazette* deemed Story's assertions "absurd and untrue," characterizing his exaggerated account and those of other cattlemen as part of a ruse to make the government lower reservation grazing fees and protect the open range by discouraging settlers.[51] Story remained adamant, however, and estimated the value of the lost animals at nearly two hundred thousand dollars.[52] He had one of his dead Angus bulls skinned and tanned to serve as a reminder of the twenty thousand dollars' worth of bulls alone that perished over the winter.[53]

Regardless of any dispute over the specific figures, the winter of 1886–87 indisputably proved among the worst ever for cattlemen on the northern plains. Granville Stuart claimed losses of

Treaty Com.
1879

A.M.Quivey   Two Belly   A.R.Keller   Tom Stewart

Old Crow   Medicine Crow   Long Elk   Plenticus   Pretty Eag

Crow Treaty Commission, 1879. Young Chief Plenty Coups (front, second from right) appreciated
that Story employed Crow men to tend his cattle, but also resented that ranchers, including Story,
took advantage of the reservation's grazing lands without adequately compensating the tribe.
C. M. Bell, photographer. MHS Photograph Archives, Helena 981-231

66 percent, while those of the Niobrara Land and Cattle Company
on the Powder River exceeded 70 percent. Accounting for the lower
mortality rates sustained by ranches in west-central Montana and
the inflated reports used by some managers to hide prior losses from
their wealthy employers, Montana cattle operations likely suffered
average losses of around 60 percent, making the veracity of Story's
claim entirely possible.[54]

In the aftermath of that winter, the Crows sought to negotiate
leases directly with cattlemen in hopes of receiving better compensation for the use of their land. On April 23, 1887, some 350 tribal
members, with permission of the Interior secretary, endorsed leases

to "reliable parties" at fifty cents a head per annum for horses and cattle and twelve cents per annum for sheep and goats. Ranchers would have to pay an additional toll while moving animals from one reservation range to the next and take special care not to damage crops. Permits would be limited to the west side of the Clarks Fork, and any stock found east of the stream would result in fines and a possible forfeiture of grazing rights. Story quickly filed an application and received a lease from Williamson, who also allowed any rancher in need of forage to graze his cattle with Story's, provided they pay the fifty-cent fee per head.

Critics felt the policy favored larger and wealthier cattlemen, those with "political influence or long purses," who would fight any effort to reduce the size of the reservation and open it to settlement.[55] "It will be a cluster of petty principalities," read a letter to the *Billings Gazette*, "upon which the humble peasantry who live north of the river dare not set their feet."[56] Proponents noted that the leases required annual renewal, thus limiting permanent control by any individual stockman, and the demand for grazing rights would induce the government to shrink the reservation and open available lands for settlement.[57]

Starting in November 1887, Story made the required payments on his own herd, some six thousand head, but was only able to collect fees from James Dilworth for two thousand head, J. J. Walk for three hundred head, and Ed Cardwell for four hundred head. Story's lease would be renewed in large part due to Chief Plenty Coups, who was grateful that Story provided the Crows with beef and flour "for three winters" and employed the young men of the tribe.[58] But eight cattlemen who failed to pay the grazing fee to Story found themselves excluded.[59]

Questions regarding the county taxation of cattle further complicated the system. On February 23, 1887, a portion of Gallatin County east of the Bozeman Pass had become Park County, with Livingston designated as its seat.[60] Park became one of three counties that tried to collect back taxes on Story's cattle. In December, Yellowstone County officials at Merrill Station had seized twenty carloads of Story's Chicago-bound beef cattle, claiming he owed $2,184.55. Story deposited $2,500 to release the lien, and eventually won the court case when Yellowstone County's right of "judicial purposes" on reservation land west of the Bighorn River was ruled invalid. The outcome was the same in a similar effort by Custer County. Park County, after failing to win a judgment against Story for back taxes on his cattle, was fined $1,247.52 for making an "unjust assessment."[61]

Story did not always fare so well in the courts. Stray, unbranded cattle found during roundups were usually auctioned to defray costs. Story bought most of these cattle, but, according to small owners like William Anderson of Red Lodge, failed to pay in full for the animals. In 1888, Anderson began holding his own separate roundup, excluding Story from access to any strays.[62] Story accused Anderson and his foreman T. J. Williams of illegally branding his cattle mixed with the strays, vowing the two "will be made to taste the law."[63] They were arrested and brought to Bozeman, but the charges were dismissed following a hearing in late June.[64]

THROUGHOUT 1887 and into 1888, the city of Bozeman continued its slow process of refinement as it emerged from its rough-and-tumble past. In September 1887, Pastor Robert Stevenson opened the Presbyterian Academy on Main Street as an alternative to the public education system, which he described as patronized by "recognized infidels and saloon keepers."[65] Story and a few others donated slightly more than six thousand dollars to the cause. Story also remodeled his roller skating rink into the academy's classrooms, deeds that earned him a seat on the school's board of directors.[66] When a fire destroyed seventeen downtown buildings in December 1887, Ellen Story served coffee and refreshments to firefighters throughout the night until the blaze was contained at daybreak. The blaze left a two-hundred-foot gap on Main Street's north side, but the rebuilding effort was mostly wrapped up by June 1888. That same month the Story Mansion was completed.[67]

The *Courier* rightfully called the $120,000, Second Empire–style structure a palace "that far outshines anything heretofore attempted in the territory."[68] The residence featured three stories and a full basement.[69] The first-floor ceilings stood fourteen feet high, those of the second story thirteen feet, and a mansard roof capped the third floor at sixteen feet. Bricks for the twenty-inch-thick exterior walls were dipped in stale beer to seal their color. Beltings, projections, entablatures, shafts, and copings were made of either Kasota sandstone or polished red granite from Sioux Falls. A stone balcony covered the outer vestibule, and stone steps flanked by blue granite buttresses led to the entryway, adorned with arch panels also made of blue granite and carved figures *en relief*.[70]

The steam-heated, gas-lit home had four fireplaces as well as hot and cold running water. The basement housed a boiler room, laundry, drying room, fuel rooms, and vegetable and general storerooms. By the first-floor entrance, a vestibule and hallway constructed of quarter-sawed oak with an antique finish were flanked on each side by 378-square-foot parlors trimmed in cherrywood. A series of folding doors allowed the hall and parlors to combine into one huge room for receptions and dances. The library, drawing room, and master bedroom all featured either walnut or maple finishes, and the raw dimensions of the bathrooms, dining room, and kitchen, respectively measuring 54, 315, and 216 square feet, made a strong impression. Story spared little expense—the front door lock alone cost $50—but remained a stickler for detail, refusing to pay a $710 bill for doors, transoms, and sash window frames because they still contained sap.[71] William Alderson believed the mansion was the most expensive residence in the territory, making it, in his words, "pretentious."[72]

Though the plumbing work was incomplete, Ellen and Rose began with the decoration of the home's interior while Nelson and his sons tended to the herd along the Yellowstone. They hung fine art on the walls and placed imported statuary, red satin furniture, deep wool carpets, and damask draperies throughout. In subsequent years, Story would replace the gas lighting with electricity and add several outbuildings to the property, including a barn, garage, chicken coop, and storehouse.

The mansion quickly became Bozeman's centerpiece, known as the finest house on the Northern Pacific's route between Saint Paul and Seattle. Its magnificence awed many, but irritated others. The *Courier* deflected such criticism, promising that all of Story's friends would find the home welcoming and tasteful, as "Story is a matter-of-fact man and naturally despises any and all ostentations."[73] Such claims aside, the grand residence resembled no other in town, and visitors to Bozeman frequently mistook it for the courthouse, only to be shooed away by an irritated Story. Story traveled to Helena to compare his mansion with the elaborate homes of that city, and upon his return stated without hesitation, "By Gawd, I like mine best."[74]

The completion of the Story Mansion coincided with the laying of the cornerstone for the new city hall and opera house during Bozeman's 1888 Fourth of July celebration. Festivities began with a parade from Mayor Bogert's house to the construction site at Main and Rouse, where the guest of honor, Territorial Governor Preston Leslie, listened as keynote speaker William Alderson praised the people of Bozeman for building a courthouse, schools, churches, "handsome residences and substantial business blocks."[75] He noted

The Story Mansion boasted three floors and a water system that preceded that of the city.
Museum of the Rockies, Bozeman x80.6.493

Story Mansion parlor, c. 1900 Museum of the Rockies, Bozeman x80.6.495

that founders like John Bozeman, Leander Black, and Nelson Story had used "their enterprise, generosity and other good qualities of head and heart" to compensate for whatever "mistakes they may have made in their business, political, or social lives."[76] Alderson continued along these unexpected lines by promising that the opera house would be for everyone. Perhaps with the pretentious west-side mansion in mind, he encouraged his audience to "banish forever any and every feeling of jealousy, animosity, or hatred which may have been unguardedly engendered in our hearts and candidly and sincerely join hands and noble purposes in fidelity and friendship forever."[77]

The existence of any such feelings would have mattered little to Nelson Story. His interests came first. In August, the city announced plans to create its own water system by connecting a pipe to Lyman Creek, a tributary of Bridger Creek that served as a major source of waterpower for the mill, particularly when the East Gallatin froze in winter.[78] Story put up one thousand dollars and raised another five thousand dollars from a group of forty investors to locate an artesian well on his north-side property to supply the city's needs, thus reserving the flows of Lyman Creek for his own purposes.[79] In turn, the Bozeman Artesian Well, Natural Gas, Coal and Oil Prospecting

Company purchased a well-boring machine to find an aquifer and perhaps coal deposits, petroleum, gold, or silver. The city, skeptical of Story's gamble, awarded the waterworks contract to Walter Cooper and three associates. In February 1889, seven and a half miles of cast-iron pipe arrived at the Northern Pacific Depot.[80]

In the first two weeks of March, the drilling operation penetrated 210 feet, striking only sandstone and granite. In June, after reaching a depth of 415 feet with still no results, work was suspended, and on July 3, Story sued the Bozeman Water Works to prevent the diversion of water from Lyman Creek during the winter.[81] He also named several area farmers as codefendants, claiming that they possessed water rights only during the irrigating season and could not therefore use these rights during winter.[82]

Story family, c. 1888. Left to right: Rose, Nelson, Bud, Walter, Ellen, Bine.
Gallatin Historical Society Museum, Bozeman

Story's approach to the matter did not sit well with the community of Bozeman. One of the richest men in Montana, certainly in Gallatin County, Story lived in an elaborate home with its own waterworks and now sought to deny his fellow citizens the same convenience. Even Story's ally, the *Courier*, expressed chagrin at his behavior, suggesting he divert water from Bridger Creek via a mile-long, non-freezable system of flumes and pipes. It would take Story a year to find an alternative that both sides found agreeable. In the meantime, the court of public opinion left little impression on him, though the controversy was one reason he did not seek reelection as alderman in 1889.[83]

Chapter Eleven

Push and Energy, 1889–1892

ELSON AND ELLEN STORY enjoyed singing, frequently performing duets for their children. A favorite tune was "The Wisconsin Emigrant," a folk song in which a woman dissuades her husband from migrating to California by pointing out the dangers of Indians who "murder by night." It concludes with a peaceful resolution to the debate, as the husband acquiesces to his wife's wishes and professes his love for his children and especially for his spouse, whom he declares "more precious than all." The lyrics paint a rosy picture of marital disagreement and one that bore little resemblance to the Storys' own relationship.

Later in life, Ellen Story revealed to an in-law that she never could get used to Nelson's temper, evidenced by a small scar above her eyebrow.[1] Beyond such anecdotes, however, her innermost thoughts can only be surmised as she left no diary. Ellen enjoyed access to modern comforts like a horse-drawn phaeton, jewelry, clothing, furniture, and art, but according to friend Mary Long Alderson, the daughter-in-law of William Alderson, there was nothing about her "put on for appearance's sake." She was "a true western woman in always respecting merit and worth of character, regardless of the social status or the wealth or poverty of the individual."[2]

To be sure, Ellen Trent Story was tough, a survivor of mining camp mayhem and frontier town uncertainties as she bore and buried children while tending to an endless stream of housework and societal appointments. As she had at the cottage, Ellen cleaned the new mansion with a black-handled duster, churned butter from the Jersey cows she grazed on the lawn, and, when time allowed, quilted.[3] A member of the Bozeman State Housekeeper's Society, an organization with the motto "Our Kingdom is Our Home," she kept up with the latest childcare practices and studied history, literature, and national issues.[4]

In no small part due to their father's generosity, the Story children lived a charmed existence. Growing up, the boys could have just about any pet they wanted, including dogs, ponies, and goats,

Nelson and Ellen Story portrait, 1890. Family members frequently became the target of Nelson's temper, and Ellen was not spared his violent hand. Though she did not leave her husband, she did occasionally take refuge at the home of Rose and Garrett Hogan. Gallatin Historical Society Museum, Bozeman

and as teenagers they enjoyed free rein of their father's charge account at Benepe's store. Story never objected to any purchase, even when Bud spent $4.50 on silver-mounted spurs. "Well, Bud," he said, "I hope those silver mounted spurs keep your heart warm."[5]

The family rarely attended Sunday services, but enjoyed church-sponsored lectures and discussions, particularly those relating religion to state, national, and world affairs. Nelson once participated in the Methodist Episcopal Church's Children's Days by reading contemporary literature to youngsters.[6] Ironically, his favorite such work was Sarah Myers's *Margaret Ashton; or, Work and Win*, in which a little girl struggles to overcome a "perverse and willful" temper before becoming a "lovely Christian." While reading the family Bible, Story often jotted down comments in the mar-

Left to right: Bud, Walter, and Bine Story in 1886 or 1887 Hamilton Studios, photographer. Museum of the Rockies, Bozeman x72.16.13

gins. Next to a passage in the book of Revelation describing the city streets of the new heaven as "pure gold, as it were transparent glass," he wrote, "Fools, don't they know that if gold is that plentiful it will be cheaper than horse manure?"[7] Story also read the works of poet and philosopher Alexander Pope, memorizing many passages by transcribing them on envelopes or scrap paper.[8]

Story personally delivered food to needy families during Christmas, transporting the goods with a hand-drawn sled. On one occasion, he came upon a lost thirteen-year-old boy who was in tears. Story comforted the youth, put him in his carriage, and returned him to his family. When another boy came to the Story home to elude his abusive father, Story gave him a bath, food, saddle horse, blankets, and money, and sent him to live with friends on the Shields River. When the youth's father eventually abandoned the family, the boy, his mother, and his siblings were given free use of one of Story's rentals.[9]

A visit to Bozeman by Montana Stockgrowers Association treasurer Russell Harrison in the 1880s led to another act of Good Samaritanism on the part of Story. Harrison happened upon a fistfight in Pat Worsham's saloon, and when one of the combatants accidentally dropped his pistol, Harrison picked it up. Worsham and another man, thinking Harrison might shoot one or both of the fighters, attacked and severely beat him. Drawn by the commotion, Story broke up the fracas, took Harrison home, and tended to his cuts and bruises. The son of soon-to-be President Benjamin Harrison, Russell vowed never to visit Bozeman again.[10]

Story's protective instincts revealed themselves on another occasion while he inspected cattle in the Yellowstone Valley. A Crow girl on horseback approached Story's buggy, her eyes admiring his lap robe. Feeling generous, Story tossed it to her, but the girl's pony shied and bucked her into a cactus plant. While Story was pulling cactus-points out of her backside, one of his men rode by, doffed his hat, and began laughing at the scene. Story replied by patting his six-shooter, and the drover wisely rode away.[11]

Yet despite these instances of goodwill, there remained no doubt that Nelson Story could be intractable—"light on fancy but hell for stout," as one man remembered.[12] He enjoyed startling pedestrians by driving his horse team onto a sidewalk, a premeditated "dash of deviltry" fueled by the few times he over-imbibed.[13] On a cold winter evening, he locked Ellen and the children out of the mansion for their tardiness returning home from an outing, forcing Bine to enter a cellar window and climb through a heating duct to open the front door.[14] "Good Lord" was an expletive commonly heard in Story's presence, as was "God damn little shit asses," frequently directed toward his sons.[15]

In one instance, Story sent Bud and Bine to the north-side ranch to retrieve a mule, with specific orders not to rope it. On the way home, Bud could not resist lassoing the animal, but unfortunately lost his grip, allowing the mule to break away and trot onto the mansion lawn trailing the rope around his neck. "I thought I told you not to rope that mule," bellowed Nelson. As Bud tried to explain, his father cut him off: "Shut up. And the first damn one of you that says anything, I'll knock you off your horse." After a brief silence, Bine further provoked his father by proclaiming, "We can drive the mule as well as you can." At that, Nelson picked up a brick and hurled it at his son, who was fast enough out of the saddle to dodge the brick and then fast enough on his feet to outrun his father. Bine wisely remained downtown for several hours until Nelson cooled off.[16]

Story once fired Peter Koch after the faithful employee protested the bank's rejection of a loan application for his brother John's planing mill. Koch returned a few months later as assistant cashier, but, determined to break from Story, he began studying law and, after later passing the bar exam, became legal counsel and cashier at the Bozeman National Bank. Only rarely did Story yield to the demands of others. When he bought a pick handle in John Tilton's grocery, he promised to send his daughter Rose with the payment. Tilton, a strict cash-only businessman refused, forcing Story to pay up on the spot.[17]

Like other wealthy western families, the Storys sent their children east for higher education. In August 1888, Rose enrolled at the Episcopalian St. Mary's Hall School in Faribault, Minnesota. Ever since the death of Alice five years earlier, Nelson and especially Ellen doted on and spoiled their only surviving daughter. When they learned that Rose was depressed during her first time away from home, Nelson and Ellen took her out of St. Mary's in November for a sightseeing tour of New York City. The excursion achieved its intended effect, as Rose recovered and reenrolled. At the end of the school year, on June 25, 1889, the Benepe family hosted a welcome home reception for her back in Bozeman. Among the guests was their family physician, Dr. Garrett Lansing Hogan, a graduate of the Albany Medical College in his native New York. The two began a courtship.[18]

Rose Story Hogan. As a young woman, Rose had few suitors and those who did court her— including her future husband, Garrett Hogan—were eyed with suspicion. Gallatin Historical Society Museum, Bozeman

To this point, the plain-looking Rose had enjoyed the attention of few suitors. In 1886, forty-five-year-old farmer Owen McCann sent her love letters and, despite a warning from Nelson, boldly appeared at the Story home to propose. Ellen ordered him away, and Story, hearing the exchange, confronted McCann with a pistol in hand. Ellen then grabbed a shotgun and pulled the trigger, missing her target, at which point Nelson chased McCann from the yard and tried to get off a shot of his own, but the pistol jammed. McCann escaped, and all three were taken into custody. No charges were made against the Storys, but McCann was eventually declared insane and briefly committed to the territorial asylum. The episode led gossipers to conclude that any man interested in Rose was either demented or after her money. Dr. Hogan, Rose's senior by twelve years, fell into the latter category.[19]

An elaborate gathering at the family mansion on August 1, 1889, marked Rose's social debut. Some two hundred guests enjoyed dancing in the third floor and a "sumptuous repast," while marveling at the home's elaborate rooms and elegant art. Next came an excursion to Yellowstone National Park with her girlfriends and a ball at Helena's Broadwater Hotel, where she was escorted by Hogan. Rose then returned to Minnesota accompanied by Bud, who was entering his first year at the Shattuck Military Academy.[20]

Rose's husband, Dr. Garrett Hogan failed to win the admiration of his father-in-law. Rather, Nelson Story regarded Hogan as an interloper interested in Story's money. Gallatin Historical Society Museum, Bozeman

When Rose returned for Christmas, she and Hogan announced their engagement. It would be a short one, and the wedding was held at the family mansion on January 22, 1890, with nearly one hundred guests in attendance. The Storys spared no expense. Helena florist Levi Wells designed the entryway bridal arch of smilax, evergreens, carnations, roses, and lilies. Ferns and smilax adorned curtains, draperies, chandeliers, and pictures throughout the house. As an orchestra played Mendelssohn's "Wedding March," Episcopal minister Frank Lewis led the bridal party procession, followed by young Walter Story carrying a kneeling pillow of blue satin. Rose walked down the aisle in a dress of "white ottoman silk, entraine, with an overdress of embroidered tulle."[21]

Among the many wedding gifts received by the couple were gold-plated silverware, including a tea set given by Nelson and Ellen, tablespoons from Bine, and a butter knife and sugar spoon from Walter. Bud gave the Hogans a set of pearl-handled knives, while other guests proffered Dresden china, a silver cake basket, oil paintings, etchings, vases, bisque figures, and a crocheted toilet set.[22] Story paid for the couple's three-thousand-dollar honeymoon trip to Chicago and New York, and eventually purchased Samuel Langhorne's drugstore, the Bozeman Pharmacy, for his son-in-law. Another of his gifts was a new residence on South Black Avenue, but Rose, claiming the house was too cold, often stayed at the mansion during the winter months.[23]

MONTANA had a coming-out party of its own in 1889 with the long-awaited transition to statehood. After the failed attempt in 1866, another, more viable effort was launched in 1884. Voters approved a constitution, only to have it rejected by Congress, as the

Republican-controlled Senate worried about the influence of Montana's Democratic majority. But the landscape had changed in the intervening years. Due to the railroads and the mining and cattle industries, Montana's population ballooned from 39,000 in 1880 to nearly 143,000 in less than a decade.[24] Congressional approval of an enabling act in early 1889 opened the door not only for Montana's full admission to the Union, but for the Dakotas' and Washington's as well.

A constitutional convention convened in Helena on July 4, 1889, and voters approved the resultant plan of government on October 1. On November 8, President Harrison signed a bill making Montana the forty-first state.[25] One of the new constitution's provisions called for the electorate to select the new state capital. The Lewis and Clark County Courthouse in Helena had housed the territorial government for the past few years, and delegates thought it fitting to leave the choice to the people before investing funds in a more ornate statehouse.[26] By then, Helena was the state's most populous city, and its residents were confident that their community would remain the capital, but the contest would prove highly competitive.

Montana's astounding growth over the prior decade allowed several communities to make a strong case for the distinction, however, and most of them enjoyed the backing of capitalist powerbrokers whose successes paralleled those of Nelson Story in Bozeman. Sheep rancher Paris Gibson, with the backing of transportation mogul James J. Hill, had platted a new city at the Great Falls of the Missouri in 1883. Hill's St. Paul, Minneapolis & Manitoba Railroad reached Great Falls from Minot in Dakota Territory in 1887, followed a few months later by the Montana Central's connection with Helena. Great Falls would become a major trade center in northern Montana.[27] To the south, miner-turned-investor William Andrews Clark became extremely wealthy by purchasing and developing several silver and copper mines in Butte. Clark's chief rival, Marcus Daly, helmed the Anaconda Copper mining empire, and their efforts, coupled with the Utah Northern Railroad, fueled Butte's rise as the largest copper-producing city in the world and the second most populous city in Montana. Daly expanded his operations to the west, establishing a smelter in what came to be the town of Anaconda, where he invested heavily in several ventures, including the elegant Montana Hotel.[28] All of these cities entered the capital contest, as did the smaller communities of Deer Lodge, Boulder, and Bozeman.

The *Bozeman Chronicle* launched publicity campaigns, extolling the town's recent growth and promising future. The arrival of the railroad, the installation of electricity, telephones, and sidewalks, and new graded streets with names like Curtis and Beall and north-south avenues named Third, Fourth, Black, Central, Templar, and Grand were held up as evidence of Bozeman's sophistication.[29] "Besides this, Bozeman is healthy," opined the *Chronicle*. "It has public and private schools to be proud of. It has more churches than any town of its size in the West. It has handsome houses, surrounded by green yards and shade trees, nourished by water from the mountains."[30]

Steps were taken to further enhance Bozeman's appeal. The coded vigilante warnings reemerged, and "3-7-77-3" was chalked or painted on downtown sidewalks to encourage tramps and "hard cases" to move on. Story, a man of "push and energy," had already convinced Governor Benjamin White to designate the Fort Ellis grounds for the weeklong encampment of the territorial militia in October, and was seriously considering construction of a downtown hotel.[31] The foundation for Bozeman's new city hall and opera house was laid that summer, triggering additional construction projects that would amount to more than $770,000 in costs by the end of 1890.[32]

IN FEBRUARY 1890, White Caldwell and other Gallatin Valley farmers formed an alliance to correct "those evils and abuses which oppress them unnaturally," a reference to the practices of mill operators who hedged on grain payments.[33] Without naming Story, Caldwell decried the operators as having "other occupations than looking after our interests" and called for farmers to unite as a means of improving their financial and social lot.[34] Local producers also expressed dismay at the long waits to unload grain at Story's mill, which forced some to line up their wagons at nightfall in order to speed the process the following morning.[35] Story was encouraged to follow the example of Frank Benepe's new grain elevator near the Northern Pacific Depot, where farmers saved time by driving onto a wagon dump, raising the end gate, and "let 'er go Gallagher," as was the phrase at the time.[36]

But Story paid little attention to the alliance's demands. Four years earlier, he and several investors proposed county bonds to finance a short line to Butte that would lower shipping costs and boost prices for wheat and oats (something of a departure from his stance on the Utah Northern). After then-governor Benjamin Carpenter vetoed the measure, the Northern Pacific stepped in to build the connection. Story felt that local farmers only needed patience, as the project was nearly complete.[37] Besides, he was preoccupied. As he had feared, an interruption in flows from Bozeman Creek caused by frozen diversion ditches forced a temporary closure of his mill. In February, he and Elias imported a 125-horsepower engine and two 70-horsepower boilers from Wisconsin to pick up the slack. He also decided not to build the new hotel he had been considering, instead opting to erect a series of brick buildings on Main Street. William Tracy oversaw the excavation, and ground was broken in late April.[38]

Development in Bozeman continued at a fevered pace. Soon enough, Boston investors answered the community's need for an upscale hotel when they announced plans to build a structure on Main Street. Peter Koch raised one-fifth of the one-hundred-thousand-dollar cost for "The Bozeman" from local investors, despite the thought that its location at Couselle Corner was too close to Chinatown and the red-light district.[39] The developers may have in fact seen such proximity as an asset, as western hotel proprietors were known to arrange trysts for their male clientele.[40] The city council granted Edward Franklin Ferris of Sebree, Ferris & White and his brother Edwin a contract to design and construct an electric street railway, or cable car track, to connect the Northern Pacific's recently built brick depot with the city's newer residential sections. Story sold a large tract of land to Minneapolis banker Louis Menage and his partner H. B. Beard, which became Bozeman's "Capitol Hill" addition.[41] The *Courier* claimed the capital belonged in Bozeman, "a good, lively business town . . . a city of intelligent and happy families . . . benevolent societies, literary organizations, and social society clubs."[42]

ROSE AND GARRETT returned to Bozeman in April and were welcomed home with a reception sponsored by Nelson, at which attendees were served refreshments by "a corp [*sic*] of colored assistants." Then Story traveled to Kansas City seeking treatment from a specialist for persistent hemorrhoids and a rectal ailment.[43] When he returned, Story began plans for a ten-thousand-dollar grain warehouse near the train depot in Butte.[44] This came just before the "Butte and Bozeman's Day" celebration of May 26, when three hundred prominent Butte citizens journeyed to Bozeman to mark completion of the shortline. Ellen missed the event; instead, she, Bud, and Bine traveled to Kansas for a final visit with her father, whom she had not seen in twenty-seven years.[45]

The Bozeman Opera House, completed in 1890, also housed city offices. This photograph was taken about a decade later. Museum of the Rockies, Bozeman x85.2.161

Construction of the new city hall and opera house finished in June 1890. The three-story building cost forty-five thousand dollars and featured a cut-stone exterior and a capped bell tower. The building housed all city offices, including police and fire, and a one-thousand-seat auditorium with an eighteen-hundred-square-foot stage, luxury boxes, and orchestra pit. Though some thought the interior too confining and the entrances too narrow, it was heralded as the finest government building in the state.[46] That same month, a pair of saloon proprietors, "in order to keep pace with the present boom of the future capital of Montana," refitted their bar and began calling it "The Senate."[47]

Story continued with the development of his various concerns in Bozeman as summer turned to fall that year. He finished two of his Main Street brick buildings in September, each covered by a fireproof roof. More importantly, he abandoned his lawsuit over the waterworks system after the installation of new engines and boilers at his mill. This was a huge relief for the city, as close to ninety thousand dollars had already been invested in the project.[48] Story then installed a private telephone line connecting the mill with the Gallatin Valley National Bank, but October brought a temporary setback when the state examiner determined his new boilers were defective and needed replacing. Still, Story's mill faced a more serious disaster later that month when newcomer Herman Schultz tried to destroy it.[49]

A Wisconsin native, Schultz came to Bozeman earlier that year from Billings, where he had been unsuccessful in raising money to construct a flour mill. Smartly dressed and carrying a few thousand dollars in his pocket, he soon leased George Thomas's Empire Mill at Springhill. He made a courtesy call days later at the Story Mill, introducing himself to Elias and receiving a tour of the facility by the aptly named head of operations, W. C. Miller. Schultz returned on October 10 and requested a second tour, this time questioning Miller about change of shifts, the engine house, and any alternative accesses to the building.

Shortly after midnight, mill employee George Payson was making his rounds when the smell of smoke drew him to the building's fourth story. There he found Schultz, holding a five-gallon oilcan and a sack of shavings over a recently ignited blaze. Upon being discovered, Schultz charged, and as the two men tussled they fell down a flight of stairs, knocking Payson temporarily unconscious. Coming to a few minutes later, Payson sounded the alarm, rousing Miller, packer William Dorr, and two others, who used the mill's large rotary pump and hose to extinguish the fire. Schultz, having made his way back up the steps, climbed through a window to the fire escape, but fell after losing his footing. With a broken hip, he crawled twenty-five feet to an empty railcar on the sidetrack. He tied two handkerchiefs into a loop, connected one end to a rung on the car's side ladder, placed the other end over his neck, and hung himself. He was found dead the next morning.[50]

Story, on his way to Washington, D.C., to lobby for a reduction in the size of the Crow Reservation, made no public comment on the incident. All agreed that Schultz was deranged enough to think destroying Story's mill would give his newly acquired Empire Mill a monopoly. It was later learned that Schultz was suspected of burning down a mill in Wisconsin and had only departed for Montana when the investigation intensified. His relatives initially planned to have the body embalmed and shipped back to Wisconsin, but, after learning the circumstances of Schultz's death, arranged instead for a burial in Bozeman in a "common cheap casket."[51]

Nelson Story returned home in time for Christmas, allowing him to meet the newest addition to the family: Rose and Garrett's first child, a son named Nelson Story Hogan, born in late October. Before leaving for Los Angeles in January 1891, he and Ellen entertained Byron and his wife visiting from Ohio. By the time Nelson, Ellen, and Walter returned in March, the Bozeman Hotel had opened. The four-story, steam-heated building boasted numerous parlors, ninety-two guest rooms, a first-floor dining room, a private dining space for unaccompanied women, a barber shop, card rooms, and three mercantile stores. The establishment added to Bozeman's

Bozeman Hotel and Tilton Building, Main Street, Bozeman, 1898 McGill Collection, Museum of the Rockies, Bozeman x83.13.13

growing list of assets that qualified it for the state capital, but rival newspapers campaigning for either Anaconda or Helena continued to highlight the city's shortcomings, including the bordellos that had survived a half-hearted crackdown during the prior summer.[52] One paper gleefully noted "that a wonderfully depraved state of society exists in the 'Garden of Eden,'" and that lasciviousness was wildly rampant in the "city of homes and churches."[53]

After returning from California, Story planned on resting a few days before taking an excursion to New York and Washington, D.C., with Bud.[54] However, he postponed that trip after Miles City cattle-man Matt Murphy approached him about buying Story's horse and cattle herd. Story had been losing interest in ranching, and most of his attention had shifted to the mill, his bank, and expanding real estate investments in Los Angeles. He knew the open-range era was over, and that most of the land ceded by the Crows would probably be snapped up by homesteaders. The opportunity to sell his herd was too appealing to pass up.

The previous November, Nelson's nephew, W. D. Story, who had just purchased a one-half interest in the operation for fifty thousand dollars, attended a meeting at the Crow Agency that, by then, had been relocated to the Little Bighorn River. For the past few winters, the Storys had moved their herd from the Clarks Fork to lands west of Pryor Creek, and now wanted to run their cattle east of Pryor Creek. But the Crows objected, claiming that Story's cattle had dam-aged their crops. Chief Plenty Coups had always endorsed Story's use of the reservation, but had recently grown frustrated by his friend's gifts of "lump-jawed" cows and unmarketable flour and by his sudden decision to stop hiring Crow herders. As a result, agent Moses Wyman refused W. D.'s request. W. D. ignored the order, prompting inspector James Cisney to warn the Interior Department that the Storys' operation could cause serious trouble, as the two were putting "many cattle across Pryor Creek in the night & at other times."[55]

In the spring, Story knew it was time to get out. Murphy and Paul McCormick, with the financial backing of Senator Thomas Power, formed the Ox Yoke Cattle Company.[56] Story agreed to sell his herd, which ranged on the eastern side of Park County, Lake Basin, the Boulder River, or on the Crow Reservation, to the Ox Yoke for twenty-three dollars a head. In all, 13,074 animals produced a net profit of $300,702.[57] W. D. used his share from the sale to purchase a 480-acre farm two miles west of Park City, where he settled down with his wife, Kate Payne.[58]

Tragedy severed Story's ties to the cattle industry even further in the summer of 1891. That July, one of James Dilworth's former employees, twenty-four-year-old French Canadian Godfrey Demers, filed a homestead claim on property near Rock Creek that Dilworth, though he had no title, used for a hayfield. On the morning of July 10, Demers and companion Lee Ferguson ordered Dilworth's hay cutters off the land. The cutters in turn alerted Dilworth and watched from a distance as their boss rode alone to Demers's tent. As the two men talked, a pair of shots suddenly rang out and Dilworth fell from his saddle. By the time the hay cutters arrived, Dilworth was dead, leaving behind a wife and eight children. Nelson Story, Walter Cooper, Lester Willson, and Peter Koch served as pallbearers at his Bozeman funeral.[59]

Demers claimed self-defense, and went to trial in October. Ferguson maintained that Demers had only fired his Winchester rifle after Dilworth reached for his pistol. Other witnesses for the defense held that Dilworth was short-tempered and had on more than one occasion pulled a gun on an employee. Prosecution witnesses Garrett Hogan and fellow physician Henry Foster disputed the defendants' account of the event. Their examination of the fatal wounds led them to believe Dilworth was most likely twenty feet away when the shots were fired, suggesting the killing was premeditated. Nonetheless, on October 30, the jury acquitted both men, infuriating Story, residents of Red Lodge, and the editors of the *Chronicle*, who felt two assassins had gone "scot free."[60]

IN THE FALL of 1891, Bine and a few friends followed in the steps of Bud Story by enrolling at Shattuck Military Academy.[61] Although a similar institution had opened in Bozeman that September and promised standard classroom instruction, music lessons, and "military tactics," the upstart academy failed to prevent young men from leaving the state to pursue their educations. One of the new school's instructors grumbled that $40,000 would remain in Bozeman each year if students heading east could be convinced to attend the new school. Not only did Story keep his sons at Shattuck, he also outfitted Bine with a wagon, a four-horse team, and saddle horses so he and a few friends could enjoy a three-week excursion through Yellowstone National Park before heading to Minnesota. Weeks later, he outfitted son-in-law Garrett Hogan for a far more elaborate undertaking.[62]

Earlier in the year, Story and Elias Jr. paid Thomas Quaw $1,000 for a twenty-acre site in Belgrade, where they immediately began construction of a new grain elevator to allow valley farmers to forgo trips to Bozeman. The $100,000 structure was completed in the fall. Hogan now wanted to open a pharmacy in the promising community. His two-month-old Bozeman operation was adorned with mahogany furniture and a $1,000 soda fountain purchased by his father-in-law, and Hogan had no qualms about soliciting additional financial assistance to outfit a new Belgrade store in similar fashion.[63] Always willing to keep his daughter happy, Nelson accompanied Garrett and Rose on a trip to New York to purchase additional medicines and supplies. Again, Story footed most of the bill and then departed for California to join Ellen and the Benepes. The Hogans, meanwhile, remained in New York so that Garrett could complete a month-long postgraduate course in medicine and surgery.[64]

Upon returning to Montana, Hogan partnered with Thomas and Irene Hill to open the Belgrade pharmacy, but the arrangement showed little promise of success. The Hills and Hogan rarely saw eye-to-eye on matters pertaining to management of the store, and the Hills occasionally denied Hogan access to the property. Within a year, $3,000 in unpaid debts saddled the operation. The court put the property into receivership and the partnership dissolved.[65] Hogan's Bozeman store was not doing well either, and he accused his main competitor, pharmacist Richard May of the White Front Store, of selling imitation and aged drugs at a 10 to 15 percent discount. Hogan openly dubbed May "the cut rate patent medicine fiend."[66] May countered, accusing Hogan of using "valueless and dangerous" medicines left over from his predecessor, Samuel Langhorne. By mid-January 1892, the dispute faded, with May still receiving the bulk of local business. Though Garrett and Rose hosted more than their share of card and dancing parties, he never enjoyed much popularity in the community, even after the March birth of their second child, a boy named Romaine, added to their family's presence in the growing community.[67]

The optimistic forecast over the siting of the new state capital fueled further investment and entrepreneurial activity in the Gallatin Valley. The year 1892 saw the establishment of the Commercial Exchange Bank with E. Broox Martin as president. Martin also teamed with George Ramsey to form the Bozeman Milling Company, and together they sold $75,000 in capital stock to build a flour mill near the railroad tracks, in effect partnering with the Story Flour Mill. Nelson added new equipment to his operation, and began construction of an eight-foot-wide, two-foot-deep water canal to supply

The flurry of city improvements in Bozeman during the 1890s included an electric streetcar, shown here in the early 1900s. Gallatin Historical Society Museum, Bozeman 9860

extra power. In so doing, he tore down a fence on property belonging to Elmyra Frazier, and after she filed a court complaint, Story paid for the damages but continued construction nonetheless.[68]

That summer, Bozeman took yet another step to prove its worthiness as the state capital. After a rousing Fourth of July celebration complete with a parade, speeches, baseball games, barbecue, and fireworks, the Bozeman Electric Streetcar line began operation. Three Laclede Company Cars ran on three miles of track that zigzagged from the Northern Pacific Depot south to the Capitol Hill addition.[69] Opening day drew a huge crowd of locals, many of whom had never before seen an electric car. Worries that the cars would spook horses proved unfounded.[70]

Story was one of nine men who joined the Bozeman for the Capitol Committee, chaired by Walter Cooper.[71] Together with Gallatin County businessmen, the committee issued a letter to all state newspapers in September, predicting voters would reject Bozeman's rivals, particularly "the unsightly, barren and worked out gravel heaps of Helena, where there is ample evidence of premature decay."[72] The committee also issued aluminum "Bozeman for the Capitol" promotional medals that some residents used as watch charms or scarf pins. Helena's medal, according to the *Chronicle,* was made out of a cracker, "just the thing for the Cracker City."[73]

As election day approached, an upsurge in corruption and bribery tainted the contest. Promoters of Helena were accused of sending agents, or "rats," across the state offering "boodle" for those who would vote to keep the capital in Helena. The *Chronicle* claimed one of these agents warned Park County voters that Bozeman would steal Livingston's railroad machine shops if she became the capital.[74] Other Helena backers said Bozeman had withdrawn from the race, making a vote for her a waste. Cooper convened a special town meeting in the opera house on October 14 to reaffirm Bozeman's commitment to the effort. Speakers accused Helena, through the "hoggishness and the venality of her millionaires," of bribing newspaper editors for endorsements. William Alderson told the crowd that Helena had raised $100,000 for the capital fight, and Lester Willson denied rumors that Bozeman was running a bribery campaign, the committee having raised only $5,775 to mail ninety-one thousand fliers to voters throughout the state. Story did not speak, but pledged his continued support.[75] A resolution condemning Helena's "odious and disgraceful tactics . . . and its corrupt use of money" was unanimously passed at a second public meeting a week later.[76]

Just days before the vote, the *Helena Independent* accused Marcus Daly of the Anaconda Copper Company of funding Bozeman's campaign. Daly, according to the *Independent*, hoped Bozeman would gain enough votes to prevent a plurality for Helena, thus forcing a run-off that would give him more time to garner support for Anaconda. As it turned out, the *Independent*'s accusations had merit. Daly had indeed given seventy-five thousand dollars to "a leading banker and capitalist of Bozeman": Nelson Story, who used the money to offer loans to prospective donors to the Bozeman campaign if they could not afford an out-of-pocket contribution.[77] If Bozeman became the capital, the borrower would repay the loan with interest, which Story would split with Daly. If the Bozeman bid failed, Story and Daly would forgive the debt entirely. There was no financial risk

Bozeman for the Capitol [sic] token. In spite of efforts by Story and others, Bozeman lost its bid to become the state capital. Gallatin Historical Society Museum, Bozeman

for Story, who was merely using "Daly's gold."[78] A similar scheme promised free real estate to those who agreed to vote for Bozeman. This ploy seemed to be more popular, and citizens from Butte lined up for hundreds of Bozeman lots.[79]

The *Courier* brushed the *Independent* aside, saying Story contributed his own funds liberally to the Bozeman campaign for "legitimate expenses" or the "sinues [*sic*] of war" and adding that he "waded personally into the thickest of the fight, thus subjecting himself to the poisoned arrows and cowardly calumny of Helena's boodlers and her subsidized newspapers."[80] Nonetheless, the *Independent* confidently predicted a fourth-place finish for Bozeman, "the beautiful and busted."[81]

The *Independent* was right. Helena garnered 13,892 votes, followed by Anaconda with 10,014, Butte with 7,757, and Bozeman with 7,636. Great Falls, Deer Lodge, and Boulder finished fifth, sixth, and seventh respectively, setting the stage for a run-off between Anaconda and Helena.[82] The *Independent* saluted the "sober judgment and common sense of the people," exclaiming that "bossism and boodleism" were now gone forever.[83] Both of Bozeman's papers consoled their readers by reminding them that the local committee had run "a noble and honorable fight" free from bribery and corruption.[84] Perhaps in an effort to validate the committee's efforts even further, the *Courier* printed a front page story about a Butte boy whose life was saved by a "Bozeman for the Capitol" medal worn proudly on his shirt when he accidentally discharged a pistol. The bullet that could have punctured his heart instead ricocheted off the front of the medal. Every night before he went to bed, the boy thanked God that Bozeman had entered the capital race.[85]

Chapter Twelve

A Worthy Candidate, 1893–1895

B
Y 1893, Nelson Story's new Belgrade elevator was "filled to the roof with wheat."[1] The Story & Company Mills in Bozeman had a capacity of 250 barrels a day and the elevators 250,000 bushels. After the Bozeman Milling Company's new Farmers Mill was completed on January 3, Elias added new machinery, extra water buckets, tanks, hoses, hydrants, and a new office.[2] A cold snap that month forced both flour mills to close temporarily in order to prevent dampened wheat, unable to thaw, from bunching in the bins.[3]

That winter, Bud and Bine transferred to the Ogden Military Academy in Utah, where Bud would graduate at the end of the academic year. Ellen joined Nelson, Walter, and the Hogans for a sojourn to Los Angeles. There, the Storys hosted friends from Montana in their new California residence at 840 West Adams Street, the part of town "occupied entirely by the elite."[4] They were among fifteen thousand tourists who wintered in Los Angeles in 1893, using the city's street-car and steam-train system to visit the coast at Santa Monica, the orange groves of San Bernardino, and, occasionally, "Old Mexico." With money from the cattle sale in his pocket, Story purchased rental properties in Los Angeles, hiring fellow Montanan Herb Morrill to collect rents and pay the taxes.[5]

While the Storys basked in sunny California, the Montana legislature debated the future site of a new agricultural college. The Gallatin Valley's central location, livestock and grain industries,

Preparing to ship grain, Belgrade Museum of the Rockies, Bozeman x80.6.580

and forty-five-hundred-foot altitude, which closely approximated two-thirds of the state, made it preferable to the other candidate, Miles City. Amenities like the opera house, the Bozeman Hotel, a reconstructed two-story West Side School building, and several new avenues and streets (one of them named Story) tipped the scale, and on February 16, 1893, the legislature voted to locate the Montana State College of Agriculture and Mechanic Arts within three miles of Bozeman.[6]

In accordance with the Hatch Act of 1887 and the Second Morrill Act of 1890, the federal government promised just over thirty-three thousand dollars to support a land-grant college. Governor John Rickards wanted the school established as quickly as possible, and

he proposed an opening date of July 1 so that the federal appropriation could be claimed for the fiscal year 1894. With the Presbyterian Academy closing, Story offered use of his skating rink for classes in order to meet the governor's deadline.[7] Rickards, at the urging of the Bozeman Board of Trade, then named Story one of three advisors to the school's governing body, the Local Executive Board of Education. Its first charge was the selection of the school's exact location.[8]

Certainly, the acquisition of the agricultural college was a better "grab" for Bozeman than the capital, especially with the impending "liberal appropriation" from the government. The *Bozeman Chronicle*, with the Storys and other wealthy families in mind, revived the sentiment that such a first-class institution negated the need of any student to travel out-of-state for an education.[9] All desired prompt action, and proposed sites included land near Belgrade, Fort Ellis, and the area intended for the capital. Walter Cooper rightly predicted that the college would ultimately become a university and, therefore, should be located as close to Bozeman as possible: "The college will derive a great deal of its support from Bozeman. I do not care where it is placed as long as it is in or near the town."[10] Cooper's wish came true the following week when the Board of Education, meeting at the Bozeman Hotel, accepted a 160-acre parcel donated by the county adjacent to the Capitol Hill addition. Though absent from the meeting, Story donated fifteen hundred dollars so the board could purchase an additional 40 acres that had been set aside

Story provided land for the Montana State College for Agriculture and Mechanic Arts, shown here around 1900. The school is now Montana State University. Museum of the Rockies, Bozeman x83.13.1317

for the state capital.[11] He returned in June, "in excellent health and with unabated confidence in Bozeman's future."[12]

❖

AMERICA'S MONETARY SYSTEM had been based on a ratio between silver and gold of 16:1, the silver in a silver dollar weighing sixteen times the amount of gold in a gold dollar.[13] That changed in 1873, when the U.S. government adopted a solely gold standard by demonetizing silver. Story, like most westerners, believed adherence to the silver and gold ratio would keep more money in circulation,

and the resulting inflation would raise wages and grain prices alike. In 1878, the government restored silver as legal tender and began subsidizing its production by purchasing bullion at a maximum rate of four million dollars per month, and the subsequent issue of silver certificates stimulated silver mining in the West, particularly in Montana and Colorado. Eastern investors backed silver operations near Butte and Helena, and by 1887, Montana was the number one silver producer, with a total yield of $15.5 million.

But the increase in the country's silver supply led to its devaluation—the price for silver in 1889 was ninety-three-and-a-half cents an ounce, compared to $1.32 in the 1870s. Congress, under pressure from the "Silverites," responded with the Sherman Silver Purchase Act, allowing the Treasury Department to buy nearly the entire national production of silver at market prices and issue notes redeemable in silver and gold at the sixteen-to-one ratio. The act allowed the silver mining boom in Montana to continue, but foreign investors, rendered uneasy by the glut of silver, began moving their gold reserves overseas. Treasury gold stocks fell below the one-hundred-million-dollar reserve limit on April 21, 1893, leading to bankruptcies and a massive sell-off on Wall Street. Speculation in railroads that were vastly overbuilt in the 1880s left companies like the Philadelphia and Reading Railroad and the Northern Pacific overextended, forcing them into bankruptcy. A run of depositors

Walter Cooper sitting at his desk, 1890s. Cooper was elected to the Montana legislature in 1895. Museum of the Rockies, Bozeman x85.3.179

demanding their money forced banks to close their doors. Unemployment in Montana and other states rose.[14]

In an interview with the *Courier*, Story blamed the panic on foreign investors hoarding gold and the Democratically controlled House's repeal of tariffs on lead and wool. He worried that fewer tariffs would hurt American businesses and force the government to levy an income tax: "It takes $2,000,000 a day to support this government and if the 'tariff is a tax' it is not felt by us so much as it would be if we had to provide funds to meet the running expenses of the government by direct taxation; our state and county taxes are all we feel like paying that way."[15] Story, believing more silver in circulation would lower farm and ranch debt, advised the government to call in greenbacks and bank bills of small denominations. "The treasury vaults would thus be speedily relieved, the mints would be coining up to their capacity and the price of silver would advance because of the increased demand for it."[16]

In late June, England stopped the coinage of silver rupees in India, triggering closures and layoffs at several Montana mines. Story joined Walter Cooper, John Mendenhall, Lester Willson, and several others as Bozeman delegates to the statewide silver convention on July 6 in Helena.[17] The two hundred attendees formed the Montana Silver Association, hoping to "usher in an unexampled era of prosperity, contentment, and happiness."[18] The following week, after visiting idle silver mines in Butte, Interior Secretary Michael Hoke Smith listened to arguments by Story, Garrett Hogan, and others at the Northern Pacific Depot, all demanding that silver be coined on a sixteen-to-one ratio with gold. Meanwhile, the spreading depression crept into town. The Bozeman Hotel shut down, and the Bozeman National Bank closed on July 19. Story surrendered the following week by closing the Gallatin Valley National, leaving the Commercial Exchange as Bozeman's lone bank. He felt the closure was preferable to watching the bank's assets of $474,000 "dwindle to nothing," and promised to pay all depositors in full over a two-year period before withdrawing his holdings.[19]

In reality, Story had made his decision shortly after his return to Bozeman. Before leaving for Los Angeles in January, he instructed the bank's board of directors to give him first option on any bonds the bank might sell. But while he was in Los Angeles, the directors, worried about the Panic, instead sold the bonds on the open market. They felt the institution needed cash, and if Story bought the bonds no net gain would be realized, as he would probably do so with his seventy thousand dollars in deposits. When Story returned and learned of the sale, he was furious. As the majority stockholder, he controlled the vote for liquidation and used the Panic as an excuse to exact his revenge. "If they had written and consulted him, it would not have happened, but it was the secrecy they maintained and the bank's ignoring him and what he had told it that made him so mad," claimed Bine. "He admitted to me years after that it was a mistake, but he did not propose to be ignored."[20]

Dr. Henry Wright Foster, one of the bank's directors, told a cohort that Story should be hanged. While the seriousness of the suggestion was doubtful, when Story got wind of the threat he confronted the doctor on Main Street and beat him with his hickory cane.[21] Fearing retaliation, a lynching, "or something akin thereto," he sent word for Bine to bring his shotgun and six-gun, as he intended to face any trouble "standing up."[22] Bine obliged, but there was no further violence, only assault charges, for which Story paid a $2,100 fine. He also paid Foster $25,000 to drop a civil lawsuit, which the doctor used to begin construction of Bozeman's first major hospital, the Bozeman Sanitarium.[23] Story's short fuse had resulted in another civic improvement.

THE ONLY INDUSTRY in the Gallatin to weather the Panic nearly unscathed was malting barley. Beginning in 1889, Henry Altenbrand, president of the New York and Brooklyn Malting Company, planted harvest samples in several states, including Montana. Results showed that the crop grown in the central part of the Gallatin Valley was fuller, heavier in weight, and brighter in color, thanks primarily to the natural soil and lack of rain during the harvest season.[24] The community of Hamilton, which relocated closer to the Northern Pacific right-of-way, had been renamed Moreland, but when Altenbrand's new Manhattan Malting Company purchased the townsite and thousands of additional acres, it became Manhattan.

Altenbrand also helped form the West Gallatin Irrigation Company to build and maintain a water canal into the area. In 1891, a colony of ten Dutch families settled on company lands to raise barley and exported fifty thousand bushels to Europe that year alone. The chief commissioner of Germany's Department of Agriculture, Professor Delbruck, was most impressed with the yields of the Gallatin Valley, deeming the irrigation system employed by the Dutch ideal, thanks to the water of the nearby West Gallatin River.[25]

While barley held steady, Bozeman's two flour mills had to shut down in the summer of 1893. Dealers in Helena, Butte, and Great Falls were annually importing 275,000 barrels of flour from Minnesota, the Dakotas, and other northwestern states, spending an estimated amount of one and a half-million dollars. They claimed that production and delivery of Montana wheat was inconsistent and unable to keep up with demand, and that urbanites considered wheat from outside the state superior. As a result, Gallatin Valley farmers were realizing only thirty-five to forty cents a bushel. A frustrated Nelson Story bemoaned that he had two hundred thousand bushels of "No. 1" wheat at the elevator in Belgrade and a similar amount in his mill and warehouses in Bozeman.[26]

To aid local producers, Bozeman Milling Company general manager E. Broox Martin and Helena National Bank president Erastus Edgerton began a campaign to encourage Montanans to "buy at home." They accused Montana dealers of prejudicing local tastes by selling only third-rate flour from western Montana.[27] Edgerton claimed the Gallatin Valley was "burdened down" with the weight of its "generous crop," and Montana's preoccupation with silver had caused her citizens to forget about other resources such as wheat. With Gallatin Valley wheat at thirty-five cents, why support eastern farmers who could garner sixty cents a bushel?

> The Nelson Story mill has a capacity of three hundred barrels a day, and the Bozeman Milling company has a capacity of two hundred barrels a day, making a total of five hundred barrels a day. First-class in every particular, costing thousands of dollars to build and equal to any mill of the same size in Minneapolis, these mills are sufficient to supply the demands of the entire state.[28]

Nelson Story & Company stepped up its advertising in several Montana newspapers, boasting that the company's hard and soft wheat, the "Saskatchewan" and "Montana Belle" brands, were better than any imported product. To prove his point, Story sent samples to the Montana agricultural exhibit at the Chicago World's Fair. The Bozeman Milling Company sent its "Royal" and "Economy" brands. In baking contests against flour from Minnesota, Montana's flour, both soft and hard wheat, fared quite well, with Story's hard wheat winning special praise.[29]

These campaigns, supported by the Farmers Institute of Montana, helped the state's wheat markets rebound. With Nelson Story & Company establishing a branch in Butte, sales grew. In a newspaper advertisement, Fred Buchler of Bozeman's Tivoli Saloon proclaimed, "Butte is going to use our flour and therefore I sell Butte beer, which by the way is the best in the market."[30] Elias, realizing people needed bread, "the staff of life," and that perhaps the worst of the Panic was over, made plans to resume full operations at the mill in the fall in time for the harvest.[31]

Story left the mill in Elias's hands so that he and Ellen could visit the World's Fair in Chicago, where Ellen's portrait, one of three from the Gallatin Valley, hung in the Montana Building. Elias's optimism received a boost with the reopening of the Bozeman Hotel and the Bozeman National Bank. Work to connect telephone service between Bozeman, Helena, and Livingston led forty Bozeman residences to purchase subscriptions.[32] Story, once he returned from Chicago, helped Hogan reopen the Bozeman Pharmacy by giving him close to four thousand dollars to settle liens and various debts. He then attended a November meeting of the Board of Education in Helena.[33]

During the winter, Hogan received the contract to furnish medicines and medical attendance to the county for $420 per year, a welcome supplement to the family income as another child, Vandevere, had been born the previous August. Rose, upset with her confinement in Bozeman while her parents were in California, telegraphed her mother in March 1894 that she was ill and needed Ellen's company. Ellen, accompanied by Walter, returned April 1, and Rose quickly recovered.[34] Nelson remained in Los Angeles, entertaining visitors Lester and Emma Willson, as well as William Alderson, who afterward wrote a friend that Los Angeles was "in good shape under Mr. Story's guidance."[35] Before returning home, Story confiscated Herb Morrill's horse and buggy when Morrill failed to turn over $1,300 in collected rents and pay property taxes. On his way to Bozeman, Story joined Ellen, Rose, and Walter for Bine's June graduation in Ogden.[36]

During Story's absence, attorney and friend Cornelius Bradshaw wrote to the *Pioneer Press* in Saint Paul and the *Chicago Record,* extolling Story's potential as a candidate for the U.S. Senate.[37] "Colonel" Bradshaw cited his business ability and "unquestioned" integrity, and claimed that as a millionaire he would have great personal influence in Washington.[38] But the idea of Nelson Story as a Montana senator received lukewarm enthusiasm. An editorial in the *Yellowstone Journal* opined, "While we have no desire to nip Mr. Story's senatorial ambition in the bud, we cannot refrain from remarking in this connection that the state of Montana has probably had enough "personal influence" that is connected with seven figures with a "$" at the front."[39] The *Bozeman Chronicle* refused to back Story, diplomatically noting that while he would make a first-class senator, he remained the "rankest sort" of a Republican, "a man, who by his own individual efforts, backed by splendid judgment has made himself what he is."[40]

Story had only run in one major campaign, a failed effort in 1871 to become territorial delegate for Choteau, Gallatin, and Meagher Counties.[41] When Martin Maginnis decided not to seek another term as territorial delegate to Congress in 1882, Story was high on the Republican list of replacements, but he turned it down.[42] He also rejected a bid for the governorship. Story seemingly had no ambition beyond that of city alderman, confessing to former territorial governor Samuel Hauser that his attempted influence in political matters "has had the opposite effect intended."[43] But over time his attitude evolved, and he became more politically active. On October 8, 1894, he addressed a rally of the Young Men's Republican Club of Bozeman. Story criticized free trade and called for the coinage of silver so that the United States would have more money in circulation and pay off its foreign and domestic debt. He blamed the debt for the Panic of 1893, and held that Congress should ban paper money under ten dollars:

> The fives, the twos and the ones should all be withdrawn from circulation and the $500,000,000 of silver now in the treasury would soon find its way into the hands of the people. Then we could open our mints to the free coinage of silver and the treasury would not be glutted with it. We are a debtor nation of at least $10,000,000 and all we owe would gladly take silver. . . . If the silver we have piled in the treasury vaults were in the hands of the people we would have no surplus. One scratch of the pen, one act of Congress would settle this question. We have built up our manufacturing industries under protection until no other nation can compete with us and if we sustain our silver our money will not go from us.

Story said the Sherman Silver Purchase Act, by then repealed, was flawed because it tried to "keep up the price of silver." He said there was not enough gold in the world to back up all outstanding notes and bonds, and when the free coinage of silver ceased, America lost half its money supply. Gold became even more valuable, but made the national debt larger. With silver out of circulation, America's creditors reaped the benefits.[44] In another speech two weeks later in the opera house, Story emphasized the need for protectionism:

> That gold has been going from the United States the last year to pay for goods abroad, and in order to return to the free coinage of silver, it will be necessary for us to change the trade in our favor and when the trade of nations is in our favor we can resume the free coinage of silver and retain our gold basis of redemption.

Story favored selected embargoes and tariffs high enough on some imported goods that other nations would quit sending them to the United States, thus spurring manufacturing and lower taxes at home:

> And when we produce all we can consume and all that a man wears from the top of his head to the sole of his foot, when that is produced and made here and bought here, who is the tax paid to? Where does he pay a tax? He simply works or exchanges (it matters not what) with the man who produces that article, and there is no tax paid.
>
> If the industries of the United State are all pursued, and all our manufactures are made in the United States, not imported from foreign countries, you buy these manufactures from your fellow man and get such products as he may produce. Your money is here and your industries are here, and where do you pay a tax? On nothing.

In order to offset the lost tax revenue from higher tariffs, Story advocated an internal tax on big expense items. "That tax," said Story "comes up as a direct tax on the rich. The poor man will be relieved and the rich can take care of themselves."[45] Story knew that any industrial growth under his proposal would benefit the already unpopular business trusts on the East Coast, but he welcomed that consequence:

> There has never been a trust in the United States but has resulted to the benefit of the people. . . . Let trusts be formed; let the competition of America bring them down and when they fall you are getting the benefit and getting the manufacture of that article at a lower price than you otherwise could.[46]

Story then praised Republicans in office, especially former bank employee and U.S. representative Charles S. Hartman, who had won election in 1892. As to his potential senatorial candidacy, Story remained silent. Montana Republicans, impressed with both speeches, distributed twenty thousand copies in pamphlet form across the country.[47]

ON SATURDAY, OCTOBER 20, Republican National Committee chair and former congressman Thomas Carter held the first of two "Helena for Capitol" meetings in Bozeman. Hard feelings lingered from the 1892 run-off vote, and so both Bozeman papers endorsed Anaconda. Story was a member of the sparse crowd that chuckled when Carter asserted that Helena buys Gallatin Valley watermelons and corn, two crops not produced in the region. Three days later, Helena attorney Sam Word spoke for nearly two hours, claiming Helena had always been friendly to Bozeman. He cited the role played by Martin Maginnis in stopping the transfer of Company F of the Second Cavalry to Fort Custer in 1879. But when Word claimed Bozeman held a banquet to thank Maginnis for his efforts, Story jumped at the chance to shame his nemesis by correctly noting that the banquet had been held several days before the transfer was rescinded, and that it was designed to prevail on Maginnis and Department of Dakota commander General Thomas Ruger the importance of keeping Company F at Bozeman. Embarrassed, Word concluded his speech and the meeting adjourned.[48]

The "Anaconda for Capitol" rally held on October 31 was a much different affair. Bozeman rolled out the red carpet for that city's proponents, who were joined by Paris Gibson of Great Falls. Story served as one of the event's official cohosts. There was an evening parade from the courthouse to the opera house, fireworks, and music from the Queen City Cornet Band. Speeches recounted Helena's deception and poor treatment of Bozeman over the years, as well as the economic impact of Marcus Daly on the state's economy. The enthusiasm and large attendance bolstered the belief that Anaconda would win the runoff.[49]

Anaconda indeed won Gallatin County, though not by the margin many expected: 1,294 to 1,042. Statewide the results were much different, as Helena captured the long sought-after prize by nearly two thousand votes. Locally, Story's published speeches and support of Republican candidates were cited as reasons for Republican victories in ten contested Gallatin County races, including William Alderson's bid for the state house.[50]

Story traveled to Anaconda, Butte, and Helena to gauge support among legislators for his senatorial bid. His efforts, however, did not amount to much of a campaign to secure the office, but were driven more by curiosity as to how he might fare. He rented a suite of rooms at the Hotel Helena in advance of the January 1895 session, during which the senatorial appointment would be decided by the state Senate.[51] The *Helena Independent* derided Story's candidacy with a series of disparaging editorials, to which the *Courier* responded by calling him a "good, sensible, highly respected citizen, a tried and true Republican . . . a worthy and well qualified candidate."[52] Still, the *Chronicle* refused to endorse Story, saying it would be like "Dead Sea fruit."[53] The Butte *Daily Inter Mountain* was noncommittal, writing that the Republicans of Montana "might go farther and fare worse."[54]

The senate of the fourth Montana legislative session would select two U.S. senators. Since the legislature had failed to choose a senator in 1893, one would complete a partial term, the other the regular term beginning in the spring. As the Republicans enjoyed a thirteen-to-seven majority in the legislature's upper house, the winners of the Republican caucus would be all but guaranteed victory. The leading candidates were incumbent Thomas Power, former territorial house speaker Lee Mantle of Butte, Governor John Rickards, and Helena attorney Thomas Carter. Story, Wilbur Fisk Sanders, and Helena mayor Elbert Weed were considered long shots. The weekend of January 5 was reserved for handshaking, deal making, and canvassing by the leading candidates, all of whom were present save Lee Mantle, who would not arrive until Sunday, and Story, who, accompanied by Bud, would not arrive until Monday.[55] William Alderson gave scant attention to promoting Story, as he was more interested in becoming house speaker, a position that went to Wilbra Swett of Silver Bow County. Not until Story's chief booster Colonel Cornelius Bradshaw arrived on Sunday did Story's campaign get out of "still water."[56] But the odds were too heavily stacked, and Story knew it. Helena newspapers the *Herald* and the *Independent* endorsed Carter. Story doubted he would survive the first ballot, and talked openly of throwing his support behind Mayor Weed.[57]

On January 9, the frenzy of the campaigning ceased when the Republican caucus convened at the Merchants Hotel. The public and the press were excluded. Legislators agreed to choose a senator from western Montana as well as one from eastern Montana. The "short term" senator who would complete the term expiring in 1899 was chosen first, the prize going to Lee Mantle on the first ballot. Candidates for the east-side senator were placed into nomination, with William Alderson submitting Story's name. The first ballot was completed just after one o'clock in the morning. Carter received seventeen votes, Sanders and Power fourteen each, Weed seven, and Nelson Story four. None had the required majority. Three more ballots would be cast over the next hour, but still no candidate received a majority. The caucus adjourned after the fourth ballot showed Carter with nineteen votes, Power and Sanders each with fifteen, Weed with six, and Nelson Story's total cut in half to two.[58] The following evening, the caucus reconvened in the district courthouse, thought to be a location less susceptible to the prying eyes and ears of the press. After another five ballots, still no winner emerged. Story ended the night with the same two votes with which he had started.[59]

It was now evident the caucus was not going to select a candidate who, despite the appeal of his vigilante and cattle-drive days, remained dogged by the controversies of the Indian Ring years. The *Dillon Tribune*'s mockery of the John Bozeman monument in 1883 and the *Yellowstone Journal*'s recent allusion to Story's wealth kept the questions and allegations of the 1870s alive in the minds of too many Montanans. The *Chronicle*'s analogy of Dead Sea fruit was spot-on: Story's successes could not completely eclipse his reputation. Recognizing the situation for what it was, he withdrew his name from consideration, allowing Alderson to lend his support to Thomas Carter "in the interest of harmony and unanimity of choice."[60] On Friday evening, January 11, after eleven ballots, thirty votes secured a win for Carter. The actual senate vote four days later was a formality, with both Mantle and Carter receiving thirteen of the twenty votes cast for each senator.

Bud Story, 1892 Gallatin Historical Society Museum, Bozeman

Story took the expected defeat in stride. He remained in Helena for a Board of Education meeting and then returned to Bozeman on January 18.[61] As the thermometer dipped to twenty below zero, he, Ellen, Bine, and Walter left for Los Angeles, while Bud returned for a second year of study at a St. Louis, Missouri, business college. Garrett, Rose, and their children remained in Bozeman, where Hogan's brother Romaine arrived that winter to help with the drugstore.[62] Elias also assisted, but Hogan still struggled, leading Story to conclude that his son-in-law was a fine physician but a poor businessman unable to "manage a goose nest."[63] Despite growing financial setbacks, Hogan began construction of a two-story house on an eighty-acre tract east of town that he and his family would occupy by the end of the year.[64]

In California, Story purchased more real estate, much of it along or near Spring Street, soon to be known as "The Wall Street of the West" due to the concentration of banks and insurance companies. These staggered acquisitions included a lot on the southeast corner of Sixth and Broadway obtained from Los Angeles real estate speculator James Boon Lankershim for $55,000, a parcel in the 600 block of Spring Street for $63,000, and land near what would become the Arcade Theater for $8,700.[65]

The Storys returned to Bozeman in the spring to learn that a thief, John Manningham, had broken into their mansion in March and taken bedding, clothing, curtains, jewelry, and silverware. He was arrested while transporting the stolen items toward the railroad depot in a handcart and sent to the penitentiary at Deer Lodge.

Etha Mayo Story, wife of Bud Story, c. 1892 Burk, photographer. Gallatin Historical Society Museum, Bozeman

Meanwhile, in St. Louis, Bud used some playful pilfering of his own to impress the girl he had been courting for nearly a year, socialite Etha Lue Mayo. Etha was amused when Bud stole a couple of watermelons from a Missouri truck patch during a picnic. Smitten by the wealthy, handsome man from the Montana cattle ranges, she agreed to his marriage proposal.[66] Following their June 10 wedding in St. Louis and a honeymoon in New York, Bud brought his bride to Bozeman at the end of the month and immediately began construction on a new home near the mill that would be ready for the couple by year's end. In keeping with Bud's rustic bent, the home had a dirt floor, an unfamiliar and challenging situation for a woman whose father, Confederate veteran William Mayo, was president of the St. Louis Loan and Investment Company and secretary of the National Grand Lodge of the Masonic Order.[67] Her transition to Montana was eased by Ellen and Rose, who invited her to cohost tea parties, dances, and yard parties at the family mansion. Such events were more in keeping with Etha's upbringing in St. Louis and certainly made her feel more at home out West, allowing her to tolerate, at least for a few years, Bud's simple floor plans.[68]

Chapter Thirteen

Guest of the Millionaire, 1895–1897

COMMON AXIOM in the American West holds that whiskey is for drinking and water is for fighting over.[1] Nelson Story had little use for whiskey, but water to irrigate his land and power the mill was essential. In 1895, he constructed a six-foot-wide canal across farmer Daniel Maxey's land to irrigate his property to the north and east. Maxey, armed with a shotgun, confronted Story and his crew, but backed off when Story told the men to keep working while patting his holstered six-shooter. A court injunction eventually forced Story to cease the work, but, in the meantime, he won an injunction of his own against John and Carrie Aylsworth and Andrew and Ella Edsall, barring them from taking five hundred inches of water from Bozeman Creek. The victory was short-lived, however, as the court eventually ruled that the Aylsworths and the Edsalls were entitled to 705 inches, while Story and William Tracy were entitled to 225 inches, as per the 1865 appropriation. Later on, Story would enjoy better luck securing the water that he believed was rightfully his.[2]

Throughout the 1890s, Story continued his campaign for the free coinage of silver. Although officially out of the banking industry following the liquidation of the Gallatin Valley National Bank in January 1896, Story was elected a director of the National Bank of California while he and Ellen visited Los Angeles that winter.[3] He told the *Los Angeles Times* that all money should be issued by the government and secured as a first mortgage on all property, both private and public.[4] Once he returned home on May 30, 1896, Story told the *Livingston Post* that most bankers would be in favor of silver if they just studied the issue. "Most of the small bankers," he claimed, "think they have to be gold bugs just because some of the big Wall Street financial men are, the little fellows hoping by this means to be taken for big fish themselves."[5]

An ally in Story's campaign was Civil War veteran Oliver Chisholm, registrar of the U.S. Land Office in Montana, who owned interests in three mining operations, including the Bozeman-based Sixteen To One Mining & Milling Company. Knowing that silver coined at a sixteen-to-one ratio could double the worth of his investment, he teamed with Story on June 23, 1896, to host a reception for Congressman Charles Hartman's return from the Republican National Convention in St. Louis. In his speech at the opera house, Hartman renounced the Republican adherence to the gold standard, calling it an insidious system fastened upon the laboring and producing classes of the country. Story spoke after Hartman and in his hour-long speech reiterated his now-familiar position on silver.[6]

A week later, Hartman told Senator Lee Mantle, chairman of the Republican State Committee and a fellow bimetallist, that he would not support the Republican platform or the party's candidate, William McKinley. He then went to the Democratic National Convention in Chicago as a supporter of Henry Teller, but endorsed William Jennings Bryan after the former Nebraska congressman concluded his address by warning gold-standard adherents that the people would not allow them to "press down upon the brow of labor this crown of thorns. You shall not crucify mankind upon a cross of gold."[7] Bryan captured the nomination, leading Oliver Chisholm to predict that the Republicans, conspirators to the "gold wreckers of Wall Street," were doomed, their downfall "as certain as that of Rome."[8]

Charles Hartman, c. 1889
Howard J. Lowry, photographer. MHS Photograph Archives, Helena 952-036

Hartman dismissed rumors that he might accept the Democratic nomination for Congress, but with Story's encouragement he became the Silver Republican nominee.[9] Story organized a rally on August 20 at the opera house, during which the 162 attendees formed the Hartman Silver Republican Club.[10] Weeks later the Silverites dominated the Republican county convention. Story, having pledged five hundred dollars to the Bryan campaign, engineered the passage of resolutions in support of protectionism and bimetallism. William Alderson, John Bogert, Peter Koch, and even Frank Benepe remained loyal to McKinley and the gold plank, and passed a resolution denouncing the silver supporters for turning the meeting into an endorsement of the Democratic national ticket.[11] "In justice to him, it may be fair to say that less than four years ago he was a gold bug of the gold bugs," wrote Alderson of Story, "but as it is truthfully said that, wise men sometimes change, but fools never, he has gone to the other extreme." Still, Alderson felt the defection would be no more alarming than the Ghost Dance revival then sweeping across the various tribes of the Great Plains and believed that, in time, its supporters would recover from their "wild, theoretical silver infatuation."[12]

At the Democratic state convention in Missoula, electors decided not to nominate a candidate for Congress,

William White Alderson, c. 1890s Museum of the Rockies, Bozeman x83.13.1774

in effect throwing their support behind Hartman. The Bryan-Free Silver wing, including Nelson Story, withdrew its delegates from the Republican state convention in order to submit their own candidates, Hartman among them. The remaining delegates, including Alderson, nominated O. F. Goddard for Congress and endorsed the William McKinley–Garret Hobart ticket, the platform of the St. Louis Convention, and the extension of suffrage to women. When all was said and done, McKinley captured the White House, Democrat Robert Burns Smith defeated Republican Alexander Botkin for governor, and Hartman won the congressional seat.[13]

DURING 1896, southwest Montana's economy continued to recover from the lingering effects of the earlier panic. William Wylie established a series of guest camps in Yellowstone National Park, each featuring a dining tent and several large, woodstove-heated guest tents furnished with bedsteads and mattresses. Dr. Foster's hospital, the Bozeman Sanitarium, opened in June. The brick structure had eleven rooms, a kitchen, reception room, and an operating room. A new, government-backed fish hatchery neared completion just north of Bozeman, and the executive board of the College of Agriculture and Mechanic Arts, including Story, awarded a heating and ventilation contract to a Cincinnati firm for $13,200, having contracted with a Missoula builder the prior September for the construction of the school's main building, chemical lab, veterinary building, workshops, and drill hall.[14] The cornerstone for the school's new main building was laid October 21.[15]

In the valley itself, the amount of land under barley cultivation doubled from the prior year to eleven thousand acres, yielding 46.9 bushels an acre. Frank Benepe and E. J. Owenhouse, partners in a Bozeman hardware and mercantile store, exported much of it overseas to Germany, where it became a favorite.[16] Local farmers, too, appreciated the barley harvest; as the season's first crop, it was a provider of ready cash.

Those producers who took their grain to the Story Mill no longer dealt with Elias. An onset of stomach pain initially dismissed as dyspepsia worsened, and Elias took a rest from his work at the urging of his uncle. He sold his mill interest to Bud and planned a move to California, hoping that the milder climate might aid his recovery.[17] Nelson and Elias left Montana on December 13, traveling via Spokane to Portland, where they boarded a steamer that stopped briefly in San Francisco before reaching Los Angeles. Elias then decided to visit Hawaii, where ocean swims and bicycle rides might relieve his persistent stomach troubles. But after his arrival on the island, the symptoms only worsened, and physicians concluded that an abscess had formed, necessitating an appendectomy. The operation was performed on January 26, 1897, but Elias died a few hours later. Conscious until the end, but sensing his time was limited, the thirty-four-year-old asked to be buried in Bozeman's Blackmore Cemetery. Story saw to these arrangements, with the funeral held at the family mansion on Thursday, February 18. Elias's father arrived the night before, but Nelson remained in Los Angeles.[18]

Words like "exemplary" and "dignified" featured prominently in Elias's obituary. Like Nelson, Elias rarely drank. Though a bachelor, he was not chaste. His countenance and wealthy background attracted the attention of women, allowing Elias, in Bine's words, to enjoy "a little horizontal exercise."[19] His estate consisted of investments totaling almost sixty thousand dollars, mostly in real estate mortgages, the balance in sheep and the Belgrade elevator. He left five thousand dollars each to three of his sweethearts, and the remainder to his half-sisters Nora and Desta May.[20] Nora and her husband, Albert Roecher, traveled to Bozeman in July to settle the estate, and, at the urging of the Storys, they agreed to stay so that Albert, in partnership with William Alward, could take over Hogan's drugstore.[21]

Even in the face of family tragedy, Story's commitment to his various ventures remained unwavering. In February, Judge H. C. Cockrill ruled that both Story and Daniel Maxey had a right to the contested ditch for agricultural purposes, and would therefore share ownership as tenants in common. The decision brought an uneasy and short-lived resolution to the controversy that had begun two summers prior.[22] In July, Story hired another crew to repair the water canal that now also encroached on the property of Daniel's sons, John and William. The brothers rejected the notion that the court ruling applied to them, and so they armed themselves and confronted Story, who stopped work only long enough to receive a court injunction barring the Maxeys from any further interference.[23]

Story's attention was quickly steered back to the silver issue after Charles Hartman convinced William Jennings Bryan, then on a western tour, to add Bozeman and three other Montana towns to his itinerary. Oliver Chisholm chaired the executive committee to oversee the town's preparations, and appointed Nelson Story to head the finance committee and Democratic state representative George Ramsey to head the reception committee. The grounds committee chose the West Side School for Bryan's August 20 speech, and erected a speaker's platform near a shaded corner of the building. Grandstands offered seating for two thousand visitors, with those making a reservation pledging to keep chatter and cheering to a minimum so that all could hear Bryan.[24]

Story met with Bryan in Butte to discuss the Bozeman itinerary, but upon his return, Etha Ellen Story, Bud and Etha's seven-month-old baby girl, suddenly died.[25] Her passing curtailed Bud and Etha's involvement with the town's preparations, and though Nelson and Ellen also felt the loss, they continued on with plans for Bryan's arrival, now just two days away. So, too, did others. Charles Eggleston's poem, "When Bryan Came To Butte," published the week before in the *Anaconda Standard*, inspired William Davies to pen a pro-silver ode to Bryan in the August 19 edition of the *Chronicle*, sung to the tune of "Marching thro' Georgia" and featuring the chorus:[26]

Oh come, oh come, and sing this song with me;
Oh come, oh come, from mountain and the sea;
And we will march in triumph, with our banners
    floating free
Shouting a welcome to Bryan.[27]

Alderson would not be outdone. Playing on the heralded sixteen-to-one ratio, he printed a sixteen-verse poem, "The *Avant Courier's* Royal Welcome to Bryan," on the front page of the August 21 issue. The composition drew on McKinley's victory, Story's money, and Bozeman's homes of "peace and plenty" to ridicule the silver movement:

Four years of free trade racket, of broken banks and
    stores,
Brought thousands to starvation, as beggars to our doors,
But times have changed, O! Bryan, a Chief is in
    command;
Calamity's discharged, Prosperity takes a hand.

We welcome thee, O! Bryan—guest of the millionaires—
We'll join in adulation and mix thee with our prayers;

Its halls, and schools, and churches; its hearts, both old
    and new,
All swell with kindly impulse, and open unto you.
Just bask in daily sunshine; at night repose on down;
No cross of gold shall harm you, no thorns compose
    your crown;
For Bozeman, the Beautiful, [is] a city of renown,
And the writer of this WELCOME is,

ONE WHO NAMED THE TOWN.[28]

Sandwiched between the publication of Davies's and Alderson's poems was Bryan's visit itself. On Friday, August 20, 1897, Bozeman celebrated "Bryan Day." Main Street businesses were adorned with flowers and bunting. Seven thousand people came from throughout the region, the single largest gathering in the young community's history, exceeding the size of the crowd who witnessed the arrival of the railroad and the visit by former president Grant.

The train carrying Bryan, his family, Congressman Hartman, and

Northern Pacific Depot, Bozeman, Montana Territory, c. 1885   F. J. Haynes, photographer. MHS Photograph Archives, Helena H-4651

Senator Mantle arrived at the Northern Pacific Depot early in the afternoon. Thousands were in attendance, including a band and the reception committee. Sheriff William Fransham cleared a path through the excited throng so that Nelson Story could escort Bryan to a waiting barouche, decorated with garlands and pulled by four white horses. The Bryan children took seats in one of two small carts drawn by a Shetland pony, while Mrs. Bryan and her niece joined the ladies of the reception committee in a separate carriage. Led by the band and a military escort, the entourage headed for Main Street and

William Jennings Bryan, 1896
Library of Congress

then on to Charles Hartman's south-side home for lunch. The crowd cheered along the entire route, and the parade went off "without a single hitch or disaster."[29]

After a brief rest, the party continued on to the West Side School. Bryan held on to Story's arm as he climbed to the speaker's podium, where he was welcomed by a loud shout from the multitude, "a veritable sea of uplifted and anxious faces."[30] George Ramsey offered a formal introduction, and after another round of applause and welcoming shouts, Bryan began his speech by asking those shielding the sun with umbrellas to lower them, so all could see and hear.

Bryan, like Story three years earlier, insisted America's switch to the gold standard had primarily benefited foreign creditors and America's upper class, while saddling the farmer with lower crop prices and land values. He reiterated a portion of his now-famous 1896 "Cross of Gold" speech by rejecting the argument that benefits to the wealthy would cascade down to the laborer and farmer. Using a biblical analogy, Bryan noted that Lazarus was satisfied to eat the crumbs from Dives's table, but that the American people were not obliged to eat the crumbs from the businessman's table. Instead, he offered a vision of the social order in which the lower classes were most important:

> Instead of the laborer and the farmer depending upon the business man, they are the foundation of our society . . . the businessman builds upon the structure of the financier instead of on the foundation of the farmer and laboring man. It is like removing a roof from a building. You can easily take off the roof of a building and improve it and rise it, but if you destroy the foundation you destroy the entire building.[31]

To bolster his argument, Bryan quoted an 1890 report by then-congressman William McKinley noting that prosperity in agriculture led to progress in the country's other economic sectors. While acknowledging a recent bump in wheat prices, Bryan attributed the development to the ongoing famine in India rather than the gold standard, contrary to the claims of the McKinley administration. In short, he asserted, bimetallism would make for a fairer nation, allowing the farmer to pay his debts and maintain his property. The gold standard was making Americans poorer and European financiers richer. Rather than appease foreign and domestic business interests, the United States should simply announce it was adopting silver and gold, and invite them to come along.

Bryan's speech lasted an hour and twenty minutes, and was interrupted several times by applause and cheers. He concluded by thanking the Silver Republicans for caring more about their country than their party, and claimed there were now three "great branches of one great medium; the Democratic, Silver Republican Party, and the Populists":

> No matter how long I live, I can never do as much for
> the American people as they have done for me. And if
> you ask me what is my fondest wish and hope; what is
> my highest ambition, I tell you that it is that I may not
> do anything that will alienate my heart from the hearts
> of these people who have fought for the cause that lies
> deepest in my heart.

Mantle and Hartman echoed Bryan's sentiments. Mantle maintained that he never left the Republican Party, but that the Republican Party left him. Bryan introduced Hartman by saluting the congressman for standing as firm on silver as the mountains around Bozeman stood on their bases. Hartman told the audience the Silver Republicans were not a wing of the Republican Party, but altogether separate. Besides, he said, both wings of the Republican Party "bird are yellow."[32]

Afterward, Mr. and Mrs. Bryan were escorted to a hallway in the West Side School to shake hands with well-wishers. They then returned to the Hartman home, where Bryan answered telegrams and letters and received additional visitors while Ellen Story helped entertain the children with a party on the lawn, which had been decorated with electric lights and Chinese lanterns for the occasion. The Bryans spent the night at the Hartman home, catching a train for Billings the next day. While the *Chronicle* praised Bryan's appearance and his speech, the *Courier* predictably ridiculed the effort, calling the talk an "unpolished product of an average school boy."[33]

This visit marked the climax of the silver movement in Bozeman. Nationally, prices for farm produce rose, and with passage of the ultra-protective Dingley Tariff Act, the monetary debate began to wane.[34] In 1898, only ten people, seven Silver Republicans and three spectators, one of them a *Courier* reporter who spotted "that millionaire Story and Bonanza King Chisholm," attended the Silver Republican convention held at the Spieth and Krug building. The meager assembly chose eleven delegates, exceeding the number of those in attendance, to represent the faction at the party-wide state convention. Story and Chisholm were among those selected, but another delegate and two of the alternates had already quit the silver movement and returned to the Republican fold.[35] In something of an about-face, Frank Benepe would join with Bud to publish a pro-silver newspaper, the *Gallatin County Republican,* in 1900, but it failed to rally the support of those who had once been so vociferous for Bryan and bimetallism.[36] Story thereafter abandoned his engagement with the issue, concluding yet another episode in which his undeniable abilities as a man of business failed to translate into the arena of politics.

Chapter Fourteen

Waterloo, 1897–1905

D ESPITE HIS GRUFF PERSONA and his penchant for ruth-
lessness in affairs of business, Story maintained a small
circle of close friends throughout the years, among them
William Alderson, William McKenzie, Lester Willson,
Frank Benepe, and Albert Roecher. He also maintained close ties
with mild-mannered, religious Matthew Bird until the reverend's
relocation to Washington State in 1885. In many ways, Bird was the
complete opposite of Story, yet he shared some of Story's courage.
In the early 1880s, Story and Bird, returning to Bozeman from the
Crow Agency, stopped for dinner at Hoppers Station, a stage stop
just west of Livingston.[1] Upon being seated, Story felt a jab in his side
and, looking down, noticed the octagonal barrel of a Sharps buffalo
rifle. Holding the weapon was a haycutter named Huntsman, whom
Story had recently fired for shortchanging him on deliveries. That
termination had resulted in a fistfight, with Story prevailing. Now
Huntsman had the upper hand, or so he thought. Without warning,
Bird lunged at Huntsman's rifle just as it discharged, causing the
bullet to graze Story's side before penetrating the wall behind him.
Incensed by the wound, Story administered another drubbing of
Huntsman, who thereafter wisely decided to drop the matter.[2]

With the exception of these friends and his family, Story merely
tolerated most people, instead keeping with one of his favorite
maxims: Geoffrey Chaucer's line that "too much familiarity breeds
contempt."[3] At times, however, his usual indifference turned into

Reverend Matthew Bird in Bozeman, c. 1870s. Despite their differences, Story and Bird remained friends until Bird left the area in 1885. D. Marsh, photographer. Museum of the Rockies, Bozeman x85.3.118

unrestrained disdain. Such was the case in 1897, with former cattleman Joe Lindley, when the two began feuding over property near the Bozeman Hotel.

A native of Indiana, Lindley had farmed briefly in Minnesota before graduating from college in Jacksonville, Illinois. He tried farming in Kansas and Colorado over the following months, but was unsuccessful, which he attributed to drought. With the outbreak of the Civil War, Lindley volunteered to serve, and in May of 1861 was mustered into Company K, First Regiment, of the Kansas Volunteer Infantry. He was wounded just a few months later at Wilson Creek, Missouri, and received an honorable discharge. Afterward, he worked as a freighter between Nebraska City and Denver, as well as Salt Lake City and Virginia City, Montana, where, in 1864, he took up residence. His stay there was brief; like so many others, Lindley saw a promising future for himself in the Gallatin Valley, where he farmed and freighted goods to and from Fort Benton. In 1871, Lindley started a cattle operation along the Shields River, declaring himself the "first cattleman of the Yellowstone," which irritated Story, who had established his ranch in the valley five years earlier, to no end. In 1882, Lindley married a widow, Rachel Miles, quit the cattle business, and settled in Bozeman, where he opened an insurance and loan operation while selling real estate on the side. He served two terms as city alderman, and would serve two more.[4]

In January 1891, Lindley and his wife mortgaged six downtown lots housing five bordellos to Nelson Story for five thousand dollars. When Bozeman lost the state capital bid, Lindley wrongly assumed the loan was forgiven.[5] He only made two hundred dollars in payments, which Bine attributed to Lindley's lack of self-control.[6] "Joe used to go down the line to collect rent," he later recalled, "but instead of collecting, the sirens would ply him with ambrosia, braid ribbons in his whiskers, get him stinko and before he could get any money he'd owe them more than they owed him."[7]

Story had warned Lindley three times that the loan was delinquent before he finally foreclosed in August of 1897. Rather than contest the action, Lindley reminded Story of the capital clause, but Story denied that the terms applied, and insisted that the property itself, despite Lindley's investment, "ain't worth a damn."[8] He dismissed his debtor's fears of financial ruin with the cold observation that he could always retire to a soldier's home. The court granted Story a default judgment on September 24.

Contrary to his statements to Lindley, Story saw the bordellos as a solid investment, and he eventually gifted them to Bud. They enjoyed a steady clientele, and Story took pleasure in the fact that patronage from his mill employees represented something of a partial reimbursement for the wages he paid. In 1895, the city council ignored cries from the Citizen's League to close all saloons and brothels, opting instead to collect fines from prostitutes and bawdy house owners.[9] These fines averaged only ten to twenty-five dollars, considerably less than the five-hundred-dollar maximum allowed by a law that also provided for a six-month jail sentence for "renting houses to parties for the purposes of prostitution."[10] Few, if any, of the madams were jailed, and property owners never faced charges. The council acknowledged that bordellos were public nuisances, but continued to allow their operation. In early 1898, Story instructed Bine to paint and re-shingle the buildings, after which he doubled the rents. Lindley demanded restitution, intensifying the conflict with Story.[11]

Joseph Lindley, n.d. Lindley and Story never saw eye-to-eye. MHS Photograph Archives, Helena 943-504

Another feud erupted that fall between Story and August Kling, a manual laborer who had emigrated from Sweden. Story let Kling live in one of his north-side cabins rent-free, hoping he would save enough money to buy the property outright. In October 1897, Story sent four migrant threshers, Albert Garlock, C. V. Boyer, Morris Lemar, and a man known only as "Smith," to room for free with Kling until they found work. Kling, a short-tempered man once arrested for chasing another man with an ax, at first welcomed the new tenants, but after a week grew tired of the company and asked them to leave. His demand was ignored.

On October 25, the men dined heartily on rice, sausage, bacon, lemon jelly, bread, and coffee. Within a few hours, Garlock was seized with cramps. Boyer went to town to find a doctor, only to be stricken by similar symptoms at a Bozeman saloon. He was attended to by Dr. Lewis Safley, while another physician, Charles Chambliss, went to the cabin, where he found Garlock dead. Lemar also grew ill, but both he and Boyer eventually recovered. Suspiciously, only Kling and Smith, who had not consumed the sugar that night, were unaffected by the mysterious affliction. Dr. Frank Traphagen of the agricultural college examined the sugar and determined it had been laced with strychnine. Kling was then jailed until a six-member coroner's jury failed to bring an indictment, although most in the community considered him guilty.[12]

A few weeks later, Story and his sons came to the property to do some field work. After a few hours, they dropped their tools and took a dinner break in Bozeman. When they returned, Story was startled to find his pick covered with animal dung. Knowing immediately who the culprit was, Story tossed the pick to the ground, took off his gloves, pulled out his six-shooter, and yelled at the top of his lungs, "Goddamn Kling!" and headed toward the cabin. While Bine and Walter deterred their father, Bud escorted Kling off the property to a safe haven until he could catch a train to California. The Swede was never heard from again.[13]

THE GALLATIN VALLEY welcomed the onset of the Spanish-American War in April 1898 with a patriotic rally outside the Bozeman Hotel, complete with fireworks and music. More than four hundred men, of whom about eighty hailed from Bozeman, composed the Montana Cavalry.[14] Despite their military academy education, neither Bud nor Bine enlisted, Bine later claiming he only took orders from his father.[15]

Bine, however, had another good reason to remain in Montana while others of his generation heeded the call to arms: his recent engagement to Katherine Ferris. The nineteen-year-old daughter of successful businessman and banker Edward Franklin Ferris, "Kate" briefly taught school after attending the Montana College of Agriculture and Mechanic Arts. She and Bine took serious note of each other while attending the Presbyterian Academy, and during the summer of 1895, Bine bought a spring wagon on his father's account at Benepe-Owenhouse to accompany Kate, her family, and a girlfriend to Yellowstone National Park. During one night's campout, Bine and Kate probably became the first, and perhaps only, couple ever to cook fudge over an open fire within the park's borders. This trip initiated a three-year courtship that culminated with an Episcopalian wedding on May 4, 1898, attended only by family and a few

Bine Story (front row, center) married Kate Ferris (seated, second from left) in 1898. Gallatin Historical Society Museum, Bozeman 6676

close friends. More than one hundred came to the reception at the mansion, and Bine and Kate left late in the evening for a three-week honeymoon in Los Angeles, Nevada, and Utah. When they returned in the summer, Bine began work at the Commercial National Bank and the newlyweds moved into their wedding present from Nelson Story, the house on South Black Avenue recently vacated by the Hogans.[16]

Earlier in the year, Dr. Hogan had been offered a contract surgeon's post in the regular army with the pay of a captain, but he turned it down, instead borrowing twenty thousand dollars from Nelson to settle personal and drugstore-related debts and to move his family to Helena, where he hoped to rebound his lagging medical practice.[17] His personality and East Coast arrogance had alienated many in Bozeman, who did not appreciate his remark, printed in the *Courier,* that "Montana is a fine country, but New York City is the place in which to do business."[18] So, too, did his characterization of Californians as the biggest liars on earth fail to win him friends in the community.[19] After Nelson's assault on Dr. Foster following the disputatious liquidation of the Gallatin Valley National Bank, Hogan was slammed by a *Livingston Post* editorial: "Had he [Story] administered a thrashing to that supercilious son-in-law of his . . . he would probably have been presented with a medal as a token of his good judgment."[20] Hogan's only regular patients were the Storys and Benepes, and, after a few weeks in Helena, Ellen asked him to return to Bozeman to treat her for an undisclosed illness. Following her recovery, Hogan relocated his family to Lewistown, where he would partner with Dr. T. H. Monahan.

But, just like in Bozeman, Hogan's Lewistown practice floundered. Rose missed her parents and the mansion socials. In 1898, she accompanied Nelson and Ellen to the Trans-Mississippi Exposition in Omaha, followed by a trip to New York, in each instance leaving Garrett in Lewistown to care for the children. The birth of Bine and Kate's first child, Katherine, in March 1899 and that of a boy, Nelson Story III, to Bud and Etha the following January, exacerbated Rose's feelings of isolation from her immediate family. His practice's dismal prospects and his wife's unhappiness propelled Garrett to return the family to Bozeman in 1900, where, after briefly contemplating the idea of setting out for the north as part of the Alaska gold rush, he instead accepted reappointment as Bozeman's city health officer. A year later, Rose gave birth to a girl named Amelia.[21]

IN APRIL 1899, Bud, Bine, and their wives attended a fundraiser for the Elks Ladies, at which each received a dollar's fine for "working their father so hard."[22] In actuality, Nelson needed no encouragement, showing little interest in slowing the growth of his commercial empire. He and Bud, having constructed a new storage building at the Bozeman mill, drew plans for a ten-thousand-dollar brick warehouse in Butte to store company flour. Two hundred thousand bushels of Gallatin Valley barley were exported to Europe in 1897, and spring wheat yields were averaging more than thirty bushels an acre. Flour from the Story Mill was being shipped to Portland, Seattle, and San Francisco, and in 1899, the company sold fifteen thousand sacks to markets in Hong Kong. Story & Company now began a heavy advertising campaign to secure business with local producers, promising top dollar for barley as well as offering excellent storage facilities for those waiting for higher prices.[23]

In order to expand his footprint in the industry, Story purchased the Gallatin Mills operation from Perry McAdow, which included eight hundred miner's inches of Bozeman Creek water.[24] The dam used by McAdow was old and in need of repair, so Story decided to relocate the "cut" to Mill Creek further north. The chosen site, partly out of necessity but probably also out of spite, happened to sit on Joe Lindley's land. Story cut down half a dozen of Lindley's cottonwoods with which he built a log-and-sandstone check dam to divert water from Bozeman Creek. Unusually high rainfall caused the ditch to overflow, flooding not only Lindley's land but also a portion of the town's east side. Lindley was not as upset about his cottonwoods as he was the location of the dam, and the fact that Bozeman Creek no longer offered its melodious gurgle at night to help him fall asleep.[25] Ignoring a friend's warning that Story "will put any man in the ditch who stands up against him," Lindley hired blacksmith James Pratt to blow up the structure. When the pipe bomb failed to explode, Story confiscated the device and chained it to a downtown telephone pole to humiliate Lindley.[26] Though the dam was modified to prevent further flooding, city workers tried to dismantle the structure on March 8, 1900. They were chased away by Story, who struck one of the men across his back, for which he was charged with third degree assault.[27]

In response, Story filed a lawsuit seeking damages of one hundred dollars and received a temporary restraining order barring the dam's destruction. The city maintained that Story possessed the right to only 705 inches, and that the dam had to be dismantled as it had caused five hundred dollars' worth of damage to the town's east side. The city also claimed Bozeman Creek was a natural watercourse that required eighteen hundred miner's inches for drainage, and that Story's diversion of an additional ninety-five inches violated an 1893 ordinance that prohibited any obstruction of the creek within city limits.[28] With the lawsuit pending, Story went to court to answer the assault charge. He claimed there was no criminal intent; he had only been attempting to get the workman's attention. Remarkably, a county jury agreed, and acquitted Story of the charge on March 20.[29] The temporary restraining order allowed Story & Company to process 9.6 million pounds of wheat and 4 million pounds of oats in 1900, roughly one-sixth of the valley's total grain production.[30]

The diminished flow of Bozeman Creek, however, caused raw sewage from the Bozeman Hotel, city hall, and the opera house to accumulate and stagnate in the watercourse, producing an unbearable stench and heightening fears of an outbreak of typhoid, diphtheria, or another infectious disease. Five years earlier, after finding most of Bozeman's well water contaminated by cesspools,

Dr. Hogan had urged the city to invest in a sewer system, but his recommendation fell on deaf ears. This time Hogan, seeking to avoid a squabble with his father-in-law and frustrated by the city's foot-dragging, resigned as city health officer. In December, the city council finally acted, passing an ordinance to build a sewer line that would still deposit the sewage into Bozeman Creek, but further downstream. The total cost amounted to $8,300, most of it to be paid by adjacent property owners.[31]

Story demonstrated little concern about the sewage problem, instead focusing his attention on improving several of his Main Street properties. He installed Bozeman's first cement sidewalk in front of the Old Boston Store; designed a one-story, fireproof brick building; and helped Bud complete plans for a foundry capable of high-quality iron work, including what would become the firm's specialty: the production of hay stackers.[32] Story had added additional real estate to his holdings throughout the 1890s, including George Wakefield's Northern Pacific Hotel property. Shortly after his return in October from a month-long visit to Los Angeles, the hotel caught on fire. No alarm bell was sounded, however, ostensibly to avoid panicking a group of Democrats holding a meeting in the nearby opera house. Given that no one was injured, the loss of the structure proved a fortunate turn of events. Story planned to demolish it anyway and replace it with a new, brick commercial building, aptly named the Story Block.[33]

IN EARLY NOVEMBER 1900, Story received a threat through the mail:

> Bozeman, Mont.,
> November 5, 1900
>
> Nelson Story, Esq.
>
> You think that if I cannot stand your indignity, "I may move"—no, here it is: "If Montana is not large enough for you it may be well for you to move out." Business men, and [those] of level heads, have talked it, and it has been said to me, that if I should kill Story "nothing would be done to you," and if you should kill me, it would amount to little so far as I am concerned, but to you it would be that which I told you in the first place, it would be your Waterloo.

The author was Joe Lindley, still beside himself over the dam, but angrier still over the property foreclosure three years earlier.

> You advanced money in my name on the Capital fight on the conditions that it was not to be paid by me unless we won the fight, which is the only condition which I would have done it. It was an understanding between us to that effect; you collected it just the same from me; while I am of the combative [type] when willfully and maliciously imposed on, I have not killed anybody except, under the rules and regulations. No, No, I am getting too old to kill now, except I get crazy and that I do not propose you do, you must open up the dam again or there will be a breezy time.[34]

Many of the sentences in a note sent two days later were written in red ink, Lindley explaining it was "for the same reason a red flag is waved at a bull—to make him mad:"[35]

> Nov. 7th. I have been waiting to see if you would open up the dam of your own accord. I will wait no longer; so get a move on you, or I will blow the dam to ____ and you with it if necessary.
>
> Hoard up your ill-gotten gains, and we will stick it in your 4x6 hole, up on the hill with you.[36]

If Lindley indeed hoped to enrage Nelson Story, he succeeded. On Friday, November 23, Story confronted Lindley outside the post office. The conversation became heated, and after Story ordered him away, Lindley reached for his revolver. But Story drew first, and with his other hand pushed Lindley into Main Street, kicking him three or four times while advising him "not to resent the assault, you cowardly son-of-a-bitch!"[37] The confrontation ended when Lindley retreated to his office. He later filed charges, and the state agreed to prosecute Story for second degree assault.[38]

On January 14, 1901, district judge William Holloway ended the water lawsuit with the city by ruling in Story's favor. Holloway said the original Cover-McAdow water right was vested prior to the issuance of the 1893 ordinance and exempted from the city's 1872 patent. Story could have his eight hundred inches, but no more. Anything left over belonged to the city.[39] The following month, Story again appeared before Judge Holloway, this time facing the assault charge.

Story's mill, with Northern Pacific train cars in front, 1895 Dawes and Davies,
photographer. MHS Photograph Archives, Helena PAc 93-41 F2.2

Both men claimed the other had drawn his gun first. Story produced
the threatening letters as evidence that he was in fear of bodily
harm, and the jury agreed. It deliberated for only ten minutes before
acquitting Story.[40] The dam remained, and Story again escaped
criminal charges. Joe Lindley's slow burn festered.

EXCAVATION for the Story Block on Main Street began in 1901.
Large column pillars and other hardware were cast at the Story
Iron Foundry, where Bud had just installed a new seven-and-a-half-
horsepower electric motor to replace the gas engine.[41] Installation
of a new six-thousand-dollar engine for the Story Mill, along with
some minor upgrades, wrapped up on August 26. Some of the year's
crop had already been stored in the elevator: one hundred thousand
pounds of wheat and seventy thousand pounds of oats.

The following day, while most mill workers were at lunch, a spark
from the new engine fell on a canvas apron close to the dust house,
and within minutes the structure ignited in fire. Workers tried to
subdue the blaze, but by the time firefighters arrived with a hose reel,
hook-and-ladder wagon, and steam-powered fire engine, a southwest
wind had carried the flames to engulf the elevator. Story came on

Story's newly renovated mill caught on fire in 1901. Museum of the Rockies, Bozeman x80.6.25

the scene shortly thereafter, directing and assisting volunteers carrying hoses. Young boys dashed to Bozeman Creek to fill water pails, which they threw on buildings not yet touched by the fire. When it became apparent the elevator could not be saved, the hoses were turned on the office, storage house, and other buildings to prevent them from catching fire. Volunteers moved two carloads of flour out of harm's way, the only contents of the mill that would be saved. So intense was the heat that firefighters doused themselves with water

Nelson Story grilling worker after mill fire,
1901 Schlecten Brothers, photographer. Museum of the
Rockies, Bozeman x80.6.26

to prevent their clothes from igniting. The roar of the flames from inside the elevator was terrific, and observers compared the collapse of its roof to a volcanic eruption. Only two brick warehouses, a part of the engine house, and the boiler were saved. The rest of the facility, including the elevator and flouring plant, was in ashes. Several hundred yards of the foothills east of the mill, the Story Hills, were charred, resembling the aftermath of a prairie fire.[42]

It was the largest and costliest fire in Bozeman's young history, with damages listed at two hundred thousand dollars. The year before, Story had allowed his fifty-thousand-dollar insurance policy to lapse, meaning he would have to absorb the entire loss. This he took in stride, claiming he had saved one hundred thousand dollars in premiums for the mill and other nearby properties.

As area farmers worried about getting their product to market, Story, Bine, Wilbur Williams, and Ed Lamme launched an aggressive bid to buy up shares of the Bozeman Milling Company. By the end of the year, Story controlled four-fifths of the $125,000 initial capital stock. He named Bine company president and gave him $50,000 in stock in what now became Nelson Story & Company, Merchant Millers, Grain Dealers. In its first year, the operation would clear a profit of $75,000, and $85,000 in its second. It had the largest payroll in Bozeman, produced up to 650 bushels per day, and had an overall capacity of 500,000 bushels, including 1,000 barrels of flour and 300 barrels of cereal.[43]

Story's water dispute with John Maxey re-erupted in the summer of 1902. Maxey and some of his neighbors complained that Story was diverting too much water into his ditch, and that the overflow was damaging their property. Story agreed to enlarge the ditch, but did not tell Maxey when he planned to do so. On June 25, as Maxey was irrigating his field, Story shut off the water intake so that his crew could begin work. Maxey confronted Story at the mansion, demanding he restore the water, but Story refused, saying he was only enlarging the ditch as requested. Vowing to restore the water himself, Maxey headed back to the farm, with Story following behind, shotgun in hand. Maxey was armed as well, and, when the altercation came to a head at the ditch site, half a dozen shots rang out. Each man had a grudging respect for the other, however, since Maxey had once worked at Story's mill, so neither fired with deadly aim, although Maxey did sustain a slight foot wound. Story called for a cease-fire, and after a brief cooling-off period restored the water. Neither pressed charges against the other.[44]

On July 31, the city council convened to decide yet another land issue involving Nelson Story. Earlier that year, a Bozeman librarian sent a letter to industrialist-millionaire Andrew Carnegie seeking assistance to build a new library. In March, alderman Joe Lindley received a reply: an offer of $15,000 for construction, provided that annual funding from the city would be a minimum of $1,500. This the city council quickly agreed to, and voters approved a boost in funding from one-half to a full mill.[45] Of the sites under consideration for the new library, one was owned by Story, but local taxpayers were leery of the potential deal. Only a year earlier, school trustees had paid him $2,500 for land just east of the mansion to build the new Gallatin County High School, although three other tracts were cheaper.[46] Since Bud had been elected alderman in April, some believed another dandy land deal for his father, who again sought $2,500 from the city, was a fait accompli.

But the council raised eyebrows when it announced the selection of a nine-hundred-dollar parcel on the north side owned by Elmyra Frazier. The land stood adjacent to Chinatown and the red-light district, Bozeman's "Bad Lands," which now had no fewer than nine "female boarding houses."[47] The location led one dismayed citizen to exclaim, "I don't think Mr. Carnegie meant the library to be used for missionary purposes."[48] Given the earlier controversy surrounding the high school, a majority of the council had been hesitant to purchase another Story-owned parcel, no matter how well-situated. Lindley, unwilling to support any deal with Nelson Story, said the Frazier property was "the best we could agree on at the time."[49] Further complicating the matter was the pressure applied by north-side residents who felt entitled to at least one public building. Of the six councilmen only two, one being Bud, opposed the Frazier site, seeing it as a "penny wise and pound foolish compromise."[50]

The selection reawakened the public outcry about vice in Bozeman, spurring new demands for permanent removal of the city's "objectionable features." Just a few months earlier, madam Lizzie Woods, dubbed by the *Courier* "the fairy queen of the Bad Lands," received a fine of $150 for harboring a fourteen-year-old girl in one of her houses. This generated anxiety about the prospect of children visiting a library so close to the "Tenderloin District."[51] The fear and anger eventually subsided, but not before another call to fine the "demimondes" the maximum allowed under the law and price them out of business.[52]

The controversy spurred Bud to find a buyer for the brothels given to him by Nelson a few years earlier. The madams were paying him $150 per month in rent, but having ties to the red-light district hampered his ability to pursue his own political aspirations. Bud later noted that "the stigma attached to owning such property—that did not compensate a man."[53] Otherwise, his prospects as a candidate for elected office seemed promising. He had a recognizable last name, and his image as a family man was strengthened on August 13, when Etha gave birth to a girl they named Mayo. In November, Bud won a seat in the state House of Representatives. He took a sixty-day leave from the city council, and, accompanied by his father, traveled to Helena on January 3, 1903.[54] Four young boys vying to serve as Bud's page mistook Nelson for Nelson Jr., each receiving the same curt reply: "I am the old man and not in politics . . . go and look up Bud."[55] Bud soon sold the east-side brothels to Robert Dawes for $3,250, and in 1904, won election as the mayor of Bozeman.[56]

After returning home from Helena, Nelson, Ellen, and Walter boarded the North Coast Limited for Los Angeles.[57] While in California, Story wrote Bine with instructions to dispatch two employees to survey the latest industry improvements in Montana and the Midwest to ensure that his own new mill would be the "best and most perfect flouring mill that money would put up."[58] Bine, with Nelson's approval, began the work in the spring, with machinery and fixtures supplied by the Nordyke and Marmon Company of Indianapolis.[59]

During this California trip, Walter married Geraldine "Mamie" Baird of Los Angeles. A year earlier, having completed studies at Shattuck and then at Eastman Business College in Poughkeepsie, New York, Walter became a bookkeeper and teller at the Commercial National Bank. He was often seen proudly driving a Victor Steam Carriage, likely the first automobile to traverse the streets of Bozeman, frightening people and livestock alike.[60] On one occasion, Walter took his father for a spin. Nelson became unnerved when a safety valve popped off and, as soon as the car slowed, he "hit for the timber."[61] Nelson would soon lose his fear of the automobile.

But Walter would forever be plagued by the consequences of his promiscuous bachelorhood, as a case of gonorrhea rendered him infertile, most likely dooming his marriage.[62] It was no doubt on Nelson's mind when he wrongly predicted to Bine that the "poor boy . . . will have a rough time of life."[63] Walter brought his bride to Bozeman that spring, but the two soon decided to make Los Angeles their permanent home.[64]

Back in Bozeman, Nelson Story was making life rough for Joe Lindley. Still smarting from his Main Street rebuke, Lindley continued to send rambling letters to Story while he was in Los Angeles. The first was a copy of one sent earlier to Judge Holloway on July 10, 1902, protesting Story's acquittal by referencing his past confrontations with Bill Carter and John Maxey:

> You were blind to the fact that he can, and does manufacture any evidence desired and that he is the most perjured of the lot. From the earliest days of this territory the revolver has been his constant companion. Early in the

Walter Story is at the wheel of the automobile. Nelson Story and an unidentified woman (possibly Mamie Baird) are passengers. Gallatin Historical Society Museum, Bozeman 3785

60's he crippled his man; as late as the 25th ult. he tried his shotgun on one of our esteemed citizens, in which case he found one he could not bulldoze.[65]

Enclosed with the letter to Holloway was another addressed directly to Story that included references to the Indian Ring, a heretofore unreported assault on Ellen, and the attack on Dr. Foster:

> You who have robbed the government with both hands, bribed U.S. deputy marshals, held up a U.S. army officer (Capt. Ball of 2nd U.S. cav.), attempted to do so because he was true to his trust; . . . you who kicked the prostrate form of the woman you swore to protect; kicked her after knocking her down with that ever-ready revolver. Such an inhuman assault in my judgment is as bad, unpardonable, as the assassination of Lincoln, Garfield, or McKinley.
>
> Now, Sir, I might have added another attack of yours which you made on one of the most respected of our citizens, and with revolver and club you pounded that man over the head while holding him at the point of your revolver.[66]

In a follow-up note, Lindley claimed money had made Story a "miserable man," leading him to treat others as "chaff."[67]

Story found the letters amusing, and forwarded them to the *Gallatin County Republican* and the *Gallatin Farmer and Stockman* in Belgrade to be published as advertisements. In one forwarded to the *Republican* on August 13, 1903, Story referred to his nemesis as "a notorious thief that infested the Shields River country for a number of years and made heroic raids upon the cattle of that locality. This hero sends this to me, evidently for publication in order to establish his heroism."[68] Lindley finally ended his correspondence, but Story was having too much fun. To the *Republican*, he sent another of the letters, written three years earlier, containing a vague proposition: "That you would, cancel the indebtedness, and give me $500 (for the Mort'g; property)."[69] Story saw this as proof that Lindley all along designed to blackmail him, noting in an addendum, "I owe Lindley nothing and am under no obligations to trade property with him or give him anything. Of his hundred or more letters to me, every one has a threat if he is not paid money. How long he is going to keep up this kind of business is hard to tell."[70]

BY 1904, Bozeman's population had reached nearly six thousand. The first tenant in the just-completed, twenty-five-thousand-square-foot Story Block was the Willson Company Store, which boasted among its many amenities a restroom, still something of a novelty in many parts of the West.[71] January saw the dedication of the new Carnegie Library, built of red and white brick and Billings sandstone, which offered a lecture hall of "ample size" and two reading rooms, one for men and the other for ladies and children.[72] The new Story flour mill, "as nearly fire-proof as it is possible to make it," began full operations the first week in April.[73] All told, the reconstruction cost $111,528.59. As promised, the water-powered operation had a capacity of three hundred barrels a day.[74] In Belgrade, where the population now totaled four hundred, Story's elevator had a capacity of 225,000 bushels. Frank Benepe's Gallatin Mill processed four million pounds of barley in 1903, while the Gallatin Valley Milling Company, operated by Oliver Fisher and his three sons, produced more than two hundred barrels daily.[75]

Meanwhile the "vexatious misunderstanding," as the *Avant Courier* called the Story-Lindley squabble, continued.[76] In May, just weeks after Lindley filed a twenty-thousand-dollar damage suit over the "private" letters printed in the *Gallatin County Republican*, Story poured water on Joe's head while Lindley stood on the street beneath his downtown office.[77] This was soon followed by another Main Street confrontation in which Story hit Joe between the eyes with the butt-end of his Colt .44 Dragoon revolver. Lindley let out an agonizing yell and ran across the street to Phillips Bookstore, his Prince Albert coat tails sailing out behind him and Nelson Story in close pursuit. Lindley begged the clerk to "stop him, he is going to kill me!" The clerk, later noting that he did not want Lindley's "inwards" splattered around the store, closed the front door and put his weight against it just as Story reached the entrance. Story managed to push the door partially open and, waving his pistol, demanded the clerk retreat. The man complied, as by then Lindley had escaped through the back door.[78] Bine, who had been in his father's office and heard the commotion, now ran into the store, calmed his father and walked him home for a talk. "I told him this damn fighting settled nothing & we would immediately have Joe arrested & try him for his sanity."[79] From that point forward, Story's Colt, which he had referred to as his "old cannon," became known as the "old Lindleyizer."[80]

The day after the Main Street ruckus, Lindley went to Schlechten's photo studio, smeared ink on his face to give the appearance of a bloody visage, and had his picture taken as evidence of the assault. He then filed charges, and Story was arrested November 21. Bond was set at $1,000 pending a plea, but a few weeks later Story forfeited the bond and left for Los Angeles with Ellen. In February, the court ordered Story to enter a plea by April 1, 1905.[81] Story responded with letters from five Los Angeles physicians who swore that minor heart trouble and a stomach ailment made his return to Montana inadvisable. The court deferred, and allowed Story to appear upon his return later in the spring. Nelson and Ellen returned home on June 2, 1905, and the next day he pleaded guilty to third degree assault, paying a fine of $250.[82]

After receiving still more threatening letters, Story pressed the county attorney to hold insanity hearings for Lindley. The two-day procedure began on June 20.[83] A panel of three physicians, plus a representative of the Warm Springs Asylum, questioned Lindley, and concluded that though he had certainly demonstrated unhinged behavior, there was not enough evidence to declare him mentally unsound. The jury deliberated for several hours before finding Joe Lindley not guilty, and he was released from jail.[84] But the county attorney charged Lindley with extortion, claiming his threatening letters were meant to extract money. In November a jury agreed, fining Lindley five hundred dollars. He defiantly sat in jail for one week before paying the fine.[85]

Though able to continue his insurance business and remain active as a veteran of the Grand Army of the Republic, Joe's spirits never mended.[86] His "Waterloo" for Story did not come to pass, and in fact would prove to be his own downfall. In a 1907 letter to the city council, he called Story a "maligner, blackmailer, perjurer, and wife-whipper."[87] Two years later, when the Storys replaced the cottonwood dam with one of cement and gravel, Lindley blew up the old structure with a homemade explosive. He was convicted of willfully and maliciously destroying property, and fined $250.[88]

Chapter Fifteen

The End of Us All, 1905–1926

THE APRIL 23, 1905, issue of the *Los Angeles Herald* carried an article updating its readers on the progress of construction projects in downtown Los Angeles, in particular those along Main and Broadway Streets. Among the notations was this: "What Nelson Story will do with the southeast corner of Broadway and Sixth, the Lord only knows, but he's rich a-plenty and can do wonders if he wants to. He's the Montana banker, you know."[1] As it turned out, the former Montana banker would be involved with development of the property, but in a subordinate role. A few years earlier, he gave the parcel to Walter, and pledged financial support when his youngest son decided the site was ideal for a commercial retail and office building.

It was the beginning of a number of generous gifts to all of the Story children, with Bine receiving a Spring Street parcel valued at $190,800 and Bud the lot near the future Arcade Theater site, worth $30,000, as well as another at Fifth and Spring adjoining the Alexandria Hotel.[2] In addition, Bud became vice president of the Bozeman Milling Company and bought $50,000 worth of company stock from Nelson for $38,000 in cash.[3] Rose and Garrett took ownership of the family's winter home on West Adams so they could relocate permanently to Los Angeles. Story paid half their moving expenses, and also promised Garrett stock in a Los Angeles hospital.[4] But his mood soured after the Hogans complained that the home's roof leaked. As far as Nelson was concerned, the ungrateful couple should pay for any repairs and upkeep.[5] In a letter to Bine, Story wrote that the two "can help themselves a little at least and not go to the beach and sit around idle the year around." He regretted another gift to Rose, the Story Block in Bozeman, believing Hogan "has played every trick and plan[s] to get hold of my property . . . he has been a secret enemy to all of us and naturally so." Nelson considered cutting them off entirely, as "poverty makes dogs gentle and that is the only remedy for the Hogan outfit."[6] Despite his harsh words, Rose would soon receive from her father a commercial building on Spring Street.[7]

Nelson Story turned sixty-seven in 1905, but age did little to slow his pace. He accompanied his old Leavenworth friend Tom Allen to the Portland Exposition in Oregon, making various stops in California, and, together with Ellen, hosted his brother Elias and his wife on a visit from Ohio.[8] He also served as pallbearer at the July funeral of Wilbur Fisk Sanders in Helena, and before returning home made plans for his and his family's final rest by purchasing a twenty-thousand-pound block of granite—believed the largest ever sold in the state to that time—from the Montana Monument Works to mark the family plot at Blackmore Cemetery.[9]

In December, Nelson and Ellen again departed Bozeman for Los Angeles. On this and all subsequent trips, they stayed at either the Lankershim or Hayward Hotel.[10] This was a brief visit for Ellen, as she opted to return to Montana alone in February 1906 to hear Bud's keynote address during the annual meeting of the Pioneers' Society of Gallatin County, an affiliate of the Society of Montana Pioneers, of which Ellen and Nelson were charter members. Mayor Bud Story told the one hundred–plus attendees that the soldiers at Fort Ellis had saluted his birth with a volley of cannon fire, and the report had nearly knocked his mother from her bed. Ellen never corroborated Bud's tale, and for good reason: given the opinions army officers held of Nelson Sr., it was probably fictional.[11]

The annual sojourns the Storys and other "snowbirds" made to California played a role in establishing a tradition that, despite a lengthy hiatus, became Bozeman's annual signature event. When wealthy Montanans returned from California, they shared descriptions of the La Fiesta de Los Angeles and the Rose Carnivals of Santa Rosa and San Jose. This inspired the *Courier* to crusade in 1896 for a flower festival that would not only draw tourists, but also offer "elevating, artistic and educative influence" for Bozeman residents.[12] A lack of interest tabled the idea until 1906, when the newly formed Civic League decided to promote an event celebrating the sweet pea flower. In April, the league, backed by several local businesses, announced that the Bozeman Sweet Pea Carnival would occur the weekend of August 11.[13]

On the appointed day, a mixture of sweet peas and other flowers, as well as pink, green, and white bunting decorations, festooned Main Street businesses. A carriage carrying Mayor Bud Story, Senator Thomas Carter, and several other dignitaries led a mile-long parade of nearly 140 floats. Sweet Pea Queen Kathryn Hanley, chosen by popular vote of the community, had her own carriage, escorted by trumpeters dressed in medieval costumes and maids of honor. It took forty-five minutes for the procession to travel west on Main Street to the new high school. Next came the queen's coronation in Bogert Park, a baseball game in which Bozeman defeated Livingston

Sweet Pea Festival (Carnival) parade on Main Street, Bozeman, 1906. Museum of the Rockies, Bozeman x83.13.131

Pioneer Jubilee, 1914. In the center are Nelson and Ellen Story. Gallatin Historical Society Museum, Bozeman 12338

16–15, and demonstrations by drill teams and the Bozeman Fire Department's hook-and-ladder squad. The evening featured musical concerts, a "battle of the flowers" with carnival goers pelting one another with sweet peas and confetti, and two festive balls.[14]

A few months later, Nelson Story was elected to a two-year term as president of the Pioneers' Society of Gallatin County. In his November 24 acceptance speech, he called for an end to "strife and enmity," urging the remaining pioneers to "work together harmoniously for the good of all."[15] The source of the ill-will to which he referred remained unspecified, although there were any number of likely guesses: his ill-gotten gains, the waterworks controversy, his mill's part in the floods on the east side, or his dubious treatment of Joe Lindley. Story's call for reconciliation in the community may have stemmed from a realization that his best years were behind him, a point driven home not only by the death of Sanders, but also the recent passing of William Davies and William Alderson.[16] Story was especially close to Alderson, having just helped him merge the

Avant Courier and the *Gallatin County Republican* into the *Republican-Courier*, where Alderson remained managing editor until his death in October.[17]

❖

NELSON AND ELLEN's wealth gave their children a leg up in life, but Bud, Bine, and Walter deserve credit for their ambitions and energy. In 1906, Walter was ready to break ground at Sixth and Broadway, but Nelson, fearing inflated material costs after the San Francisco earthquake, talked him out of it.[18] Walter briefly partnered with Arthur Tandy in a real estate firm before breaking out on his own, and over the next few years he fine-tuned the drawings and design for an eleven-story skyscraper to be called the Walter P. Story Building.

He borrowed half of the one-million-dollar budget from his father, the other half from area bankers. The two-year-long construction period began on April 1, 1908. The steel alone cost $143,000, the marble work $77,650.[19] Twelve plate glass windows, valued at $1,000 each, and the largest in any building west of Chicago, were installed on the ground floor. The Mullen & Bluett Clothing Company leased the basement and first floor for $48,000 a year, while a variety of firms and businesses snatched up the four hundred office spaces on the remaining floors, totaling an annual rental income in excess of $300,000.[20]

In Bozeman, Bud and Bine were able to flaunt their success by moving their families into better homes. Ornate and elegant residences lined Bozeman's south side in the early 1900s, with the finest on South Central Avenue, soon to be renamed South Willson. They were larger and incorporated the Queen Anne,

The Walter P. Story Building in Los Angeles, California California History Room, California State Library

Colonial Revival, and Mission Revival styles. In 1910, Bine built a three-story, twenty-two-room late Victorian mansion on South Central Avenue. The 19,500-square-foot residence featured a ballroom on the third floor and a 4,600-square-foot carriage house.[21] By now,

Members of the Gallatin County Farmers' Alliance drive wagonloads of grain down Main Street, Bozeman, 1905. Schlecten Brothers, photographer. Museum of the Rockies, Bozeman 92.36.1

Bine and Kate had four children: Katherine, Byron, Malcolm, and Virginia.[22] Bine hired two maids to assist Kate, African American Frances Miller and her daughter Viola. Bud and Etha owned a home on South Grand, but after the death of Etha's father in 1907, her mother, Ella, had moved into the household.[23] With two young children, Nelson Story III and a daughter named Mayo, they too wanted more room, and Etha successfully pressed Bud to buy Oliver Fisher's luxurious South Central home, kitty-corner from Bine and Kate, when Fisher moved his family to Seattle.[24] Like his brother, Bud hired a maid, German immigrant Emilie Walshfer [25]

Oliver Fisher was the owner of the Gallatin Valley Milling Company, and prior to his relocation to Seattle, the Story boys invested thirty-five thousand dollars in new equipment and a warehouse to compete with Fisher's four new elevators along the Gallatin Valley

Railway between Salesville and Manhattan. Shipping connections for Gallatin Valley produce received a boost in 1908 when the Chicago, Milwaukee, St. Paul & Puget Sound Railway, soon to be known as the Milwaukee Road, purchased a rail line north of Gallatin County to connect with its transcontinental route to Puget Sound. The railroad soon extended the line to Three Forks and, eventually, other points in the valley.[26] In 1909, Bine hired close friend and Belgrade State Bank cashier Charles Vandenhook as company treasurer and operations manager for the mill. Vandenhook quickly established a five-hundred-thousand-dollar line of credit with a bank in Saint Paul, Minnesota, allowing the Storys to purchase new machinery and add a cereal mill closer to town with a capacity of two hundred barrels a day.[27] By the end of the year, the mill marketed the Ceretana flour brand in attractively designed bags promoting the "Famous Gallatin Valley, the Egypt of America."[28] The upgrade, along with Bine's decision to widen Mill Creek to prevent any more east-side flooding, was intended to stave off competition from the Farmers & Merchants Elevator in Bozeman, now owned by the Farmer's Alliance of Gallatin County.[29]

Though Story had turned the operational reins over to his sons, he still felt the need to call the shots. In 1911, after architect Fred Willson completed blueprints for the mill's new warehouse, Nelson looked them over and told Bud and Bine the foundation was not heavy enough. "Here's an architect," Bine answered, "who knows his business. If the foundation you want had been the proper foundation, he would have increased the foundation to that size." The patriarch, however, refused to budge, even as Bud warned that a heavier foundation would increase costs. "Well," said Nelson, "you'll build that foundation the way I want it."[30] While Nelson entertained his visiting brothers with various outings, among them a gopher-shooting contest, Willson changed the plans.[31]

Shortly after Byron and Elias departed, Story decided to make one last trip to Ohio. After taking in a speech by President William Howard Taft at the Northern Pacific Depot on October 19, 1911, Nelson, without Ellen, headed for Meigs County.[32] Grandniece Emma Gorsuch was awed by "Uncle Nelt," but surprised by his demands for clean underwear and sheets each day. "Strange for a man used to the rough life of a cowboy," she mused, "but I guess all that was behind him then."[33] Shortly after Nelson's return to Bozeman, Elias suffered a massive stroke and died on December 31. His daughter Nora attended the funeral in Ohio, but with Rose visiting for the holidays, Nelson stayed home.[34]

In 1912, Nelson and Ellen made plans for their last visit together to Los Angeles, Story having decided that "one place is enough for anyone to confine his attentions to."[35] For him, that place was Bozeman. Prior to their departure, Bud and Bine stopped by the mansion and found their mother in tears, claiming Nelson had abused her. These incidents had continued sporadically through the years. Twice Ellen had appeared at the Hogan home seeking sanctuary, and to Garrett's credit, he stood by his mother-in-law each time she defied Nelson's orders to return to her own home.[36] In this instance, Bud and Bine finally took action. They cornered their father in the basement and forced him to come upstairs and apologize. True to his defiant nature, Story became belligerent, swearing at Ellen and acting as if he would strike her. The two grabbed him, and Bud inadvertently cut Nelson's cheek with a gold ring Ellen had purchased for him in Mexico.[37] Later, Bud tried to apologize, but Nelson waved him off, telling his son, "That's alright, just don't think anything about it. I would not have much regard for a boy that didn't stand up for his mother."[38]

When the Storys returned from California, Nelson flew into another rage after learning one of Ellen's milk cow calves had died. He stomped about the mansion, blaming his sons and calling them damn fools, and swore they would receive no more money. But, like the earlier confrontation, all was soon forgiven, and Story divided a good deal of his Bozeman area property between Bud and Bine in 1913, who both agreed to pay him and Ellen five hundred dollars a month in return.[39]

For the balance of the decade, Nelson and Ellen remained close to home. In 1914, Bozeman hosted the golden anniversary of Montana Territory and silver anniversary of statehood with the largest barbecue in Montana to date, requiring eight of the best Gallatin beeves, twenty fat sheep, fifteen hundred pounds of bread, and twelve thousand "great big baked potatoes."[40] The Storys entertained Nelson's brother Byron during the event, and received a courtesy call from fellow old-timers Conrad Kohrs, Martin Maginnis, and Granville Stuart.

Ellen occasionally joined her husband for car rides, the most notable being an excursion to Virginia City with Bud and Etha for a look at the "old neighborhood."[41] Once, while being chauffeured by his driver Bernard Meade, Story became angry when the gears clashed on a downhill slope. Meade claimed it was unavoidable as the transmission was a little touchy. As the car approached Bine's home, Story noticed his grandson Malcolm and a few friends tossing around a football. He ordered Meade to stop and bring Malcolm to the car. As the unsuspecting boy approached, he heard a gruff order from Nelson: "Get in. Drive!" Young Malcolm took the wheel while Meade sat in the passenger seat. "Drive down Cleveland!" Malcolm complied. "Turn on Church . . . head for the Administration Building!" As the car approached the same slope, the gears again clashed when Malcolm downshifted. Meade, having been vindicated, breathed a sigh of relief as the car stopped at Malcolm's home, where Story gave one last command: "Out!"[42]

Nelson took daily walks in downtown Bozeman, his head always covered by a flat-topped Stetson.[43] "He was a dignified old gentleman with a long, white beard, and always dressed in dark blue broadcloth and highly polished boots," wrote an observer. "He never had a pair of shoes on in his life, and his home was full of boot jacks."[44] Story enjoyed making courtesy calls on friends from years gone by, swapping stories and memories of Bozeman's early days. But with the passage of time, the number of fellow pioneers became fewer and

View of Bozeman from Story Hills, 1915. Frank Benepe's grain elevator near the Northern Pacific Depot is visible in the foreground and the agricultural college is in the center. Museum of the Rockies, Bozeman x80.6.216b

fewer. Among the departed was Joe Lindley, who died at his Boze-man home of heart failure on December 29, 1915. Upon hearing the news, Nelson Story wept.[45]

BUD STORY had three main passions: sports, the outdoors, and cars. He served as president of the Intermountain Baseball League in 1909, the same year he captured the Northwest Sportsmen's Asso-ciation's highest shooting honor, the Globe Trophy, in Walla Walla, Washington.[46] In 1912, he founded a wholesale and retail automobile business, the Story Motor Supply Company, that soon specialized in servicing Cadillacs, Studebakers, and Fords.[47] Two years later, Bud purchased a several-hundred-acre ranch in the Gallatin Canyon that bordered Yellowstone National Park, won election to the Gallatin County commission, became exalted ruler of the Bozeman Elks Lodge, and agreed to a term as president of the Gallatin Auto Club.[48] Though he won notice for a record-setting 224-mile round-trip from Bozeman to Henrys Lake, Idaho, in one day, Bud was a careless driver. He once lost control of his vehicle and rolled down an eighteen-foot embankment, miraculously sustaining only a few bad bruises. He later ripped out the oil pan of his Mitchell automobile in a failed attempt to drive into the West Fork Basin of Gallatin Canyon.

Bud's political experience as alderman, mayor, state represen-tative, and now county commissioner propelled his candidacy for lieutenant governor in 1916. Those hopes were dashed, however, when he and fellow commissioners Charles Callaghan and Charles Overstreet were ousted in September by Helena judge Robert Word, son of Sam Word, who agreed with a grand jury that all three had ille-gally collected per diem fees over several days when viewing county roads. In Bud's case, the amount was substantial: $3,409.40.[49]

Bine, though an avid bicyclist, focused his attention on busi-ness.[50] In 1912, after the Milwaukee Road announced plans to build a second spur line to the facility, he expanded the elevator capacity to five hundred thousand bushels. Soon the Story operation was shipping flour and cereals throughout the United States and as far away as Japan. In 1916, after becoming president of the Boze-man Chamber of Commerce, Bine purchased Peter Koch's interest in a sheep company formed years earlier in partnership with John Work. Upon Work's death, his interest went to his son Lester, and in November of 1916, Bine gave Koch $50,000 worth of preferred stock bearing 8 percent annual interest. Bine and Lester changed the

Bozeman Canning Company MHS Photograph Archives, Helena 940-528

name to the Story-Work Sheep Company, a livestock operation with a primary focus on wool production. Nelson put up $192,500 worth of bonds in 1917 as collateral, and Bine agreed to pay his father an additional $4,437.50 on July 1 and January 1 annually.[51] Bine and Lester purchased the 27,222-acre Clear Range Ranch in the Smith River Valley, together with fifteen thousand sheep, one hundred forty cattle, seventy-five horses, twelve hundred tons of hay, and assorted equipment for several hundred thousand dollars. The two then sold 4,500 yearling ewes to a Helena firm for $36,000, and before the year was out, the company sold a quarter million pounds of wool to an eastern buyer.[52]

The following year, Bud, Bine, Lester Work, and a few others formed a pea-processing firm, the Bozeman Canning Company. The men had eyed the possibility since the spring of 1911, when the Jerome B. Rice Seed Company of New York secured contracts to plant seed peas on three thousand acres of Gallatin Valley farmland. By the end of that year, several Manhattan farmers had reaped anywhere from forty to fifty bushels an acre at $1.80 per bushel. In 1913, seventeen thousand acres were planted, allowing the Gallatin Valley to produce 75 percent of the seed peas raised in the United States. Plans called for the hire of fifty men and women to work in

Bozeman Milling Company building, c. 1910 Museum of the Rockies, Bozeman 85.44.56

the cannery to be built near the mill, with the first year's capacity at one million cans.[53]

To lighten their load, the Story brothers accepted an offer from the Montana Milling Company to buy the Bozeman Milling Company for $375,000. By that time, they and their new partners, Van and Chester Sweet, had acquired all interest in the mill from Nelson, Wilbur Williams, and Ed Lamme. The deal closed on June 19, 1919. At the time, the mill employed seventy-five men and women, so with other mills in Great Falls, Harlowton, and Lewistown, the Montana Milling Company, known also as the Montana Flour Mills Company, became the largest operation between the Twin Cities and Seattle. Bud and Bine purchased stock in the new venture, and Bine stayed on as one of the directors.[54]

Due in large part to World War I, the Sweet Pea Carnival was discontinued, and a poor crop yield in 1919 led to the cancellation of the county fair.[55] To fill the void with some form of entertainment, Bud organized the first annual "Wildest West Roundup," and purchased enough lumber to build a twenty-thousand-seat arena at the north-side fairgrounds. The show, featuring "the greatest riders, ropers, and bulldoggers in the world," entertained thousands in mid-August, and together with the state Elks convention, drew twelve thousand visitors.[56]

While organizing the roundup, Bud and Bine decided Bozeman needed yet another entertainment venue. The opera house's seating capacity no longer met demand, and patrons frequently were turned away. With the rising popularity of motion pictures, Bozeman's movie houses, the Lyric and Gem Theaters, also struggled to keep pace.[57] Together with the Gem's owners, Howard Greene, Erwin Kleinschmidt, and Otto Schmidt, the Storys invested one hundred thousand dollars to build a new Main Street theater—one that could showcase movies, vaudeville acts, major dramas, and musicals—that would also serve as a lasting tribute to their mother.[58] Designed by architect Fred Willson, the Ellen Theater featured ornamental cornices, terrazzo floors, glass-paneled doors, marble walls, a balcony, theater boxes, dressing rooms, and a second-floor banquet and dance hall. Overall seating capacity exceeded eight hundred. The

The Ellen Theater, shown here in 1931, is still operating today. F. Bertil Linfield, photographer. Museum of the Rockies, Bozeman x83.13.38

Ellen opened on December 1, 1919, with the photoplay *The Miracle Man*, starring Lon Chaney. Vaudeville productions were booked for Friday nights, and within a few years the Ellen rendered the Lyric and Gem Theaters nearly obsolete.[59]

ROSE made it a point to visit her parents nearly every year. Though Garrett's eyesight was faltering due to the onset of glaucoma, he realized a modicum of success by investing in the fish-canning industry.[60] The first two ventures were salmon-canning operations in Eureka and Wilmington, California, his investment in the latter alone being twenty thousand dollars.[61] Later, he put money in a tuna-canning plant.[62] Still, he had nowhere the foothold in Los Angeles as that of Walter, and he turned again to his father-in-law for assistance, discreetly doing so through his wife.

Rose, claiming she and Garrett were tired of the constant repairs to their Los Angeles home, asked her mother if she and Nelson would buy them a different house. In 1918, while Walter was visiting, Ellen persuaded her three boys to broach the subject with Nelson. Walter was chosen the spokesman because, according to Bud, "he was the smallest and the old man probably would not jump onto him so hard, we figured."[63] But when Walter made the proposition, Story flew into a rage. He broke the armrest on his chair and told his boys he was still the boss and the Hogans had received all they were going to get. Rose didn't need a new home, Story said, since the one they had "was alright for me, I cannot see why it isn't good for them."[64]

Rose fared better in 1919. While Garrett took Amelia to New York City to resume studies at Jessica Finch's post-secondary school, Rose received four parcels of commercial real estate in downtown Bozeman. Story was still hesitant to put any more property in the hands of the Hogans, but he again yielded.[65]

Bine's financial situation also started to weigh on Nelson's mind. Suspecting a collapse in prices at the conclusion of World War I, he had advised Bine to curtail his involvement in the wool industry. Bine, however, remained confident in his operation's future. At one point, the company ran fifty-three thousand head of sheep and produced up to 225,000 pounds of wool annually, 10 percent of Montana's total wool production during the war. In 1919, they purchased thirty thousand acres near the Clear Range Ranch from John Ringling for one million dollars to accommodate their herd, which by then had grown to one hundred thousand head.[66]

But just as Story feared, the price of wool began a steady drop in May of 1920. Sheep once valued at $20 to $22.50 a head were worth only $3.50 to $5 a head when the market bottomed out in November 1921. Toward the end of the year, Lester severed all ties with the company, now in debt to the tune of $307,326.69. Imports of inexpensive foreign wool had Montana sheep men, including Bine, lobbying Congress to pass an emergency tariff. Many blamed the government for placing price controls in 1918 that left them selling wool at prices 10 to 20 percent less than that on the open market. The Montana Wool Growers Association cut wages for sheepherders and ranch hands, and since the association effectively functioned as a trust, workers were hard-pressed to earn more than the set rate of forty to fifty dollars per month.[67] Bine was slowly going broke, the stress making him "a physical and mental wreck."[68] To keep afloat, he and Kate sold their mansion to the Sigma Alpha Epsilon fraternity in 1922, and rented a house one block to the north. Though Peter Koch had died in 1918, Bine still owed his widow Laurie interest on the wool stock. Nelson, his differences with Peter long forgotten, liquidated some property and paid the obligation.[69]

Walter, too, was about to face adversity, but not to the same degree. After his discharge from the service in World War I, Walter received a commission as an infantry captain in the California National Guard in December 1920. A year later he was promoted to the rank of major and organized a new infantry company that would evolve into the Third Separate Battalion. He also organized Battery A of the California Field Artillery, and took command of the 160th Infantry of the California National Guard, later given the honorary title of Los Angeles's Own. Despite these accomplishments, his personal life was crumbling as his marriage eroded and ended in divorce. Walter turned his attention to Italian actress Marie Louise Lorenn, who had landed a few minor roles in Hollywood under the screen name of Lorenza Lazzarini. The two married, and by the early 1920s split their time between a sixteen-acre country estate and ranch house outside Hollywood and a luxurious penthouse on the top floor of the Walter P. Story Building.[70]

Bud, meanwhile, took another crack at political office. Having helped establish the Bozeman Rotary Club and serving as president of the Montana Highway Improvement Association, he again sought the Republican nomination for lieutenant governor. The GOP gubernatorial candidate was former congressman and senator Joseph Moore Dixon, and together the two promised to stem the rising tide of socialist groups like the Industrial Workers of the World, the American Society of Equity, and the Nonpartisan League. They hosted a rally on September 29, 1920, at Bozeman's Gem Theater. Seated on stage in a huge leather chair, Nelson listened as Bud promised to deal with the radicals much like his father had the Virginia City road agents when he pulled the box out from underneath George Ives.[71] Dixon and Story went on to victory in November.

Bine managed to hold on financially. He borrowed money from Kate's family and deeded his Spring Street commercial building in Los Angeles to Walter, who paid off the six-hundred-thousand-dollar mortgage and later used the site to construct the Los Angeles Stock Exchange.[72] This allowed Malcolm, after graduating from the Culver Military Academy in June of 1921, to enroll at Eastman Business College. Daughter Katherine, having studied at the American Conservatory of Music in Chicago for one year, was able to continue her studies in Portland, where she sang in the 1921 Portland Rose Festival.[73] But Nelson decided to rework his estate primarily to ease Bine's situation and hopefully limit any future meddling by Garrett Hogan. In a letter to Walter, he stated the Hogans "are all able to work and earn their bread and should make an effort before all is gone."[74]

A will he had drawn up in 1910 proclaimed that his children had all received enough, and that the full value of his estate should go to Ellen. His new will substituted "sons" for "children." Ellen was to receive a life estate in all of Story's property with "the net rents, issues and profits derived therefrom during her life." Upon Ellen's death, the estate was to be divided in half. Walter was named trustee for Rose's half, and, upon her death, the remainder would go to her four children. Kate was named trustee for the other half, which was to benefit her children. But unlike Rose, Kate could use income from her share for personal needs. Bine's name was omitted to deter creditors from the sheep debacle. Another provision called for Bine and Walter to divide the property among the trustees should Ellen die before Nelson. Story told attorney Roy Keister, who wrote the will, that he had wanted Bine to have more, but his son refused.[75]

Story executed a new agreement with Bud and Bine in 1923 that acknowledged total receipts from Bine of $72,625 and $63,000 from Bud. He now gave each of them securities worth the respective amounts, so long as he and Ellen received the interest. Bine also received stocks, bonds, and a promissory note, Bud a bank certificate of deposit. Story felt the boys had earned these securities because both had abided by the 1913 contract, and Bine, in his view, had lived up to the 1917 arrangement. The 1923 agreement called for Kate to receive the securities upon the death of Nelson and Ellen to settle outstanding debts with the Ferris family.[76]

These arrangements, particularly the latter, helped Bine rebound. A few years later, with the help of Bud, Roy Keister, and attorney Hubert Bath, he formed a general trade, real estate loan, construction, and auctioneering concern, Story Land & Livestock. He and Bud also purchased shares in a Madison County placer operation they named the Mayo Mining Company.[77]

IN APRIL OF 1922, Nelson and Ellen became great-grandparents with the birth of Nelson Story IV, or "Fourthy."[78] By then, Ellen rarely left the mansion, often confined by various illnesses that included chronic appendicitis. She and Nelson had private nurses, and on those days when she was bedridden, Story made it a point to visit her room and talk while sitting on the side of her bed. He tried to stay busy. At age eighty-five, he climbed onto the mansion's roof to repair a leak.[79] Still, his health waned, and he became susceptible to colds. In 1923, his physician, J. Franklin Blair, drained an abscess on his neck, and after his recovery he felt well enough to take a car ride with Bine, telling Ellen afterward, "Mother, we've been on a forty-five-mile drive, and I'm just as good a man as I ever was."[80]

Story, though, remained dogged by hemorrhoids, a swollen prostate, and pain in his bladder and kidneys. He also had trouble controlling his bowels, and suffered from frequent bouts of coughing and hiccupping. He usually cupped his ear during conversations, but never complained, telling an acquaintance at least he did not have to listen to local gossip. Story often refused to take his prescribed medicines unless thoroughly coaxed by his nurses or physician. His worry over Ellen made him anxious, and according to Dr. Blair, he was very excitable and emotional. He ate his dinners at 4:00 PM, retired early and slept late, usually taking breakfast at 10:00 AM. When he felt up to it, he took walks through the house and, weather permitting, in the yard, using a cane.[81]

Tragedy would only worsen Nelson's anxiety. Bud, now president of the Pioneer Construction Company, had recently established the Story Rock Crushing Plant. Nelson III moved to Helena to oversee its operations. On Tuesday evening, September 25, 1923, he was returning from an outing in Helena with three friends when their car crashed on a muddy road. One man was killed, but Nelson III and the other two eventually recovered.[82] This mishap was a prelude to a more serious accident. On November 2, Bud and Etha were returning to Bozeman after visiting Walter in Los Angeles. Following lunch in McCammon, Idaho, Bud, anxious to get home, sped the Cadillac Roadster toward Pocatello. He successfully negotiated the first of a pair of curves in the road, but accelerated too quickly as he came to the second, causing him to lose control. The roadster veered off the road when the brakes locked, and the car rolled twice down a ten-foot embankment. Bud and Etha were both thrown from the vehicle, and Etha died at the scene. Scaling the embankment, Bud managed to signal for help before collapsing into unconsciousness and an "irrational state." He would spend weeks recovering in a Pocatello hospital.

Etha's body arrived in Bozeman by train on November 6, and was taken to the family residence on South Willson, where she lay in repose pending the funeral. Family members came to Bozeman from across the country, including her daughter Mayo, then attending college at the University of Wisconsin. Bud, visited by Walter and Etha's brother Harry in Pocatello, was unable to make his wife's funeral. The service was officiated by Reverend William Faber of Helena, Episcopal bishop of the Diocese of Montana. Nelson and Ellen attended, as did hundreds of locals and others from across the state, including Secretary of State Charles Stewart. Etha was laid to rest in the family plot. Bud returned to Bozeman later in the month, and Nelson visited him nearly every day during his recuperation.[83]

On February 9, 1924, Ellen Story's health finally gave out, and she died at the mansion at the age of seventy-nine. The woman who had endured the hardship of the frontier, the heartbreak of losing several children, and a husband who was both abusive and an able provider of untold comfort, had gone to her last reward. Nelson, fighting an illness of his own and confined to the mansion, was with his wife when she passed. Housekeeper Lizzie Long recalled how Nelson remarked tearfully while the two of them viewed Ellen's body that his wife's death meant "the end of us all."[84] The funeral was February 12, during which all stores in Bozeman paid tribute to Ellen Story by closing for business. Following an Episcopalian service in the mansion, she was laid to rest in the family plot. Immediately after the service, Rose took possession of some of her mother's clothes and jewelry.[85]

Bud, still suffering from the loss of his wife and mother in the span of four months, spent several weeks in Los Angeles, hoping the warmer weather and sunshine might hasten his recovery. Upon his return in April, he required minor intestinal surgery at the Murray

Likely the last photograph of the Story family together, taken in the early 1920s. Back, left to right: Thomas Byron Story (Bine), Rose Story, Walter Perry Story, Nelson Story II (Bud); front: Nelson Story, Ellen Trent Story. Yellowstone Gateway Museum, Livingston YGM_2006.044.3022

Hospital in Butte.[86] Bine, Kate, and their teenaged daughters Virginia and Winifred moved into the mansion to help care for Nelson. Bine and Kate repaired leaks in the roof and purchased new drapes and wallpaper. They installed adjustable shutters and an intercom system that connected virtually every room as well as the barn. They maintained the chicken coops, but Bine sent his mother's milk cow to graze near the mill, complaining that the animal drew too many flies. Nelson moved into his wife's room, and in June fired nurse Emma Parkins, who constantly squabbled with Kate over his care.[87]

Depression seized Nelson over the next several months. At one point he told Bud that "this god damned job of trying to die" was the hardest he had ever tackled.[88] Poor health confined him mostly to the mansion, and he spent many hours bedridden. He was demanding on his three private nurses, insisting someone keep him company at all times. Story would talk incessantly to Bine, the staff, and visitors about his crossing the Great Plains to Colorado, or driving the herd to Montana. He once grabbed the slumbering Frank Benepe by the lapel during one of these talks, shook him until he awoke, and then finished the tale. His walks were mostly limited to short strolls in the mansion yard on sunny days. Other times, Bine took him in a wheelchair, and Kate occasionally brought him with her to downtown Bozeman, where he sat in the car while she shopped.[89]

In 1925, at the urging of Walter and Rose, Story agreed to return to Los Angeles in hopes that the gentler climate might improve his health. Accompanied by Bine and nurse Sue Eaton, Story boarded a train on November 13, and three days later Walter met the party at the Los Angeles train station. Nelson walked off the train on the arm of Eaton, and, though he felt well, was taken by wheelchair to a waiting limousine and driven to the nursing-home wing of Angelus Hospital. Rose opposed the arrangement, instead wanting to house her father and his nurses in an apartment near her mansion. Walter felt his father could receive "special treatment" at the hospital and visited him three to four times per day, at one point buying him a new set of teeth and a new set of glasses.[90] Rose also visited daily, recalling that on one visit Story told her, "This is a very nice place for old people. I see many old people here."[91] She also arranged visits for him to her home, and occasionally took him for rides around Los Angeles.

CONSIDERING the many enemies that he accumulated throughout his lifetime, not to mention the perils of Bleeding Kansas, Alder Gulch, the Bozeman Trail, and the Yellowstone Valley, Story lived a remarkably long life. But on March 10, 1926, at 5:45 AM, he died at the Angelus Hospital, just three weeks shy of his eighty-eighth birthday. Bud was at his ranch and Bine in Los Angeles, having spoken to Nelson only hours before his death. Walter and the Hogans selected the coffin from a Los Angeles funeral home, and the train carrying Nelson Story's body reached Bozeman in the morning on Monday, March 15. Walter and Rose were also on board, accompanied by their spouses. Following the service, the coffin was hermetically sealed and transported along Main Street, lined by hundreds of people, to the cemetery, where Nelson Story was buried next to Ellen.[92]

Afterword

Trusted Son

As I knew father Story he always had dignity, more than any
of his sons have. They all have had in greater or less degree the
great streak of wit and repartee. Nelson was a very complicated
character. Utterly ruthless when mad and at such times he was
always on the defensive and attacking the offender with any
weapon at hand. The knife used at the gate when he left home,
the brick thrown at Bine in the barnyard. On the other hand,
he was quick to help anyone in trouble and always generous to
anyone with whom he had friendly relations or who had helped
him out of the various unpleasant interactions, his passions or
pursuit of gain had gotten him into. Mother Story told me sadly
when she was more than seventy years old that she 'couldn't get
used' to his tantrums. I never saw him have one.

He had an exceptionally brilliant mind which always grasped
the practical course to be pursued to further any advantage to
himself personally or to the community in which he lived, which
was of course his business also.

In fact, he was one of those people who did just as he pleased
and depended on his quick thinking mind and his influence and
his money to carry him safely on and it seems they always did.[1]

S O WROTE KATE STORY in a letter to her son Byron in 1945.
She held her father-in-law in high esteem, dismissing his
temper as a minor shortcoming of an ambitious man who,
in the end, loved his family and community. Her forgiveness,
however, never extended to Garrett Hogan, and she maintained to

her children that if Nelson had paid him to leave town and not court Rose in the first place, the family would have been better off.[2] Her uncharitable opinion of him began on the day they first met, grew over time, and intensified a few months after Story's death, when Rose filed a lawsuit accusing her three brothers of cheating her out of two hundred thousand dollars in stocks and bonds.

The legal fight started in Los Angeles, where Rose blocked Walter's attempt to become administrator of the estate, alleging he and his brothers distributed Story's property to "such persons as they saw fit."[3] On December 7, 1926, the California court granted Rose's petition to have Albert Roecher appointed administrator. She subsequently filed suit in Gallatin County, and the trial began October 20, 1930. The family was convinced that the suit came at Garrett's urging.

One of Rose's witnesses, Lizzie Long, alleged that the 1912 altercation in the mansion had in fact been an attempt by Bud and Bine to strong-arm Nelson into turning over the bonds in question. Long said she saw Story afterward bleeding from his face and that he carried a scar below his eye up until his death. She also recalled an incident right after World War I when Bine again demanded the bonds and burned papers that he took from Nelson's desk.[4] According to her testimony, Story had told Long on many occasions, "I've given the boys a million and a half, and that is enough," and that he intended to leave everything to Rose.[5]

On the stand, Rose insisted that Story had promised her the bonds and half of his property. On the evening of Ellen's funeral, she claimed, Bine and Walter had assured the Hogans that Story would leave her all of his estate and that Bine confessed he felt like a "dirty dog" for taking the bonds in 1917 to finance his sheep operation. Rose said if her brothers paid her two hundred thousand dollars, the value of the bonds, she would have dropped the matter, but that was no longer possible since Bine had lost it all. Rose also accused Bine and Kate of improperly caring for their father, asserting that Kate once refused Nelson's request to summon a doctor, a charge Kate denied. Rose also believed Bine, while overseeing his father's business affairs, had taken money from Nelson's checking account.[6]

Rose further testified that her brothers had destroyed Story's first will, so she and Garrett drew up a document outlining all that they had been promised, which her brothers then modified by excluding two pieces of Bozeman real estate, one of which was the mansion. Infuriated, Rose told Walter she wanted everything she could get. After Nelson's death, the bonds had a value of roughly sixty-five thousand dollars, and Walter agreed to hand them over to his sister if she would sign a release. Rose and her son Romaine, a Los Angeles attorney, declined the offer. They instead demanded that Bine pay them 6 percent interest on the two-hundred-thousand-dollar principal for fifteen years and then pay the full principal itself. Romaine later offered to settle with Bine for one hundred and fifty thousand dollars, but Bine refused.[7] This prompted Garrett to tell Walter that "you boys will keep on until some of you will get into the penitentiary."[8] He called the Story brothers "the three musketeers," and later told Frank Benepe he was going to "sue those sons of bitches for everything I can think of" after he got the bonds.[9] Hogan also claimed his father-in-law never delivered the promised stock in the Los Angeles hospital, so Hogan joined the staff at a different institution and opened an office of his own on West Third Street.[10]

Witnesses for the defense painted a different picture. They claimed Nelson wanted all of his children to share in his wealth and that he had never promised Rose all the bonds, only a fair share of the estate. From 1890 until his death, Story on numerous occasions had given his children real estate, stock, cash, and personal property. Bine received more than $513,000, Bud $601,000, but Rose had received $772,200.[11] Some witnesses maintained Story wanted to deny Garrett access to his money for fear the doctor would waste it gambling on some frivolous enterprise, leaving Rose and her children with nothing. According to Bine, Garrett tried to get Story to sign over the bonds in 1924, but Nelson refused. The incident left his father so angry "he could bite a nail in two."[12]

Charles Vandenhook witnessed the conveyance of the bonds to Bine, adding that Bine only used the interest, not the principal. He also watched in 1924 as Story signed a deed for his home to Walter, reserving a life estate. "I'm giving this house to Walter, because I don't believe any other Story can keep it up."[13] Walter believed that since Rose did not want to live in Montana, Nelson felt she would either sell it for a song or lose it by not paying property taxes. Rose claimed her father was not mentally competent at the time to handle his own affairs, but the Story brothers held that the old man still made his own decisions.[14] They also maintained that Nelson wanted Bine, whom he trusted with the family business, to look after him and Ellen in their advanced years, noting that "he is our main support at the present time and has been in the past."[15]

A plumber who worked for the Storys in the early 1920s claimed that Rose referred to her father as "the old fool," a charge she later refuted.[16] Bine denied referring to himself as a "dirty dog," and said that he never tried to influence Nelson's business decisions. The papers he had burned were old and of no value. He said he was very close to his father, who carried his son's picture in his locket. Walter admitted he and his brothers planned on abrogating their father's will, and that he and Bine had only promised Rose four of the real estate pieces from the beginning. At the time, they observed, Rose seemed satisfied with the arrangement, suggesting that Hogan was the one pushing for the bonds.[17]

On August 7, 1931, district judge Benjamin Berg ruled in favor of the Story boys and against Rose. He decided she should receive nothing more, as she had already realized her fair share of the estate and that the boys had not committed any conspiracy. Bine, said the judge, was a "trusted son" helping his father manage his affairs toward the end of his life. He held that the agreement of December 14, 1923, between Nelson and the Story boys was legitimate, and that Nelson had freely intended to give both the securities in exchange for the cash they had paid him. The judge also rejected the notion that Bine had assaulted his father in 1912, leaving open questions pertaining to Bud's actions during the incident. The state supreme court would later uphold Judge Berg's ruling.[18]

Rose, Garrett, and Romaine left town hurriedly. Evidently, Rose never returned. Malcolm's daughter, Martha Story Drysdale, who spent the first five years of her life in Los Angeles before moving to the ranch near Emigrant, claimed never to have met her, though Rose lived until 1953 and Garrett until 1956. Rose only kept in touch with Walter, as they both were Los Angelinos.[19]

The lawsuit left Bine, as he later described it, "screwed up in a knot."[20] The same could be said for Bud who, on October 21, 1932, died unexpectedly of a massive stroke while visiting friends in the Gallatin Canyon. He was fifty-eight.[21]

Within a year of Bud's death, the Montana State Board of Equalization and the Internal Revenue Service concluded that Nelson Story had transferred ownership of the bonds, real estate, certificates of deposit, and stocks in the manner that he did so that his children's inheritance would not be subject to taxation. The development drew Walter, Bine, and Kate into yet another legal fight, which took four years to resolve. The Board of Tax Appeals reduced the value of the estate by ruling most of the property given to Story's children was not done so in contemplation of death and, therefore, should not be taxed. That did not include the mansion, valued at $37,250, for which Walter was liable for taxes.[22]

Given Nelson's fear that the Hogans would one way or another lose the mansion, he must have wanted it to stand for generations to

Walter P. Story (right) and Johnnie Shaeles at the Story Mansion, 1936. A year later the mansion was demolished. Museum of the Rockies, Bozeman 84.81.4

come. Many of the ornate homes built by his contemporaries, such as those of Thomas Power and Samuel Hauser in Helena, have since been preserved in Montana. Stately residences that belonged to capitalists like Charles Conrad of Kalispell and Preston Boyd Moss of Billings became museums, as did that of Marcus Daly in Hamilton. Despite Nelson's hopes, however, the Story Mansion was doomed by several factors. Foremost was Bine's financial misfortune in the 1920s, which left him and Kate in need of housing. Subsequently, Bud's death, Rose's estrangement, and Walter's focus on his affairs in California all combined to preclude any family or community effort to preserve the home.

Walter and Lorenza deeded the mansion to Kate in 1930, and she and Bine lived there for several years. Save for a few leaks, not uncommon for a structure of its vintage, the home was as sound as the day it was built: no tight doors, cracks, or settling of the foundation.[23] They hosted occasional parties and get-togethers, but not as many as Ellen had. In August 1936, the cash-strapped Storys sold the mansion to the county school district for twenty thousand dollars, and the district agreed to pay back taxes on the property.[24]

The transaction would prove to be the building's death knell. In 1937, school trustees decided to raze the structure to accommodate a Works Progress Administration–financed expansion of the county high school.[25] Any private or public fundraising for a last-minute rescue was out of the question given the ongoing depression. Many Gallatin County residents were struggling to keep their own homes out of foreclosure, and an improved school facility at government expense took higher priority. Edward Haggerty, who promised to demolish the structure in exchange only for the interior materials, won the contract. Before starting, he held an open house and organized public tours of the mansion, and when the job was done, doors, staircases, and other materials were used in the construction and remodeling of local residences and businesses. Bine and Kate retained all of the mansion's chandeliers, the first-floor bathroom set, as well as other assorted items, including two granite columns from the mansion's front that now mark the family burial site.

After living in a rented home for a few years, Bine and Kate tore down the old Alderson home on South Willson and built a new one

From left to right, Nelson Story III, Bud Story, Nelson Story IV ("Fourthy"), and Nelson Story, 1922
Gallatin Historical Society Museum, Bozeman 1010

in 1941.[26] For the balance of their years, they led a quiet life, frequently dining out. Holidays, Christmas especially, were spent with their children and grandchildren; Bine played the piano and led family sing-alongs.[27] He died in 1954, Kate in 1959.

Professionally, Walter proved the most successful of the Story boys. In 1926, he was promoted to the rank of brigadier general and took command of the Eightieth Brigade, and later persuaded the California legislature to establish Camp Merriam, a training site for the state national guard. In 1937, he was promoted to major general, eventually commanding the Ninth Army Corps and then the Fortieth Infantry Division. Protracted illness forced his retirement in 1942. His many citations included a twenty-five-year Service Medal, Medal of Merit, World War I Victory Medal, American Defense Service Ribbon, and the Order Crown of Italy. At the California State Military Museum, one of the finest repositories of military history in the western United States, the Walter P. Story Memorial Library and Research Center is named in his honor.

Walter was also involved in many corporate and nonprofit organizations. He served as president of the Story Building Corporation, commissioner of the Los Angeles Fire and Police Pension Board, and board chairman of the Mullen & Bluett Clothing Company, which he aided in establishing the Miracle Mile District along Wilshire Boulevard. He and his second wife enjoyed membership in various elite California social clubs, including the Overland Country Club, the Bel Air Bay Club, the Bohemian Club, and the Rancho Visitadores. After their divorce in 1951, Walter converted to Catholicism and married Evelyn Smith four years later. He died on June 18, 1957, with an estate of roughly ten million dollars. One-third went to Evelyn, with the balance distributed to his nieces, nephews, second wife Lorenza, and various institutions, including the University of Southern California, Loyola University, and Shriners Hospital.[28]

WHEN NELSON AND ELLEN attended the Pioneers' Society of Gallatin County meeting in 1917, keynote speaker and attorney George Pease praised the ambition of those westward emigrants who had settled the Treasure State. "The east was not large enough for you. You coveted the empire of the West. You wanted the world, at least this magnificent part of it which we call Montana . . . you were men who wanted the company of your wives, for you brought them to share with you the life where the opportunity for human companionship was limited."[29] His words, considered alongside the intimate recollections of Kate Story, captured the broader arc of Nelson Story's life.

Story wanted more than what Ohio could offer, and like so many others headed west in search of opportunity. In Montana he realized his dreams of being a self-made man. For better or worse, he was a remarkable individual. His personal and professional conduct was at times unconscionable, according to both present-day sensibilities and those of his contemporaries, but that truth does little to negate his industriousness, courage, and accomplishments. Without excusing the shortcomings and rougher edges of her great-grandfather, Martha Drysdale concluded that it was only fair to judge Story according to the times in which he lived:

> I suppose in those days, [of] the Wild-Wild West, one had to be pretty rough, at times ruthless in business interests and protecting family in order to survive. I've always thought he probably did business as business was done in those days and probably was not doing anything very different than anyone else.[30]

As it did throughout the American West, the federal government—through generous expenditures that underwrote the creation of Fort Ellis, the Crow Agency, and the State College of Agriculture and Mechanic Arts—kept Bozeman afloat and facilitated its growth during the late nineteenth and early twentieth centuries. Hard-eyed entrepreneurs like Nelson Story, who were willing to seize the opportunities for personal gain, built on that backing. His legacy in Bozeman still survives, but with newcomers raising the city's population by about 4.5 percent annually, more and more people seem to know less and less about him.[31] They, and the millions of tourists who visit southwest Montana annually, are drawn by the lifestyle and outdoor opportunities, such as hiking, fishing, skiing, hunting, and touring nearby Yellowstone National Park. At the dawn of the twenty-first century, Montana State University is the state's fastest growing university, thanks largely to its schools of agriculture, business, and engineering. The campus serves as a regional hub for the arts, intellectual life, and athletics, adding greatly to the area's cultural appeal and offering continuing education programs and lectures to the general public.[32] Although Story's support for the school was by no means equivalent to that, say, of fellow western tycoon Leland Stanford to the university that bears his name, his role in the institution's development warrants greater recognition.

A life like Story's is the fodder of classic Westerns and a dime-novelist's dream, but thus far only one aspect has been depicted in literature and film: the cattle drive from Texas. Paul Wellman's *The Greatest Cattle Drive*, published in 1964, offers an accurate description of the event, albeit in heroic terms with some artistic license. Henry Wilson Allen's *The Tall Men*, published in 1954, includes many incidents from the drive to weave a fictional tale featuring lead character Nathan Stark, whose name has the same initials and number of letters as Nelson Story.[33] The book was eventually made into a motion picture. Perhaps most famous of all, Larry McMurtry's novel *Lonesome Dove*, set along a cattle drive from Texas to Montana, is loosely based on Story, but the events portrayed in the book and subsequent television miniseries in fact more closely resemble Charles Goodnight and Oliver Loving's 1867 cattle drive from Fort Belknap, Texas, to Fort Sumner, New Mexico.[34] In any event, it was the cattle drive that, in 1959, won Story a place in the National Cowboy & Western Heritage Museum's Hall of Great Westerners, and in 2008 Story was inducted into the Montana Cowboy Hall of Fame. His involvement in freighting, banking, milling, and real estate—the less glamorous foundation of communities like Bozeman—remains underappreciated.

Were Nelson Story to return to Bozeman today, he would without a doubt be furious that the family mansion no longer stands. But he might be consoled by the prominence of many landmarks bearing his name. A statue of Malcolm stands on Main Street, and historical structures like the Bozeman Armory exist in large part due to the generosity of the Story family. Story Tower provides family and graduate housing on the Montana State University campus. The Ellen Theater is still in operation, and the block where Bine and Kate's elegant home still stands is now known as Story Mansion Park. In 2003, the city of Bozeman purchased the residence from the Sigma Alpha Epsilon fraternity and rents it for weddings, receptions, and meetings. Ground has been broken for a nature sanctuary and city park on fifty-five acres that includes the Story Mill property, and private developers have started construction of a downtown hotel at the armory site with the working name Etha, for Etha Mayo Story.

The surrounding region bears numerous other testaments to Story's influence. In neighboring Park County, the family ranch near Emigrant, passed down through the generations, now operates as Story Cattle Company and Outfitting, offering accommodations and guides for hunters pursuing bear, elk, and deer. In one of the property's warehouses, a treasure trove of artifacts survives, including

The Bozeman Centennial Committee commissioned this statue of Nelson Story, which was created by metal artist Jim Dolan. Ironically, the larger-than-life statue is located at Lindley Park, a picturesque city park named for the man who both feared and fought against Story. Courtesy Marie Schenck

saddles that belonged to Nelson, Bud, and Bine; the tin box Story used to transport his gold in 1866; the jail doors battered down by the mob prior to the 1873 lynching of Triplett and St. Clair; as well as a horse carriage, wagons, and automobiles. The beautiful Soldier's Chapel located near Big Sky in the Gallatin Canyon sits on land donated by Nelson Story III and his wife Velma. The heavy stone and log structure is a memorial to their son "Fourthy," Lieutenant Nelson Story IV, killed in action in New Guinea, and to the eighty-one men of his unit, the 163rd Infantry Regiment of Montana, who also lost their lives in World War II.[35]

But the ironic location of one monument in Bozeman is worthy of reflection. In 1918, Joe Lindley's widow Rachel sold a parcel of land to the city that would become Lindley Park, the site of the Sweet Pea Festival of the Arts. In 1968, the Kiwanis Club constructed a park pavilion, followed in 1984 by a statue that probably still has Joe spinning in his grave: a metal likeness of Nelson Story, astride his horse, as he may have looked during the legendary cattle drive from Texas.[36]

Notes

Abbreviations used in the notes include:

Annual Report of the Commissioner of Indian Affairs (ARCIA)

Commissioner of Indian Affairs (CIA)

Crow Indian Agency Fraud Hearings Collection (CIAF)

Fort Ellis Record Collection (FERC)

Fort Ellis Records, 1869–1876, Microfilm reel 123 (FERM)

Gallatin County Clerk and Recorders Office, Bozeman, Montana (GCCR)

Gallatin County District Court Office, Bozeman, Montana, Records of the Clerk (GCC)

Gallatin Historical Society Research Center (GHSRC)

Government Printing Office, Washington, D.C. (GPO)

Investigation on the Conduct of Indian Affairs (ICIA)

Office of Indian Affairs (OIA)

Montana Historical Society Research Center, Helena, Montana (MHS)

Montana The Magazine of Western History (Montana)

Roecher Family File (RFF)

Senate Committee on Indian Affairs (SCIA)

Story Family Files (SFF)

United States Office of Indian Affairs, Crow Indian Agency Records (USCIAR)

INTRODUCTION

1. James F. "Bud" Day, "The Day Family History," www.findagrave.com/cgi-bin/fg.cgi?page=gr&GRid=75085239, accessed March 17, 2017.

2. Churchman Associates, *The Churchman* 125 (Jan. 28, 1922): 27; *Great Falls Daily Tribune*, Feb. 20, 1919.

3. Dee Brown, *The American West*, 314-15.

4. William L. Lang, "Charles A. Broadwater and the Main Chance in Montana," *Montana* 39 (Summer 1989): 31-34.

5. William G. Robbins, "The Deconstruction of a Capitalist Patriarch: The Life and Times of Samuel T. Hauser," *Montana* 42 (Autumn 1992): 23-25.

6. Greg Gordon, *When Money Grew on Trees: A. B. Hammond and the Age of the Timber Baron*, 13-14.

7. Paul F. Sharp, "Merchant Princes of the Plains," *Montana* 5 (Winter 1955): 7-9, 14.

8. Byron Story, "Nelson Story Sr. Was One of Montana's First Gold Miners," *Bozeman Courier*, May 6, 1938.

9. *Rocky Mountain Husbandman*, Apr. 13, 1876.

10. Joe Lindley to Nelson Story, *Gallatin County Republican*, Aug. 11, 1903.

11. Joaquin Miller, *An Illustrated History of the State of Montana*, 742. Miller was the pen name used by Cincinnatus Heine Miller.

Nineteenth-century journalist Ambrose Bierce considered Miller, for the most part, a liar.

12. *Bozeman Courier*, Mar. 19, 1926.

CHAPTER ONE

1. Nelson Story in the *Washington Post*, n.d., cited in Byron Story, "Nelson Story Sr. Was One of Montana's Outstanding Pioneers," *Bozeman Courier*, Apr. 22, 1938.
2. Elliott West, *The Contested Plains: Indians, Goldseekers, and the Rush to Colorado*, 177–78; Michael A. Leeson, ed., *History of Montana*, 1739–1885, 1163–64.
3. His apprenticeship was under Samuel Dix. See George Francis Dow, ed., *Records and Files of the Quarterly Courts of Essex County, Massachusetts*, vol. 2, 67; *Progressive Men of the State of Montana*, 1256; Ezra S. Stearns, William Frederick Whitcher, and Edward Everett Parker, *Genealogical and Family History of the State of New Hampshire: A Record of the Achievements of her People in the Making of a Commonwealth and the Founding of a Nation*, 1: 314.
4. John was executed, Elizabeth was spared. See http://salem.lib.virginia.edu/texts/tei/BoySal2R?term=&div_id=BoySal2-n2.346&chapter_id=n107&name=goowil.
5. Office of the Secretary of State of Massachusetts, Volume 15 of *Massachusetts Soldiers and Sailors of the Revolutionary War: A Compilation from the Archives, Prepared and Published by the Secretary of the Commonwealth in Accordance with Chapter 100, Resolves of 1891*, 138. George Madison Bodge, *Soldiers in King Philip's War*, 156–57.
6. Everett H. Tribett, "Andrews and Story, Andrews Family History of Massachusetts, Story Genealogy of Mass. & Ohio," Film 391, Item 4, LDS Family History Library. Upon his return to Ipswich, John Jr. spent several months recovering from fever, ague, and smallpox.
7. *Meigs County Ohio History Book*, 316, 327; Keith Ashley, genealogist, to the author, Sept. 8, 1995; *Pomeroy Weekly Telegraph*, Aug. 14, 1860. Story's middle name occasionally appears as Giles.
8. Edgar Ervin, *Pioneer History of Meigs County, Ohio, to 1949; including Masonic History of the Same Period*, 236–37; *Meigs County Ohio History Book*, 10–11; D. B. Story, *A Brief History of Bedford Township*, 57.
9. Charlene Hoeflich, "The Legacy of Nelson Story: Son of Meigs County Pioneer Family," Gallipolis, Pomeroy, Ohio, *Sunday Times-Sentinel*, Oct. 11, 1998. For years, the community displayed signs reading "Welcome to Historical Bungtown" and "Bungtown, the Center of the World."
10. Sheppard Black, Special Collections Librarian, Ohio University, to the author, Sept. 9, 1995.
11. Malcolm Story, interview by Kenneth J. Swenson, History of Nelson Story audiotape recordings, 1967, Merrill G. Burlingame Papers, Collection 849 (hereafter Malcolm Story, interview).
12. Albert D. Richardson, *Beyond the Mississippi; From the Great River to the Great Ocean*, 53.
13. West, *Contested Plains*, 6. Originally incorporated as the Massachusetts Emigrant Aid Company.
14. Lawrence was named for abolitionist Amos Lawrence.
15. Frederick Merk, *History of the Westward Movement*, 391–93; Thomas Goodrich, *War to the Knife: Bleeding Kansas, 1854–1861*, 22.
16. Thomas "Bine" Story to Byron "Budge" Story (hereafter Bine to Budge), Apr. 23, 1945, Story Family Files (hereafter SFF), Gallatin Historical Society Research Center (hereafter GHSRC); Goodrich, *War to the Knife*, 135; Leeson, *History of Montana*, 1163; Bud and Mary Burkhart, interview by the author, Apr. 23, 2008, (hereafter Burkhart, interview), GHSRC Oral History Collection; Malcolm Story, interview.
17. David Roberts, "The Brink of War," *Smithsonian* (June 2008): 50; Leroy R. Hafen and Ann W. Hafen, eds., *Mormon Resistance: A Documentary Account of the Utah Expedition, 1857–1858*, 23, 13–14.
18. Percival G. Lowe, *Five Years a Dragoon ('49 to '54) and Other Adventures on the Great Plains*, 309–10.
19. Ibid., 320.
20. Leeson, *History of Montana*, 1163; Lowe preferred the Wilson Wagon made in Philadelphia to tote cargo, but on this trip, was stuck with substandard wagons. See Lowe, *Five Years a Dragoon*, 313–17, 320.
21. West, *Contested Plains*, 104–10, 213, 219; Leeson, *History of Montana*, 1163.

22. Horace Greeley, *An Overland Journey, from New York to San Francisco, in the Summer of 1859*, 138.

23. West, *Contested Plains*, 179; Leeson, *History of Montana*, 1164.

24. Greeley, *An Overland Journey*, 122.

25. Leeson, *History of Montana*, 1164.

26. *1850 U.S. Federal Census*, Lee, Platte, Missouri, Roll M432_410, p. 354B, p. 355A, image 144; *1860 U.S. Federal Census*, Stranger, Leavenworth, Kansas Territory, Roll M653_350, p. 879; Family History Library, film 803350; Meta Strickler, interview by the author (hereafter Strickler, interview), May 16, 2008, GHSRC Oral History Collection; W. J. Davies, "Off For California," *Avant Courier*, Jan. 20, 1894.

27. Leeson, *History of Montana*, 1164.

28. West, *Contested Plains*, 219; Margaret A. Parker, "The Cattle King, II," *River Currents*, Apr. 2, 1988; Ray Pomplun, "Epitome Northwest," *Empire Magazine* (Oct. 24, 1976): 36; Leeson, *History of Montana*, 1164; Lewis Atherton, *The Cattle Kings*, 225.

29. Glenda Riley, *The Female Frontier: A Comparative View of Women on the Prairie and Plains*, 48.

30. Malcolm Story, interview.

31. Mrs. Matthew W. Alderson, "Mrs. Nelson Story Sketch," Mary Long Alderson Papers, 1894-1936 (hereafter ML Alderson Papers), Special Collections, Montana Historical Society Research Center, Helena, MT (hereafter MHS); Davies, "Off For California."

32. William J. Trimble, "The Mining Advance into the Inland Empire" (PhD diss., University of Wisconsin, 1914); "See it Now, Historic Montana: A Present Day Tourist Paradise," *Montana* 9 (July 1959): 36.

33. Merrill G. Burlingame, *The Montana Frontier*, 86.

34. Jefferson for President Thomas Jefferson, Madison for Secretary of State James Madison, and Gallatin in honor of Treasury Secretary Albert Gallatin.

35. George Black, *Empire of Shadows: The Epic Story of Yellowstone*, 479, n. 2.

36. Merrill G. Burlingame, *John M. Bozeman, Montana Trailmaker*, 7-8; Merrill G. Burlingame, *Gallatin County's Heritage: A Report of Progress, 1805-1976*, 4.

37. M. L. Wilson, "The Evolution of Montana Agriculture in its Early Period," *Proceedings of the Mississippi Valley Historical Association* 9 (1917-1918): 432.

38. Michael P. Malone, "The Gallatin Canyon and the Tides of History," *Montana* 23 (Summer 1973): 2.

39. Mrs. E. Lina Houston, *Early History of Gallatin County*, 4.

40. *Republican-Courier*, Sept. 8, 1905.

41. Variations include Absaroka or Absarokee, the translation being "Children of the Large Beaked Bird" or "Children of the Raven." A misinterpretation led whites to call them Crows. See Frank B. Linderman, *Plenty-Coups, Chief of the Crows*, 28.

42. Frederick E. Hoxie, *Parading Through History: The Making of the Crow Nation, 1805–1935*, 86–87.

43. W. J. Davies, "John Bozeman—Peculiarities of his Character," *Avant Courier*, Jan. 21, 1893.

44. *Bozeman Courier*, Feb. 28, 1923.

45. Burlingame, *John M. Bozeman, Montana Trailmaker*, 8.

46. Susan Doyle, *Journeys to the Land of Gold, Emigrant Diaries From The Bozeman Trail, 1863–1866*, vol. 1: 47–49; W. S. McKinzie, "John Bozeman," *Avant Courier*, Dec. 19, 1891; "jack," or male mules, were preferred over females for packing.

47. Leeson, *History of Montana*, 1164.

48. Ellen Baumler, ed., *Girl From the Gulches: The Story of Mary Ronan as told to Margaret Ronan*, 26–27; Mary Ellen McWilliams, "Nelson Story," Merrill G. Burlingame Papers, 1880-1980, Collection 2245.

49. Baumler, *Girl From the Gulches*, 26–28. The attackers could have been Shoshones, Paiutes, or Bannocks. See John Hailey, *The History of Idaho*, 49.

50. Baumler, *Girl From the Gulches*, 28.

51. Richard Wharton, *An Oral History of the Settlement of the Gallatin Valley*, 9, GHSRC.

52. Davies, "Off For California."

53. Dan L. Thrapp, *Vengeance! The Saga of Poor Tom Cover*, 114-16; Muriel Sibell Wolle, *Montana Pay Dirt: A Guide to the Mining Camps of the Treasure State*, 42; *Bozeman Chronicle*, Sept. 7, 1899.

54. Larry Barsness, *Gold Camp: Alder Gulch and Virginia City, Montana*, 7–8; Leeson, *History of Montana*, 1164.

55. *Kalispell Times*, June 19, 1941.

56. Richardson, *Beyond the Mississippi*, 479.

57. Robert E. Strahorn, *The Resources of Montana Territory and Attractions of Yellowstone National Park*, 22.

58. John W. Grannis Diaries, 1863–1878, SC 301, MHS, cited in Barsness, *Gold Camp*, 9.

59. Baumler, *Girl From the Gulches*, 31.

60. R. E. Mather and F. E. Boswell, *Vigilante Victims: Montana's 1864 Hanging Spree*, 47–50; Gregory Aydt, *A Radical Cure: Thomas Dimsdale, Radical Republicanism, and the Montana Vigilantes During the Civil War* (master's thesis, Eastern Illinois University, 1999), 17-18. Plummer actually spelled his name with only one "m," but it has most commonly been spelled with two.

61. The victim was Jack Cleveland, and the fight occurred in the Goodrich Hotel. See Mark C. Dillon, *The Montana Vigilantes, 1863–1870: Gold, Guns and Gallows*, 28–29.

62. Leeson, *History of Montana*, 318; Mather and Boswell, *Vigilante Victims*, 38; Dillon, *The Montana Vigilantes*, 32.

63. Aydt, *A Radical Cure*, 22–23.

64. Thomas J. Dimsdale, *The Vigilantes of Montana, or Popular Justice in the Rocky Mountains*, 70.

65. Ashley, letter to the author, Sept. 8, 1995; Roecher Family File (hereafter RFF), GHSRC.

66. Dorothy Johnson, *The Bloody Bozeman, The Perilous Trail to Montana's Gold*, 104; Ellen Louisa Gordon Fletcher Diary, Aug. 20, 1866, Ellen Louisa Gordon Fletcher Papers, 1866–1910, Merrill G. Burlingame Papers, Collection 335 (hereafter Fletcher Diary).

67. Wolle, *Montana Pay Dirt*, 44.

68. Leeson, *History of Montana*, 784; Wolle, *Montana Pay Dirt*, 44; Michael S. Kennedy, "Tall in the Saddle—First Trail Drive to Montana Territory," in *Cowboys and Cattlemen: A Roundup from Montana*, 113.

CHAPTER TWO

1. Burlingame, *John M. Bozeman*, 9-11; McKinzie, "John Bozeman."

2. Burlingame, *John M. Bozeman*, 12-13.

3. Johnson, *The Bloody Bozeman*, 83.

4. Nathaniel P. Langford, *Vigilante Days and Ways*, 145-51.

5. Tiebalt's name has also been spelled Tbalt, Tiebolt, and Tbolt.

6. Helen Fitzgerald Sanders, *History of Montana*, vol. 1, 201-2; Llewellyn Link Callaway, *Montana's Righteous Hangmen: The Vigilantes in Action*, 22-34; Dillon, *The Montana Vigilantes*, 91.

7. Dillon, *The Montana Vigilantes*, 93.

8. Sanders, *History of Montana*, vol. 2, 868-69.

9. Ibid.

10. Ibid.

11. Mather and Boswell, *Vigilante Victims*, 15.

12. Johnson, *The Bloody Bozeman*, 93.

13. Merrill G. Burlingame, "Montana's Righteous Hangmen: A Reconsideration," *Montana* 28 (Autumn 1978), 44.

14. Aydt, *A Radical Cure*, 35-38.

15. Mather and Boswell, *Vigilante Victims*, 125; Conrad Kohrs, *An Autobiography*, 35-36.

16. Leeson, *History of Montana*, 292, 297.

17. Mather and Boswell, *Vigilante Victims*, 146-49. Great-grandson Bud Burkhart claimed Nelson Story was a posse member, but this is unsubstantiated. See Burkhart, interview.

18. *Saint Cloud Democrat*, May 26, 1864.

19. Helen McLure, "Bad Men, Unsexed Women, and Good Citizens: Outlaws and Vigilantes in the American West," in *Making of the American West: People and Perspectives*, ed. Benjamin H. Johnson, 266.

20. Aydt, *A Radical Cure*, 52-53; Burlingame, "Montana's Righteous Hangmen," 37.

21. Burlingame, *John M. Bozeman*, 13.

22. Mrs. W. J. Beall, "Montana's Early History. A Pioneer Woman's Recollections of People and Events Connected with Montana's Early History," *Contributions of the Historical Society of Montana* 8 (1917): 295.

23. Doyle, *Journeys to the Land of Gold*, vol. 1: 146-47.

24. John S. Gray, *Custer's Last Campaign: Mitch Boyer and the Little Bighorn Reconstructed*, 3, 21.

25. Bridger Canyon was allegedly named by Kit Carson, who survived an Indian attack with Bridger and another man in the area. See *Bozeman Chronicle*, May 18, 1899.

26. Doyle, *Journeys to the Land of Gold*, vol. 1: 151-52.

27. *Avant Courier*, Dec. 19, 1902.

28. William White Alderson, "The Diary of William W. Alderson: Across the Great Plains to Montana in 1864, Settlement in Bozeman and in the Gallatin Valley, Montana, 1864-1877" (hereafter Alderson Diary), 7, GHSRC.

29. Mrs. E. L. Houston, "Mass Meeting of Citizens Chose Name of Intrepid Scout for Town," *Weekly Courier*, Aug. 5, 1914.

30. Work Projects Administration for the State of Montana, *Montana: A State Guide Book*, 138.

31. Trimble, "The Mining Advance into the Inland Empire," 82.

32. Mrs. W. J. Beall, "Mrs. W. J. Beall Tells of Early-Day Social Affairs in Gallatin County," *Bozeman Courier*, Feb. 25, 1925; *Avant Courier*, Dec. 19, 1902. The hotel was located at the northwest corner of Main Street and Bozeman Avenue.

33. W. W. Alderson, "Early Day Reminiscences," I, *Avant Courier*, Mar. 24, 1900.

34. C. H. Waterman, "Comparisons by a Pioneer," *Bozeman Weekly Chronicle*, Mar. 5, 1914.

35. Burlingame, *Gallatin County's Heritage*, 6; W. W. Alderson, "Marketing Their First Crop of Potatoes," *Avant Courier*, Feb. 24, 1900; *Weekly Courier*, Sept. 9, 1914; Robert G. Dunbar, "The Economic Development of the Gallatin Valley," *Pacific Northwest Quarterly* 14 (Oct. 1956): 118; also known as McAdow Ditch and later, Story Ditch. McAdow received the eight hundred miner's inches in 1866. Millers relied on waterpower to operate machinery, and allotments were based on a system used to measure water that extracted gold from gravel and dirt. An orifice two inches thick with a one-inch square hole was placed in the sluice box. One-fortieth of a cubic foot of water, or one miner's inch, passed through the hole per second, the equivalent of 16,200 gallons per day. The system was complicated, arbitrary, and inexact, but it sufficed.

36. Deeds recorded in the Madison County Clerk and Recorder Office, Virginia City, Montana: B. F. Christenot to Nelson Story, Oct. 17, 1864, Deed Book B: 496; John M. Keefer to Nelson Story, July 1, 1865, Deed Book F: 436; Edward Burins to Nelson Story, July 1, 1865 (filed Aug. 17, 1865), Deed Book F: 437; Wm. D. Wright to Nelson Story, July 11, 1865, Deed Book F: 513; Leeson, *History of Montana*, 1164; Nick Shrauger, "B. F. Christenot, Where are You?" *In Celebration of Our Past* 7 (1995): 20.

37. Fletcher Diary, Aug. 20, 1866.

38. *Montana Post*, Mar. 25, 1865.

39. Story, "Nelson Story Sr. Was One of Montana's First Gold Miners." Carter sued Story for civil damages, but dropped the matter when Story agreed to pay him five dollars a month for the balance of his life. See *Montana Post*, June 10, 1865; Malcolm Story, interview; and Wharton, *An Oral History*, 12.

40. Barsness, *Gold Camp*, 179–81; *Montana Post*, Apr. 22, 1865.

41. Wolle, *Montana Pay Dirt*, 44.

42. *Avant Courier*, Feb. 28, 1902.

43. Wilson, "Evolution of Montana Agriculture," 434.

44. *Montana Post*, Feb. 17, 1866.

45. Malcolm Story, interview.

46. Michael Malone, Richard Roeder, and William Lang, *Montana: A History of Two Centuries*, 99–100.

47. *Montana Post*, Apr. 15, 1865. The company also dreamed of a telegraph line from Fort Laramie all the way to "Russian America" (Alaska), across the Bering Sea and into Europe.

48. Under the 1851 Treaty of Fort Laramie, much of what is now eastern Montana and western South Dakota was unceded tribal territory and not open for American settlement.

49. Houston, *Early History*, "Foreword."

50. E. S. Topping, *The Chronicles of the Yellowstone*, 34–35; *Montana Post*, Sept. 2, 1865.

51. *Bozeman Weekly Chronicle*, Feb. 25, 1915. Rosa eventually divorced A. H. Van Vlierden, who took their two daughters and returned east, where they both soon died. Rosa married William Beall in November 1868.

52. *Montana Post*, Sept. 2, 1865.

53. Alderson, "Marketing Their First Crop of Potatoes." The others included brothers Rouse, Penwell, and Dunbar, William Beall, Jacob Gumm, and O. D. Loutsenhizer.

54. Beall, "Montana's Early History," 299; Burlingame, *Gallatin County's Heritage*, 22.

55. John W. Grannis Diaries, 1863–1878, 4, 7, SC 301, MHS.

56. Diary of James A. Sawyers, Oct. 5, 1865, in *Letter from the Secretary of the Interior, in answer to a resolution of the House of February 16, relative to a wagon road from Niobrara to Virginia City*, 39 Cong., 1 sess., H.R. Doc. No. 58, 1866, 28.

57. Charles Cook, David E. Folsom, and William Peterson, *The Valley of the Upper Yellowstone. An Exploration of the Headwaters of the Yellowstone River in the Year 1869*, 8.

58. *Montana Post*, Oct. 14, 1865.

59. Robert V. Hine and John Mack Faragher, *The American West: A New Interpretive History*, 304.

60. Garnet M. and Herbert O. Brayer, *American Cattle Trails, 1540–1900*, 45, 51; James S. Brisbin, *The Beef Bonanza, or, How to get rich on the Plains: being a description of cattle-growing, sheep-farming, horse-raising and dairying in the West*, 24.

61. Many western writers claim Story intended to take cattle from Fort Worth to the Missouri Pacific Railway at Sedalia, Missouri, for shipment to Chicago, then decided on Montana when blockaded at Baxter Springs, Kansas. However, primary sources, namely Story's account published in Michael Leeson's 1885 *History of Montana*, an interview he gave to the *Washington Post*, his personal letters, and family documents suggest Montana was his intended destination all along.

62. Malone, Roeder, and Lang, *Montana*, 100.

63. *Montana Post*, Jan. 22, 1866.

64. Marlene Smith Baranzini, *A Golden State: Mining and Economic Development in Gold Rush California*, 130–31. The proposal would eventually fail.

65. *Montana Post*, Feb. 17, 1866.

66. Dillon, *The Montana Vigilantes*, 239.

67. *Montana Post*, Nov. 25, 1865.

68. Joseph G. McCoy, *Historic Sketches of the Cattle Trade of the West and Southwest*, 23; Parker, "The Cattle King, II." During winter, Holladay's six-horse, seventeen-passenger Concord Coach took passengers to Salt Lake City once a week. See Frank C. Robertson, *Fort Hall, Gateway to the Oregon Country*, 276.

69. H. A. Trexler, "Missouri-Montana Highways," *Missouri Historical Review* 12 (Apr. 1918): 158–60; Carlos A. Schwantes, *Long Day's Journey: The Steamboat and Stagecoach Era in the Northern West*, 187.

70. Leeson, *History of Montana*, 1164; Wharton, *An Oral History*, 12; Pomplun, "Epitome Northwest," 37.

71. Dillon, *The Montana Vigilantes*, 239.

72. *Montana Post*, Mar. 31, 1866.

73. Ibid.

74. Dillon, *The Montana Vigilantes*, 243.

CHAPTER THREE

1. Leeson, *History of Montana*, 1164; Carol Schmidt, "Bozeman's Legend of a Story," *Bozeman Daily Chronicle Centennial Edition*, Apr. 1, 1983; Granville Stuart, *Forty Years on the Frontier*, vol. 2, 98; Wharton, *An Oral History*, 13.

2. Frank M. King, *Longhorn Trail Drivers: Being a True Story of The Cattle Drives of Long Ago*, 47.

3. His last name was also spelled Trojio. See Office of Indian Affairs, "Annual Report of the Commissioner of Indian Affairs (hereafter ARCIA) to the Secretary of the Interior for the Year, 1875," 302.

4. Jefferson Jones, "The Murder of John Bozeman?" *Quest for Knowledge Men's Club*, Dec. 13, 1955, GHSRC.

5. Also referred to as the Baxter Springs or Sedalia Trail.

6. Hine and Faragher, *The American West: A New Interpretive History*, 304.

7. Harvey Griffin, "Ox Yoke Was First State Cattle Brand," *Billings Gazette*, n.d. SFF; Edward Everett Dale, *The Range Cattle Industry: Ranching on the Great Plains from 1865–1925*, 34; King, *Longhorn Trail Drivers*, 47; *Ismay Journal*, Nov. 7, 1924.

8. "Held the herd" or "holding the herd" is a common cowboy term for keeping the cattle under control. See Theodore Roosevelt, "The Round-Up," *The Century* 35 (6): 860.

9. Cattleman Charles Goodnight is credited with creating the first chuck wagon in June of 1866, when he and Oliver Loving herded Texas longhorns to New Mexico. Therefore, the term was probably not in the American lexicon when Story left Texas. Hence the use here of the term supply wagon. See Brown, *The American West*, 285.

10. Ibid; Dee Brown, *Trail Driving Days*, 6.

11. Donald Emmet Worcester, *The Chisholm Trail: High Road of the Cattle Kingdom*, 156; Brayer, *American Cattle Trails*, 42.

12. William G. McLoughlin, *After the Trail of Tears*, 112–13; Daniel N. Vichorek, *Montana's Cowboys: Living the Heritage*, 17.

13. Walter Gann, *Tread of the Longhorns*, 45.

14. Kansas "Jayhawkers" were Free-State supporters who, during the Civil War, battled pro-slavery men. Following the war, they garnered a reputation as plunderers and looters.

15. Jerome Constant Smiley, *Prose and Poetry of the Live Stock Industry of the United States: With Outlines of the Origin and Ancient History of Our Live Stock Animals*, 1: 433; Brown, *Trail Driving Days*, 6; McCoy, *Historic Sketches*, 29, 36–37.

16. King, *Longhorn Trail Drivers*, 74; Burkhart, interview; Charles Henderson, "The Amazing Story," *Wild West Magazine* 7 (Aug. 1994): 54.

17. *Kansas Patriot*, June 23, 1866.

18. Although the Osage had ceded these lands the year before, the counties of Labette, Montgomery, Chautauqua, Elk, and Cowley had not yet been formed.

19. Bine to Budge, n.d.; Bine to Budge, Dec. 13, 1944.

20. Leeson, *History of Montana*, 1164.

21. General Order No. 27, issued by General John Pope at St. Louis, Feb. 28, 1866, cited in Robert G. Athearn, *William Tecumseh Sherman and the Settlement of the West*, 38.

22. Bine to Budge, July 12, 1944; Leeson, *History of Montana*, 1164; *Avant Courier*, July 24, 1879.

23. Walt House, "The Real Story about Nelson Story," *Remington Society of America Journal* 3 (2013): 26.

24. Paul I. Wellman, *The Greatest Cattle Drive*, 104; Robert S. Fletcher, "The End of the Open Range in Eastern Montana," in *The Montana Past: An Anthology*, eds. Michael P. Malone and Richard B. Roeder, 26.

25. Kennedy, "Tall in the Saddle—First Trail Drive to Montana Territory," 104.

26. Bine to Budge, Aug. 30, 1944; Doyle, *Journeys to the Land of Gold*, vol. 2, 423. George Overholt, George Dow, and Frank Mounts were part of the drive, but whether they were hired back in Texas, in Leavenworth, or Fort Kearny is unclear. Arthur L. Stone, *Following Old Trails*, 212; *Daily Missoulian*, July 31, 1917. Catlin served in the 87th Indiana Regiment for the war's duration.

27. Doyle, *Journeys to the Land of Gold*, vol. 2, 431–32.

28. Ibid., 2, 427–34.

29. *Weekly Courier*, Apr. 4, 1917.

30. Vichorek, *Montana's Cowboys*, 18–19.

31. Leeson, *History of Montana*, 1164.

32. Stone, *Following Old Trails*, 214.

33. Leeson, *History of Montana*, 1164–65.

34. Benjamin Dailey, diary, Aug. 4, 1866, cited in Doyle, *Journeys to the Land of Gold*, vol. 2, 680–81.

35. Leeson, *History of Montana*, 1165; Story, "Nelson Story Sr. Was One of Montana's First Gold Miners."

36. Stone, *Following Old Trails*, 216.

37. Story, "Nelson Story Sr. Was One of Montana's First Gold Miners."

38. Stone, *Following Old Trails*, 214.

39. Kennedy, "Tall in the Saddle," 105–6.

40. Dee Brown, *Fort Phil Kearny, An American Saga*, 136; Henderson, "The Amazing Story," 57.

41. Paul I. Wellman, *The Trampling Herd*, 98–99.

42. Brown, *Fort Phil Kearny*, 136.

43. Stone, *Following Old Trails*, 214.

44. Ibid., 215. Many travel books, such as *Moon Handbooks: Wyoming*, claim Nelson Story's brief stay made him the namesake of the nearby town of Story. However, the community is in fact named for Charles Story (no known relation), who operated a ranch near the site in later years.

45. Henderson, "The Amazing Story," 58.

46. Brown, *Fort Phil Kearny*, 137–38.

47. David Dary, *Cowboy Culture: A Saga of Five Centuries*, 231–32.

48. Stone, *Following Old Trails*, 215.

49. Leeson, *History of Montana*, 1165.

50. The boat was one from William Davies's boatyard, recently stolen by two men who were forced to flee from Indians and return to Bozeman. See *Avant Courier*, Feb. 11, 1893.

51. Story, "Nelson Story Sr. Was One of Montana's First Gold Miners."

52. Kathryn Wright, "Fort Nelson Story," *Billings Gazette Sunday Magazine*, Dec. 3, 1972. The site has since been referred to as Stockade Hill. The stones that protected Story and his men were used years later to construct a homestead and schoolhouse.

53. Bine to Budge, Dec. 13, 1944; Martha Story Drysdale, interview by the author, Apr. 28, 2008 (hereafter Drysdale, interview), Oral History Collection, GHSRC; Story, "Nelson

Story Sr. Was One of Montana's First Gold Miners."

54. Brown, *The American West*, 313

CHAPTER FOUR

1. Story's family claims he purchased scrip from Union veterans to buy land. See Vichorek, *Montana's Cowboys*, 21.

2. Mrs. W. J. Beall, "Bozeman's First Schools," *Contributions to the Historical Society of Montana* 7 (1910): 307-8; Alderson, "Early Day Reminiscences," and Davis Willson, "Back in the '60's," *Avant Courier*, Mar. 11, 1899.

3. Leeson, *History of Montana*, 1165.

4. *Montana Post*, Feb. 17, 1866; Ibid., Mar. 30, 1867; Tom Haines, "McAdow Mill," in *Flouring Mills of Montana Territory*, 15; Thrapp, *Vengeance!*, 216. Cover's armed escort consisted of John Richard, Jr., Jim Bridger, and Henry "Hank" Williams. See Barry J. Hagan, *Exactly in the Right Place: A History of Fort C. F. Smith, Montana Territory, 1866–1868*, 68.

5. Oscar, Merritt, and John Penwell. Also known as the Springhill Flouring Mills. See Haines, "Union or Spring Hill Flouring Mills," in *Flouring Mills of Montana Territory*, 19.

6. Beall, "Bozeman's First Schools," 307; Beall, "Montana's Early History," 300-302. The church was located on the northwest corner of Olive Street and South Willson Avenue. It is now the Bozeman United Methodist Church.

7. Alderson, "Early Day Reminiscences," *Avant Courier*, Mar. 31, 1900; W. W. Alderson, "In The Interests of Historic Accuracy," *Republican-Courier*, Feb. 2, 1906; Kim Allen Scott, "The Willson Brothers Come to Montana," *Montana* 49 (Spring 1999), 62; Esther C. Niebel, *A Century of Service—History of The First Methodist Church, Bozeman, Montana 1866–1966*, 5.

8. Willson, "Back in the '60's."

9. Burlingame, *John M. Bozeman*, 28.

10. Ibid., 22-23; Davies, "John Bozeman—Peculiarities of his Character."

11. William Davies, cited in Burlingame, *John M. Bozeman*, 24.

12. Elmyra Frazier's maiden name was Bozeman. The two believed they were related, but could never prove it.

13. *Weekly Courier*, Mar. 19, 1913. McKenzie's name was often spelled McKinzey, Mackinzie, Mckinzie or MacKenzie. Early Bozeman historian Lina Houston spelled it McKenzie, and that is how it is engraved on his tombstone.

14. Burlingame, *John M. Bozeman*, 26.

15. Story, "Nelson Story Sr. Was One of Montana's First Gold Miners."

16. Merrill G. Burlingame, and K. Ross Toole, *A History of Montana*, vol. 1, 311-13; Clyde A. Milner and Carol A. O'Connor, *As Big as the West: The Pioneer Life of Granville Stuart*, 55-56; *Progressive Men of the State of Montana*, 258.

17. *Montana Post*, Feb. 9, 1867; Merrill D. Beal, *The Story of Man in Yellowstone*, 160-61; Burlingame and Toole, *A History of Montana*, vol. 2, 316-17.

18. Gray, *Custer's Last Campaign*, 54-55. The army rejected Richard's vouchers for being "exorbitant."

19. Ibid., 54; "Bannack and Gallatin City in 1862-1863. A Letter by Mrs. Emily R. Meredith," cited in Clyde McLemore, *Frontier Omnibus*, 244. The governor held administrative control over Indians within the territory. This made Meagher territorial superintendent of Indian Affairs.

20. John Bozeman to Francis Meagher, Mar. 25, 1867, cited in Leeson, *History of Montana* 119.

21. Thrapp, *Vengeance!*, 224.

22. McKinzie, "John Bozeman."

23. *Boulder Monitor*, Oct. 25, 1919, cited in Burlingame, *John M. Bozeman*, 34.

24. T. W. Cover to T. F. Meagher, Apr. 22, 1867, cited in Leeson, *History of Montana*, 119. Cover gave differing accounts of what happened. The version printed by Leeson is privileged here.

25. Ibid.

26. Jones, "The Murder of John Bozeman?" 9.

27. Ibid., 7; Gray, *Custer's Last Campaign*, 57.

28. Jones, "The Murder of John Bozeman?" 8. "Spanish Joe" refers to Jose Pablo Tsoyio, "Mexican Joe."

29. Ibid., 9.

30. The employee Story shared his version with was Lester Pierstorff. See Pierstorff Family File, GHSRC.

31. Nelson Story to E. A. Brininstool, Oct. 5, 1920, SFF.

32. Nelson Story, Sr., letter, Feb. 11, 1911, SFF.

33. Houston, *Early History*, 13.

34. Estate of John M. Bozeman, July 13, 1869, box 34, Gallatin County District Court Office, Bozeman, Montana, Records of the Clerk (hereafter GCCC). Cover would acquire large orange groves near Riverside, a town he purportedly helped "lay out." In 1884, he disappeared in the California desert while looking for the mythical Peg-Leg Gold Mine.

35. Stuart, *Forty Years on the Frontier*, vol. 2, 64-65; John Y. Simon, ed., *The Papers of Ulysses S. Grant*, vol. 7, 106-7; *Montana Post*, Apr. 13, 1867.

36. Ibid., Apr. 27, 1867.

37. *Annual Report of the Secretary of War, 1867*, H.R. Doc. No. 1, 40 Cong., 2nd sess., 33.

38. *Montana Indian War Claims*, H.R. Doc. No. 98, 41 Cong., 3rd sess., 1871, 4.

39. *Avant Courier*, June 8, 1901; Stuart, *Forty Years on the Frontier*, vol. 2, 65.

40. Thomas H. Leforge, *Memoirs of a White Crow Indian (Thomas H. Leforge) as told by Thomas B. Marquis,* 19; George M. Templeton, diary (hereafter Templeton Diary), June 14, 1867, cited in Hagan, *Exactly in the Right Place*, 98.

41. Malone, Roeder, Lang, *Montana*, 100-103.

42. *Annual Report of the Secretary of War*, 1867, H.R. Doc. No. 1, 40 Cong., 2nd sess., 53.

43. *Montana Indian War Claims*, H.R. Doc. No. 98, 41 Cong., 3rd sess., 1871, 8.

44. Davis Willson to "Folks at Home," May 29, 1867, folder 2, Lester S. Willson Family Papers, 1861-1922, Merrill G. Burlingame Papers, Collection 1407.

45. *Montana War-Claims*, H.R. Rep. No. 82, 42 Cong., 2nd sess., 1872, 5.

46. Ibid., 36.

47. Robert G. Athearn, *Thomas Francis Meagher: an Irish Revolutionary in America*, 162.

48. Dennis Seibel, *Fort Ellis, Montana Territory, 1867–1886: The Fort that Guarded Bozeman*, 5.

49. *Annual Report of the Secretary of War*, 1867, H.R. Doc. No. 1, 40 Cong., 2nd sess., 53.

50. Gail Schontzler, "Who Killed John Bozeman? Historians find new suspect," *Bozeman Daily Chronicle*, Oct. 4, 2014.

51. *Annual Report of the Secretary of War*, 1867, H.R. Doc. No. 1, 40 Cong., 2nd sess., 51.

52. R. S. LaMotte to Adjutant General Dept.

of Dakota, Aug. 31, 1867, Fort Ellis Record Collection (hereafter FERC), GHSRC.

53. LaMotte to Fort Shaw, Aug. 28, 1867, FERC; Thomas Charles Rust, "Settlers, Soldiers and Scoundrels: The Relationship Between Army and Civilian Society in the Development of Bozeman, Montana, 1867-1886," 37-38, GHSRC.

54. Wilson, "Evolution of Montana Agriculture," 434; Doris Whithorn, "John J. Tomlinson of Emigrant Gulch and Gallatin Gateway," *In Celebration of Our Past* 9 (1997), 9.

55. Davis Willson, "From Bozeman City," *Montana Post*, Oct. 26, 1867.

56. *Helena Herald*, Dec. 5, 1867.

57. Leeson, *History of Montana*, 608; B. Derek Strahn, "Fort Ellis Remembered," *At Home Magazine* 5 (Dec. 2004): 13.

58. Beall, "Mrs. W. J. Beall Tells of Early-Day Social Affairs in Gallatin County"; Beall, "Montana's Early History," 301-3.

59. *Helena Herald*, Dec. 19, 1867.

60. *Report of Brevet Major General Alfred H. Terry, Annual Report of the Secretary of War*, H.R. Doc. No. 1, 1868, v. 1, 40 Cong., 3rd sess., 33.

61. Four thousand dollars for the potatoes, and six thousand dollars for freighting costs. Story normally charged five cents a pound in freighting costs. See Nelson Story to Granville Stuart, June 15, 1918, Merrill G. Burlingame Special Collections.

62. Templeton Diary, Oct. 13, 1867, cited in Hagan, *Exactly in the Right Place*, 148; Templeton Diary, Nov. 19-20, 1867, cited in John D. McDermott, *Red Cloud's War: The Bozeman Trail, 1866–1868*, vol. 2, 470; Story, "Nelson Story Sr. Was One of Montana's First Gold Miners."

63. Mark Herbert Brown, *The Plainsmen of the Yellowstone: A History of the Yellowstone Basin*, 182.

64. Davis Willson, "From Bozeman," *Montana Post*, May 2, 1868; J. S. Carvell, "The Indian Raid Between Fort Ellis and the Yellowstone," *Helena Weekly Herald*, Apr. 30, 1868; Stuart, *Forty Years on the Frontier*, vol. 2, 81.

65. LaMotte to Fort Shaw, Aug. 1, 1868, FERC.

66. Willson, "From Bozeman."

67. Athearn, *William Tecumseh Sherman*, 198; LaMotte to Fort Shaw, Aug. 1, 1868, FERC; McDermott, *Red Cloud's War*, vol. 2, 517.

68. Thomas Marquis, *Custer, Cavalry & Crows:*

The Story of William White as told to Thomas Marquis, 54.

69. Hagan, *Exactly in the Right Place*, 231–32.

70. LaMotte to Fort Shaw, Aug. 1, 1868, FERC.

71. Statement of Nelson Story, Sept. 6, 1894, Claim #9481, *Records of the United States Court of Claims*, cited in McDermott, *Red Cloud's War*, vol. 2, 518.

72. Davis Willson, "Bozeman Correspondence," *Montana Post*, July 31, 1868; J. S. Carvell, "From Our Regular Ft. Ellis Correspondent," *Helena Weekly Herald*, Aug. 20, 1868; Leeson, *History of Montana*, 1165.

73. McDermott, *Red Cloud's War*, vol. 2, 522–23; *Avant Courier*, Aug. 4, 1900; Robert M. Utley, *The Lance and the Shield: The Life and Times of Sitting Bull*, 82; Brown, *The Plainsmen of the Yellowstone*, 427.

74. Leeson, *History of Montana*, 604; Merrill G. Burlingame, *Historical Report: Concerning Lands Ceded to the United States Government by the Crow Indians in the Treaty of 1868*, 48–49; Carvell, "From Our Regular Ft. Ellis Correspondent"; Burkhart, interview.

75. Mrs. W. H. Tracy, "Reminiscences of Early Days," *Avant Courier*, Mar. 11, 1899. The Guy House was located at 35 East Main Street.

76. Last names of the men killed were Leonard, Newall, Moore, McDowell, and Crowell. See J. M. Lindley, "Last Raid of the Hostile Sioux," *Avant Courier*, Dec. 5, 1902.

77. *Montana Post*, Mar. 19, 1869.

78. The meeting was at Fridley's Billiard Hall and Saloon on Mar. 22. See *Montana Post*, Apr. 2, 1869.

79. *Helena Herald*, May 7, 1868.

80. *Montana Post*, Apr. 2, 1869.

81. *Helena Herald*, July 15, 1869.

82. Seibel, *Fort Ellis*, 15, 47.

83. *Rocky Mountain News*, Aug. 18, 1874; Whether Black met Story in Kansas is unknown.

84. *Leander M. Black*, H.R. Doc. No. 871, 46 Cong., 2nd sess., 1880.

85. Horace Maynard, quoted in Simon, *The Papers of Ulysses S. Grant*, vol. 19, 356.

Chapter Five

1. Brown, *The Plainsmen of the Yellowstone*, 428.

2. The actual amount was $153,557.28. *Montana War-Claims*, H.R. Rep. No. 82, 42 Cong., 2nd sess., 1872, 39–40, Alexander Leggat Pamphlet Collection, 1863–1966, Collection 2369, Merrill G. Burlingame Papers (hereafter cited as Leggat Collection); *Avant Courier*, Mar. 21, 1872.

3. Mary A. Black v. Nelson Story, judgment, Mar. 13, 1897, box 144: 2382 (hereafter Black v. Story 2382), GCCC.

4. ARCIA, 1870, 199; Keith Algier, *The Crow and the Eagle, A Tribal History from Lewis and Clark to Custer*, 237–38, 256; Brown, *The Plainsmen of the Yellowstone*, 428–29; B. Derek Strahn, "The Savior of Eastern Montana," *At Home Magazine* 6 (Nov. 2005), 9.

5. Deeds recorded in the Gallatin County Clerk and Recorders Office, Bozeman, Montana (hereafter GCCR): Nelson Story to Leander M. Black, Jan. 3, 1870 (filed Oct. 8, 1881), Deed Book 2: 95; Leander M. Black to Nelson Story, Jan. 3, 1870, Deed Book H: 24; M. M. Black, administrator for the estate of Leander Black v. Nelson Story, Ellen Story, and Elias Story, judgment, Dec. 30, 1887, box 56: 552 (hereafter Black v. Story 552), GCCC.

6. *Weekly Courier*, Mar. 28, 1917; *Bozeman Courier*, May 7, 1948.

7. *Montana Pick and Plow*, Dec. 31, 1869.

8. Gray, *Custer's Last Campaign*, 88; Jerry Brekke, "Historical Overview of Benson's Landing, Park County, Montana."

9. The dissolution was completed by an intermediary, attorney Joseph Davis. See Black v. Story 552, GCCC.

10. Mrs. E. L. Houston, "Landmark of Bozeman Moved. Once Home of Nelson Story," *Bozeman Chronicle*, Apr. 2, 1914; "Mrs. Nelson Story Sketch," M. L. Alderson Papers. The home was located on the southeast corner of Main Street and Tracy Avenue. Since relocated, it is still used today at 322 West Mendenhall Street.

11. Merrill G. Burlingame ed., *Bozeman in 1869: The Diary and Reminiscences of Mrs. William H. Tracy*, 29.

12. Todd Wilkinson, "Here, History Really Is The Story Of Our Town," *Bozeman Daily Chronicle*, May 20, 2002; *Bozeman Chronicle*, May 30, 1907; *Weekly Courier*, Feb. 25, 1914; *Bozeman Courier*, Apr. 11, 1923.

13. *U.S. Federal Census Mortality Schedules, 1850–1855, Non-population Census Schedules*

for *Montana, 1870 and 1880,* Gallatin, Montana, M1806, Roll 1, 1869.

14. John Waller, *Health and Wellness in 19th-century America*, 96.

15. Riley, *The Female Frontier*, 52.

16. *1870 U.S. Federal Census*, Bozeman, Gallatin, Montana Territory, Roll M593_827, p. 112B, Family History Library, film 552326.

17. *Avant Courier*, Apr. 27, 1901; Leeson, *History of Montana*, 1115; *Bozeman Weekly Chronicle*, August 20, 1925. In 1877, the Metropolitan, located on the northeast corner of Main Street and Bozeman Avenue, was acquired by the Malin Brothers from St. Louis, who changed the name to match one of that city's finest hotels, the Laclede.

18. *Bozeman Chronicle*, Feb. 25, 1909.

19. Paul A. Hutton, "Phil Sheridan's Pyrrhic Victory: The Piegan Massacre, Army Politics, and the Transfer Debate," *Montana* 32 (Spring 1982): 38–39. Rodger C. Henderson, "The Piikuni and the U.S. Army's Piegan Expedition: Competing Narratives of the 1870 Massacre on the Marias River," *Montana* 68 (Spring 2018): 48–70.

20. *Montana Pick and Plow* and *New York Evening Post*, cited in Strahn, "Fort Ellis Remembered," *At Home Magazine* 5 (Dec. 2004): 10–11.

21. Hutton, "Phil Sheridan's Pyrrhic Victory," 32.

22. Dan DeQuille, *A History of the Comstock Mines: Mineral and Agricultural Resources of Silver Land*, 36–37, 39; *Bozeman Chronicle*, July 25, 1900; *Bozeman Courier*, Apr. 23, 1924; *Brooklyn Eagle*, May 12, 1886.

23. Francis Paul Prucha, *The Great Father: The United States Government and the American Indians*, vol. 1, 502.

24. Burlingame, *The Montana Frontier*, 179; Lyndel Meikle, "No Paper Trail—Crooked Agents on the Crow Reservation, 1874–1878," in *Speaking Ill of the Dead*, 25; Lawrence F. Small, ed., *Religion in Montana: Pathways to the Present*, vol. 1, 142.

25. Prucha, *The Great Father*, vol. 1, 517–19.

26. Algier, *The Crow and the Eagle*, 239–40.

27. Ibid., 290–93; Lawrence L. Loendorf and Nancy Medaris Stone, *Mountain Spirit: The Sheep Eater Indians of Yellowstone*, 167; Brigham D. Madsen, *The Lemhi: Sacajawea's People*, 73.

28. Algier, *The Crow and the Eagle*, 241–42, 296, 314.

29. *Republican-Courier*, Sept. 19, 1905; Leeson, *History of Montana*, 1165–66; Malcolm Story, interview.

30. *Bozeman Avant Courier*, Jan. 5, 1877.

31. *Avant Courier*, Sept. 13, 1871.

32. *Republican-Courier*, Sept. 15, 1905. Subscription to the paper cost six dollars a year. Advertising was eight dollars per inch per month.

33. *Avant Courier*, Sept. 13, 1871.

34. Ibid., Sept. 27, 1871; Ibid., May 9, 1872; Black v. Story 2382, GCCC; Strahn, "The Savior of Eastern Montana," 9; National Register of Historic Places, South Tracy-South Black Historic District, Bozeman, Gallatin County, Montana, National Register #87001840, sec. 8: 47–48. The residential section, an extension of the "Original Townsite," was named Black's Addition.

35. Leeson, *History of Montana*, 1166; Leander M. Black v. Nelson Story, Oct. 15, 1874, boxes 15 & 16 (hereafter Black v. Story 1516), GCCC.

36. *Avant Courier*, July 25, 1872; *Bozeman Avant Courier*, Jan. 31, 1873; F. R. Brunot to C. Delano, Aug. 28, 1873, cited in Algier, *The Crow and the Eagle*, 294.

37. *Avant Courier*, July 25, 1872. The bank could sell United States bonds and disburse public funds to the War and Interior Departments. The initial capital was fifty thousand dollars. Black was president, George Fox cashier, and William Roe, C. J. Lyster, and John Bruce officers. The First National Bank building was located on the southeast corner of Main Street and Black Avenue.

38. The Cooper/Black Building is located at 118 East Main Street.

39. Bill Skidmore, *Treasure State Treasury. Montana Banks, Bankers, & Banking 1864–1984*, 27.

40. *Gallatin County Tribune* and *Belgrade Journal*, Apr. 21, 1955; Strickler, interview.

41. Alderson Diary, 79: entry of Apr. 15, 1872.

42. Houston, *Early History*, 13.

43. *Weekly Courier*, Apr. 1, 1914. Blackmore sent a pyramid-shaped headstone from Salt Lake City that still marks his wife's grave, and later a mountain to the south

of Bozeman was named in honor of the Blackmores.

44. Haines, "McAdow Mill," and "Salesville or Tomlinson Mill," in *Flouring Mills of Montana Territory*, 7, 16; David Kennedy, "Walter Cooper, 'Old Reliable,' and the Bad Business of Buffalo," *Pioneer Museum Quarterly* 32 (Summer 2009), 25; Peter Koch to Laurentze Koch, Jan. 14, 1873, cited in Kim Allen Scott, ed., *Splendid on a Large Scale*, 248; *Bozeman Avant Courier*, July 25, 1902.

45. *Avant Courier*, Sept. 19, 1872.

46. Robert W. Larson, *Gall: Lakota War Chief*, 83.

47. *Avant Courier*, Nov. 30, 1871; *Bozeman Avant Courier*, Aug. 22, 1872; M. John Lubetkin, "'No Fighting Is To Be Apprehended': Major Eugene Baker, Sitting Bull, and the Northern Pacific Railroad's 1872 Western Yellowstone Surveying Expedition." *Montana* 56 (Summer 2006): 33–40.

48. Kim Allen Scott, "Anatomy of a Lynching," *In Celebration of Our Past* 15 (2003), 72–75.

49. *Weekly Courier*, July 8, 1914.

50. Scott, "Anatomy of a Lynching," 76–77.

51. *Bozeman Avant Courier*, Feb. 7, 1873.

52. The execution site was at the corner of Broadway Avenue and West Main Street.

53. Scott, "Anatomy of a Lynching," 71; *Weekly Courier*, July 8, 1914; Bine to Budge, Dec. 13, 1944.

54. *Bozeman Avant Courier*, Feb. 7, 1873.

CHAPTER SIX

1. *Bozeman Avant Courier*, May 2, 1873.

2. Gray, *Custer's Last Campaign*, 101.

3. *Bozeman Avant Courier*, Nov. 7, 1872.

4. Black v. Story 1516, GCCC.

5. Leforge, *Memoirs of a White Crow Indian*, 60–61.

6. Ibid., 62.

7. *Montana War-Claims*, H.R. Rep. No. 82, 42 Cong., 2nd sess., 1872, 45, 47.

8. *Montana Indian War Claims*, H.R. Doc. No. 98, 41 Cong., 3rd sess., 1871, 1; *Montana War-Claims*, H.R. Rep. No. 82, 42 Cong., 2nd sess., 1872, 8; *Montana Indian War Claims of 1867*, H.R. Doc. No. 9, 43 Cong., 2nd sess., 1874, 2, Leggat Collection.

9. *New York Sun*, Nov. 17, 1871.

10. *Helena Gazette*, cited in *Avant Courier*, Dec. 7, 1871.

11. Sam Word was with John Bozeman's ill-fated wagon train of 1863, joining those who turned back to the Platte.

12. *Bozeman Avant Courier*, Dec. 5, 1872; Ibid., Feb. 14, 1873; Ibid., Mar. 28, 1873.

13. Ibid., Apr. 11, 1873.

14. Robert G. Athearn, "Railroad to a Far Off Country: The Utah & Northern," *Montana* 18 (Autumn 1968): 4–6; *Avant Courier*, May 2, 1873.

15. Leeson, *History of Montana*, 619.

16. *Bozeman Avant Courier*, May 30, 1873.

17. Ibid., Apr. 18, 1873; Ibid., May 9, 1873; Ibid., May 16, 1873.

18. *New York Times*, May 21, 1873.

19. *Bozeman Avant Courier*, Apr. 18, 1873; *New York Times*, May 17, 1873.

20. F. D. Pease to Commissioner of Indian Affairs, Dec. 28, 1872, cited in Algier, *The Crow and the Eagle*, 298.

21. ARCIA, 1873, 249.

22. *Investigation on the Conduct of Indian Affairs*, H.R. Rep. No. 778, 43 Cong., 1st sess., 1874, 227 (hereafter ICIA No. 778).

23. ARCIA, 1871, 418.

24. Ibid., 1873, 115–16; Leforge, *Memoirs of a White Crow Indian*, 95–96.

25. ARCIA, 1873, 133.

26. *Bozeman Avant Courier*, Sept. 19, 1873.

27. ARCIA, 1873, 129.

28. Ibid.

29. Gray, *Custer's Last Campaign*, 102; *Agreement with Crow Indians*, H.R. Doc. No. 89, 43 Cong., 1st sess., 1874, 12.

30. *Bozeman Avant Courier*, Aug. 22, 1873.

31. Ibid., Sept. 5, 1873; Topping, *The Chronicles of the Yellowstone*, 99–100.

32. *Bozeman Avant Courier*, Jan. 23, 1874; Jan. 30, 1874.

33. Ibid., Sept. 19, 1873.

34. Niebel, *Century of Service*, 11–13.

35. Richard White, *Railroaded: The Transcontinentals and the Making of Modern America*, 56, 73, 83.

36. Daniel S. Tuttle to E. G. Dimmick, Oct. 10, 1873, in *Bozeman Avant Courier*, Nov. 7, 1873.

37. Peter Koch to Laurentze Koch, Oct. 2, 1873, cited in Scott, ed., *Splendid on a Large Scale*, 277.

38. *Madisonian*, Nov. 20, 1875.

39. James S. Brisbin, report to General Sheridan on Indian agency fraud, 1878 (hereafter

40. Brisbin to Sheridan, 1878), 15, James Sanks Brisbin Papers, 1850–1891, MC 39, MHS.

40. Gray, *Custer's Last Campaign*, 102–3.

41. Brisbin to Sheridan, 1878, 7.

42. Ibid., 5–6, 24.

43. *Gallatin County Republican*, Nov. 15, 1904.

44. Peter Koch to Laurentze Koch, Dec. 25, 1873, 286, and Peter Koch to Laurentze Koch, Feb. 28, 1874, cited in Scott, ed., *Splendid on a Large Scale*, 302. The post was also as known as Fort Sherman and Fort Defiance.

45. *Bozeman Avant Courier*, Mar. 27, 1874.

46. *New York Times*, Nov. 2, 1873.

47. *Bozeman Avant Courier*, Dec. 12, 1873.

48. Gray, *Custer's Last Campaign*, 104–5.

49. Leeson, *History of Montana*, 619; *Bozeman Avant Courier*, June 27, 1873; Ibid., July 4, 1873; *Weekly Courier*, Mar. 27, 1918. Other officers were George Fox, S. B. Bowen, John Mendenhall, Charles Rich, Charles Clark, Perry McAdow, Charles Hoffman, Alexander McPherson, and H. N. McGuire. Story owned six hundred shares of capital stock at twenty-five dollars a share.

50. A. J. Noyes, *In The Land of The Chinook, the Story of Blaine County*, 106; *Bozeman Avant Courier*, Jan. 23, 1874; Ibid., Jan. 30, 1874. Story briefly considered sending Peter Koch from the Judith to the Tongue River to help carpenters begin construction of a townsite, but scrapped the idea.

51. Benjamin Franklin Grounds was elected captain, William Wright lieutenant, Eli B. Way adjutant, and Hugh O'Donovan signal officer. See *Bozeman Avant Courier*, May 15, 1874.

52. James S. Hutchins, "Poison in the Pemmican: A detailed account of The Yellowstone Wagon-Road Prospecting Expedition of 1874," *Montana* 8 (Summer 1958): 10–11; Utley, *The Lance and the Shield*, 118; *New York Times*, Mar. 15, 1874.

53. *Helena Herald*, cited in *Bozeman Avant Courier*, Mar. 27, 1874.

54. W. E. Ellsworth, *A History of the Gallatin Valley and City of Bozeman, with Sketches of Men, Firms, and Corporations*, 6.

55. *Bozeman Avant Courier*, May 15, 1874; Hutchins, "Poison in the Pemmican," 9–10. Though the Yellowstone Expedition committee labeled Vernon a lunatic, they tried to merge the two forces before the Bozeman departure. Vernon initially resisted, but by then had changed his mind.

56. *Madisonian*, Mar. 7, 1874; *New York Times*, Mar. 15, 1874.

57. Leeson, *History of Montana*, 1166; RFF.

58. Lee Silliman, "The Carroll Trail: Utopian Enterprise," *Montana* 24 (Spring 1974): 2–3; *Bozeman Avant Courier*, Mar. 6, 1874. Dawes would eventually sell the post to Major A. S. Reed and Jim Bowles, who relocated portions near the present site of Lewistown.

59. *Bozeman Avant Courier*, Mar. 13, 1874.

60. ICIA No. 778, 178–83.

61. Ibid., 283.

62. Other investors included A. Bart Henderson and C. J. Lyston.

63. *Bozeman Avant Courier*, July 24, 1874; Aubrey L. Haines, *The Yellowstone Story: A History of Our First National Park*, vol. 1, 188–89.

64. David R. Miller, Dennis J. Smith, Joseph R. McGeshick, James Shanle, and Caleb Shields, *The History of the Fort Peck Assiniboine and Sioux Tribes, 1800–2000*, 81.

65. "Paul J. McCormick—Grand Old Man of Montana," Yellowstone Genealogy Forum, https://www.ancestry.com. Ed Fenlason and Mel Gemmill, "Villainous Vernon," *In Celebration of Our Past* 12 (2000), 73–74.

66. *Bozeman Avant Courier*, May 8, 1874.

67. Brown, *The Plainsmen of the Yellowstone*, 217–18.

68. *Bozeman Avant Courier*, May 1, 1874; *Sheridan Wyoming Enterprise,* cited in *Bozeman Chronicle*, July 28, 1898; Addison Quivey, "The Yellowstone Expedition of 1874," *Contributions to the Historical Society of Montana* 1 (1876), 284.

69. Utley, *The Lance and the Shield*, 119; Burlingame, *The Montana Frontier*, 209.

70. B. F. Potts to Columbus Delano, May 7, 1874, cited in Brown, *The Plainsmen of the Yellowstone*, 214.

71. Mark H. Brown, "Muddled Men Have Muddied The Yellowstone's True Color," *Montana* 11 (Winter 1961): 35; James Bruce Putnam, *The Evolution of a Frontier Town: Bozeman, Montana and Its Search for Economic Stability, 1864–1867*, 40.

72. ARCIA, 1874, 262.

73. Ibid., 1874, 261.

74. Brown, *The Plainsmen of the Yellowstone*, 336; Park County Historical Society, "3rd Annual Historical Tour," *A Collection of Historical Tours of Park County and the Surrounding Areas*, 3, GHSRC.

75. Brown, *The Plainsmen of the Yellowstone*, 432; ARCIA, 1874, 261.

76. Special Requisition, May 4, 1874, cited in Algier, *The Crow and the Eagle*, 300.

77. Malcolm Story, interview; *Madisonian*, Dec. 4, 1875.

78. William (Billy) Frazier, interview by Bessie Benham, Apr. 3–4, 1940, GHSRC (hereafter Frazier, interview).

79. Brisbin to Sheridan, 1878, 15–16.

80. Ibid., 17–18.

81. *Madisonian*, Jan. 8, 1876.

82. Brisbin to Sheridan, 1878, 10–11, 18–19, 30.

83. J. A. Wright to E. P. Smith, June 2, 1874, cited in Algier, *The Crow and the Eagle*, 245.

84. *Helena Weekly Herald*, July 23, 1874.

85. *Madisonian*, July 11, 1874.

86. *Bozeman Avant Courier*, July 31, 1874.

87. Ibid., Aug. 7, 1874.

88. Ibid., Sept. 18, 1874.

89. Ibid., Nov. 7, 1874.

90. Accusations of fraud and bribery in the election forced the matter into the courts, and it would be a year before the Montana Supreme Court ruled in Helena's favor. *Helena Weekly Herald*, Aug. 6, 1874; Malone, Roeder, Lang, *Montana*, 109–10.

91. *Bozeman Avant Courier*, Nov. 7, 1874; Ibid., May 16, 1878.

92. *Bozeman Times*, Nov. 13, 1874.

93. *Bozeman Chronicle*, Oct. 3, 1907.

94. Tracy, "Reminiscences of Early Days."

95. *Bozeman Avant Courier*, Dec. 21, 1871.

96. *Avant Courier*, Nov. 13, 1874.

97. *St. James Episcopal Church, Eighty Years . . . 1868–1948*.

98. Algier, *The Crow and the Eagle*, 247; Gray, *Custer's Last Campaign*, 113.

99. Clapp to E. P. Smith, Dec. 23, 1874, cited in Gray, *Custer's Last Campaign*, 114.

100. Clapp to E. P. Smith, Dec. 31, 1874, ibid.

101. N. B. Sweitzer to the Assistant Adjutant General, Department of Dakota, Apr. 25, 1875, Fort Ellis Records, 1869–1876, Microfilm reel 123 (hereafter FERM), MHS.

102. *Bozeman Times*, June 3, 1875.

103. *New York Times*, May 7, 1875; *Madisonian*, Nov. 20, 1875.

104. Contract of William Kiskadden, May 26, 1875, Deposition of William Kiskadden, Nov. 12, 1877, in Nelson Story v. L. M. Black, boxes 23 and 24: 201 (hereafter Story v. Black 201), GCCC; Deposition of William Kiskadden, Apr. 15, 1879 (hereafter Kiskadden Deposition), in Nelson Story v. Leander M. Black, box 30: 225 (hereafter Story v. Black 225), GCCC. Kiskadden was married to Maria Slade, widow of alleged road agent Joseph Slade, hung by the vigilantes. The other surety was D. J. McCann.

105. *Letter from the Secretary of the Treasury . . . relative to the settlement of the accounts of Dexter E. Clapp, late agent of the Crow Indians, Montana Territory*, S. Doc. No. 19, 46 Cong., 3rd sess., 1880, (hereafter S. Doc. No. 19) 3, 4, 7, 10. All of these payments were rejected by the Committee of Indian Affairs.

106. Statement of Dexter E. Clapp, Apr. 18, 1876, folder 4, Crow Indian Agency Fraud Hearings Collection, 1876–1877, Collection 2146 (hereafter CIAF), Merrill G. Burlingame Special Collections.

107. Statement of Dexter E. Clapp, Apr. 18, 1876, folder 4, CIAF.

CHAPTER SEVEN

1. William E. Lass, "Steamboats on the Yellowstone," *Montana* 35 (Autumn 1985): 27–28; Charles W. Bryan Jr., "Dr. Lamme and His Gallant Little 'Yellowstone,'" *Montana* 15 (Summer 1965), 25.

2. *Bozeman Avant Courier*, June 18, 1875; Utley, *The Lance and the Shield*, 119; James Brisbin to Assistant Adjutant General, Department of Dakota, Mar. 6, 1876, FERM.

3. *Bozeman Avant Courier*, June 25, 1875.

4. *Bozeman Times*, June 29, 1875. The *Maggie Hoppe* was named for Hugh Hoppe's daughter Margaret.

5. Utley, *The Lance and the Shield*, 119; *Helena Weekly Herald*, July 29, 1875; Gray, *Custer's Last Campaign*, 118.

6. *Bozeman Avant Courier*, Dec. 4, 1874; *Madisonian*, Nov. 20, 1875; Ibid., May 1, 1875.

7. *Bozeman Times*, June 29, 1875; Ibid., July 6, 1875.

8. S. Doc. No. 19, 10. Payment was suspended;

Story also expanded his freighting into other areas of the territory, charging clients nearly twice the going rate of five cents a pound if forced to use unestablished roads. See Henry Blake and Cornelius Hedges, Story, respondent, v. Maclay, appellant, *Reports of Cases Argued and Determined in the Supreme Court of Montana Territory, from the August Term, 1877 to the August Term, 1880, Inclusive*, vol. 3, 482.

9. *Madisonian*, July 10, 1875.

10. Algier, *The Crow and the Eagle*, 328–29. A small tributary of the Stillwater River near where Joe was killed is still called Mexican Joe Creek. A nearby hill is known as Joe Hill. Thomas Leforge claims Tsoyio's remains may have been found a year later, several miles downstream. See Leforge, *Memoirs of a White Crow Indian*, 119.

11. *Madisonian*, July 10, 1875.

12. D. W. Benham to the Assistant Adjutant General, District of Montana, July 9, 1875, FERM; Joseph Lindley, "Last Raid of the Hostile Sioux," *Avant Courier*, Dec. 12, 1902.

13. Lieutenant Jerome's cousin Jennie Jerome married Lord Randolph Churchill and was mother of British Prime Minister Winston Churchill.

14. Lindley, "Last Raid of the Hostile Sioux"; *Bozeman Avant Courier*, July 16, 1875. The group included James Latta, Ed Fridley, and Madison Black.

15. ARCIA, 1875, 302; *Madisonian*, July 17, 1875; Lindley, "Last Raid of the Hostile Sioux."

16. D. W. Benham to the Assistant Adjutant General, Department of Dakota, June 23, 1875, FERM.

17. Benjamin F. Potts to U. S. Grant, July 8–9, 1875, in Simon, *The Papers of Ulysses S. Grant*, vol. 26, 513.

18. D. W. Benham to the Acting Assistant Adjutant General, District of Montana, July 14, 1875, FERM; *Helena Weekly Herald*, July 22, 1875; Leeson, *History of Montana*, 636.

19. Gray, *Custer's Last Campaign*, 119–20.

20. *Bozeman Avant Courier*, July 23, 1875. Fort Pease was occupied by the army during the 1876 Sioux campaign, and eventually abandoned.

21. Belknap was the first cabinet officer to ever visit Montana. He received red-carpet treatment, including music by the cornet band, a firing of cannons, and a display of national flags. See *Helena Weekly Herald*, July 29, 1875.

22. The other two were Frank Murray and Sam Malin. Story filed a $2,250 claim against the U.S. government for the loss of cattle and equipment from these raids. It would take more than ten years to settle, but the government eventually agreed to pay $2,000. See *Weekly Avant Courier*, June 16, 1887.

23. Leforge, *Memoirs of a White Crow Indian*, 120; *Bozeman Avant Courier*, Aug. 6, 1875.

24. *Helena Independent*, Aug. 12, 1875.

25. ARCIA, 1875, 303.

26. Algier, *The Crow and the Eagle*, 330; Captain Benham shared the same concerns about the agency relocation as Major Sweitzer, telling his superiors in July, "That the whole thing is gotten up for the benefit of the Traders who by the removal will secure the entire trade of the Crow Indians without competition, in short it is a movement in the interests of the Indian Ring." See D. W. Benham to the Assistant Adjutant General, District of Montana, July 8, 1875, FERM.

27. ARCIA, 1875, 302; S. Doc. No. 19, 11. Payment was suspended.

28. Gray, *Custer's Last Campaign*, 121; *Bozeman Avant Courier*, Aug. 20, 1875; Carroll Van West, *Capitalism on the Frontier: Billings and the Yellowstone Valley in the Nineteenth Century*, 40.

29. Wilson, "Evolution of Montana Agriculture," 439.

30. Prucha, *The Great Father*, 1: 517–19; Henry Hartshorne, ed., "An Important Address," in *Friends' Review: A Religious, Literary and Miscellaneous Journal* 28 (1874–1875): 810.

31. Stuart, *Forty Years on the Frontier*, vol. 2, 80.

32. J. M. Yandell to C. Delano, Apr. 1, 1875, cited in Algier, *The Crow and the Eagle*, 301–2.

33. Leforge, *Memoirs of a White Crow Indian*, 56–57.

34. West, *Capitalism on the Frontier*, 41.

35. Frazier, interview.

36. Hartshorne, "An Important Address," 810–11.

37. *Bozeman Avant Courier*, Aug. 6, 1875.

38. *Bozeman Times*, Aug. 24, 1875.

39. Ibid., Sept. 14, 1875.

40. *Bozeman Avant Courier*, Oct. 22, 1875; *Madisonian*, Oct. 23, 1875.

41. The jurors were L. B. Olds, S. R. Buford, George Ramsey, James Smith, H. N. Veeden, George Young, Jacob Housel, R. M. Goin, George Flanders, N. M. Farnum, G. Barnes, Henry Monforton, Robert Gillespie, Joseph Plumb, Thomas Deyarmon, P. D. Hayward, and Charles Anceney. See *Madisonian*, Oct. 23, 1875.

42. Vivian A. Paladin, ed., "Memoirs of a Many-Sided Man: The Personal Record of a Civil War Veteran, Montana Territorial Editor, Attorney, Jurist," *Montana* 14 (Autumn 1964): 34-35, 49-50; Simon, *The Papers of Ulysses S. Grant*, vol. 26, 512.

43. Yale University, *The Twenty Years' Record of the Yale Class of 1862*, 92.

44. Brisbin to Sheridan, 1878, 48-52; Scott, ed., *Splendid on a Large Scale*, 331-32.

45. *Madisonian*, Nov. 6, 1875. The true identity of "Witness" remains unknown. Mounting debt had forced Leander Black to temporarily cease publication of the *Bozeman Times*, making an anonymous letter campaign in the *Madisonian* his only recourse to discredit Story. See *Bozeman Times*, Sept. 14, 1875. Another viable candidate is Sam Word, or any of the agency employees who had witnessed Story's misdeeds.

46. Ibid., Nov. 4, 1875; *Bozeman Avant Courier*, Nov. 19, 1875.

47. Ibid., Oct. 29, 1875.

48. *Madisonian*, Oct. 23, 1875.

49. Ibid., Oct. 30, 1875.

50. *Bozeman Avant Courier*, Nov. 19, 1875.

51. *Madisonian*, Nov. 6, 1875.

52. *Bozeman Avant Courier*, Nov. 12, 1875.

53. *Bozeman Times*, Sept. 14, 1875.

54. West, *Capitalism on the Frontier*, 41; *Bozeman Avant Courier*, Nov. 12, 1875.

55. M. Maginnis to C. Delano, Sept. 27, 1875, cited in Algier, *The Crow and the Eagle*, 289.

56. *Madisonian*, Nov. 20, 1875.

57. *Bozeman Avant Courier*, Nov. 12, 1875.

58. Ibid.

59. Ibid., Nov. 19, 1875.

60. Simon, *The Papers of Ulysses S. Grant*, vol. 26, 513.

61. *Bozeman Avant Courier*, Oct. 8, 1875; Ibid., Oct. 15, 1875; Ibid., Nov. 5, 1875; Ibid., Dec. 31, 1875; Bryan, "Dr. Lamme and His Gallant Little 'Yellowstone,'" 29.

62. *New York Tribune*, cited in *Bozeman Avant Courier*, Nov. 26, 1875.

63. Lass, "Steamboats on the Yellowstone," 27-28.

64. Dexter E. Clapp to E. P. Smith, n.d., Crow Indian Agency Records, 1872–1900, Collection 883, MHS.

65. *Bozeman Avant Courier*, Jan. 21, 1876; *Bozeman Times*, Feb. 3, 1876; Miller, et al., *Fort Peck Assiniboine and Sioux Tribes*, 87; *Republican-Courier*, Oct. 16, 1906.

66. *Bozeman Times*, Feb. 3, 1876.

67. *New North-West*, Feb. 18, 1876; *Bozeman Times*, Apr. 6, 1876.

68. S. Doc. No. 19, 16. Payments were suspended.

CHAPTER EIGHT

1. Nelson Story v. Leander M. Black, Dec. 31, 1877, box 25: 219, GCCC.

2. *Bozeman Avant Courier*, Jan. 14, 1876.

3. Deposition of DeWitt C. Marshall, Sept. 16, 1878 (hereafter Marshall Deposition), in Story v. Black 201, GCCC.

4. The contract provision called for a dollar and a quarter per hundred pounds per hundred miles, yielding the rate of ninety-one and one-quarter cents for transportation.

5. Contract of William Kiskadden, May 26, 1875 (hereafter Kiskadden Contract), in Story v. Black 201, GCCC; William Kiskadden to E. P. Smith, Oct. 12, 1875 (hereafter Kiskadden to Smith), ibid.; Edward Smith to Secretary of Interior, Oct. 22, 1875 (hereafter Smith to Interior), ibid.; Marshall Deposition, ibid.

6. Ed Ball to Col. L. M. Black, Sept. 25, 1875, in Story v. Black 201.

7. Deposition of Dexter E. Clapp, May 1, 1879 (hereafter D. Clapp Deposition), Story v. Black 201; Marshall Deposition, ibid.

8. Dexter Clapp to the Commissioner of Indian Affairs, Dec. 30, 1876, 22-23, folder 1, CIAF (hereafter Clapp to CIA); Marshall Deposition, Story v. Black 201; Deposition of William Kiskadden, Nov. 12, 1877 (hereafter Kiskadden Deposition), ibid.; Interrogatories Propounded to Dexter Clapp, Mar. 13, 1878 (hereafter D. Clapp Interrogatories), ibid.

9. Interrogatories Propounded to James Hall, Apr. 11, 1878 (hereafter Hall Interrogatories), Story v. Black 201; D. Clapp

Interrogatories, Amended Complaint, Nov. 15, 1877, ibid.; Thomas Lewis v. L. M. Black, Sept. 14, 1876, box 25, GCCC; Story v. Black 225.

10. Edward Ball to the Commissioner of Indian Affairs, Feb. 18, 1876, CIAF (hereafter Ball to CIA).

11. Ibid.

12. D. Clapp Interrogatories, Story v. Black 201.

13. Ball to CIA.

14. D. Clapp Deposition, Story v. Black 201.

15. Ball to CIA.

16. Proceedings and Debates, 46 Cong., 2nd sess., 1880, 10, 2449.

17. Ibid., 2450.

18. Ibid.

19. Jurors were Leroy Southmayd, John D. Thomas, J. H. Baker, Henry S. Gilbert, J. B. Snapp, Hugh Edwards, A. H. Sennett, John Willhart, F. R. Merk, R. P. Bateman, James Word, and Isaac Underwood. Trial jurors were M. D. Johnson, J. H. Pfeil, John T. Ingram, A. Lambrecht, E. H. Bartlett, G. Cowell, Nick Carey, M. D. Platney, W. B. Webb, and three others. See *Madisonian*, Feb. 26, 1876.

20. *Bozeman Times*, Mar. 30, 1876; *Madisonian*, Mar. 25, 1876.

21. Ibid.

22. Ibid.

23. Brisbin to Sheridan, 1878, 45–47.

24. Ibid., 53.

25. *Helena Independent*, Apr. 5, 1876.

26. *Madisonian*, Apr. 8, 1876.

27. *Rocky Mountain Husbandman*, Apr. 13, 1876.

28. *Bozeman Avant Courier*, Apr. 14, 1876; *Bozeman Times*, Apr. 27, 1876.

29. *Madisonian*, Apr. 15, 1876.

30. *Bozeman Avant Courier*, Apr. 14, 1876.

31. *Bozeman Times*, Apr. 20, 1876.

32. Jean Edward Smith, *Grant*, 540, 590–94.

33. Walter Joachim, "Hiester Clymer and the Belknap Case," *Historical Review of Berks County* 36 (Winter 1970–71), 13.

34. *New York Times*, Mar. 30, 1876.

35. Ibid., Apr. 5, 1876. When Brisbin forwarded Ball's report, William Belknap was secretary of war. By the time it reached Washington, he had been succeeded by Alphonso Taft.

36. *Bozeman Avant Courier*, Mar. 31, 1876.

37. *Bozeman Times*, Apr. 27, 1876; *Madisonian*, Apr. 22, 1876.

38. Simon, *The Papers of Ulysses S. Grant*, vol. 27, 394.

39. *Bozeman Avant Courier*, May 5, 1876; *Bozeman Chronicle*, Jan. 4, 1912; Clapp to CIA.

40. Marshall Deposition, Story v. Black 201.

41. Kiskadden Deposition, Story v. Black 201; Nelson Story v. Fellows D. Pease and Leander Black, Mar. 24, 1877, box 25: 182, GCCC.

42. Proceedings and Debates, 44 Cong., 1st sess., 1876, H3639.

43. *Bozeman Avant Courier*, July 28, 1876.

44. Ibid.

45. Ibid.

46. Jim Annin, *Horace Countryman: Unsung Hero*, 6.

47. *Madisonian*, Aug. 10, 1876.

48. *Yankton Press & Dakotan*, cited in *Bozeman Avant Courier*, June 16, 1876; Bryan, "Dr. Lamme and His Gallant Little 'Yellowstone,'" 30–31.

49. Nelson Story to Thomas A. Thompson, Nov. 17, 1876, quoted in Story, "Nelson Story Sr. Was One of Montana's First Gold Miners."

50. Bryan, "Dr. Lamme and His Gallant Little 'Yellowstone,'" 35; *Helena Independent*, July 31, 1876.

51. "Officers of the Army That Know Capt. Ed. Ball," folder 6, CIAF.

52. Brisbin to Sheridan, 1878, 56.

53. Rey is the spelling in his military record. Records of the Adjutant General's Office, 1780s–1917, Appointment, Commission and Personal Branch Files, box 400, 9w/6/26/6, RG 94, National Archives; Randall A. Johnson, "The Ordeal of the Steptoe Command," *The Pacific Northwesterner* 17 (Winter 1973).

54. Algier, *The Crow and the Eagle*, 303–5; *New North-West*, Sept. 1, 1876; *Bozeman Times*, Nov. 30, 1876.

55. Statement of Nelson Story, Jan. 3, 1877, folder 2, CIAF (hereafter Story Statement).

56. Clapp to CIA.

57. Story Statement.

58. Ibid.

59. *Bozeman Times*, Oct. 19, 1876.

60. Simon, *The Papers of Ulysses S. Grant*, vol. 27, 394.

61. Ibid.; Merritt C. Page to U. S. Grant, Nov. 13, 1876, ibid.

62. Nelson Story to Thomas A. Thompson,

Nov. 17, 1876, quoted in Story, "Nelson Story Sr. Was One of Montana's First Gold Miners."

63. Ibid.

64. Clapp to CIA.

65. Story Statement.

66. Ibid.

67. Kiskadden Deposition, Story v. Black 225; *Bozeman Avant Courier*, Mar. 15, 1877.

68. *Helena Independent*, Mar. 11, 1877; Ibid., May 31, 1877.

69. *Bozeman Times*, Dec. 21, 1876.

70. *Bozeman Avant Courier*, Jan. 5, 1877; Ibid., Jan. 30, 1877.

71. *Madisonian*, May 17, 1877; *Bozeman Avant Courier*, May 24, 1877; *Yale University, The Twenty Years' Record*, 93. Blackmore Cemetery is now Sunset Hills Cemetery.

72. Amended Complaint, Nov. 15, 1877, Story v. Black 201.

73. Answer, July 18, 1877, Story v. Black 201.

74. Complaint, Feb. 28, 1878, Story v. Black 225.

75. Judgment on Verdict, Nov. 2, 1878, Story v. Black 201; Judgment on Verdict, May 12, 1879, Story v. Black 225.

76. Brown, *The Plainsmen of the Yellowstone*, 436.

77. Richard White, *It's Your Misfortune and None of My Own: A History of the American West*, 176.

Chapter Nine

1. Bruce Hampton, *Children of Grace: The Nez Perce War of 1877*, 107.

2. *Bozeman Avant Courier*, Aug. 9, 1877.

3. Hampton, *Children of Grace*, 179–80.

4. Ibid., 194, 202, 211.

5. Leeson, *History of Montana*, 1166; *Bozeman Avant Courier*, Aug. 30, 1877; *Bozeman Courier*, Apr. 13, 1921.

6. *Bozeman Avant Courier*, Dec. 13, 1877.

7. Bine to Budge, Aug. 12, 1944. Constructed by William Beall for fifteen thousand dollars, it was located on West Babcock Street between South Fourth and South Grand Avenues.

8. *Bozeman Avant Courier*, May 2, 1878. Including costs of grading and fencing, the total investment for stockholders came to $4,500.

9. *Bozeman Avant Courier*, May 16, 1878; *Republican-Courier*, Jan. 2, 1912.

10. Near present-day Manhattan, Montana.

See *Bozeman Avant Courier*, July 9, 1875; Ibid., Sept. 6, 1877.

11. *Bozeman Avant Courier*, Oct. 11, 1877; Ibid., Jan. 10, 1878; Ibid., Feb. 14, 1878.

12. The operation now became "Willson & Lewis." *Bozeman Avant Courier*, Jan. 16, 1879; Ibid., Sept. 26, 1878.

13. *Bozeman Avant Courier*, Nov. 7, 1878; Ibid., Apr. 3, 1879.

14. George W. Woodson to Nelson Story, Dec. 29, 1878, SFF.

15. Thomas Lewis v. Jeanette Lewis, decree of divorce, Nov. 19, 1879, No. 307, GCCC. The timing of the divorce coincided with territorial law that required a minimum of one year of marriage before a divorce could be granted; *Bozeman Avant Courier*, Nov. 6, 1879; Ibid., Feb. 26, 1880; *Weekly Avant Courier*, Dec. 21, 1882.

16. *Bozeman Avant Courier*, Nov. 8, 1877.

17. Ibid., Aug. 29, 1878.

18. Skidmore, *Treasure State Treasury*, 28.

19. Financial Records, Henry Elling Papers, 1864–1911, MC 262, MHS, folder 13, box 15.

20. *Bozeman Avant Courier*, Oct. 10, 1878; *Weekly Courier*, Jan. 9, 1918; Black v. Story 552.

21. *Bozeman Avant Courier*, May 23, 1878; Ibid., Sept. 5, 1878; *Pettengill's Newspaper Directory and Advertiser's Handbook*, 178. The newspaper, like the *Courier*, had a circulation of eight hundred, and the closure came just months after the death of thirty-seven-year-old publisher Henry Wilkinson.

22. *Bozeman Avant Courier*, Oct. 8, 1875; Ibid., June 26, 1879; Ibid., Jan. 2, 1879; Ibid., Jan. 23, 1879; Nelson Story v. Madison & Rosa Black, Aug. 31, 1875, No. 335, GCCC; *Avant Courier*, Dec. 15, 1894; L. S. Willson v. L. M. Black, Oct. 28, 1878, box 4: 278, GCCC. Stewart Wellson, Samuel Bradbury, Theophilus A. Ashburner, and S. Allen Evans also won judgments against Black, Fellows Pease, and William Kiskadden.

23. *Bozeman Courier*, May 7, 1948; Leander M. Black, H.R. Doc. No. 871, 46 Cong., 2nd sess., 1880; *Inter-Mountains Freeman*, July 24, 1881; *Bozeman Avant Courier*, July 28, 1881; Ibid., Aug. 18, 1881; *Helena Independent*, July 19, 1881; Ibid., Nov. 13, 1881.

24. Bryan, "Dr. Lamme and His Gallant Little 'Yellowstone,'" 35–36.

25. Named for Sanford Coulson, head of the Missouri River Transportation Company;

West, *Capitalism on the Frontier*, 48, 50–51; *Rocky Mountain Husbandman*, Jan. 10, 1878.

26. *Bozeman Avant Courier*, May 9, 1878; J. W. Allen, "How To Successfully Navigate the Upper Yellowstone," *Avant Courier*, July 4, 1878.

27. Named for passenger Bertie Railey, the first woman to travel that far up the Yellowstone by steamship.

28. Bryan, "Dr. Lamme and His Gallant Little 'Yellowstone,'" 38–39; *Bozeman Avant Courier*, June 27, 1878.

29. Some of the boat's timber was recovered and used to construct buildings in Miles City. See Bryan, "Dr. Lamme and His Gallant Little 'Yellowstone,'" 35–36, 39–42; Lass, "Steamboats on the Yellowstone," 35–36; *Bozeman Avant Courier*, June 12, 1879; Ibid., July 3, 1879.

30. Bine to Budge, July 12, 1944; *Bozeman Avant Courier*, July 24, 1879; Ibid., July 31, 1879; Ibid., Aug. 7, 1879.

31. Story, "Nelson Story Sr. Was One of Montana's First Gold Miners."

32. In the Matter of the Estate of Thomas A. Thompson, July 25, 1879, box 37, GCCC.

33. Territory of Montana v. Nelson Story, Dec. 13, 1879, boxes 27–28: 259, GCCC; Bine to Budge, Apr. 3, 1945.

34. Riley, *The Female Frontier*, 71, 96.

35. *Bozeman Avant Courier*, Feb. 3, 1881; W. S. Trent to Nelson Story, May 15, 1880, SFF.

36. *Bozeman Avant Courier*, Mar. 25, 1880 (Martin & Myers were second at $1,189); Ibid., Feb. 12, 1880; Ibid., July 15, 1880.

37. *Bozeman Avant Courier*, Dec. 9, 1880; Ibid., Dec. 16, 1880; *Helena Independent*, Apr. 13, 1878. Seventeen of the children were of "African descent." Beginning in 1878, when there were only three enrolled in Bozeman's schools, black children were seated with white students on a temporary basis until "other arrangements" could be found. Evidently, those other arrangements had yet to be made.

38. *Bozeman Avant Courier*, Sept. 30, 1880; Ibid., Nov. 18, 1880; Ibid., Jan. 1, 1881.

39. B. Derek Strahn, "A Once-Thriving Red Light District," *At Home Magazine* 4 (Mar. 2003), 5. Couselle Corner was on the northwest corner on Main Street and Rouse Avenue.

40. No two sources concur on livestock statistics in Montana. For example, historian James Hamilton says there were 165,000 head of cattle in the territory in 1880, while Mike Malone and Richard Roeder claim 428,279. Tables provided in the "First Annual Report of the Bureau of Agriculture, Labor and Industry of Montana for the Year Ended November 30, 1893 for livestock estimates," are relied upon here.

41. Leeson, *History of Montana*, 1135; Myers Family File, GHSRC. Moreton Frewen was married to Clarita "Clara" Jerome, sister of Jennie and aunt of Winston Churchill.

42. Burlingame and Toole, *A History of Montana*, vol. 1, 318; Stuart, *Forty Years on the Frontier*, vol. 2, 188. Saddle and Sirloin Club and Edward Norris Wentworth, *A Biographical Catalog of the Portrait Gallery of the Saddle and Sirloin Club*, 140; Thompson P. McElrath, *The Yellowstone Valley: What it is, Where it is, and How to get to it: A Handbook for Tourists and Settlers*, 69.

43. *First Annual Report of the Bureau of Agriculture, Labor and Industry of Montana for the Year Ended November 30, 1893*, 272, table 71.

44. Strahorn, *The Resources of Montana Territory*, 25–26; *Bozeman Avant Courier*, July 4, 1878; Leeson, *History of Montana*, 1143; *Omaha Daily Bee*, Mar. 24, 1882.

45. Brisbin, *The Beef Bonanza*, 163.

46. *Bozeman Avant Courier*, Mar. 3, 1881; Ibid., Dec. 1, 1881; Ibid., July 21, 1881; Ibid., Aug. 11, 1881; Ibid., Sept. 8, 1881. A few years later, Story reverted to the ox-yoke brand he first used in 1866.

47. *Pioneer Press*, cited in *Bozeman Avant Courier*, Sept. 4, 1879. Twenty-two hundred head of steers were brought to Bismarck during the fall of 1879. One of the largest processing firms in Chicago was operated by Rosenbaum Brothers & Company. See Strahorn, *The Resources of Montana Territory*, 26.

48. Malcolm Story, interview.

49. Brisbin, *The Beef Bonanza*, 144.

50. Charles Anceney was vice president, Edward Gardner secretary, and Joe Lindley treasurer. See *Bozeman Avant Courier*, Feb. 24, 1881.

51. Athearn, "Railroad to a Far Off Country," 18, 22.

52. *Bozeman Avant Courier*, Aug. 11, 1881.

53. B. Derek Strahn, "Bozeman's Historic Story Mill District," *At Home Magazine* 3 (Aug. 2002), 9.

54. West, *Capitalism on the Frontier*, 121–22.

55. Haines, *The Yellowstone Story*, vol. 1, 259–60; *Avant Courier*, Jan. 22, 1904. The McAdow brothers later platted a portion of their land into the Northern Pacific Addition.

56. Haines, *The Yellowstone Story*, vol. 1, 260. Story had promised Norris his financial support for a branch railroad line from Bozeman to the park during a reception in July of 1878 and wrongly concluded Norris would support the proposition. See *Bozeman Avant Courier*, Aug. 1, 1878.

57. Ibid., June 1, 1882.

58. John Tomlinson, et ux., to Nelson Story, Aug. 18, 1875, *Deed Book K*, 285, GCCR; May 15, 1877, *Deed Book K*, 413, GCCR.

59. James T. Shed, et al., to Nelson Story, Aug. 3, 1880, *Deed Book 2*, 131, GCCR; Aug. 29, 1881, *Deed Book 2*, 78, GCCR; *Avant Courier*, Sept. 7, 1901.

60. *Gallatin County Republican*, Sept. 3, 1901.

61. Merk, *History of the Westward Movement*, 447–49.

62. *Bozeman Avant Courier*, Mar. 30, 1882; National Register of Historic Places, Northern Pacific—Story Mill Historic District, Bozeman, Gallatin County, Montana, National Register #96000479 (hereafter HD 96000479), sec. 8: 3; *Avant Courier*, Sept. 7, 1901. Shed's last name was often spelled Shedd.

63. *Weekly Avant Courier*, Jan. 11, 1883.

64. James Martin was made cashier. See *Bankers' Magazine and Statistical Register* 38 (July 1883 to June 1884, incl.), 478.

65. *Bozeman Avant Courier*, June 26, 1879; Ibid., Aug. 31, 1882; Leeson, *History of Montana*, 1166.

66. Gary Forney, "Bozeman's Charles Hartman, Man of Many Hats, Many Parties," *Montana Pioneer*, Mar. 1, 2012, 11; Gary Forney, "Trials of Martin Peel," *In Celebration of Our Past* 15 (2003), 34.

67. *Bozeman Avant Courier*, May 4, 1882; Ibid., May 11, 1882; Ibid., May 18, 1882; Ibid., May 25, 1882.

68. Waller, *Health and Wellness*, 99.

69. *Bozeman Avant Courier*, May 18, 1882.

70. Ibid., June 8, 1882.

71. *Bozeman Avant Courier*, Aug. 3, 1882; *Weekly Avant Courier*, Dec. 28, 1882; Lucia B. Mirrielees, ed., "Pioneer Ranching in Central Montana, From the Letters of Otto Maerdian, Written in 1882–83," cited in McLemore, *Frontier Omnibus*, 402.

72. *Bozeman Avant Courier*, July 6, 1882; Ibid., Aug. 3, 1882.

73. *Bozeman Weekly Chronicle*, Dec. 30, 1915; Ibid., Feb. 7, 1883. Joe Lindley was the paper's president.

74. *Weekly Avant Courier*, Nov. 23, 1882.

75. Bine to Budge, Oct. 9, 1944.

76. *Weekly Avant Courier*, Feb. 22, 1883.

77. Ibid., Mar. 1, 1883.

78. Bine to Budge, Sept. 15, 1944.

79. *Weekly Avant Courier*, Mar. 8, 1883.

80. Ibid., Mar. 22, 1883. A lone Northern Pacific locomotive actually arrived in Bozeman a week earlier.

81. *Weekly Avant Courier*, May 10, 1883. Story represented Ward three. Other aldermen were W. W. Alderson, Walter Cooper, Will Davis, Peter Koch, William McAdow, Daniel Rouse, and William Tracy.

82. National Register of Historic Places, Main Street Historic District, Bozeman, Gallatin County, Montana, National Register #87001848, (hereafter HD 87001848), sec. 8: 6. The Spieth & Krug Building is located at 240–246 East Main Street.

83. *Weekly Avant Courier*, Apr. 5, 1883. The building was known as St. Lawrence Hall. The rink was open three evenings a week for the general public, two for ladies and their escorts. Admission was twenty-five cents. Afternoon admission was free, and Story offered nickel-plated skates for rent.

84. *Dillon Tribune*, cited in *Livingston Enterprise*, July 11, 1883. A portion of the monument's inscription perpetuated the myth of Bozeman's death, stating Bozeman was "killed by Blackfoot Indians on the Yellowstone, Apr. 18, 1867." See Burlingame, *John M. Bozeman*, 42. Story assisted other civic efforts in 1883, serving on the Reception Committee for the Old Folks' Ball in February, and donating money for the city's Fourth of July celebration. See *Weekly Avant Courier*, Feb. 15, 1883.

85. *Bozeman Avant Courier*, Aug. 3, 1882; Ibid., Aug. 24, 1882. Theories about the meaning of the "3-7-77" used by Helena vigilantes

range from the dimension of a grave (three feet wide, seven feet long, seventy-seven inches deep), a warning to leave town (within three hours, seven minutes, and seventy-seven seconds), the composition of the Alder Gulch Vigilance Committee (three lawyers, seven merchants, and seventy-seven miners), or a Masonic code denoting the number of masons who attended the first three major events of the "brethren" in Montana (three at the first Masonic meeting, seven who founded the vigilance committee in 1863, and seventy-seven for the first funeral for a mason held at Bannack in 1862, i.e. the deceased and seventy-six mourners). See Dillon, *The Montana Vigilantes*, 352–53.

86. *Weekly Avant Courier*, June 5, 1884.
87. Ibid., Sept. 13, 1883. Cook had relied on European investors to help him finish the railroad.
88. White, *Railroaded*, 218.
89. *Helena Independent*, July 7, 1883; *Weekly Avant Courier*, May 10, 1883.
90. *Bozeman Chronicle*, July 4, 1883.
91. Alfred Terry to Lilly Terry, July 4, 1883, cited in Roger Darling, *A Sad and Terrible Blunder*, 273.
92. Robert L. Peterson, "The Completion of the Northern Pacific Railroad System in Montana: 1883–1893," in *The Montana Past: An Anthology*, eds. Michael P. Malone and Richard B. Roeder, 161; *Bozeman Chronicle*, Sept. 12, 1883.
93. *Weekly Avant Courier*, Sept. 13, 1883.
94. *Bozeman Chronicle*, Sept. 12, 1883; Peterson, "The Completion of the Northern Pacific Railroad System in Montana," 163. The ceremonial site, near Gold Creek, is not far from where gold was first discovered in 1852.
95. *Weekly Avant Courier*, Jan. 24, 1884.

CHAPTER TEN

1. *First Annual Report of the Bureau of Agriculture, Labor and Industry of Montana for the Year Ended November 30, 1893*, 275–76, table 73; Burlingame and Toole, *A History of Montana*, vol. 1, 318; Stuart, *Forty Years on the Frontier*, vol. 2, 188.
2. *Helena Daily Enterprise*, June 12, 1883; *Weekly Avant Courier*, Oct. 2, 1884; United States Office of Indian Affairs, Crow Indian Agency Records (hereafter USCIAR), box 1, book 2, MC 87, MHS.
3. Hoxie, *Parading Through History*, 116–21, 150; Burton M. Smith, "Politics and the Crow Indian Land Cessions," *Montana* 36 (Autumn 1986): 30–33.
4. *Rocky Mountain Husbandman*, Apr. 2, 1885.
5. H. J. Armstrong to Nelson Story, Apr. 17, 1882, SFF.
6. Letter from the Secretary of the Interior, regarding the leasing of land on the Crow reservation in Montana Territory 48 Cong., 2nd Sess., Senate Executive Document No. 22, 1, 140–41, cited in Fletcher, "The End of the Open Range."
7. *Bozeman Chronicle*, July 15, 1891; Donald G. Tolman, "James Rolandson Dilworth," 1–2, GHSRC. *The condition of the Indians in the Indian Territory, and other Reservations, etc.*, S. Rep. No. 1278, 49 Cong., 1st sess., 1886, (hereafter SCIA No. 1278), 134, 141, 149, 166.
8. Also signing on was Dakota Territory rancher Theodore Roosevelt.
9. *Daily Yellowstone Journal*, Sept. 4, 1884; *Weekly Avant Courier*, Jan. 15, 1885; SCIA No. 1278, 150.
10. Fletcher, "The End of the Open Range," 140–41.
11. Tolman, "James Rolandson Dilworth," 2; Robert H. Fletcher, *Free Grass to Fences*, 95; *Rocky Mountain Husbandman*, Feb. 12, 1880; Roosevelt, "The Round-Up," 851–52.
12. Bine to Budge, Aug. 12, 1944.
13. Ibid.
14. Roosevelt, "The Round-Up," 855.
15. Bine to Budge, Aug. 12, 1944; Roosevelt, "The Round-Up," 856, 862.
16. *Weekly Avant Courier*, July 24, 1884; Bine to Budge, Aug. 12, 1944. A few years earlier, Flathead Indians stole fifty of Nelson Story's horses in the Yellowstone Valley. All were recovered. See *New North-West*, May 7, 1880.
17. *Bozeman Weekly Chronicle*, Aug. 12, 1885.
18. Brown, *Trail Driving Days,* 190.
19. *Weekly Avant Courier*, Aug. 27, 1885; Milner and O'Connor, *As Big as the West*, 219–21; William Kittredge and Steven M. Krauzer, "Mr. Montana Revised: Another Look at Granville Stuart," *Montana* 36 (Autumn 1986): 19; Bine to Budge, Aug. 12, 1944; Brown, *Trail Driving Days*, 190–91.

20. Fletcher, *Free Grass to Fences*, 76.

21. Milner and O'Connor, *As Big as the West*, 240. Story was one of the seventy members who attended the August 26, 1885, meeting, where his primary concern was lowering the annual dues from fifteen dollars to ten dollars. He remained in good standing with the Stockgrowers Association through 1889, though the 1885 meeting was the only one he attended. See Minute Book, 1885–1889, Montana Stockgrowers Association Records, 1885–1912, MC 45, MHS.

22. *Weekly Avant Courier*, Sept. 20, 1883.

23. *Bozeman Avant Courier*, Mar. 30, 1882; *Avant Courier*, Sept. 7, 1901. The McAdow brothers' Gallatin Mills had by this time ceased operations.

24. *Weekly Avant Courier*, June 19, 1884; Ibid., Sept. 4, 1884; HD 96000479, sec. 8: 3; *Bozeman Weekly Chronicle*, Jan. 14, 1885.

25. *Weekly Avant Courier*, Mar. 9, 1885; *Bozeman Weekly Chronicle*, Dec. 16, 1885; Ibid., Jan. 20, 1886; Ibid., Mar. 24, 1886.

26. *Weekly Avant Courier*, Jan. 7, 1886.

27. *Bozeman Weekly Chronicle*, July 7, 1885; *Weekly Avant Courier*, Feb. 18, 1886.

28. *Weekly Avant Courier*, May 13, 1886; Ibid., May 20, 1886; *Bozeman Weekly Chronicle*, Aug. 8, 1888; *Bozeman Courier*, Feb. 1, 1935; Ibid., May 7, 1948; Leeson, *History of Montana*, 1121.

29. *Weekly Avant Courier*, Aug. 5, 1886. Since the army's departure, locals helped themselves to windows, doors, partitions, walls, and anything else that could be carted away. Some of these materials were reused as far away as Red Lodge and the Crow Reservation. See *Avant Courier*, Mar. 28, 1889.

30. *Avant Courier*, Nov. 13, 1890.

31. *Weekly Avant Courier*, Mar. 5, 1885.

32. Story, "Nelson Story Sr. Was One of Montana's First Gold Miners"; *Weekly Avant Courier*, May 14, 1885; Ibid., Sept. 10, 1885; Ibid., Apr. 8, 1886; *Bozeman Weekly Chronicle*, Apr. 27, 1887. The Story Mansion was located on the southeast corner of Fifth Avenue and Main Street.

33. *Weekly Avant Courier*, May 6, 1886.

34. Ibid., May 27, 1886; Ibid., Sept. 9, 1886; *Bozeman Weekly Chronicle*, Jan. 12, 1887.

35. *Weekly Avant Courier*, Oct. 28, 1886.

36. Brisbin, *The Beef Bonanza*, 148.

37. *Billings Gazette*, Nov. 8, 1886.

38. *New North-West*, Oct. 22, 1886; *New York Times*, June 21, 1886; *Weekly Avant Courier*, Oct. 14, 1886.

39. *Report on the Internal Commerce of the United States*, Bureau of Statistics, 1885, 154; *Bozeman Weekly Chronicle*, Mar. 30, 1887.

40. "Capture of the Crow Reserve," *Forest and Stream: A Weekly Journal of the Rod and Gun* 26, no. 21 (June 17, 1886), 405; *Billings Gazette*, Dec. 18, 1886; Ibid., July 5, 1887.

41. *Billings Gazette*, Dec. 11, 1886.

42. Ibid., Dec. 23, 1886.

43. Stuart, *Forty Years on the Frontier*, vol. 2, 234.

44. *Bozeman Weekly Chronicle*, Jan. 12, 1887.

45. Ibid., Jan. 19, 1887; Ibid., Mar. 30, 1887.

46. Ibid., Mar. 30, 1887.

47. John K. Rollinson, *Wyoming Cattle Trails: History of the Migration of Oregon-raised Herds to Midwestern Markets*, 260.

48. *Bozeman Weekly Chronicle*, Mar. 30, 1887.

49. Bine to Budge, Aug. 30, 1944; *Bozeman Weekly Chronicle*, Mar. 23, 1887.

50. Burlingame, *The Montana Frontier*, 284; *Billings Gazette*, Mar. 14, 1887.

51. *Billings Gazette*, cited in *Bozeman Weekly Chronicle*, Mar. 16, 1887. Gallatin County rancher Charles Anceney noted that native cattle raised in Montana suffered losses of no more than 15 percent. But trail, or "Pilgrim" cattle, sustained losses of 50 percent or more—hence the reason so many absentee owners were bankrupted. He encouraged all cattlemen to buy Montana cattle but to breed only as many as the ranges could support, rather than figuring profits "at desks in New York or London." See *Bozeman Weekly Chronicle*, Apr. 27, 1887.

52. *River Press*, Mar. 23, 1887; *Bozeman Weekly Chronicle*, Mar. 9, 1887.

53. Ibid., Apr. 6, 1887.

54. Stuart, *Forty Years on the Frontier*, vol. 2, 237; Sam Gordon in the *Yellowstone Journal*, cited in Fletcher, *Free Grass to Fences*, 90–91;. Malone, Roeder, and Lang, *Montana*, 166; W. M. Elofson, *Frontier Cattle Ranching in the Land and Times of Charlie Russell*, 138; "First Annual Report of the Bureau of Agriculture, Labor and Industry of Montana for the Year Ended November 30, 1893," Table 71—Horse and Cattle Industries, 272.

55. *Billings Daily Gazette*, June 27, 1887.

56. Ibid., July 5, 1887.

57. Ibid., June 24, 1887; Ibid., July 6, 1887.

58. Letters received, Office of Indian Affairs, RG 75, National Archives, 7432–1890, cited in Hoxie, *Parading Through History*, 165; Ibid., 152–53. Story and Plenty Coups had a mutual respect for each other, and the Crow chief often entertained Story and his sons in his two-story log cabin on Pryor Creek. See Story, "Nelson Story Sr. Was One of Montana's First Gold Miners."

59. Henry Williamson to Nelson Story, Nov. 22, 1887; Dec. 19, 1887; Jan. 18, 1888, USCIAR; *Billings Gazette*, June 24, 1887.

60. Jerry Brekke, *Our Time & Place: Tales from Cooke City to the Crazies*, 25–27. When Gallatin County was created, it encompassed all of present-day Park and Sweet Grass Counties, and portions of Carbon, Yellowstone, Fergus, Meagher, and Cascade Counties.

61. Board of County Commissioners of Yellowstone County v. Nelson Story, Feb. 13, 1888, box 60: 1428, GCCC; *Bozeman Chronicle*, Dec. 14, 1887; Ibid., July 22, 1891; *Weekly Avant Courier*, Dec. 15, 1887; Ibid., Feb. 14, 1889.

62. Ibid., June 14, 1888.

63. *Bozeman Weekly Chronicle*, June 6, 1888.

64. Ibid., June 27, 1888.

65. Robert Stevenson to Hervey Ganse, Sept. 2 and 23, 1885, cited in Norman J. Bender, "The very atmosphere is charged with unbelief . . . Presbyterians and Higher Education in Montana—1869/1900," *Montana* 28 (Spring 1978): 21.

66. *Bozeman Weekly Chronicle*, June 22, 1887; *New York Evangelist*, Apr. 29, 1886.

67. The mansion was located on the southeast corner of Main and Fifth. See *Weekly Avant Courier*, Dec. 29, 1887.

68. Ibid., June 7, 1888.

69. *Bozeman Weekly Chronicle*, May 2, 1888.

70. *Bozeman Weekly Chronicle*, Apr. 27, 1887.

71. D. W. Crowley v. Nelson Story, Nov. 14, 1888, box 145: 1558, GCCC; *Bozeman Weekly Chronicle*, Apr. 27, 1887.

72. Alderson, "Early Day Reminiscences."

73. *Weekly Avant Courier*, June 7, 1888.

74. Story, "Nelson Story Sr. Was One of Montana's First Gold Miners."

75. *Weekly Avant Courier*, July 12, 1888. The opera house was located at the southwest corner of Rouse Avenue and Main Street.

76. Ibid.

77. Ibid.

78. *Avant Courier*, Jan. 10, 1889; Ibid., Jan. 24, 1889; Ibid., June 6, 1889.

79. Among the investors were A. P. Clark, E. J. Owenhouse, and Lester Willson. See *Avant Courier*, July 11, 1889.

80. Ibid., Mar. 21, 1889; Ibid., June 6, 1889; *Bozeman Weekly Chronicle*, July 3, 1889.

81. *Avant Courier*, Mar. 21, 1889; Ibid., June 20, 1889.

82. Nelson Story v. Bozeman Water Works Company, et al., July 3, 1889, box 86: 1594, GCCC.

83. *Avant Courier*, July 3, 1889.

CHAPTER ELEVEN

1. Katherine Story to Byron Story, Apr. 11, 1945, SFF.

2. "Mrs. Nelson Story Sketch," M. L. Alderson Papers, 102–3; Mary was William Alderson's daughter-in-law.

3. Amanda Sehulster, "The Silent Story: A Bozeman Founding Mother," 16, GHSRC; *Avant Courier*, Dec. 4, 1897.

4. Phyllis Smith, *Bozeman and the Gallatin Valley: A History*, 255.

5. Bine to Budge, Apr. 4, 1945.

6. *Weekly Avant Courier*, June 18, 1885.

7. Story, "Nelson Story Sr. Was One of Montana's First Gold Miners."

8. Bine to Budge, Dec. 13, 1944.

9. Evelyn Young, "Another Gallatin Family," *Gallatin County Tribune* and *Belgrade Journal*, Feb. 26, 1970; Bine to Budge, Apr. 3, 1945.

10. Bine to Budge, Dec. 2, 1944; *Republican-Courier*, Nov. 21, 1905. Harrison had Worsham and Williams arrested the next day, and each received a fifty-dollar fine.

11. SFF.

12. Don Anderson to Mrs. Meloy, Mar. 10, 1977, SFF.

13. Malcolm Story, 80 Bzn. Families, Private Collection of Clippings and Notations, Nov. 14, 1970, GHSRC.

14. Malcolm Story, interview.

15. Bine to Budge, Apr. 3, 1945.

16. Ibid.

17. *Republican-Courier*, Sept. 19, 1905.

18. *Weekly Avant Courier*, Nov. 28, 1888; *Bozeman Chronicle*, Dec. 5, 1888; Ibid., Dec. 12, 1888; *Avant Courier*, June 27, 1889;

Rose Story Hogan, plaintiff, v. Thomas Byron Story, Katherine F. Story, his wife, and A. C. Roecher, as administrator of the estate of Nelson Story, Sr., deceased, defendants, vols. I–IV, case nos. 8895, 8896, 8897, Oct. 20, 1930, GHSRC (hereafter Hogan v. Story), 2: 517; *Gallatin County Tribune* and *Belgrade Journal*, Jan. 10, 1957. Hogan relocated to Bozeman in 1886.

19. Bine to Budge, Nov. 6, 1944; *Billings Gazette*, Dec. 16, 1886; *River Press*, Dec. 22, 1886; *Bozeman Weekly Chronicle,* Jan. 12, 1887.

20. *Avant Courier*, Aug. 8, 1889; Ibid., Sept. 5, 1889; *Bozeman Weekly Chronicle*, Aug. 21, 1889; Ibid., Sept. 4, 1889.

21. *Avant Courier*, Jan. 29, 1890.

22. *Avant Courier*, Jan. 23, 1890; *Bozeman Chronicle*, Jan. 29, 1890.

23. *Bozeman Weekly Chronicle*, Mar. 12, 1890; Hogan v. Story, 1: 362; Ibid., 4: 1540, 1853. The pharmacy was housed in the Black/Cooper Building at 118 East Main Street.

24. U.S. Census Bureau, "Resident Population and Apportionment of the U.S. House of Representatives." www.census.gov/dmd/www/resapport/states/montana.pdf.

25. Malone, Roeder, and Lang, *Montana*, 94–98.

26. Kirby Lambert, Patricia Mullan Burnham, and Susan R. Near, *Montana's State Capitol: The People's House*, 4–5.

27. Roeder, Richard B. "A Settlement on the Plains. Paris Gibson and the Building of Great Falls." *Montana* 42 (Autumn 1992): 7–8.

28. Malone, Roeder, and Lang, *Montana*, 202–5.

29. *Bozeman Weekly Chronicle*, Jan. 16, 1889.

30. Ibid.

31. *Avant Courier*, Jan. 31, 1889; *Bozeman Weekly Chronicle*, Oct. 2, 1889; *Bozeman Chronicle,* May 8, 1889; Ibid., Oct. 9, 1889. During that encampment, Fort Ellis would be known as Camp B. F. White.

32. *Avant Courier*, June 20, 1889; B. Derek Strahn, "Of Ballots, Boodle and Boomtowns," *Pioneer Museum Quarterly* 35 (Summer 2012): 13–14; *Bozeman Weekly Chronicle*, July 24, 1889. Transients were never welcome, particularly during the capital campaign. Eventually, railroad men at the depot formed a "Kangaroo Club,"

bluntly telling tramps that only gentlemen were allowed on the premises. See *Avant Courier*, May 30, 1891.

33. *Bozeman Chronicle*, Feb. 5, 1890. The Gallatin Farmer's Alliance No. 4 was open to farmers twenty-one and older and their wives and daughters, provided they were eighteen or older.

34. *Bozeman Chronicle*, Feb. 5, 1890.

35. Ibid., Oct. 15, 1890.

36. *Avant Courier*, Oct. 24, 1889. J. B. Virtue, employed by Story for four years, now went to work for Benepe as foreman, in charge of weighing grain. George Trent was the mill's engineer. The grain elevator was located at the corner of East Tamarack and Front Streets.

37. *Weekly Avant Courier*, Feb. 26, 1885; *Daily Inter Mountain*, cited in *Weekly Avant Courier*, Mar. 26, 1885; *Weekly Avant Courier*, Apr. 16, 1885; Ibid., Oct. 22, 1885; Bill and Jan Taylor, *Over Homestake Pass on the Butte Short Line: The Construction Era, 1888–1929*, 17–19. Other investors in the Montana Central Railroad Company included Walter Cooper, Lester Willson, and William Alderson. Their proposal to the legislature called for Gallatin and Silver Bow Counties, with voter approval, to each provide $250,000 to be repaid over a thirty-year period by railroad bonds bearing 6 percent annual interest.

38. *Avant Courier*, May 1, 1890; *Bozeman Chronicle*, Mar. 19, 1890.

39. *Avant Courier*, May 22, 1890. North Dakota architect George Hancock, who had also designed the recently refurbished St. James Episcopal Church in Bozeman, was hired to design the hotel. See Strahn, "Of Ballots, Boodle and Boomtowns," 14.

40. Riley, *The Female Frontier*, 116.

41. *Avant Courier*, Mar. 27, 1890; *Northwest Magazine*, cited in *Bozeman Chronicle*, Mar. 19, 1890; Ibid., Apr. 9, 1890; Ibid., Apr. 16, 1890; Ibid., Nov. 19, 1890.

42. *Avant Courier*, Mar. 27, 1890.

43. *Bozeman Chronicle*, Apr. 9, 1890.

44. *Livingston Enterprise*, cited in *Bozeman Chronicle*, Jan. 22, 1890.

45. *Avant Courier*, Apr. 10, 1890; Ibid., May 29, 1890; Ibid., June 12, 1890; Ibid., June 26, 1890; *Bozeman Weekly Chronicle*, May 28, 1890;

45. Hogan v. Story, 2: 678; Matthew Trent died in 1895. See *Kansas, Deaths and Burials, Index, 1855–1930*, FHL film number 1411966.

46. *Bozeman Chronicle*, July 2, 1890.

47. *Avant Courier*, July 3, 1890.

48. Ibid., Sept. 18, 1890; *Bozeman Weekly Chronicle*, June 11, 1890. Story's block at 2–12 East Main Street would be named for his daughter-in-law, Etha Mayo Story. See HD 87001848, sec. 8: 13, 18.

49. *Bozeman Chronicle*, Oct. 1, 1890; Ibid., Oct. 7, 1890; Ibid., Oct. 15, 1890.

50. Ibid., Oct. 15, 1890; *Avant Courier*, Oct. 16, 1890.

51. *Anaconda Standard*, Aug. 31, 1901.

52. *Bozeman Weekly Chronicle*, Jan. 21, 1891; *Bozeman Chronicle*, July 2, 1890; Ibid., Mar. 25, 1891; *Avant Courier*, May 22, 1890; Ibid., Sept. 26, 1891.

53. *The Exchange*, cited in the *Avant Courier*, Oct. 31, 1891. Professor Hayden nicknamed the valley the "Egypt of America" years before. It was named after the southern Illinois area known as "Little Egypt" because of its role in feeding the rest of that state after the harsh winter of 1830–31. See *Bozeman Chronicle*, May 13, 1891.

54. *Avant Courier*, June 27, 1891.

55. Charles Crane Bradley Jr., "After the Buffalo Days: Documents on the Crow Indians from the 1880's to the 1920's," 74–76.

56. *Daily Yellowstone Journal*, Dec. 10, 1890; Ibid., Oct. 16, 1892; *Helena Independent*, July 30, 1891; *Fergus County Argus*, Oct. 29, 1891.

57. William Courtenay v. Nelson Story and W. D. Story, Nov. 21, 1892, box 86: 2006, GCCC; Bob Fudge, "Long Trail from Texas," *Montana* 12 (Summer 1962), 44 n. The Murphy Cattle Company would make additional livestock purchases that summer, increasing the size of its cattle herd from twelve thousand head to eighty-two thousand, valued at $1.5 million. See *Buffalo Wyoming Echo*, cited in the *Billings Gazette*, May 28, 1891; *Bozeman Chronicle*, May 6, 1891.

58. Bine to Budge, Oct. 9, 1944; *Meigs County Ohio History Book*, 329.

59. *Bozeman Chronicle*, July 15, 1891; Ibid., July 29, 1891; *Avant Courier*, July 18, 1891.

60. *Bozeman Chronicle*, Nov. 4, 1891.

61. Willie Alexander, Roy Martin, and Perry McAdow. See *Avant Courier*, Aug. 29, 1891.

62. *Avant Courier*, Aug. 8, 1891; Ibid., Aug. 29, 1891.

63. Burlingame, *Gallatin County's Heritage*, 66; *Bozeman Chronicle*, Apr. 22, 1891; Ibid., Oct. 14, 1891; Ibid., Dec. 30, 1891.

64. Ibid., Nov. 11, 1891; Ibid., Nov. 18, 1891; Ibid., Dec. 2, 1891.

65. Garrett L. Hogan v. Irene Hill & Thomas Hill, Nov. 25, 1892, box 81: 2010, GCCC.

66. *Avant Courier*, Jan. 16, 1892.

67. *Avant Courier*, Jan. 9, 1892; Ibid., Oct. 5, 1895; *Bozeman Chronicle*, June 15, 1892. The controversy triggered closer scrutiny from the state board of pharmacy, and three years later, May's license was suspended.

68. Elmyra Frazier v. Nelson Story, June 6, 1892, box 78: 1945, GCCC; *Bozeman Chronicle*, Mar. 9, 1892; *Avant Courier*, Mar. 19, 1892. Among the officers and trustees were Walter Cooper and Peter Koch. P. T. Morris eventually won the bid for board work and material for the mill for $15,300. See *Bozeman Chronicle*, June 1, 1892.

69. The Northern Pacific Depot was located at 820 Front Street. The streetcar line ran south to Peach Street, west to Church Street, south to Main Street, and then west and south to Capitol Hill.

70. *Bozeman Chronicle*, July 6, 1892; Ibid., Aug. 3, 1892; *Avant Courier*, July 30, 1892.

71. *Bozeman Chronicle*, Aug. 10, 1892; Ibid., Oct 18., 1892.

72. Bozeman for the Capitol Committee to "Dear Sir," Sept. 29, 1892, Merrill G. Burlingame Collections.

73. *Bozeman Chronicle*, Oct. 25, 1892.

74. Ibid., Oct. 18, 1892.

75. Ibid.

76. *Avant Courier*, Oct. 22, 1892.

77. *Helena Independent*, Nov. 3, 1892; Ibid., Nov. 5, 1892; *Bozeman Chronicle*, Oct. 25, 1894.

78. *Helena Independent*, Nov. 5, 1892.

79. Bozeman for the Capitol Committee to "Dear Sir," Sept. 29, 1892; *Helena Independent*, Nov. 6, 1892.

80. *Avant Courier*, Nov. 12, 1892.

81. *Helena Independent*, Nov. 7, 1892.

82. *Avant Courier*, Dec. 3, 1892.

83. *Helena Independent*, Nov. 9, 1892.

84. *Bozeman Chronicle*, Nov. 15, 1892.
85. *Anaconda Standard*, cited in *Avant Courier*, Nov. 26, 1892.

CHAPTER TWELVE

1. *Avant Courier*, Nov. 26, 1892.
2. He also grazed 130 head of the "fattest and slickest cattle in the entire West" near the mill. See *Avant Courier*, Feb. 11, 1893.
3. Ibid., Dec. 17, 1892; Ibid., Jan. 7, 1893; Ibid., Feb. 4, 1893; Ibid., Feb. 11, 1893.
4. *Bozeman Chronicle*, Mar. 28, 1893. Adams Street is now Adams Boulevard.
5. *Avant Courier*, Dec. 3, 1892; *Bozeman Weekly Chronicle*, Mar. 1, 1894; *Bozeman Daily Chronicle*, Oct. 22, 1932.
6. *Avant Courier*, Dec. 10, 1892; Ibid., Jan. 21, 1893; *Bozeman Chronicle*, Jan. 21, 1893. The state university would go to Missoula, the school of mines to Butte, and the penitentiary to Deer Lodge.
7. Rydell, Robert, Jeffery Safford, and Pierce Mullen, *In the People's Interest: A Centennial History of Montana State University*, 9. The skating rink property was eventually given to Bud, who in 1906 sold it to the Roman Catholic Diocese of Helena. Holy Rosary Church now stands on the site, located at the southeast corner of Main Street and Third Avenue. See *Bozeman Chronicle*, Sept. 12, 1906.
8. John Rickards to Nelson Story, Mar. 8, 1893, Montana Governors Records, 1889-1905, MC 35a, MHS. Story was the only board member from Bozeman. See *Avant Courier*, Mar. 4, 1893; Ibid., Mar. 18, 1893; Ibid., Mar. 25, 1893.
9. *Bozeman Chronicle*, Feb. 21, 1893.
10. *Avant Courier*, Mar. 18, 1893.
11. Ibid., Mar. 25, 1893; Burlingame, *Gallatin County's Heritage*, 98–99; Walter Cooper, E. H. Talcott, George Kinkel, Lester Willson, and Peter Koch were appointed to the school's local executive board.
12. *Avant Courier*, June 10, 1893.
13. Dillon, *The Montana Vigilantes*, 47; White, *It's Your Misfortune and None of My Own*, 374.
14. Robert A. Chadwick, "Montana's Silver Mining Era: Great Boom and Great Bust," *Montana* 32 (Spring 1982): 18–19, 25, 27.
15. *Avant Courier*, June 10, 1893.
16. Ibid.
17. *Bozeman Chronicle*, July 6, 1893.
18. Ibid., July 13, 1893. Marcus Daly was elected president and Carl Hans of Butte first vice president.
19. Ibid., July 20, 1893; Ibid., June 15, 1893; Burlingame, *Gallatin County's Heritage*, 95; Chadwick, "Montana's Silver Mining Era," 31; *Avant Courier*, July 22, 1893; Ibid., July 29, 1893.
20. Bine to Budge, Sept. 15, 1944.
21. Volney Steele, *Bleed, Blister, and Purge: A History of Medicine on the American Frontier*, 222.
22. Bine to Budge, Oct. 9, 1944.
23. Located on West Lamme Street between North Willson and North Tracy Avenues. *Livingston Post*, Dec. 9, 1893; Steele, *Bleed, Blister, and Purge*, 222; *Bozeman Chronicle*, Aug. 3, 1893.
24. *Bozeman Chronicle*, July 20, 1893; Ibid., July 28, 1898.
25. Francis L. Niven, *Manhattan Omnibus—Stories of Historical Interest of Manhattan and Its Surrounding Communities*, 177, 180. In 1893, the West Gallatin Irrigation Company, a partner of the Manhattan Malting Company, owned thirty thousand acres near Moreland. By 1898, there were more than fifty Dutch families. See *Bozeman Chronicle*, July 28, 1898.
26. *Avant Courier*, Aug. 26, 1893; Ibid., Sept. 2, 1893.
27. *Bozeman Chronicle*, Aug. 24, 1893; *Avant Courier*, Sept. 2, 1893.
28. Ibid.
29. *Daily Inter Mountain*, Nov. 26, 1894; *Helena Independent*, Apr. 9, 1894; *Bozeman Chronicle*, Feb. 28, 1893; *First Annual Report of the Bureau of Agriculture, Labor and Industry of Montana for the Year Ended November 30, 1893*, 174.
30. *Avant Courier*, Sept. 2, 1893.
31. *Bozeman Weekly Chronicle*, Mar. 29, 1894.
32. The other two portraits being Mrs. Beall and Mrs. J. W. Mardis. See *Avant Courier*, June 3, 1893; *Bozeman Chronicle*, Sept. 7, 1893.
33. *Avant Courier*, Oct. 14, 1893; Ibid., Oct. 28, 1893; *Bozeman Chronicle*, Sept. 28, 1893; Ibid., Oct. 26, 1893; Gallatin Valley Mercantile Company v. Garrett L. Hogan,

Apr. 20, 1893, box 83: 2086, GCCC; Noyes Bros. & Cutler v. Garrett Hogan, Apr. 20, 1893, box 84: 2088, GCCC; H. M. Parchen & Company v. Garrett L. Hogan, May 1, 1893, box 83: 2085, GCCC.

34. *Avant Courier*, Mar. 17, 1894; Ibid., Mar. 31, 1894; *Bozeman Chronicle*, Apr. 5, 1894.

35. Ibid., May 17, 1894.

36. Ibid., Mar. 1, 1894; *Avant Courier*, May 12, 1894; Ibid., June 2, 1894.

37. Ibid., May 19, 1894; *Bozeman Chronicle*, May 31, 1894.

38. Ibid., May 17, 1894.

39. *Yellowstone Journal*, May 9, 1894.

40. *Bozeman Chronicle*, Dec. 6, 1894.

41. Ellis L. Waldron, *Montana Politics since 1864: An Atlas of Elections*, 29.

42. *Bozeman Avant Courier*, June 1, 1882; Ibid., Sept. 7, 1882.

43. Nelson Story to S. T. Hauser, Dec. 6, 1892, folder 6, box 21, Samuel Thomas Hauser Papers, 1864–1914, MC 37, MHS.

44. *Avant Courier*, Oct. 13, 1894.

45. Ibid., Oct. 27, 1894.

46. Ibid.

47. Miller, *Illustrated History*, 742–43. Even the *Chronicle* offered praise, but not enough to make an endorsement: "Mr. Story has the physical force to give his utterances weight, but this will not save the Republican party in this county, this year." See *Bozeman Chronicle*, Oct. 11, 1894.

48. *Bozeman Chronicle*, Nov. 1, 1894; *Avant Courier*, Oct. 27, 1894.

49. Ibid., Nov. 3, 1894.

50. *Bozeman Chronicle*, Aug. 9, 1894; *Avant Courier*, Nov. 17, 1894; Ibid., Nov. 24, 1894.

51. Ibid., Nov. 17, 1894; *Bozeman Chronicle*, Dec. 20, 1894.

52. *Avant Courier*, Dec. 8, 1894.

53. *Bozeman Chronicle*, Dec. 6, 1894.

54. *Daily Intermountain*, n.d., cited in *Avant Courier*, Dec. 8, 1894.

55. *Helena Independent*, Jan. 5, 1895; *Helena Herald*, Jan. 5, 1895; *Bozeman Chronicle*, Jan. 10, 1895.

56. *Helena Independent*, Jan. 6, 1895.

57. *Avant Courier*, Jan. 12, 1895.

58. *Helena Herald*, Jan. 10, 1895.

59. Ibid., Jan. 11, 1895.

60. *Avant Courier*, Jan. 19, 1895.

61. Ibid.

62. Ibid., Sept. 22, 1894; Ibid., Jan. 12, 1895; Ibid., Feb. 2, 1895.

63. Hogan v. Story, 3: 1180.

64. *Avant Courier*, Dec. 14, 1895.

65. The deal was finalized by cablegram, as Lankershim was in Paris, France, at the time. The property is located at 610 South Broadway. See *Los Angeles Express*, cited in *Bozeman Weekly Chronicle*, Mar. 14, 1895; Hogan v. Story, 3: 1227–28.

66. *Bozeman Weekly Chronicle*, Mar. 14, 1895; Ibid., Apr. 25, 1895; Burkhart, interview.

67. *Salt Lake Herald*, June 9, 1895. The Mayos were believed to be distant relatives of Dr. William Worrall Mayo, founder of the Mayo Clinic.

68. Drysdale, interview; *Bozeman Chronicle*, May 30, 1895; Ibid., Nov. 7, 1907; *Avant Courier*, June 1, 1895; Ibid., June 29, 1895; Ibid., Oct. 5, 1895.

CHAPTER THIRTEEN

1. The quote has been attributed to Mark Twain. Malcolm Story, interview.

2. *Avant Courier*, July 27, 1895; SFF; Nelson Story & W. H. Tracy v. J. H. Aylsworth, C. L. Aylsworth, Andrew Edsall, & Ella Edsall, July 1895, box 126: 2493, GCCC.

3. Besides Nelson and Elias Story, other stockholders were J. E. and Berry Martin, Lester Willson, Joseph Radford, and Ed Lamme. See *Bozeman Weekly Chronicle*, Jan. 9, 1896. *The Bankers' Magazine, Rhodes' Journal of Banking and The Bankers' Magazine, Consolidated* 52 (Jan. to June 1896), 511.

4. *Los Angeles Times*, cited in *Bozeman Weekly Chronicle*, Feb. 28, 1895; Ibid., June 4, 1896.

5. *Livingston Post*, cited in *Bozeman Chronicle*, June 25, 1896.

6. *Avant Courier*, June 27, 1896; Permanent Files, 12-H, 11-IJK, 43-S, GCCR; B. Derek Strahn and Thomas Lee, *Historic Homes of Bozeman*, 67.

7. Democratic Party National Convention, Chicago, 1896, *Official Proceedings of the Democratic National Convention Held in Chicago, Illinois*, July 7, 8, 9, 10, and 11, 1896, 234.

8. *Avant Courier*, July 4, 1896; *Bozeman Chronicle*, July 16, 1896.

9. *Avant Courier*, Aug. 15, 1896.

10. *Bozeman Weekly Chronicle*, Aug. 27, 1896.

11. *Bozeman Chronicle*, Sept. 10, 1896; *Avant Courier*, Sept. 12, 1896; Ibid., Oct. 3, 1896.

12. Ibid., Aug. 22, 1896.

13. *Bozeman Chronicle*, Sept. 10, 1896; *Avant Courier*, Sept. 19, 1896; Ibid., Oct. 24, 1896. Bryan won nearly 80 percent of the vote in Montana.

14. *Avant Courier*, Sept. 28, 1895.

15. Ibid., Aug. 15, 1896; *Bozeman Chronicle*, Dec. 10, 1896.

16. Benepe-Owenhouse Hardware was located at 108 West Main Street, and later moved to its present location at 36 West Main Street. See *Bozeman Chronicle*, Jan. 13, 1898.

17. Permanent Files 47S, 60S, 61S, GCCR; *Bozeman Chronicle*, Nov. 5, 1896.

18. *San Francisco Call*, Dec. 22, 1896; *Bozeman Chronicle*, Feb. 11, 1897; *Avant Courier*, Feb. 13, 1897; Ibid., Feb. 20, 1897.

19. Bine to Budge, Oct. 9, 1944.

20. *Bozeman Chronicle*, Mar. 4, 1897. The three girls were Miss Aline Anceney of San Francisco (daughter of the late Charles Anceney), Sarah Lowe of Bozeman, and Mrs. Rhoda A. Neilson of Canon City, Colorado.

21. *Bozeman Chronicle*, Feb. 18, 1897; RFF.

22. Daniel Maxey v. Nelson Story, judgment and decree, Feb. 6, 1897, box 129: 2495, GCCC.

23. Nelson Story v. John & William Maxey, July 24, 1897, boxes 112–13: 2792, GCCC.

24. *Bozeman Chronicle*, July 29, 1897; Ibid., Aug. 5, 1897; Ibid., Aug. 19, 1897.

25. Family Burial Records, St. James Episcopal Church, Bozeman, MT, 40.

26. Charles H. Eggleston, "When Bryan Came To Butte," in *Montana Margins: A State Anthology*, 346.

27. *Bozeman Chronicle*, Aug. 19, 1897.

28. *Avant Courier*, Aug. 21, 1897.

29. *Bozeman Chronicle*, Aug. 26, 1897. The Hartman home is located at 619 South Willson Avenue.

30. Ibid.

31. Ibid.

32. Ibid.

33. *Avant Courier*, Aug. 28, 1897.

34. Merk, *History of the Westward Movement*, 482.

35. *Avant Courier*, Aug. 13, 1898.

36. Permanent File 20R, GCCR. Two years later, Hartman would align himself with the Democratic Party. In 1913, he was appointed ambassador to Ecuador by President Woodrow Wilson.

Chapter Fourteen

1. Run by J. J. and Emma Hopper.

2. Story, "Nelson Story Sr. Was One of Montana's First Gold Miners." Bird's action was unusual, given his timid nature. A band of mischief-makers once hoisted the preacher's buggy to the top of the Methodist Episcopal Church in Bozeman the night before Sunday services. Though consoled by Ellen, Bird was deeply hurt by the prank. See *Bozeman Avant Courier*, June 13, 1873.

3. Bine to Budge, Aug. 30, 1944.

4. *Weekly Courier*, Jan. 5, 1916.

5. Mortgage from J. M. and R. M. Lindley to Nelson Story, Jan. 6, 1892, Mortgage Book 7, 525, GCCR.

6. Nelson Story v. J. M. Lindley & R. M. Lindley, Aug. 20, 1897, box 113: 2798, GCCC.

7. Bine to Budge, Jan. 20, 1945.

8. Joe Lindley to Nelson Story (hereafter Lindley to Story), Nov. 5, 1900, in *Bozeman Chronicle*, Aug. 2, 1905.

9. Ibid., Dec. 14, 1895.

10. Ibid., Aug. 8, 1902.

11. Larry Bishop and Robert A. Harvie, "Law, Order & Reform in the Gallatin, 1893–1918," *Montana* 30 (Spring 1980): 23; Bine to Budge, Jan. 20, 1945.

12. *Bozeman Chronicle*, Nov. 4, 1897.

13. Malcolm Story, interview.

14. Composed of Troops A (Billings), B (Bozeman), C (Custer County), and D (Missoula), the commander was Lieutenant Bruce Wallace, U.S. Army. As Company B prepared for deployment, word arrived from Washington that a hastily formed company of cavalry from Butte would take their place. The sudden change was backed by Senators Carter and Mantle, who felt western Montana was not fully represented. Company B commander Captain James F. Keown and more than half his men reluctantly accepted the offer. The *Chronicle* called Company B's treatment an outrage, noting that "riders are almost unknown" in Butte. *Bozeman Chronicle*, May 12, 1898.

15. *Bozeman Chronicle*, Apr. 28, 1898; Thomas Byron Story to Malcolm Story, July 3, 1932, SFF.

16. *Avant Courier*, May 7, 1898; *Bozeman Courier*, May 7, 1948; Drysdale, interview. The home was on the twenty-east block of Babcock Street.

17. *Avant Courier*, Mar. 5, 1898; *Bozeman Chronicle*, Apr. 28, 1898; Hogan v. Story, 4: 1540–42.

18. *Avant Courier*, Oct. 6, 1894.

19. *Bozeman Chronicle*, Apr. 13, 1893.

20. *Livingston Post*, Aug. 31, 1893.

21. *Avant Courier*, May 14, 1898; Ibid., June 17, 1899; Ibid., Feb. 24, 1900; Ibid., Apr. 14, 1900; *Fergus County Argus*, Aug. 31, 1898; *Bozeman Chronicle*, Jan. 17, 1900; Ibid., Oct. 20, 1898; Ibid., Oct. 27, 1898; Ibid., Nov. 13, 1901; Family Baptismal Records, St. James Episcopal Church, Bozeman, 14.

22. *Bozeman Chronicle*, May 4, 1899.

23. Nelson Story v. the City of Bozeman, judgment, Jan. 14, 1902, box 132: 3030 (hereafter Story v. Bozeman no. 3030), GCCC; *Bozeman Chronicle*, Mar. 30, 1899; Ibid., Aug. 31, 1899; *Avant Courier*, Sept. 16, 1899.

24. Ibid., July 22, 1899; *Bozeman Chronicle*, Aug. 18, 1898; Ibid., July 28, 1898; S. M. Emery, "Agriculture of Gallatin," *Bozeman Chronicle*, Aug. 11, 1898.

25. The Lindley Home, now the Lindley House Bed and Breakfast, is located at 202 Lindley Place.

26. Bine to Budge, Jan. 20, 1945; Bine to Budge, n.d.

27. J. M. Lindley to Hon. Mayor and Council [City of Bozeman], Apr. 6, 1909, SFF.

28. Story v. Bozeman no. 3030.

29. *Bozeman Chronicle*, Mar. 21, 1900.

30. *Avant Courier*, Nov. 27, 1900.

31. Ibid., Mar. 9, 1895; Ibid., Nov. 10, 1900; Ibid., Nov. 17, 1900; *Bozeman Chronicle*, Dec. 26, 1900.

32. *Avant Courier*, Mar. 17, 1900, 3; Ibid., Apr. 7, 1900; Ibid., Sept. 15, 1900. The machine shop was located on the southwest corner of Main Street and Grand Avenue.

33. George Wakefield, et ux., to Nelson Story, Oct. 16, 1897, *Deed Book 24*: 317, GCCR; *Avant Courier*, Sept. 29, 1900; Ibid., Oct. 20, 1900; *Gallatin County Republican*, Nov. 6, 1900.

34. Lindley to Story, Nov. 5, 1900, in *Bozeman Chronicle*, Aug. 2, 1905.

35. R. E. Brown to Byron Story, Dec. 28, 1944, SFF.

36. Lindley to Story, Nov. 7, 1900, in *Bozeman Chronicle*, Aug. 2, 1905.

37. Lindley to Story, June 19, 1903, in *Gallatin County Republican*, July 7, 1903.

38. *Avant Courier*, Dec. 1, 1900.

39. Story v. Bozeman no. 3030. While eating supper with his wife and five-year-old son, a Bozeman city attorney mentioned he was working on the Story dam case. A few days later the woman—a strict Presbyterian—was stunned to find the boy playing lawyer and addressing several empty chairs. "Gentlemen of the jury," he exclaimed, "I don't want anything to do with this damned case anyhow." See "Had A Precedent," *Law Notes* 4 (1900/1901), 39.

40. *Avant Courier*, Dec. 1, 1900; Ibid., Feb. 23, 1901. Until his return in June, Dr. L. Holmes of Butte handled what there was of Hogan's Bozeman practice.

41. *Bozeman Chronicle*, Apr. 3, 1901; Ibid., Aug. 14, 1901; *Avant Courier*, May 18, 1901. The Story Block is located at 33–39 East Main Street.

42. *Anaconda Standard*, Aug. 28, 1901; *Bozeman Chronicle*, Aug. 28, 1901.

43. *Avant Courier*, Aug. 31, 1901; *Bozeman Chronicle*, Sept. 4, 1901; B. Derek Strahn, "Bozeman's Other Mill," *At Home Magazine* 7 (Feb. 2006), 10; Bine to Budge, Dec. 2, 1944.

44. *Avant Courier*, July 14, 1894; Ibid., June 27, 1902; *Bozeman Chronicle*, July 2, 1902.

45. *Bozeman Chronicle*, Mar. 26, 1902; Ibid., Apr. 9, 1902.

46. *Bozeman Chronicle*, Dec. 4, 1901; *Avant Courier*, Dec. 7, 1901; Ibid., Aug. 1, 1902. The Gallatin County High School, later renamed the Willson School, is located on the southwest corner of 3rd Avenue and Main Street.

47. The library building, now a law office, is on the southwest corner of North Bozeman Avenue and Mendenhall Street.

48. *Gallatin County Republican*, Aug. 5, 1902.

49. *Bozeman Chronicle*, Aug. 6, 1902.

50. *Gallatin County Republican*, Aug. 5, 1902.

51. *Avant Courier*, Nov. 23, 1901.

52. Strahn, "A Once-Thriving Red Light Dis-

NOTES TO PAGES 244–249

trict," *At Home Magazine* 4 (Mar. 2003), 6. Not until 1917 would Montana's attorney general order all red-light district houses closed, though the operations continued in Bozeman until 1918.

53. Hogan v. Story, 3: 1116–17.

54. *Bozeman Chronicle*, Nov. 12, 1902; *Avant Courier*, Jan. 9, 1903.

55. *Helena Independent*, cited in *Avant Courier*, Jan. 9, 1903.

56. *Bozeman Chronicle*, Apr. 5, 1905.

57. Ibid., Jan. 30, 1903.

58. *Gallatin Farmer and Stockman*, Jan. 31, 1903. The two employees were W. F. Williams and A. J. Thurston.

59. *Gallatin County Republican*, May 26, 1903.

60. Walter purchased the car from Fred Fielding. See *Avant Courier*, Aug. 15, 1902.

61. *Bozeman Courier*, Aug. 2, 1952.

62. Wharton, *An Oral History*, 14; Mark J. Denger, "Major General Walter Perry Story, CNG—The Man behind the Founding of Camp San Luis Obispo, Original Home of the California National Guard," California Center for Military History. www.militarymuseum.org/story.html.

63. Nelson Story to T. B. Story, Mar. 25, 1909, Exhibit 25, Hogan v. Story, 4: 1592.

64. *Avant Courier*, May 1, 1903; Ibid., June 24, 1904.

65. J. M. Lindley to Hon. W. L. Holloway, July 10, 1902, in *Gallatin County Republican*, July 7, 1903.

66. Lindley to Story, June 19, 1903, in *Gallatin County Republican*, July 7, 1903.

67. Lindley to Story, July 22, 1903, in *Gallatin County Republican*, Aug. 11, 1903.

68. Nelson Story to Republican Publishing Co., Aug. 13, 1903, in *Gallatin County Republican*, Aug. 18, 1903.

69. Ibid., Sept. 25, 1903, in *Gallatin County Republican*, Sept. 29, 1903.

70. Ibid., Oct. 24, 1903, in *Gallatin County Republican*, Nov. 10, 1903.

71. The Willson Company Store was located at 101 East Main Street.

72. *Gallatin County Republican*, Aug. 26, 1902; *Avant Courier*, July 3, 1903; Ibid., Oct. 16, 1903; B. Derek Strahn, "Our Fourth Boom: The Progressive Years, 1900 to 1918," *At Home Magazine* 2 (Dec. 2001), 8; *Avant Courier*, Apr. 8, 1904; *Madisonian*, cited in *Avant Courier*, July 8, 1904.

73. *Bozeman Chronicle*, Apr. 6, 1904.

74. Bozeman Milling Co. v. Northern Pacific Railroad Company, Oct. 31, 1911, box 234: 4456, GCCC.

75. *Gallatin County Republican*, May 3, 1904.

76. *Avant Courier*, June 16, 1905.

77. *Bozeman Chronicle*, May 11, 1904; Ibid., May 25, 1904.

78. R. E. Brown to Byron Story, Dec. 28, 1944, SFF.

79. Bine to Budge, Jan. 20, 1945.

80. Nelson Story III to Professor M. G. Burlingame, Feb. 8, 1956, SFF.

81. Bine to Budge, Jan. 20, 1945; *Avant Courier*, Dec. 2, 1904; *Bozeman Chronicle*, Feb. 1, 1905.

82. State of Montana v. Nelson Story, Sr., Assault in the 2nd Degree, Nov. 26, 1904, GCCC.

83. *Gallatin County Republican*, June 27, 1905.

84. *Avant Courier*, June 23, 1905.

85. State of Montana v. Joseph M. Lindley, judgment, Nov. 4, 1905, GCCC; Bine to Budge, Jan. 20, 1945.

86. Lindley served three terms as commander of the William English Post. See *Weekly Courier*, Jan. 5, 1916; Bine to Budge, Apr. 3, 1945.

87. J. M. Lindley to the City Street Comm't. or City Council, Oct. 31, 1907, SFF.

88. State of Montana v. Joseph M. Lindley, Aug. 22, 1909, box 189: 4074-E, GCCC.

Chapter Fifteen

1. *Los Angeles Herald*, Apr. 23, 1905.

2. *Los Angeles Herald*, Feb. 24, 1910; Los Angeles Department of City Planning. City Cultural Heritage Commission, Case Number: CHC-2013-1551-HCM Approval of Expansion of Historic-Cultural Monument #80 (Palm Court) to include Alexandria Hotel and additions 501 S. Spring Street. Aug. 12, 2013. Nelson purchased the lot at Fifth and Spring in the early 1890s for thirteen thousand dollars. Bud miscalculated the property's value, leasing it to the Alexandria Hotel Company for a mere five hundred dollars a month. After a twelve-story annex was added in 1911, Bud realized the land could have gone for a lot more. See Hogan v. Story, 3: 1049–50, 1227–28; Ibid., 4: 2033.

3. Ibid., 3: 1216.

4. *Bozeman Chronicle*, Jan. 27, 1904; Ibid., Mar. 9, 1904; Hogan v. Story, 4: 1857.

5. Ibid., 4: 1858.

6. Nelson Story to T. B. Story, June 25, 1906, Exhibit S, Hogan v. Story, 3: 1503–4.

7. Ibid., 4: 2004.

8. *Republican-Courier*, Aug. 15, 1905; Ibid., Aug. 29, 1905; *Bozeman Chronicle*, Dec. 13, 1905; Bine to Budge, July 12, 1944.

9. *Bozeman Chronicle*, July 12, 1905; Ibid., Aug. 2, 1905.

10. Located on Broadway and Spring Streets, respectively.

11. *Bozeman Chronicle*, Feb. 14, 1906; *Republican-Courier*, Feb. 23, 1906.

12. *Avant Courier*, May 2, 1896.

13. *Republican-Courier*, Apr. 17, 1906.

14. Ibid., Aug. 14, 1906; *Bozeman Chronicle*, Aug. 15, 1906.

15. Ibid., Nov. 27, 1906.

16. Ibid., Oct. 3, 1906; *Republican-Courier*, Nov. 16, 1906.

17. Ibid., Oct. 16, 1906.

18. Nelson Story to T. B. Story, Apr. 29, 1906, SFF.

19. *Los Angeles Herald*, Feb. 23, 1908; *The Bridgemen's Magazine* 8 (Jan. 1908), 476. The building permit alone cost six hundred thousand dollars. See *Los Angeles Herald*, July 26, 1908.

20. Nelson Story to T. B. Story, Mar. 25, 1909, in Hogan v. Story, 4: 1592; *Los Angeles Herald*, Oct. 11, 1908; Eric Richardson, "History Lesson: What's the Story with the New Story Building?" http://blogdowntown.com/2006/08/2314-history-lesson-whats-the-story-with-the-new; *Bozeman Chronicle*, Feb. 24, 1910.

21. Everett, Erin, "Living history: Story Mansion's architecture tells story of Bozeman's past," *Bozeman Daily Chronicle*, May 17, 2003; Strahn, "Bozeman's Historic Story Mill District," *At Home Magazine* 3 (Aug. 2002), 10. Bine bought the twenty-six lots four years earlier at an average price of $125; Warranty deed from Wyman Ellis to T. Byron Story, June 7, 1905, *Deed Book 36*: 42; Deed from Nels Knutson and John L. Olson to T. Byron Story, June 8, 1905, *Deed Book 36*: 43; Warranty deed from Basmath A. Morse, Mary A. Morse, Nellie J. Page, Lucy M. Stevens, and Charles H. Morse, being all of the heirs of the late Frank R. Morse, to T. Byron Story, Aug. 4, 1905, *Deed Book 36*: 58; Warranty deed from George F. and Bertha M. Booth to T. Byron Story, Aug. 24, 1905, *Deed Book 36*: 57, GCCR. The property is located at 811 South Willson Avenue.

22. *1920 U.S. Federal Census*, Bozeman Ward 3, Gallatin, Montana, Roll T625_970, p. 1A, enumeration district 74. A fifth child, Winifred, would be born a few years later.

23. *Bozeman Chronicle*, Nov. 7, 1907.

24. Warranty deed from O.W. and Euphemia Fisher to Etha M. Story, September 20, 1913, *Deed Book 53*: 171.

25. The site, 722 South Willson Avenue, is now occupied by the Sigma Chi fraternity.

26. William S. Hoy, "Railroad Stations in the Gallatin Area," *Montana*, 3. The Milwaukee also purchased the Bozeman streetcar railway line.

27. *Bozeman Chronicle*, Apr. 27, 1911; Ibid., June 13, 1912; Hogan v. Story, 2: 879; Ibid., 3: 1216. The cereal mill was located on Oak Street between North Montana and North Rouse Avenues.

28. *Bozeman Chronicle*, Oct. 21, 1909.

29. Ibid., Mar. 3, 1910; Ibid., Aug. 29, 1907.

30. Hogan v. Story, 2: 871–72. Fred was the son of Lester and Emma Willson.

31. *Bozeman Chronicle*, June 22, 1911; Ibid., Mar. 10, 1968. Accompanying Byron on this trip was his granddaughter Bessie, who, while in Bozeman, met and fell in love with cowboy Welcome Neeff. They would marry and have two children. See Meigs County Pioneer and Historical Society, *Meigs County Ohio History Book*, 327.

32. *Bozeman Chronicle*, Oct. 19, 1911. Taft was the first sitting president to come to the Gallatin Valley.

33. Margaret A. Parker, "Nelson Story: The End (But the Meigs' Legend lives on)," *River Currents*, Aug. 20, 1988.

34. *Bozeman Chronicle*, Jan. 4, 1912.

35. Nelson Story to A. J. Noyes, Nov. 25, 1909, SFF.

36. Hogan v. Story, 4: 1875–80.

37. Ibid., 2: 999–1000.

38. Ibid., 2: 1014.

39. Bine to Budge, Apr. 3, 1945; Hogan v. Story, 1: 32, 38.

40. *Weekly Courier*, Aug. 12, 1914; Ibid., July 29, 1914.

41. Hogan v. Story, 1: 192.

42. Uncredited newspaper, "Pioneer Profile," Aug. 1977, Malcolm Story File, GHSRC. Meade kept his job before voluntarily moving on.

43. *Bozeman Weekly Chronicle*, Apr. 8, 1920.

44. Don Anderson to Mrs. Meloy, Mar. 10, 1977, SFF.

45. Hogan v. Story, 3: 1505.

46. *Bozeman Chronicle*, May 20, 1909. The Intermountain Baseball League eventually became the Montana State League. See *Bozeman Chronicle*, July 8, 1909; *San Francisco Call*, July 9, 1909.

47. *Bozeman Chronicle*, July 22, 1909; Janet Cronin and Dorothy Vick, *Montana's Gallatin Canyon: A Gem in the Treasure State*, 191; Permanent File, 146-S, GCCR. Bud eventually sold a one-half interest in the motor company to Charles Buford of Virginia City. See *Weekly Courier*, Apr. 29, 1914; Ibid., May 13, 1914.

48. Robert George Raymer, *Montana, The Land and the People*, 17; *Weekly Courier*, Mar. 18, 1914; Ibid., July 29, 1914; Ibid., Nov. 4, 1914. Over the years Bud would add additional land, and today it is known as the Black Butte Ranch. See Cronin and Vick, *Montana's Gallatin Canyon*, 83.

49. *Weekly Courier*, July 19, 1916; Ibid., Sept. 27, 1916; Ibid., Oct. 11, 1916.

50. *Bozeman Chronicle*, Sept. 12, 1895.

51. Hogan v. Story, 1: 33; Ibid., 3: 1457.

52. Elers Koch to Carl B. Cone, May 24, 1945, Carl B. Cone Papers, cited in Scott, ed., *Splendid on a Large Scale*, 340; *Weekly Courier*, May 10, 1916; Ibid., Sept. 13, 1916; Ibid., Nov. 29, 1916; *Livingston Enterprise*, Sept. 16, 1916.

53. Permanent File 353B, GCCR; *Bozeman Chronicle*, Apr. 13, 1911; Ibid., Feb. 1, 1912; *Weekly Courier*, Oct. 10, 1917.

54. *Bozeman Courier*, Aug. 20, 1919. Nelson's interest alone was worth $35,000. See Bine to Budge, Nov. 21, 1944.

55. *Bozeman Courier*, July 16, 1919.

56. Ibid., Aug. 20, 1919. The lumber was purchased from Kenyon-Noble.

57. The Lyric Theater was housed in what eventually became the American Legion building, and was later destroyed by the March 5, 2009, natural gas explosion in downtown Bozeman. The Gem Theater was housed at 18 East Main Street.

58. The five formed the Gallatin Theater Company, also known as the Gem Theatre Company, on May 1, 1919. See Permanent File, 186G, GCCR.

59. Rick Boylan, "The Elegant Ellen," *Bozeman Daily Chronicle Centennial Edition*, Mar. 29, 1963; *Bozeman Courier*, Nov. 26, 1919; *Bozeman Daily Chronicle*, Dec. 2, 1919. The Ellen is located at 17 West Main Street.

60. Burkhart, interview.

61. *Los Angeles Evening Herald*, Apr. 2, 1913, cited in *Bozeman Chronicle*, Apr. 10, 1913.

62. *Gallatin County Tribune* and *Belgrade Journal*, Jan. 10, 1957; *Republican-Courier*, Dec. 24, 1912.

63. Hogan v. Story, 3: 1397.

64. Ibid., 3: 1399.

65. *Bozeman Courier*, Oct. 1, 1919; Hogan v. Story, 2: 982; Nelson Story and Ellen Story, quitclaim deed to Rose Story Hogan, Oct. 29, 1919, *Deed Book 60*: 618, GCCR.

66. Hogan v. Story, 4: 1598; *Bozeman Courier*, Oct. 1, 1919; B. Derek Strahn, "Montana and the War to End all Wars," *At Home Magazine* 6 (Dec. 2005), 10.

67. Hogan v. Story, 3: 1402; Permanent File 322S, GCCR; *Bozeman Courier*, Dec. 20, 1920; Ibid., Mar. 23, 1921.

68. Hogan v. Story, 2: 1213.

69. *Bozeman Courier*, Sept. 12, 1923; Elers Koch to Carl B. Cone, May 24, 1945, cited in Scott, ed., *Splendid on a Large Scale*, 340.

70. Denger, "Major General Walter Perry Story, CNG," 2–3; *Bozeman Courier*, Mar. 25, 1925.

71. *Bozeman Courier*, Dec. 10, 1919; Ibid., Oct. 6, 1920; *Bozeman Weekly Chronicle*, May 6, 1920.

72. Ibid., 3: 1289–98.

73. *Bozeman Courier*, Oct. 5, 1921; Ibid., June 29, 1921.

74. Nelson Story to Walter Story, Feb. 23, 1921, Exhibit G, Hogan v. Story, 3: 1195–96.

75. Exhibits L & M, Hogan v. Story, 3: 1360–70.

76. Hogan v. Story, 1: 28–29, 35.

77. Permanent Files 232M and 353S, GCCR.

78. *Bozeman Courier*, Apr. 26, 1922.

79. Hogan v. Story, 3: 1171–72.

80. A. C. Roecher, As Administrator of the Estate of Nelson Story, Sr., Deceased v. Thomas Byron Story, Defendant, 8902

(hereafter Roecher v. Story), Bill of Exceptions, 78–80, GHSRC.

81. Ibid., 86; Hogan v. Story, 1: 196; Ibid., 2: 674, 693, 722, 735–36, 823; Ibid., 3: 1488.

82. Permanent File, 343S, GCCR; *Bozeman Courier*, Sept. 26, 1923. Others in the car were Harold "Hap" Ferguson, his younger brother Roy Ferguson, and Wallace Keown.

83. *Bozeman Courier*, Nov. 7, 1923; Ibid., Nov. 14, 1923; Hogan v. Story, 2: 960.

84. Hogan v. Story, 1: 155.

85. Ibid., 4: 1899; *Bozeman Courier*, Feb. 13, 1924.

86. *Bozeman Weekly Chronicle*, Apr. 17, 1924.

87. Roecher v. Story, 335; Hogan v. Story, 2: 791.

88. Ibid., 2: 1023.

89. Hogan v. Story, 2: 804; Ibid., 4: 1659; Roecher v. Story, 88–89, 91–92.

90. Ibid., 87; Hogan v. Story, 3: 1327–29.

91. Ibid., 4: 1899.

92. Death Certificate of Nelson Story, Sr. Certificate No. 2698, Los Angeles County Office of Registrar-Recorder/County Clerk, Norwalk, CA; *Bozeman Daily Chronicle*, Mar. 11, 1926; Ibid., Mar. 16, 1926; *Bozeman Courier*, Mar. 12, 1926; Ibid., Mar. 19, 1926.

Afterword

1. Katherine Story to Byron Story, Apr. 11, 1945, SFF.

2. Grant deed from Walter P. and Lorenza L. Story to Katherine F. Story, Oct. 31, 1930, *Deed Book 79*: 48, GCCR; *Gallatin County Tribune* and *Belgrade Journal*, Jan. 10, 1957.

3. In the Matter of the Estate of Nelson Story, Sr., Deceased, in the Superior Court of the State of California, in and for the County of Los Angeles, case no. 81, 490, Nov. 13, 1926, GHSRC.

4. *Bozeman Courier*, Dec. 3, 1926; Hogan v. Story, 1: 126, 134, 146.

5. Ibid., 1: 189–90. After Nelson's death, Lizzie Long went to Los Angeles to live with the Hogans.

6. Hogan v. Story, 1: 472; Ibid., 3: 1511.

7. Ibid., 1: 323–25, 337–46, 450–52; Ibid., 3: 1158, 1461, 1495; Roecher v. Story, 46.

8. Hogan v. Story, 1: 394.

9. Ibid., 2: 550.

10. Ibid., 4: 1860, 1865.

11. Ibid., 4: 1550, 1558.

12. Ibid., 2: 980, 996; Ibid., 4: 1561–62. *Bozeman Courier*, May 17, 1922; Ibid., Dec. 20, 1922; Permanent File 315S, 353S & 232M, GCCR. After a devastating downtown fire in December of 1922, Nelson refused to help the Hogans with damages of forty thousand dollars to their properties. Bud, without his father's knowledge, procured an eighteen-thousand-dollar certificate of deposit from Ellen and gave it to the Hogans to use for repairs. A portion of the repairs left the Hogans unsatisfied: they refused to pay three contractors for repair work they considered shoddy. The three had to pursue the Hogans in court, taking nearly four years to win a judgment against Rose for one thousand dollars.

13. Hogan v. Story, 2: 854.

14. Ibid., 2: 868.

15. Nelson Story to Walter Story, Dec. 14, 1923, Exhibit D, Roecher v. Story, 95a–95b; 36 B.T.A. 239 (1937). The Commercial National Bank, Petitioner, v. Commissioner of Internal Revenue, Respondent. Walter P. Story, Petitioner, v. Commissioner of Internal Revenue, Respondent. Katherine F. Story, Petitioner, v. Commissioner of Internal Revenue, Respondent. Thomas B. Story, Petitioner, v. Commissioner of Internal Revenue, Respondent. Nelson Story, III, and Charles Vandenhook, As Administrators of the Estate of Nelson Story, Jr., Deceased, Petitioner, v. Commissioner of Internal Revenue, Respondent. Docket nos. 66959, 66960, 66961, 66962, 66963. Board of Tax Appeals. Promulgated June 25, 1937.

16. Hogan v. Story, 2: 784.

17. Ibid., 3: 1158, 1461, 1495; Roecher v. Story, 46.

18. *Helena Daily Independent*, Nov. 20, 1931.

19. Drysdale, interview.

20. Thomas Byron Story to Malcolm Story, Mar. 12, 1932, SFF.

21. *Bozeman Daily Chronicle*, Oct. 22, 1932.

22. 36 B.T.A. 239 (1937). The Commercial National Bank, Petitioner, v. Commissioner of Internal Revenue, Respondent.

23. Story, "Nelson Story Sr. Was One of Montana's First Gold Miners."

24. Warranty deed from Katherine F. and T. B. Story to Gallatin County High School District, Aug. 20, 1936, *Deed Book 79*: 531, GCCR; Resolution of the Board of Trustees

of the Gallatin County High School at a Special Meeting held at 8:00 P.M., June 1, 1937, SFF; *Bozeman Courier*, Dec. 3, 1937.

25. The school board's primary reason for demolition was the fear the mansion's height would block "valuable light" from the new addition. See Resolution of the Board of Trustees of the Gallatin County High School, June 1, 1937, SFF; *Bozeman Courier*, Dec. 17, 1937; Ibid., Aug. 28, 1936.

26. Located at 624 South Willson Avenue.

27. Drysdale, interview.

28. Denger, "Major General Walter Perry Story, CNG," 3-4; *Gallatin County Tribune* and *Belgrade Journal*, June 27, 1957; Ibid., July 25, 1957.

29. *Weekly Courier*, Feb. 28, 1917.

30. Drysdale, interview.

31. Eric Dietrich, "Bozeman's growth rate tops 4 percent, population likely past 45,000," *Bozeman Daily Chronicle*, July 21, 2016.

32. Tracy Ellig, "MSU sets new enrollment record with 15,688 students," MSU News Service, Sept. 25, 2015.

33. Written with the pen name of Will Henry.

34. Larry McMurtry, "The Making of *Lonesome Dove*," *American Heritage* 52 (1): 14; Brown, *The American West*, 286-87.

35. Cronin and Vick, *Montana's Gallatin Canyon*, 71, 231-32; Malone, "The Gallatin Canyon and the Tides of History," 16. The chapel was dedicated October 2, 1955.

36. Doug Eisenman, Bozeman Parks foreman, e-mail message to author, Oct. 29, 2009.

Bibliography

Manuscript Materials

Gallatin Historical Society Research Center, Bozeman, Montana

Alderson, William White. "The Diary of William W. Alderson: Across the Great Plains to Montana in 1864, Settlement in Bozeman and in the Gallatin Valley, Montana, 1864–1877."

Aydt, Gregory. "A Radical Cure: Thomas Dimsdale, Radical Republicanism, and the Montana Vigilantes During the Civil War." Master's thesis. Eastern Illinois University, 1999.

Burkhart, Bud and Mary. Interview by the author. Bozeman, MT, Apr. 23, 2008.

Drysdale, Martha. Interview by the author. Bozeman, MT, Apr. 28, 2008.

Fort Ellis Record Collection

Frazier, William (Billy). Interview by Bessie Benham. Bozeman, MT, Apr. 3 and 4, 1940.

Hogan, Rose Story, plaintiff, v. Thomas Byron Story, Katherine F. Story, his wife, and A. C. Roecher, as administrator of the estate of Nelson Story, Sr., deceased, defendants. Plaintiff's Proposed Bill of Exceptions, Vols. I–IV. Case nos. 8895, 8896, 8897. Oct. 20, 1930.

In the Matter of the Estate of Nelson Story, Sr., deceased. In the Superior Court of the State of California, in and for the County of Los Angeles. Case No. 81, 490. Nov. 13, 1926.

Jones, Jefferson. "The Murder of John Bozeman?" *Quest for Knowledge Men's Club.* Dec. 13, 1955.

Myers Family File

Park County Historical Society. *A Collection of Historical Tours of Park County and the Surrounding Areas.* Livingston, MT: Privately published, 1985.

Pierstorff Family File

Roecher, A. C., As Administrator of the Estate of Nelson Story, Sr., Deceased v. Thomas Byron Story, Defendant. Bill of Exceptions. 8902. Sept. 19, 1930.

Roecher Family File

Rust, Thomas Charles. "Settlers, Soldiers and Scoundrels: The Relationship Between Army and Civilian Society in the Development of Bozeman, Montana, 1867–1886." Master's thesis. University of Denver, 1995.

Sehulster, Amanda. "The Silent Story: A Bozeman Founding Mother." Privately published.

Story Family Files

Story, Malcolm. 80 Bzn. Families. Private Collection of Clippings and Notations. Nov. 14, 1970.

Strickler, Meta. Interview by the author. Bozeman, MT, May 16, 2008.

Tolman, Donald G. "James Rolandson Dilworth."

Wharton, Richard. "An Oral History of the Settlement of the Gallatin Valley." Anthropology 204, Montana State University, Apr. 23, 1993.

LDS Family History Library, Salt Lake City, Utah

Tribett, Everett H. "Andrews and Story, Andrews Family History of Massachusetts, Story Genealogy of Mass. & Ohio." Film 391, Item 4.

Montana Historical Society Research Center, Helena, Montana

Alderson, Mary Long. Papers, 1894-1936, Special Collections 122.

Brisbin, James Sanks. Papers, 1850-1891, Manuscript Collection 39.

Crow Indian Agency Records, 1872-1900, Collection 883.

Elling, Henry. Papers, 1864-1911, Manuscript Collection 262.

Fort Ellis Records, 1869-1876, Microfilm Reel 123.

Grannis, John W. Diaries, 1863-1878, Special Collection 301.

Hauser, Samuel Thomas. Papers, 1864-1914, Manuscript Collection 37.

Montana Governors Records, 1889-1905, Manuscript Collection 35a.

Montana Stockgrowers Association Records, 1885-1912, Manuscript Collection 45.

Montana Territorial Legislative Assembly (1st: 1864), records, 1864-1865.

Montana Territorial Legislative Assembly (4th: 1867), Senate Journal.

U.S. Office of Indian Affairs: Crow Indian Agency Records, Manuscript Collection 87.

Montana State University Libraries, Bozeman, Montana

Bozeman for the Capital Committee to "Dear Sir." Sept. 29, 1892. Merrill G. Burlingame Special Collections.

Alexander Leggat Pamphlet Collection, 1863-1966, Collection 2369. Merrill G. Burlingame Special Collections.

Bradley, Charles Crane, Jr. "After the Buffalo Days: Documents on the Crow Indians from the 1880's to the 1920's." Master's thesis, Montana State University, 1970.

Fletcher, Ellen Louisa Gordon. Papers, 1866-1910, Collection 335. Merrill G. Burlingame Special Collections.

McWilliams, Mary Ellen. "Nelson Story." Merrill G. Burlingame Papers, 1880-1980, Collection 2245. Merrill G. Burlingame Special Collections.

Museum of the Rockies, Crow Indian Agency Fraud Hearings Collection, 1876-1877, Collection 2146. Merrill G. Burlingame Special Collections.

Story, Nelson. Letter to Granville Stuart, June 15, 1918. Merrill G. Burlingame Special Collections.

Swenson, Kenneth J. History of Nelson Story audiotape recordings, 1967, Collection 849. Merrill G. Burlingame Special Collections.

Trimble, William J. "The Mining Advance into the Inland Empire." PhD diss., University of Wisconsin, 1914.

Willson, Lester S. Family Papers, 1861-1922, Collection 1407. Merrill G. Burlingame Special Collections.

St. James Episcopal Church, Bozeman, Montana

Family Baptism and Burial Records

GOVERNMENT RECORDS AND PUBLICATIONS

City and County

Gallatin County Clerk and Recorders Office, Bozeman, MT. Records of Deeds, Mortgages, and Permanent Files.

Gallatin County District Court Office, Bozeman, MT. Records of the Clerk.

Los Angeles County Office of Registrar-Recorder\County Clerk, Norwalk, California.

Madison County Clerk and Recorders Office, Virginia City, MT. Record of Deeds, Mortgages, and Permanent Files.

State Documents

First Annual Report of the Bureau of Agriculture, Labor and Industry of Montana for the Year Ended in November 30, 1893. Helena, MT: State Publishing Company, 1893.

Office of the Secretary of State of Massachusetts. *Volume 15 of Massachusetts Soldiers and Sailors of the Revolutionary War: A Compilation from the Archives, Prepared and Published by the Secretary of the Commonwealth in Accordance with Chapter 100, Resolves of 1891.* Boston: Wright and Potter Printing Company, 1907.

Work Projects Administration for the State of Montana. *Montana: A State Guide Book.* Compiled and written by the Federal Writers' Project. New York: Viking Press, 1939.

U.S. Government Documents

National Archives. Records of the Adjutant General's Office, 1780s–1917, *Appointment, Commission and Personal Branch Files.* Record Group 94.

Office of Indian Affairs, *Annual Reports of the Commissioner of Indian Affairs for the years 1870, 1871, 1874, 1875.* Government Publishing Office (hereafter GPO).

U.S. Congress. Proceedings and Debates, 44 Cong., 1st sess., 1876.

U.S. Congress. Proceedings and Debates, 46 Cong., 2nd sess., 1880.

U.S. Congress, House. H. Doc. No. 58, 39 Cong., 1 sess., 1866, *Letter from the Secretary of the Interior, in answer to a resolution of the House of February 16, relative to a wagon road from Niobrara to Virginia City.* GPO, 1866.

———. H. Doc. No. 1, 40 Cong., 2nd sess., *Annual Report of the Secretary of War, 1867.* GPO, 1867.

———. H. Doc. No. 1, *Report of Brevet Major General Alfred H. Terry, Annual Report of the Secretary of War, 1868,* v. 1, 40 Cong., 3rd sess., GPO, 1868.

———. H. Doc. No. 98, 41 Cong., 3rd sess., 1871, *Montana Indian War Claims.* GPO, 1871.

———. H. Rep. No. 82, 42 Cong., 2nd sess., 1872, *Montana War-Claims.* GPO, 1872.

———. H. Doc. No. 9, 43 Cong., 2nd sess., 1874, *Montana Indian War Claims of 1867.* GPO, 1874.

———. H. Doc. No. 778, 43 Cong., 1st sess., 1874, *Investigation on the Conduct of Indian Affairs.* GPO, 1874.

———. H. Doc. No. 89, 43 Cong., 1st sess., 1874, *Agreement with Crow Indians.* GPO, 1874.

———. H. Doc. No. 871, 46 Cong., 2nd sess., 1880, *Leander M. Black.* GPO, 1880.

U.S. Congress, Senate. S. Doc. No. 19, 46 Cong., 3rd sess., 1880, *Letter from the Secretary of the Treasury, in response to Senate resolution of the 21st Ultimo, copies of all papers in his office relative to the settlement of the accounts of Dexter E. Clapp, late agent of the Crow Indians, Montana Territory.* GPO, 1880.

———. S. Rep. Report No. 1278, 49 Cong., 1st sess., 1886, Senate Committee on Indian Affairs, *The condition of the Indians in the Indian Territory, and other Reservations, etc.* GPO, 1886.

U.S. Department of the Interior. National Register of Historic Places. Main Street Historic District, Bozeman, Gallatin County, MT, National Register #87001848, 1987.

———. Northern Pacific–Story Mill Historic District, Bozeman, Gallatin County, MT, National Register #96000479, 1996.

———. South Tracy–South Black Historic District, Bozeman, Gallatin County, MT, National Register #87001840, 1987.

———. Reed and Bowles Trading Post, Lewistown, Fergus County, MT, National Register #10000520, 2010.

U.S. Department of the Treasury. Bureau of Statistics, *Report on the Internal Commerce of the United States.* GPO, 1885.

Books and Articles

Algier, Keith. *The Crow and the Eagle: A Tribal History from Lewis and Clark to Custer.* Caldwell, ID: Caxton Printers, 1993.

Annin, Jim. *Horace Countryman: Unsung Hero.* Columbus, MT: Stillwater Historical Society, 1976.

Athearn, Robert G. "Railroad to a Far Off Country: The Utah & Northern." *Montana* 18 (Autumn 1968): 2–23.

———. *Thomas Francis Meagher: an Irish Revolutionary in America.* Boulder: University of Colorado Press, 1949.

———. *William Tecumseh Sherman and the Settlement of the West.* Norman: University of Oklahoma Press, 1956, reprint with a foreword by William M. Ferguson and J. Thomas Murphy, 1995.

Atherton, Lewis. *The Cattle Kings.* Bloomington: Indiana University Press, 1961.

Bankers' Magazine, Rhodes' Journal of Banking and The Bankers' Magazine, Consolidated 52 (Jan.–June 1896): 511.

Bankers' Magazine and Statistical Register 38 (July 1883-June 1884, inclusive): 478.

Baranzini, Marlene Smith. *A Golden State: Mining and Economic Development in Gold Rush California*. Berkeley: University of California Press, 1999.

Barsness, Larry. *Gold Camp: Alder Gulch and Virginia City, Montana*. New York: Hasting House, 1962.

Baumler, Ellen, ed. *Girl From the Gulches: The Story of Mary Ronan as told to Margaret Ronan*. Helena: Montana Historical Society Press, 2003.

Beal, Merrill D. *The Story of Man in Yellowstone*. Caldwell, ID: Caxton Printers, 1949.

Beall, Mrs. W. J. "Bozeman's First Schools." *Contributions to the Historical Society of Montana* 7 (1910): 304-11.

———. "Montana's Early History. A Pioneer Woman's Recollections of People and Events Connected with Montana's Early History." *Contributions to the Historical Society of Montana* 8 (1917): 295-303.

Bender, Norman J. "The very atmosphere is charged with unbelief . . . Presbyterians and Higher Education in Montana—1869/1900." *Montana* 28 (Spring 1978): 16-25.

Bishop, Larry, and Robert A. Harvie. "Law, Order & Reform in the Gallatin, 1893-1918." *Montana* 30 (Spring 1980): 16-24.

Black, George. *Empire of Shadows: The Epic Story of Yellowstone*. New York: St. Martin's Press, 2012.

Blake, Henry, and Cornelius Hedges. *Reports of Cases Argued and Determined in the Supreme Court of Montana Territory, from the August Term, 1877, to the August Term, 1880, Inclusive*, vol. 3. San Francisco: Bancroft-Whitney Company, 1880.

Bodge, George Madison. *Soldiers in King Philip's War: Being a Critical Account of that War, with a Concise History of the Indian Wars of New England from 1620-1677*. Boston: Privately published by the author. Reprint, 1906.

Brayer, Garnet M. and Herbert O. *American Cattle Trails, 1540-1900*. Bayside, NY: Western Range Cattle Industry Study, in cooperation with the American Pioneer Trails Association, 1952.

Brekke, Jerry. *Our Time & Place: Tales from Cooke City to the Crazies*. Livingston, MT: Livingston Enterprise, 2003.

———. "Historical Overview of Benson's Landing, Park County, Montana." Livingston, MT: Anthro Research, Inc., 2007.

Bridgemen's Magazine 8 (Jan. 1908): 476.

Brisbin, James S. *The Beef Bonanza, or, How to get rich on the Plains: being a description of cattle-growing, sheep-farming, horse-raising and dairying in the West*. Philadelphia: J. B. Lippincott & Co, 1885.

Brown, Dee. *The American West*. New York: Charles Scribner's Sons, 1994.

———. *Fort Phil Kearny, An American Saga*. New York: G. P. Putnam's Sons, 1962.

———. *Trail Driving Days*. New York: Charles Scribner's Sons, 1952.

Brown, Mark H. "Muddled Men Have Muddied The Yellowstone's True Color." *Montana* 11 (Winter 1961): 28-37.

Brown, Mark Herbert. *The Plainsmen of the Yellowstone: A History of the Yellowstone Basin*. New York: Putnam, 1961.

Bryan, Charles W., Jr. "Dr. Lamme and His Gallant Little 'Yellowstone.'" *Montana* 15 (Summer 1965): 24-43.

Burlingame, Merrill G. *Gallatin County's Heritage: A Report of Progress, 1805-1976*. Bozeman, MT: Merrill G. Burlingame, 1976.

———. *Historical Report: Concerning Lands Ceded to the United States Government by the Crow Indians in the Treaty of 1868*. Bozeman, MT: Self-published, 1956.

———. *John M. Bozeman: Montana Trailmaker*. Rev. ed. Bozeman, MT: Museum of the Rockies, 1983.

———. *The Montana Frontier*. Helena, MT: State Publishing Co., 1942.

———. "Montana's Righteous Hangmen: A Reconsideration." *Montana* 28 (Autumn 1978): 36-49.

———., ed. *Bozeman in 1869: The Diary and Reminiscences of Mrs. William H. Tracy*. Bozeman, MT: Gallatin County Historical Society, 1985.

———., and K. Ross Toole. *A History of Montana*, 3 vols. New York: Lewis Historical Publishing Company, 1957.

Callaway, Llewellyn Link. *Montana's Righteous Hangmen: The Vigilantes in Action*. Ed. Llewellyn Link Callaway Jr. Norman: University of Oklahoma Press, 1982.

"Capture of the Crow Reserve." *Forest and Stream: A Weekly Journal of the Rod and Gun* 26, no. 21 (June 17, 1886): 405.

Chadwick, Robert A. "Montana's Silver Mining Era: Great Boom and Great Bust." *Montana* 32 (Spring 1982): 16-31.

Churchman Associates. *The Churchman* 125 (Jan. 28, 1922), 27.

Cook, Charles, David E. Folsom, and William Peterson. *The Valley of the Upper Yellowstone: An Exploration of the Headwaters of the Yellowstone River in the Year 1869*. Norman: University of Oklahoma Press, 1965.

Cronin, Janet, and Dorothy Vick. *Montana's Gallatin Canyon: A Gem in the Treasure State*. Missoula: Mountain Press Publishing Company, 1992.

Dale, Edward Everett. *The Range Cattle Industry: Ranching on the Great Plains from 1865–1925*. Norman: University of Oklahoma, 1960.

Darling, Roger. *A Sad and Terrible Blunder*. Vienna, VA: Potomac-Western Press, 1990.

Dary, David. *Cowboy Culture: A Saga of Five Centuries*. New York: Alfred A. Knopf, Inc., 1981.

Democratic Party National Convention, Chicago, 1896. *Official Proceedings of the Democratic National Convention Held in Chicago, Illinois, July 7, 8, 9, 10, and 11, 1896*. Logansport, IN, 1896.

DeQuille, Dan. *A History of the Comstock Mines: Mineral and Agricultural Resources of Silver Land*. Virginia City, NV: Boegle Publishing, 1889.

Dillon, Mark C. *The Montana Vigilantes, 1863–1870: Gold, Guns and Gallows*. Logan: Utah State University Press, 2013.

Dimsdale, Thomas J. *The Vigilantes of Montana, or Popular Justice in the Rocky Mountains*. Alexandria, VA: Time-Life Books, 1981.

Dow, George Francis, ed. *Records and Files of the Quarterly Courts of Essex County, Massachusetts*. Vol. 2. Salem, MA: Essex Institute, 1911-1975.

Doyle, Susan. *Journeys to the Land of Gold, Emigrant Diaries From The Bozeman Trail, 1863–1866*, 2 vols. Helena: Montana Historical Society Press, 2000.

Dunbar, Robert G. "The Economic Development of the Gallatin Valley." *Pacific Northwest Quarterly* 14 (Oct. 1956): 117-23.

Ellsworth, W. E. *A History of the Gallatin Valley and City of Bozeman, with Sketches of Men, Firms, and Corporations*. Bozeman, MT: *Avant Courier*, 1898.

Eggleston, Charles H. "When Bryan Came To Butte." In *Montana Margins, A State Anthol-ogy*. Ed. Joseph Kinsey Howard. New Haven: Yale University Press, 1946.

Elofson, W. M. *Frontier Cattle Ranching in the Land and Times of Charlie Russell*. Montreal: McGill-Queen's University Press, 2004.

Ervin, Edgar. *Pioneer History of Meigs County, Ohio, to 1949; including Masonic History of the Same Period*. Pomeroy, OH: Meigs County Pioneer Society, 1949.

Fenlason, Ed, and Mel Gemmill. "Villainous Vernon." *In Celebration of Our Past* 12 (2000): 71-76.

Fletcher, Robert H. *Free Grass to Fences*. New York: University Publishers Inc., 1960.

Fletcher, Robert S. "The End of the Open Range in Eastern Montana." In *The Montana Past, An Anthology*. Eds. Mike Malone and Richard B. Roeder. Missoula: University of Montana Press, 1969.

Forney, Gary. "Trials of Martin Peel." *In Celebration of Our Past* 15 (2003): 32-45.

Fudge, Bob. "Long Trail from Texas." *Montana* 12 (Summer 1962): 43-55.

Gann, Walter. *Tread of the Longhorns*. San Antonio, TX: Naylor Co, 1949.

Goodrich, Thomas. *War to the Knife: Bleeding Kansas, 1854–1861*. Mechanicsburg, PA: Stackpole Books, 1998.

Gordon, Greg. *When Money Grew on Trees: A. B. Hammond and the Age of the Timber Baron*. Norman: University of Oklahoma Press, 2014.

Gray, John S. *Custer's Last Campaign: Mitch Boyer and the Little Bighorn Reconstructed*. Lincoln: University of Nebraska Press, 1991.

Greeley, Horace. *An Overland Journey, from New York to San Francisco, in the Summer of 1859*. Albany, NY: C. M. Saxton, Barker & Company, 1860.

Hafen, Leroy R., and Ann W., eds. *Mormon Resistance: A Documentary Account of the Utah Expedition, 1857–1858*. Lincoln: University of Nebraska Press, 2005.

Hagan, Barry J., C.S.C. *Exactly in the Right Place: A History of Fort C. F. Smith, Montana Territory, 1866–1868*. El Segundo, CA: Upton and Sons, 1999.

Hailey, John. *The History of Idaho*. Boise, ID: Press of Syms-York Company, 1910.

Haines, Aubrey L. *The Yellowstone Story: A History of Our First National Park*. 2 vols. Yellowstone National Park, WY: Yellowstone Library and Museum Association, 1977.

Haines, Tom. *Flouring Mills of Montana Territory*. Missoula: Friends of the University of Montana Library, 1984.

Hamilton, James McClellan. *From Wilderness to Statehood: A History of Montana, 1805–1900*. Portland, OR: Binfords & Mort, 1957.

Hampton, Bruce. *Children of Grace: The Nez Perce War of 1877*. New York: Henry Holt and Company, 1994.

Hartshorne, Henry, ed. "An Important Address." *Friends' Review: A Religious, Literary and Miscellaneous Journal* 28 (1874–1875): 810–11.

Henderson, Charles. "The Amazing Story." *Wild West Magazine* 7 (Aug. 1994): 50–57, 94–96.

Henderson, Rodger C. "The Piikuni and the U.S. Army's Piegan Expedition: Competing Narratives of the 1870 Massacre on the Marias River." *Montana* 68 (Spring 2018): 48–70.

Hine, Robert V., and John Mack Faragher. *The American West: A New Interpretive History*. New Haven: Yale University Press, 2000.

Houston, Mrs. E. Lina. *Early History of Gallatin County*. Bozeman, MT: *Bozeman Chronicle*, 1933.

Hoxie, Frederick E. *Parading Through History: The Making of the Crow Nation, 1805–1935*. New York: Cambridge University Press, 1995.

Hoy, William S. *Railroad Stations in the Gallatin Area, Montana*. Montgomery Village, MD: Keystone Press, 1998.

Hutchins, James S. "Poison in the Pemmican: A detailed account of The Yellowstone Wagon-Road Prospecting Expedition of 1874." *Montana* 8 (Summer 1958): 8–25.

Hutton, Paul A. "Phil Sheridan's Pyrrhic Victory: The Piegan Massacre, Army Politics, and the Transfer Debate." *Montana* 32 (Spring 1982): 32–43.

Joachim, Walter. "Hiester Clymer and the Belknap Case." *Historical Review of Berks County* 36 (Winter 1970–1971): 13, 24–31.

Johnson, Dorothy. *The Bloody Bozeman, The Perilous Trail to Montana's Gold*, 4th printing. Missoula, MT: Mountain Press Publishing Co., 1992.

Kennedy, David. "Walter Cooper, 'Old Reliable,' and the Bad Business of Buffalo." *Pioneer Museum Quarterly* 32 (Summer 2009): 22–26.

Kennedy, Michael S. "Tall in the Saddle—First Trail Drive to Montana Territory." In *Cowboys and Cattlemen—A Roundup from Montana The Magazine of Western History*. New York: Hastings House Publishing, 1964.

King, Frank M. *Longhorn Trail Drivers—Being a True Story of The Cattle Drives of Long Ago*. Np: Privately published, 1940.

Kittredge, William, and Steven M. Krauzer. "Mr. Montana Revised: Another Look at Granville Stuart." *Montana* 36 (Autumn 1986): 14–23.

Kohrs, Conrad. *An Autobiography*. Deer Lodge, MT: Platen Press, 1977.

Lambert, Kirby, Patricia Mullan Burnham, and Susan R. Near. *Montana's State Capitol: The People's House*. Helena: Montana Historical Society Press, 2002.

Lang, William L. "Charles A. Broadwater and the Main Chance in Montana." *Montana* 39 (Summer 1989): 30–36.

Langford, Nathaniel P. *Vigilante Days and Ways*. Helena, MT: American & World Geographic Publishing, 1996.

Larson, Robert W. *Gall: Lakota War Chief*. Norman: University of Oklahoma Press, 2007.

Lass, William E. "Steamboats on the Yellowstone." *Montana* 35 (Autumn 1985): 26–41.

Leforge, Thomas H. *Memoirs of a White Crow Indian as told by Thomas B. Marquis*. With an introduction by Joseph Medicine Crow and Herman J. Viola. Lincoln: University of Nebraska Press, 1974.

Leeson, Michael A., ed. *History of Montana, 1739–1885*. Chicago: Warner, Beers & Company, 1885.

Linderman, Frank B. *Plenty-Coups, Chief of the Crows*. Lincoln: University of Nebraska Press, 2002.

Loendorf, Lawrence L., and Nancy Medaris Stone. *Mountain Spirit: The Sheep Eater Indians of Yellowstone*. Salt Lake City: University of Utah Press, 2006.

Lowe, Percival G. *Five Years a Dragoon ('49 to '54) and Other Adventures on the Great Plains*. Norman: University of Oklahoma Press, 1965.

Lubetkin, M. John. "'No Fighting Is To Be Apprehended': Major Eugene Baker, Sitting Bull, & The Northern Pacific Railroad's 1872 Western Yellowstone Surveying Expedition." *Montana* 56 (Summer 2006): 28–41.

Madsen, Brigham D. *The Lemhi: Sacajawea's People*. Caldwell, ID: Caxton Press, 2000.

Malone, Michael P. "The Gallatin Canyon and

the Tides of History." *Montana* 23 (Summer 1973): 2–17.

Malone, Michael P., and Richard B. Roeder, eds. *The Montana Past: An Anthology* (Missoula: University of Montana Press, 1969.

Malone, Michael, Richard Roeder, and William Lang. *Montana: A History of Two Centuries*. Rev. ed. Seattle: University of Washington Press, 1993.

Marquis, Thomas. *Custer, Cavalry & Crows: The Story of William White as told to Thomas Marquis*. Fort Collins, CO: Old Army Press, 1975.

Mather, R. E. and F. E. Boswell. *Vigilante Victims: Montana's 1864 Hanging Spree*. San Jose, CA: History West Publishing Co., 1991.

McCoy, Joseph G. *Historic Sketches of the Cattle Trade of the West and Southwest*. Washington, D.C.: Rare Book Shop Reprint, 1932.

McDermott, John D. *Red Cloud's War: The Bozeman Trail, 1866–1868*. 2 vols. Norman, OK: Arthur H. Clark Company, 2010.

McElrath, Thompson P. *The Yellowstone Valley: What it is, Where it is, and How to get to it: A Handbook for Tourists and Settlers*. St. Paul, MN: Pioneer Press, 1880.

McLemore, Clyde, ed. "Bannack and Gallatin City in 1862–1863. A Letter by Mrs. Emily R. Meredith." *Frontier Omnibus*. Missoula and Helena: Montana State University and Montana Historical Society, 1962.

McLoughlin, William G. *After the Trail of Tears*. Chapel Hill: University of North Carolina Press, 1993.

McLure, Helen. "Bad Men, Unsexed Women, and Good Citizens: Outlaws and Vigilantes in the American West." In *Making of the American West: People and Perspectives*, ed. Benjamin H. Johnson, 259–79, Santa Barbara, CA: ABC-CLIO, 2007.

McMurtry, Larry. "The Making of *Lonesome Dove*." *American Heritage* 52 (1): 14.

Meigs County Pioneer and Historical Society, Inc. *Meigs County Ohio History Book*. Dallas, TX: Taylor Publishing Co., 1979.

Meikle, Lyndel. "No Paper Trail—Crooked Agents on the Crow Reservation, 1874–1878." In *Speaking Ill of the Dead: Jerks in Montana History*. Helena, MT: Falcon Publishing, 2000.

Merk, Frederick. *History of the Westward Movement*. New York: Alfred A. Knopf, 1978.

Miller, David R., Dennis J. Smith, Joseph R.

McGeshick, James Shanle, and Caleb Shields. *The History of the Fort Peck Assiniboine and Sioux Tribes, 1800–2000*. Poplar, MT: Fort Peck Community College, 2008.

Miller, Joaquin. *An Illustrated History of the State of Montana*. New York: Lewis Publishing Company, 1894.

Milner, Clyde A., and Carol A. O'Connor. *As Big as the West: The Pioneer Life of Granville Stuart*. New York: Oxford University Press, 2009.

Mirrielees, Lucia B., ed. "Pioneer Ranching in Central Montana, From the Letters of Otto Maerdian, Written in 1882–83." *Frontier Omnibus*. Missoula and Helena: Montana State University and Montana Historical Society, 1962.

Niebel, Esther C. *A Century of Service—History of The First Methodist Church, Bozeman, Montana, 1866–1966*. Bozeman: Privately published, 1966.

Niven, Francis L. *Manhattan Omnibus—Stories of Historical Interest of Manhattan and Its Surrounding Communities*. Manhattan, MT: Francis L. Niven, 1989.

Noyes, A. J. *In The Land of The Chinook, the Story of Blaine County*. Helena, MT: State Publishing Company of Helena, 1917.

Paladin, Vivian A., ed. "Memoirs of a Many-Sided Man: The Personal Record of a Civil War Veteran, Montana Territorial Editor, Attorney, Jurist." *Montana* 14 (Autumn 1964): 31–56.

Peterson, Robert L. "The Completion of the Northern Pacific Railroad System in Montana: 1883–1893." In *The Montana Past, An Anthology*, eds. Michael P. Malone and Richard B. Roeder. Missoula: University of Montana Press, 1969.

Pettengill's Newspaper Directory and Advertiser's Handbook. New York: S. M. Pettengill & Co., 1878.

Pitcher, Don. *Moon Handbooks—Wyoming*. Emeryville, CA: Avalon Travel Publishing, 2003.

Pomplun, Ray. "Epitome Northwest." *Empire Magazine* (Oct. 24, 1976): 35–39.

Progressive Men of the State of Montana. Chicago: A. W. Bowen and Company, 1903.

Prucha, Francis Paul. *The Great Father: The United States Government and the American Indians*. 2 vols. Lincoln: University of Nebraska Press, 1984.

Putnam, James Bruce. *The Evolution of a Frontier Town: Bozeman, Montana and Its Search for Economic Stability, 1864–1867*. Bozeman, MT: Gallatin County Historical Society, 1988.

Quivey, Addison. "The Yellowstone Expedition of 1874." *Contributions to the Historical Society of Montana*, vol. 1 (1876): 268–84.

Raymer, Robert George. *Montana: The Land and the People*. 3 vols. Chicago and New York: The Lewis Publishing Company, 1930.

Richardson, Albert D. *Beyond the Mississippi: From the Great River to the Great Ocean*. Hartford, CT: American Publishing Co., 1869.

Riley, Glenda. *The Female Frontier: A Comparative View of Women on the Prairie and Plains*. Lawrence: University Press of Kansas, 1988.

Robbins, William G. "The Deconstruction of a Capitalist Patriarch: The Life and Times of Samuel T. Hauser." *Montana* 42 (Autumn 1992), 20–33.

Roberts, David. "The Brink of War." *Smithsonian* 39 (June 2008): 44–51.

Robertson, Frank C. *Fort Hall, Gateway to the Oregon Country*. New York: Hastings House, 1963.

Roeder, Richard B. "A Settlement on the Plains: Paris Gibson and the Building of Great Falls." *Montana* 42 (Autumn 1992): 4–19.

Rollinson, John K. *Wyoming Cattle Trails: History of the Migration of Oregon-raised Herds to Midwestern Markets*. Ed. E. A. Brininstool. Caldwell, ID: Caxton Printers, 1948.

Roosevelt, Theodore. "The Round-Up." *The Century* 35 (6): 849–68.

Rydell, Robert, Jeffery Safford, and Pierce Mullen. *In the People's Interest: A Centennial History of Montana State University*. Bozeman: Montana State University, 1993.

Saddle and Sirloin Club, and Edward Norris Wentworth. *A Biographical Catalog of the Portrait Gallery of the Saddle and Sirloin Club*. Chicago: Union Stock Yards, 1920.

St. James Episcopal Church. Eighty Years . . . 1868–1948: Pamphlet. Bozeman, MT: St. James Episcopal Church, 1948.

Sanders, Helen Fitzgerald. *History of Montana*. 3 vols. New York: Lewis Historical Publishing Co., 1913.

Schwantes, Carlos A. *Long Day's Journey: The Steamboat and Stagecoach Era in the Northern West*. Seattle: University of Washington Press, 1999.

Scott, Kim Allen. "Anatomy of a Lynching." *In Celebration of Our Past* 15 (2003): 70–84.

———. "The Willson Brothers Come to Montana." *Montana* 49 (Spring 1999): 58–70.

———., ed. *Splendid on a Large Scale. The Writings of Hans Peter Gyllembourg Koch, Montana Territory, 1869–1874*. Helena, MT: Bedrock Editions and Drumlummon Institute, 2010.

"See it Now, Historic Montana: A Present Day Tourist Paradise." *Montana* 9 (Summer 1959): 34–52.

Seibel, Dennis. *Fort Ellis, Montana Territory, 1867–1886: The Fort that Guarded Bozeman*. Bozeman, MT: Dennis Seibel, 1996.

Sharp, Paul F. "Merchant Princes of the Plains." *Montana* 5 (Winter 1955): 2–20.

Shrauger, Nick. "B. F. Christenot, Where are You?" *In Celebration of Our Past* 7 (1995): 19–24.

Silliman, Lee. "The Carroll Trail: Utopian Enterprise." *Montana* 24 (Spring 1974): 2–17.

Simon, John Y., ed. *The Papers of Ulysses S. Grant*. 31 vols. Carbondale: Southern Illinois Press, 1991.

Skidmore, Bill. *Treasure State Treasury: Montana Banks, Bankers, & Banking, 1864–1984*. Helena: Montana Bankers Association, 1985.

Small, Lawrence F., ed. *Religion in Montana: Pathways to the Present*. Vol. 1. Billings, MT: Rocky Mountain College, 1992.

Smiley, Jerome Constant. *Prose and Poetry of the Live Stock Industry of the United States: With Outlines of the Origin and Ancient History of Our Live Stock Animals*. Vol. 1. Np: National Live Stock Historical Association, 1905.

Smith, Burton M. "Politics and the Crow Indian Land Cessions." *Montana* 36 (Autumn 1986): 24–37.

Smith, Jean Edward. *Grant*. New York: Simon & Schuster, 2001.

Smith, Phyllis. *Bozeman and the Gallatin Valley: A History*. Helena, MT: Falcon Press, 1996.

Stearns, Ezra S., William Frederick Whitcher, and Edward Everett Parker. *Genealogical and Family History of the state of New Hampshire: A Record of the Achievements of her People in the Making of a Commonwealth and the Founding of a Nation*. Vol. 1. Chicago: The Lewis Publishing Company, 1908.

Steele, Volney. *Bleed, Blister, and Purge: A History of Medicine on the American Frontier*. Missoula, MT: Mountain Press Publishing Company, 2005.

Stone, Arthur L. *Following Old Trails*. Missoula, MT: Morton John Elrod, 1913.

Story, D. B. *A Brief History of Bedford Township*. Darwin, OH: D. B. Story, 1894.

Strahn, B. Derek, and Thomas Lee. *Historic Homes of Bozeman*. Bozeman, MT: *Bozeman Daily Chronicle*, 2004.

Strahn, B. Derek, "Of Ballots, Boodle and Boomtowns: Bozeman's 1889–1892 Bid to Become the State Capital." *Pioneer Museum Quarterly* 35 (Summer 2012): 12–19.

———. "Our Fourth Boom: The Progressive Years, 1900 to 1918." *At Home Magazine* 2 (Dec. 2001): 8–10.

———. "Bozeman's Historic Story Mill District." *At Home Magazine* 3 (Aug. 2002): 9–11.

———. "A Once-Thriving Red Light District." *At Home Magazine* 4 (Mar. 2003): 5–6.

———. "Fort Ellis Remembered." *At Home Magazine* 5 (Dec. 2004): 10–13.

———. "The Savior of Eastern Montana." *At Home Magazine* 6 (Nov. 2005): 9–11.

———. "Montana and the War to End all Wars." *At Home Magazine* 6 (Dec. 2005): 10–12.

———. "Bozeman's Other Mill." *At Home Magazine* 7 (Feb. 2006): 9–11.

Strahorn, Robert E. *The Resources of Montana Territory and Attractions of Yellowstone National Park*. Published and circulated by direction of the Montana Legislature. Princeton, NJ: Princeton University, 1879.

Stuart, Granville. *Forty Years on the Frontier*. 2 vols. Ed. Paul C. Phillips. Cleveland, OH: Arthur H. Clark Company, 1925.

Taylor, Bill, and Jan. *Over Homestake Pass on the Butte Short Line: The Construction Era, 1888–1929*. Missoula, MT: Pictorial Histories Publishing Company, 1998.

Thrapp, Dan L. *Vengeance! The Saga of Poor Tom Cover*. El Segundo, CA: Upton & Sons, 1989.

Topping, E. S. *The Chronicles of the Yellowstone*. Minneapolis, MN: Ross & Haines, Inc., 1968.

Trexler, H. A. "Missouri-Montana Highways." *Missouri Historical Review* 12 (Apr. 1918): 145–62.

Utley, Robert M. *The Lance and the Shield: The Life and Times of Sitting Bull*. New York: Henry Holt and Company, 1993.

Vichorek, Daniel N. *Montana's Cowboys: Living the Heritage*. Helena, MT: American & World Geographic Publishing, 1994.

Waldron, Ellis L. *Montana Politics since 1864: An Atlas of Elections*. Missoula: Montana State University Press, 1958.

Waller, John. *Health and Wellness in 19th-century America*. Santa Barbara, CA: ABC-CLIO, 2014.

Wellman, Paul I. *The Greatest Cattle Drive*. Boston, MA: Houghton Mifflin, 1964.

———. *The Trampling Herd*. Garden City, NY: Doubleday & Company, 1951.

West, Carroll Van. *Capitalism on the Frontier: Billings and the Yellowstone Valley in the Nineteenth Century*. Lincoln: University of Nebraska Press, 1993.

West, Elliott. *The Contested Plains: Indians, Gold-seekers, and the Rush to Colorado*. Lawrence: University Press of Kansas, 1998.

White, Richard. *It's Your Misfortune and None of My Own: A History of the American West*. Norman: University of Oklahoma Press, 1991.

———. *Railroaded: The Transcontinentals and the Making of Modern America*. New York: W. W. Norton & Company, 2011.

Whithorn, Doris, "John J. Tomlinson of Emigrant Gulch and Gallatin Gateway." *In Celebration of Our Past* 9 (1997): 6–10.

Wilson, M. L. "The Evolution of Montana Agriculture in its Early Period." *Proceedings of the Mississippi Valley Historical Association* 9 (1917–1918): 429–40.

Wolle, Muriel Sibell. *Montana Pay Dirt: A Guide to the Mining Camps of the Treasure State*. Denver, CO: Sage Books, 1963.

Worcester, Donald Emmet. *The Chisholm Trail: High Road of the Cattle Kingdom*. Lincoln: University of Nebraska Press, 1980.

Yale University. *The Twenty Years' Record of the Yale Class of 1862*. Bangor, ME: Press of J. H. Bacon, 1884.

Correspondence

Ashley, Keith. Genealogist. Letter to the author, Sept. 8, 1995.

Black, Sheppard. Special Collections librarian, Ohio University. Letter to the author, Sept. 9, 1995.

Eisenman, Doug. Bozeman Parks foreman. E-mail message to the author, Oct, 29, 2009.

Web Sites

36 B.T.A. 239 (1937). *The Commercial National Bank, Petitioner, v. Commissioner of Internal Revenue, Respondent. Walter P. Story, Petitioner, v. Commissioner of Internal Revenue, Respondent. Katherine F. Story, Petitioner, v. Commissioner of Internal Revenue, Respondent. Thomas B. Story, Petitioner, v. Commissioner of Internal Revenue, Respondent. Nelson Story, III, and Charles Vandenhook, As Administrators of the Estate of Nelson Story, Jr., Deceased, Petitioner, v. Commissioner of Internal Revenue, Respondent.* Docket Nos. 66959, 66960, 66961, 66962, 66963. Board of Tax Appeals. Promulgated June 25, 1937. http://scholar.google.com/scholar_case?-case=17933585661166455250&q=36+BTA+239&hl=en&as_sdt=2,27.

Day, James F. "Bud." "The Day Family History," www.findagrave.com/cgi-bin/fg.cgi?page=gr&GRid=75085239.

Denger, Warrant Officer 1 Mark J. "Major General Walter Perry Story, CNG—The Man behind the Founding of Camp San Luis Obispo, Original Home of the California National Guard." California Center for Military History. www.militarymuseum.org/story.html.

"First Meeting of Masons in Montana." Grand Lodge of AF&AM of Montana. www.grandlodgemontana.org.

"Had A Precedent," Law Notes, vol. 4 (1900/1901): 39. http://babel.hathitrust.org/cgi/pt?id=mdp.35112203937828;view=1up;seq=43.

"Hall of Great Westerners." National Cowboy & Western Heritage Museum. www.nationalcowboymuseum.org/info/awards-hof/Great-Westerners.aspx.

House, Walt. "The Real Story about Nelson Story." *Remington Society of America Journal* (2013): 20–29. Glendale, CA. www.remingtonsociety.org/the-real-story-of-nelson-story.

Johnson, Randall A. "The Ordeal of the Steptoe Command." *The Pacific Northwesterner* 17 (Winter 1973). www.historylink.org/File/8123.

Kansas Deaths and Burials, Index, 1885–1930. Retrieved from https://www.ancestry.com.

Los Angeles Department of City Planning. City Cultural Heritage Commission, Case Number: CHC-2013-1551-HCM Approval of Expansion of Historic-Cultural Monument #80 (Palm Court) to include Alexandria Hotel and additions 501 S. Spring Street. 12 August, 2013. http://clkrep.lacity.org/onlinedocs/2013/13-1075_rpt_plan_8-12-13.pdf.

"Nelson Story." Montana Cowboy Hall of Fame. http://www.montanacowboy.org/151001/180178.html.

"Petition for John Proctor and Elizabeth Proctor." Http://salem.lib.virginia.edu/texts/tei/BoySal2R?term=&div_id=BoySal2-n2.346&chapter_id=n107&name=goowil.

"Resident Population and Apportionment of the U.S. House of Representatives." U.S. Census Bureau. www.census.gov/dmd/www/resapport/states/montana.pdf.

Richardson, Eric. "History Lesson: What's the Story with the New Story Building?" http://blogdowntown.com/2006/08/2314-history-lesson-whats-the-story-with-the-new.

Schwartz, Dennis. "This unpretentious Western handles both the cattle drive and the romantic triangle with relative ease." http://homepages.sover.net/~ozus/tallmen.htm.

U.S. Census Bureau (1850), Lee, Platte Missouri. Retrieved from https://www.ancestry.com.

U.S. Census Bureau (1860), Stranger, Leavenworth, Kansas Territory. Retrieved from https://www.ancestry.com.

U.S. Census Bureau (1870), Bozeman, Gallatin, Montana Territory. Retrieved from https://www.ancestry.com.

U.S. Census Bureau (1920), Bozeman, Ward 3, Gallatin, Montana. Retrieved from https://www.ancestry.com.

U.S. Federal Census (database online). Provo, UT: Ancestry. Com Operations, Inc. https://www.ancestry.com.

U.S. Federal Census Mortality Schedules, 1850-1885, Gallatin, Montana. Retrieved from https://www.ancestry.com.

Yellowstone Genealogy Forum, "Paul J. McCormick—Grand Old Man of Montana." Retrieved from https://www.ancestry.com.

NEWSPAPERS

Anaconda Standard
Billings Daily Gazette
Billings Gazette
Boulder Monitor
(Bozeman) Avant Courier
Bozeman Avant Courier
Bozeman Chronicle
Bozeman Courier
Bozeman Daily Chronicle
(Bozeman) Montana Pick and Plow
(Bozeman) Republican-Courier
Bozeman Times
(Bozeman) Weekly Avant Courier
Bozeman Weekly Chronicle
(Bozeman) Weekly Courier
Brooklyn Eagle
Buffalo Wyoming Echo
(Burlington) Kansas Patriot
(Butte) Daily Inter Mountain
(Butte) Inter-Mountains Freeman
Daily Missoulian
(Deer Lodge) New North-West
Denver Post
(Denver) Rocky Mountain News
(Diamond City) Rocky Mountain Husbandman
Dillon Tribune
(Fort Benton) River Press
Gallatin County Republican
Gallatin County Tribune and Belgrade Journal
Gallatin Farmer and Stockman
(Gallipolis, Pomeroy, Ohio) Sunday
    Times-Sentinel
Great Falls Daily Tribune

Helena Daily Enterprise
Helena Daily Independent
Helena Gazette
Helena Herald
Helena Independent
Helena Weekly Herald
Ismay Journal
Kalispell Times
(Lewistown) Fergus County Argus
Livingston Enterprise
(Livingston) Montana Pioneer
Livingston Post
Los Angeles Evening Herald
Los Angeles Express
Los Angeles Herald
Los Angeles Times
(Miles City) Daily Yellowstone Journal
(Miles City) Yellowstone
    Journal
New York Evangelist
New York Sun
New York Times
New York Tribune
Omaha Daily Bee
Pomeroy (Ohio) Weekly Telegraph
River Currents (Ohio)
Saint Cloud (Minnesota) Democrat
(Saint Paul) Pioneer Press
Salt Lake Herald
San Francisco Call
Sheridan Wyoming Enterprise
(Virginia City) Madisonian
(Virginia City) Montana Post
Washington Post
Yankton Press & Dakotan

Index

JOHN C. RUSSELL was born in Kansas City, Missouri, and moved to Bozeman to attend Montana State University. He received his Bachelor of Arts degree in history in 1978. He has worked as a broadcast reporter in television and radio and most recently as director of the Gallatin (County) Historical Society. Russell has written several historical articles, one published in *Wild West Magazine*. He and his wife Peggy live in Bozeman.